D1679111

THE SEARCH FOR IDENTITY IN
THE NARRATIVE OF ROSA MONTERO

THE SEARCH FOR IDENTITY IN
THE NARRATIVE OF ROSA MONTERO

Vanessa Knights

Spanish Studies
Volume 4

The Edwin Mellen Press
Lewiston•Queenston•Lampeter

Library of Congress Cataloging-in-Publication Data

Knights, Vanessa.
   The search for identity in the narrative of Rosa Montero / Vanessa Knights.
      p. cm. -- (Spanish studies ; v. 4)
      Includes bibliographical references (p.   -   ) and index.
      ISBN 0-7734-7984-8
   1. Montero, Rosa--Criticism and interpretation. 2. Feminism and literature--Spain. 3. Feminism in literature. 4. Women in literature. 5. Identity (Psychology) in literature.   I. Title.
II. Series: Spanish studies (Lewiston, N.Y.) ; v. 4.
PQ6663.O554Z75   1999
863'.64--dc21
                                                                              99-26217
                                                                               CIP

This is volume 4 in the continuing series
Spanish Studies
Volume 4 ISBN 0-7734-7984-8
SpS Series ISBN 0-7734-734-X

A CIP catalog record for this book is available from the British Library.

Copyright © 1999 Vanessa Knights

All rights reserved. For information contact

        The Edwin Mellen Press   The Edwin Mellen Press
                Box 450   Box 67
           Lewiston, New York   Queenston, Ontario
        USA 14092-0450   CANADA L0S 1L0

                     The Edwin Mellen Press, Ltd.
                    Lampeter, Ceredigion, Wales
                  UNITED KINGDOM SA48 8LT

                 Printed in the United States of America

*To my goddaughter, Clémence and her sister Bérangère.
May they grow in wisdom and knowledge.*

TABLE OF CONTENTS

Acknowledgements ix

Abbreviations used xi

Introduction Questions of Methodological Practice 1

Chapter One A Study of the Equality and Difference Debate and its Implications in the Narrative of Rosa Montero 13

Chapter Two A Social Critique of the Institution of Motherhood in *Crónica del desamor* 45

Chapter Three Metafiction and the Search for Identity in *Crónica del desamor* and *La función delta* 79

Chapter Four The Function of the Bolero in *Te trataré como a una reina* 11

Chapter Five Crossing Subject-Object Boundaries in *Te trataré como a una reina* 14

Chapter Six Anti-Heroes and Heroines in *Amado amo*, *Temblor* and *El nido de los sueños* 16

Epilogue Narrative and Identity in *Bella y oscura* and *La hija del caníbal* 20

Conclusion Paradoxical and Shifting Identities 21

Appendix Three Interviews with Rosa Montero 22

Bibliography 27

Index 32

ACKNOWLEDGEMENTS

As so often thinking through theoretical issues is a collective process, it becomes very difficult if not impossible to thank all those involved in this project. This text is the product of speaking with, writing to and thinking with others. As well as those whose contributions are listed below, I wish to thank all those whose informed comments and perceptive questions have helped to shape my work particularly colleagues and students, past and present, at St. Andrews, Cambridge and Newcastle. I am especially grateful to Chris Perriam and Ian Biddle for their invaluable proofing of various stages of this text.

On an academic level I am grateful to Paul Julian Smith, for his constructive critical readings and P.J. Collier for the avenues opened by the critical theory course run by the Department of French at the University of Cambridge. The staff of various libraries gave invaluable assistance particularly Marisa Mediavilla of the Biblioteca de Mujeres in Madrid who allowed me to borrow non-borrowable books and provided personal copies of hard-to-find journals and Richard Rex of the University Library of Cambridge who constantly kept me informed of any accessions on women in Spain. Others working in the field kindly provided copies of their articles and books, not to mention support and encouragement: Concha Alborg, Annie Brooksbank Jones, Catherine Davies, Judith Drinkwater, Elena Gascón Vera, Kathleen Glenn, Ana Rubio Castro, Phyllis Zatlin.

I would especially like to thank Rosa Montero for her letters, for supplying me with material -thanks are also due here to her press agent MªÁngeles Martín and her assistant Paula for allowing me to loot their press files- and for taking time out of a very busy schedule. For setting up my first meeting with Rosa Montero I am grateful to Hilary Owen, Jo Labanyi and Helen Graham, not forgetting Antonio Gil de Carrasco of the Instituto Cervantes of Leeds who helped to arrange Rosa's visit to Cambridge in 1993.

Above all I wish to extend my heartfelt thanks to my family and friends, especially my parents Fred and Maguy, closest friends Heather and Anne, and my beloved David, for their love, support and encouragement.

ABBREVIATIONS USED

ACIS	*Journal of the Association for Contemporary Iberian Studies*
ALEC	*Anales de la Literatura Española Contemporánea*
HR	*Hispanic Review*
LF	*Letras Femeninas*
REH	*Revista de Estudios Hispánicos*
REIS	*Revista Española de Investigación Sociológica*
MLN	*Modern Language Notes*
RI	*Revista Iberoamericana*
RICS	*Revista del Instituto de Ciencias Sociales*
RLA	*Romance Languages Annual*

Excerpts from *Crónica del desamor, La función delta, Te trataré como a una reina, Amado amo, Temblor, El nido de los sueños* reproduced with permission from Agencia Literaria Carmen Barcells, *Bella y oscura* reproduced by permission of Editorial Seix Barral, S.A., *La hija del caníbal* reproduced by permission of Espasa Calpe, S.A..

Chapters Presented At Conferences And Research Seminars

Chapter One: Hispanic Research Seminar, University of Cambridge (12 October 1993): 'Feminismo de la igualdad/ feminismo de la diferencia': A Study of the Debate and its Implications in the Narrative of Rosa Montero'; Second Hispanic Postgraduate Conference (British), University of Birmingham (14 January 1994): 'Feminismo de la igualdad/ feminismo de la diferencia: A Study of the Debate and its Implications in Contemporary Spanish Women's Narrative' (publication forthcoming in *Journal of Hispanic Research*).

Chapter Two: Hispanic Research Seminar, Queen Mary and Westfield College, University of London (22 March 1995): '«Mujer-esposa-madre»: A Social Critique of the Institution of Motherhood in *Crónica del desamor*'; 'Contemporary Spanish Narrative in Context', day conference organised by the University of Leeds and Instituto Cervantes (3 May 1997): '¿Es o no una novela *Crónica del desamor*?: A Testimony of Confused Identity'.

Chapter Four: ACIS conference, Queen's University of Belfast (15 September 1995): '«Necesito un corazón que me acompañe...»: The Function of the Bolero in *Te trataré como a una reina* by Rosa Montero'; Department of Music Research Seminar, University of Newcastle (25 February 1998): 'Bittersweet Seduction: The Latin American Bolero'.

Chapter Five; Tongue in Cheek, the Modern and Medieval Languages Graduate Forum, University of Cambridge (14 January 1993): 'Three Scenes of Voyeurism: The Gaze and Feminine Identity in *Te trataré como a una reina* by Rosa Montero'.

Chapter Six; Fantasy, Science Fiction and the Fiction of the Unreal, day conference organised by the Institute of Romance Studies and the Centre for English Studies, University of London, School of Advanced Study (16 March 1996): 'The Quest for Self: Fantasy and Gender Identity in Rosa Montero's *Temblor* and *El nido de los sueños*'; AHGBI conference, King's College, University of London (14 March 1997): 'The Feminist Potential of Speculative Fiction'; Centre for Gender and Women's Studies Research Seminar, University of Newcastle (22 April 1998): 'An Imaginative Leap Beyond Epistemological Boundaries: Spanish Literary Works of Fantasy and Science Fiction' (publication forthcoming in *Paragraph*).

INTRODUCTION

TO BE OR NOT TO BE A FEMININE WOMAN?: QUESTIONS OF TERMINOLOGY AND METHODOLOGICAL PRACTICE.

Nuevamente, teoría y práctica se podrían dar la mano para sacudir el polvo a muchos conceptos que, como el de género, han sido útiles para explicar numerosas construcciones y procesos que actúan en la sociedad. Ahora son necesarias categorías más abiertas que expliquen cómo operan en las distintas situaciones "la diferencia" y "las diferencias" (con los hombres y entre las mujeres), y la naturaleza de las distintas estructuras sociales, culturales, psicológicas, en las que se manifiesta la opresión de la mujer en cada sociedad.

Again, theory and practice could be united in order to shake off the dust from many concepts such as gender which have been useful in explaining numerous constructions and processes which operate in society. What is necessary now are more open categories which explain how 'difference' and 'differences' (with men and between women) function in diverse situations and the nature of the different social, cultural and pyschological structures through which the oppression of women manifests itself in each society. (Justa Montero 1994, 44)[1]

Rosa Montero is one of a group of women writers who came to prominence during the late 1970s and early 1980s. This period is often referred to as the boom of women's writing in Spain. To date she has published seven novels *Crónica del desamor* (1979), *La función delta* (1981), *Te trataré como a una reina* (1983), *Amado Amo* (1988), *Temblor* (1990), *Bella y oscura* (1993), *La hija del caníbal*

(1997); the children's stories *El nido de los sueños* (1991), *Las barbaridades de Bárbara* (1996), *El viaje fantástico de Bárbara* (1997); numerous short stories for the press; the short stories 'Paulo Pumilio' in the anthology *Doce relatos de mujeres* edited by Ymelda Navajo (1982) and 'El puñal en la garganta' in the anthology *Relatos urbanos* (1994) containing short stories by various contemporary authors originally published in *El País*; the collection of short stories *Amantes y enemigos: Cuentos de pareja* (1998); the script for the Spanish television series 'Media Naranja' (1986); three collections of interviews *España para ti para siempre* (1976), *Cinco años de País* (1982) and *Entrevistas* (1996), one of journalistic pieces *La vida desnuda* (1994) and another of articles on famous women which were originally published in the Sunday supplement of *El País*, *Historias de mujeres* (1995). As Joan Brown, in one of a growing number of studies of contemporary Spanish women writers, notes, 'Montero is among the select group that includes Ana María Moix, Esther Tusquets, Lourdes Ortiz and Montserrat Roig, who by now have recognised places in the Spanish literary firmament' (1991b, 240).[2] Her novels are not only bestsellers but have also received the attention of critics both in Europe and the U.S.A.. Brown concludes her discussion of Montero's work by stating that 'she has emerged from a background of political journalism to become one of the most interesting and provocative novelists of the post-Franco era' (1991b, 255). Montero's novels form a diverse body of work which, considered as a whole, escapes rigid classification; they are provocative because of the feminist perspectives they reveal. Furthermore, I would argue that this diversity can be understood by situating the texts in the historical context of contemporary debates within the Spanish feminist movement and the changing situation of women in post-Franco Spain.

Overview

The first chapter of this study therefore aims to trace the socio-historical conditions which produced the polemical debate between equality and difference feminists, and the 1980s boom in women's narrative. One of the focal debates within the Spanish feminist movement has been the highly problematic issue of maternity, both as social institution and mythical possibility. In the analysis of maternity in Chapter Two I address both these views and the particularly Spanish ambivalence towards the mother figure which they represent. The use of metafiction in the creation of life narratives for women is discussed in Chapter Three. Whilst these narratives include that of motherhood, it is not necessarily the only choice open to women.[3] Indeed, Chapters Four and Five deal with the alternative figure of the spinster, her relationship to conventions of romantic love, and place in men's fantasies as both a figure of ridicule and fear. From fantasies, the analysis shifts in Chapter Six to the fantastic as a mode of discourse. The epilogue briefly examines the increasing focus on discourse within Montero's narrative and in the concluding chapter, an overview is given of the trajectory of her narrative production to date which addresses the difficulty of resignifying identity outside patriarchal paradigms. The novels are dealt with in chronological order of writing and I will be arguing that a clear trajectory can be traced in relation to changes and developments within the Spanish feminist movement.

Brief Survey of Montero Criticism

Whilst a growing number of articles are being written on the novels of Rosa Montero, particularly by Kathleen Glenn (1987, 1988, 1990b, 1991a) and Phyllis Zatlin (1987, 1992, 1993), several of which allude to feminist aspects of her work, they do not place her specifically in the context of contemporary debates within the Spanish feminist movement such as that between equality and difference which has proved so particularly divisive. To some extent this is done by Catherine Davies in a brief section of a very interesting article which makes links between Spanish feminist theory and narrative practice (1991a). In order to prevent unnecessary repetition, rather than discuss the critical work written on Montero in this introductory section of this text, I will do so when particular articles are relevant to the area of analysis. However, two book length studies have recently been published on Montero, by Alma Amell and Catherine Davies, and a brief overview of their theoretical standpoint may be useful here.[4]

Alma Amell's text *Rosa Montero's Odyssey* (1994) is, as its title suggests, a metaphysical discussion of the dialectics between the human being and the universe. Although Amell recognises that the texts are linked to a complex, rapidly changing reality, she does not tend to historicise her analysis. Instead she concentrates primarily on the universal themes of love and death in an attempt to place Montero into the context of a Spanish tradition of writing on such themes. Elements are taken from French psychoanalytic and Marxist theories but these are quoted in support of specific points rather than forming a critical backbone to the text. Although a wealth of literary references ranging from Aristotle to Francisco Umbral are included in support of Amell's argument, the relation between them and Montero's texts is never clearly traced. At times the text seems to share a masculinist bias towards feminist issues. For example, Amell does not take issue with Roberto Manteiga's questionable assertions about Montero's attitude towards feminism which will be further discussed in Chapter Two. However, it is not her intended aim to undertake a feminist analysis. As she clearly states in her introduction, Amell believes that Montero's narrative revolves around the acceptance of death as the ultimate outcome of all earthly endeavours. Perhaps the most interesting section of this text is the conclusion which, instead of summing up what has gone before, turns to the question of why these novels appeal so much to readers by focusing on the complexity of Montero's narrative technique and the often overlooked issue of the use of humour in her work.

In contrast Catherine Davies's book, *Contemporary Feminist Fiction in Spain: The Work of Montserrat Roig and Rosa Montero* (1994), builds on the 1991 article cited above and sets out to correct the masculinist bias of much traditional Spanish literary criticism with a both predominantly feminist and women-centred analysis. She begins by sketching the panorama of post-Franco women's narrative and outlining both Rosa Montero and Montserrat Roig's engagement with feminism. However, whilst texts are placed into their historical context, relatively few references are made to Spanish feminist theorists in the main body of the text which concentrates primarily on content analysis and discussions of narrative technique. It does however, prioritise an 'international, gender-defined literary framework' (Davies 1994, 2). This is because the text was intended for feminist readers not necessarily acquainted with Spanish literature or the socio-historical context these novels were written in. Its stated aim, which it fulfils admirably, was to 'introduce the narrative fiction of Montserrat Roig and Rosa Montero, two of Spain's most popular and distinguished contemporary women novelists to a broader public' (Davies 1994, 1).

Questions of Terminology

Originally, the title of this study was to have been 'The Construction of Feminine Identity in the Narrative of Rosa Montero'. I decided to change it to 'The Search for Identity in the Narrative of Rosa Montero' after much deliberation on the problematic nature of the term 'feminine', a term all too often conflated with a set of characteristics defined in opposition to the term 'masculine' to which it is linked in a seemingly indissoluble binary relationship. As I aim to go some way to blurring these clear-cut distinctions, moving in the words of Eve Tanor Bannet beyond a logic of either/or to a both/and positioning (1992, 3), I discarded this term and considered the term 'Women's' as a substitute but in turn rejected it as it too carries with it the ideological implications of what the term 'woman' means within the context of a patriarchal society. What does it mean to be a 'true woman' or 'truly womanly'? Furthermore, the positing of a generic 'we' rather begs the question of just who does this 'we' refer to? Whilst acknowledging the possibilities for empowerment achieved through solidarity between women and identification between groups of women, the insights afforded by poststructuralist theory in its contestation of terms such as truth and identity, whilst embracing terms such as difference, cannot be ignored. The danger lies perhaps in reducing difference to two terms: feminine/masculine or woman/man. By subsuming all women within the seemingly unitary term of 'Women's Identity', the differences between individual women are lost. This question has been addressed by several Spanish feminist theorists. Many adopt the position of Amelia Valcárcel who vindicates the adoption of a pragmatic 'we', whilst acknowledging its limitations, and the foregrounding of the individuality of women as opposed to an individualism which ultimately evades commitment (1997, 71-87):

> No se puede salir por la fuerza individual, así sea ella de enorme calibre, de las garras de las heterodesignaciones [...] Las mujeres comparten la característica de *la mujer*, esto es de una designación, por un lado, y, por otro, comparten una gama infinita de formas de estar en el mundo, una fenomenología, pero nunca una esencia.[5]

> One cannot escape through individual strength, even if it is of great calibre, the claws of heterodesignations [...] Women share the characteristic of *woman*, that

is to say of a designation on the one hand, and on the other, they share an infinite variety of ways of being in the world, a phenomenology but never an essence. (1991, 156 & 158)

Although certain elements of poststructural discourse analysis have been taken on board in this study, this has not been done uncritically. Instead, I have drawn on the growing body of feminist criticism which considers the problematic relationship between on the one hand theories which, whilst facilitating the discussion of marginal discourses, posit the dissolution of the subject, and on the other feminist political activism which stresses the importance of autonomy and agency for women.[6] Although I am aware that my decision to omit a gender reference from the title may suggest a universalist, androcentric approach or, ironically, once again the silencing of women within a patriarchal framework, I aim to provide such a voice within the main body of this text. In taking into account the contestation of terms such as identity, it is perhaps useful to set out how the term is being used in the context of this study. I interpret it as the narrative construct through which we attempt to construct our selves in a continual process of self-definition which involves both the conscious and subconscious. As a multiplicity of discourses are invoked it is shifting, fragmentary and even self-contradictory. Personal identity cannot be considered independently of external context as it is both relational and intersubjective. The recognition that the subject is not stable and may oscillate between several positions necessitated the final amendment to the original title: the shift from the construction of one particular identity to a search, a quest that is perhaps destined to be a never-ending story.[7] Montero herself has described the feminist project in terms of a continual search rather than a fixed ideological position:

> Es un intento continuo de conocimiento y clarificación sobre lo que una es y sobre el papel que juega en este mundo y sobre el papel que juega el hombre.
>
> It is a continual attempt to attain knowledge and clarification as to who one is, the role one plays in this world and the role played by men. (Villán 1983a)

Nonetheless, some sense of contingent collective identity is enabling or useful for the oppositional politics of marginalised groups providing that it is recognised as provisional and politically assumed in order to give agency to a positional contextually bound subject.

Literature and Daily Life[8]

The emphasis on feminist theory marks this study as part of a wider political project: the engagement by feminist academia with critical theories which through the discussion of the 'nature' of gender identity and female subjectivity facilitate in some way the construction of agency for women. How useful then is the study of literature as a basis for cultural analysis or a feminist politics? Both parts of this question were addressed during the fourth 'Jornadas de Investigación Interdisciplinarias' held in 1984 by the Seminario de la Mujer of Madrid's Autónoma University. Reflecting the growing critical attention being accorded to the boom in women's writing at that time, the papers given at this conference were on the theme of literature and women's everyday life. Although the majority of the papers dealt with images of women in the writing of canonical male writers, there was also an attempt to outline and carry out a putative gynocriticism, that is to say theorising of texts by women writers.[9] It is important to note that, perhaps due to the interdisciplinary nature of the seminar, the discourse analysis was not confined to literary texts but included essays on journalism, advertising, radio shows and cinema.[10] In her introduction to the conference proceedings, Mª Ángeles Durán addressed the question of a reciprocal relationship between literature and society. She asked: Who writes? For Whom? Why? How? (1987, 14). On the question of authorial intention I do not pretend to answer the question of why, although references will be made to statements made by Montero which cannot always be taken at face value. Paradoxically, Montero has repeatedly stated that her intention is to write neither militant nor commercial novels. Yet she is widely considered to be a writer of feminist best-sellers. The issues of both style and content will be addressed throughout the study within the thematic/discourse analysis. With regard to the question of author and reader, it is interesting to consider the comments made by Gayle Greene in the introductory essay of a recent collection co-edited with Coppélia Kahn of essays about the reconciliation of feminist politics and academia, in which she argues that 'stories, stories about the self, stories by women and about women's selves, had enormous power and continue to have enormous power in the creation of feminist consciousness' (Greene 1993, 11).[11] Novels by women, particularly those which are autobiographical or metafictive, have confronted the problematic questions surrounding notions of self and cultural identity. They do not simply reflect socio-historical circumstances but mediate them through reticulate discursive practices which can be inserted into the complex cultural networks which permeate both the text and its context, both its production and reception. Thus, narrative fiction provides a possible site for the negotiation of conflicts such as that between postmodern and feminist theory outlined above. As Catherine Davies concludes in her introduction to the fiction of Montserrat Roig and Rosa Montero, discussed above:

> Creative practice unties paradoxes and defies polarities; it simultaneously reflects on the past and imagines the future. It breaks down verbal and conceptual barriers and shifts the site of difference. (1994, 182)

One of my aims in this study is to refer to Spanish theorists and feminist writers, wherever possible, although traces of a background in Anglo-American and French feminist texts may of course be detected.[12] In 1983, in a review essay for *Signs* in which she discusses the response of American critics to Spanish women novelists between 1942 and 1980, Linda Chown stated that 'the feminist's task requires recognition of the varied cultural, political and aesthetic elements that shape literature' (1983, 91-2). She went on to point out the problems American critics have faced when trying to interpret these novels because they have projected their expectations and values onto them. Chown suggested a shift in methodological focus:

> Although we cannot push a button and shed automatically the culturally inherited assumptions that inhibit our understanding of the Spanish novel, we can at least become more fully aware of them by keeping in mind the peculiarly Spanish notions that govern and shape the world as Spanish women see it. (1983, 102)

She argued that to enable such a methodological shift to take place, it is necessary to situate contemporary Spanish women's narrative in the context of the history of Spanish women's literature and also of contemporary Spanish feminist studies.[13]

Whilst acknowledging the influence Chown's article has had on the development of this study, it is also necessary to take into account Geraldine Nichols's critique of Chown's position. Nichols argues that all readings, as shown by deconstructive criticism, are necessarily subjective (1992, 22). I would concur with her conclusion that a feminist practice must make explicit our limitations and conditioning as critics when interpreting a text. For example, this particular study in analysing Montero's work concentrates on gender as opposed to class, race, sexuality or any of a number of variables entering into the question of identity and subjectivity. It is also limited in scope in that I will be concentrating on her novelistic output as, despite their obvious interest, the sheer number of short stories and journalistic articles precludes their incorporation. As stated above, my main aim has been to examine the connections between Montero's narrative and the socio-cultural conditions in which it was produced; to place the text in its contexts. It is with this in mind that I have chosen to adopt the multi-disciplinary approach that has perhaps come to characterise feminist theory, 'enlist[ing] theory or theories to interrogate cultural assumptions and categories [and] to explore the interactions of literary conventions with social conventions, with an eye to feminist politics' (Greene 1993, 19). I feel that this approach is particularly well suited to a narrative which the author herself describes as 'agitated and eclectic' (Montero 1995b).

The overall focus on identity politics is particularly pertinent to Spain in the period I have chosen to study. During the post-Franco period in Spain, many seemingly stable identities have been deconstructed such as that of left-wing, formerly oppositional figures who found themselves in positions of power until the recent 1996 elections. However, as indicated above, this study is woman-centred and, whilst considering issues of party politics when relevant to the argument, will concentrate on the issue of exploring identities for women outside the confines of the term 'Woman'. Through analysing the modes of re-presentation or various discursive strategies employed by Rosa Montero in her narrative explorations of the term 'woman', I aim to show that she refutes an essentialist concept of woman trapped in a series of binary, hierarchical oppositions and moves towards the more open categories proposed by Justa Montero in my opening quote.[14]

[1] All translations are my own.

[2] Other studies include Pérez (1988), Fox-Lockert (1979), Miller (1983), special edition of *ALEC*, 12 (1987), special edition of *Ventanal*, 14 (1988), Valis & Maier (1988), Manteiga, Galerstein & McNerney (1988), Erro-Orthmann & Mendizabal (1990), Hart & Condé (1991), Ordóñez (1991), Hart (1993). There are also several book-length studies published in Spain: Pérez (1978), Gabancho -on women writers in Catalonia- (1982), special edition of *Litoral* (1986), Martín Gaite (1987), Durán & Rey (1987), special edition of *Poder y Libertad*, 13 (1990), López & Pastor (1990), Mayans Natal (1991), Gascón Vera (1992), Nichols (1992), special edition of *Quimera*, 123 (1994). See López Jiménez (1995, 13-15).

[3] Motherhood is used here in the biological sense of the term.

[4] There is also a book by Emilio de Miguel Martínez (1983) which analyses only *Crónica del desamor* and *La función delta*. In his introduction he states that this is a personal approximation written in a conversational tone as it originated from talks he gave for the 1983 'Cursos de Verano' at Salamanca University. As such, much time is spent on giving extensive plot summaries as well as thematic/stylistic analysis. The focus would seem to be on the evolution of Montero's narrative technique.

[5] Isabel Santa Cruz sustains a similar position which is cited in Chapter One in the discussion of the terms 'equality' and 'difference'. Other theorists such as Celia Amorós and Amparo Moreno Sardà will be discussed in Chapter Three which deals with metafiction and the construction of life narratives. There is a considerable body of work written by Anglo-American feminists on this issue. For reasons of brevity, I will only cite Donna Haraway's 1991 essay, 'A Cyborg Manifesto: Science, Technology and Socialist Feminism in the Late Twentieth Century' in which she acknowledges the painful fragmentation of a feminist movement for whom 'identities seem contradictory, partial and strategic' (1991, 155). She suggests response through 'affinity not identity' (1991, 155).

[6] At the debate of Cristina Molina Petit's book, *Dialéctica de la ilustración*, organised by the Centro de Investigación y Formación Feminista on 8 April 1994 at the Biblioteca Nacional de Madrid, the author expressed her belief in the need for a position for women as subject in order to undertake strategic action. For a discussion by Spanish theorists of the problematic relationship between feminism and postmodernist theory see Fagoaga (1989), Molina Petit (1992 & 1994) and Rodríguez Magda (1992).

[7] This view of the discourse of reality as a never-ending narrative is explored in Martín Gaite (1985).

[8] This is taken from the title of the Durán & Rey volume cited below.

[9] In her study of post-war narrative by Spanish women writers, Geraldine Nichols notes that in Spain the term 'ginocrítica' (gynocriticism) is often used as a euphemism for feminist literary studies rather than the Anglo-American use of the term to denote the study of literature written by women (1992, 1).

[10] Such cultural 'texts' will also be analysed, where pertinent, in this thesis.

[11] Feminist practice within academia (in the U.S.A.) is the subject of another collection of essays I have found very useful in helping to determine my own critical practice: Hartman & Messer-Davidow (1991)

[12] These traces also occur in the theory emerging from Spain, particularly in the work of women who have undertaken masters programs or doctorates in the U.S.A., such as Raquel Osborne or Cristina Molina Petit. Elizabeth Ordóñez, whilst applying predominantly French and Anglo-American theoretical perspectives in her analysis of strategies of articulation of 'voice' within contemporary Spanish narrative by women, notes that 'critical , theoretical voices [Montserrat Roig, Carme Riera, Helena Araújo, Marta Traba, Evelyne García], which traverse the boundaries of Hispanic nationalism, clearly urge interested readers everywhere to perceive their convergence with contemporaneous narrative strategies of Spanish women' (1991, 26).

[13] Anabel González, in her study of the beginnings of the post-Franco feminist movement criticises the importation of ideology (1980, 11-12). This criticism is quoted in the introductory section to Chown's doctoral thesis, in which she elaborates, 'superimposing a familiar Anglo-American view of women upon unfamiliar Spanish conditions both obfuscates Spanish realities and impoverishes or stunts emergent understanding' (Chown 1986, 57).

[14] The term 're-presentation' is hyphenated to suggest a revisionary reading of certain discursive modes/strategies rather than a simplistic reading of literature as a transparent representation of reality.

CHAPTER ONE

'BEYOND DISCOURSES OF DIFFERENCE AND EQUALITY': A STUDY OF THE DEBATE AND ITS IMPLICATIONS IN THE NARRATIVE OF ROSA MONTERO.[1]

> **Yo me defino feminista. Es una postura frente a la vida: vital intelectual, crítica, de revisión de la cultura sexista que nos han dado. Es intentar que esta sociedad no siga obligándonos a limitarnos por nuestro sexo.**
>
> **I define myself as a feminist. It is a stance towards life: dynamic, intellectual, critical, revisionary of the sexist culture we have been given. It is an attempt to put an end to the limitations imposed on us by society because of our sex.**
> **(Montero in Fontradona 1995, 34)**

For Rosa Montero feminism is not necessarily a question of political activism but of a personal attitude towards life, a vital condition in a patriarchal society in which women are oppressed. That notwithstanding, she was named one of the ten most influential women during the transition period and her work as a journalist and editor on the staff of *El País* undoubtedly has had an impact in the sociopolitical arena (Montero 1991a, xii). Although Montero places herself outside the organised feminist movement in Spain and furthermore refuses to accept the label of feminist narrative, because of its militant connotations, her narrative would seem to mirror closely the debates within that movement, particularly the equality/difference debate.[2] I therefore propose to begin this study with a historical account of the Spanish feminist movement since 1975 in order to trace the development of this debate.

The Spanish Feminist Movement and the Transition to Democracy

The evolution of the Spanish feminist movement cannot be considered without reference to the political context of the transition to democracy, as feminist activities have been shaped by the process of social and political change.[3] In particular feminist groups have had to address the immediate fascist past under Franco and the lack of political effectiveness of women during the regime. Consequently the feminist movement has been split into two basic groups: those who advocate double militancy and the more radical single militancy groups (Davies 1991a, 204-06). Broadly speaking, the former address questions of class and nationality as well as gender and can be interpreted in the wider political context of the fight for democratic rights in a country emerging from a long-standing dictatorship within a traditionally centralised society. During the transition period opposition parties of the Left urged women activists within those political parties to subordinate women's liberation to what they saw as the more immediate task of building a democracy. In contrast single militancy feminists stressed the need for autonomous women's organisations in order to tackle what they saw as specifically women's oppression by men of all political persuasions. Their argument was that there could not be a true democracy without a complete overhaul of the patriarchal system and so they desisted from the fight for legal equality whilst retaining the goal of equality in 'dignity and social value' (Durán & Gallego 1986, 206). Furthermore, they abstained from state politics because they did not accept the values implicit in a hierarchical political system. A more radical strand of feminists claimed superiority over men and advocated a separate, utopian feminine culture (Kaplan 1992, 428-30).[4]

María Angeles Durán and Teresa Gallego have traced the development of the feminist movement in Spain after the death of Franco. They divide the first decade into three main periods:

1975-79: creation, expansion and organisation of a general movement.

1979-82: division within the movement due to internal disputes.

1982-85: decline and fall of the organised movement but a rise in the number of micro-organisations. (Durán & Gallego, 1986)

The initial period of expansion was dominated by the double militancy groups also known as 'class struggle feminism' (Durán & Gallego 1986, 208). This may be explained by the fact that the Spanish feminist movement, along with the Greek, is distinguished within Europe because it was initially an underground movement whose members faced arrest, torture, imprisonment, and exile. Various women's organisations had been linked to the clandestine political parties and a submerged network of feminist organisations came to the surface as these parties were legalised (210-11).[5] 1975 was a particularly important year for Spanish feminists as it was the United Nations International Women's Year and although Spanish feminists were prevented from attending events the coverage in the press served to promote the feminist cause. Editions of *Urogallo* (31-32) and *Cuadernos para el Diálogo* (August) were devoted entirely to women's issues and feminist debate (Roig Castellanos 1986, 431-2).[6] The first 'Jornadas para la Liberación de la Mujer' were held soon after Franco's death on 6-8 December 1975 in Madrid. Around five hundred women attended these secret meetings in which three main feminist groups emerged: the Movimiento Democrático de Mujeres, the Seminario Colectivo Feminista of Barcelona, and the Línea Barcelona, otherwise known as the Tercera Vía. These advocated women's liberation through democratic freedom, the suppression of the class system and power based on economic relations, and the transformation of society by autonomous feminist organisations respectively.[7] The movement was given prominence in the press as it emerged from clandestinity and it has been argued that the crucial year for the development of the Spanish feminist movement was 1976. In that year several Spanish women, including the radical feminist Lidia Falcón, travelled to Brussels to testify at the International Tribunal for Crimes Against Women held on 4-8 March (Russell & Van de Ven 1976). More significantly the 'Jornades Catalans de la Dona' held in Barcelona, in May of the same year, were attended by some four thousand women indicating the growth and change in status of the feminist movement within Spain. The discussion in Barcelona revolved around the main ideological issue in Spanish feminism, that is the conflict between double and single militancy. Feminist groups sprang up all over Spain and by 1979 Anabel González was to put their number at over a hundred (Roig Castellanos 1986, 438).

As the 1977 election approached, politicians of all parties recognised the potential of the women's vote and every party was to incorporate the principle of equality in their programme, even if the Socialists and Communists were the only parties to incorporate all of the women's demands in their electoral manifestos (Alcobendas Tirado 1984, 217-19).[8] Twenty of the delegates elected in 1977 were women, including the prominent feminists Carlota Bustelo (PSOE) and María Dolores Calvet (PSUC). Whilst emphasising the political activity that characterised this period, it is important to note that theoretical analysis was also being carried out. Various feminist works were published during this period by authors such as Lidia Falcón, Carmen Alcalde, María Aurelia Capmany, and sympathetic male intellectuals such as Amando de Miguel and Carlos Castilla del Pino (Roig Castellanos 1986, 424-30, 439, 443). The views of many of these feminists -along with various women writers such as Montero, Montserrat Roig and Ana María Moix- can be found in the review *Vindicación Feminista* directed by Lidia Falcón and edited by Carmen Alcalde. It was published between July 1976 and December 1979 but folded due to lack of funding.[9] Radical feminist groups in Spain have tended to suffer from a lack of popular support, with working-class women preferring to collaborate with the parties of the Left and the trade unions Comisiones Obreras and the Unión General de Trabajadores. This may be explained by the role the unions have played in providing information and guidance on retraining and employment opportunities. and also by the perception of the feminist movement as elitist. In 1977 the first 'Jornadas de la Mujer Trabajadora' were held. This dissociation within the Spanish feminist movement between activist politics and theoretical analysis is discussed at length in Juana Gil Ruiz's study of equality politics in Spain (1996) which argues persuasively for the need to unite theory and praxis in order to increase the power base of the movement through links with the community.

The ongoing debate between the two main positions within the Spanish feminist movement came to a head in 1979 in a general meeting of the Spanish feminist movement held in Granada and attended by some three thousand women.[10] This meeting was the starting point of the disintegration of the movement as an organised whole, as the breach between the two tendencies proved to be irreconcilable and the meeting dissolved into an acrimonious debate in which the two sides failed to reach any agreement. Thereafter many women were to turn to individualistic personal transformation as their goal. This can be interpreted as part of the more general phenomenon of the *desencanto* (disenchantment) with politics in Spain in the 1980s but it could also be argued that the recognition of the basic legal claims put forward by women by the Socialist government contributed to the decline in the appeal of the movement.[11]

After Granada the movement was no longer to be dominated by party feminists. Although women's committees remained active within the socialist and communist parties, the Partido Comunista de España in particular was to suffer an internal crisis in the early 1980s, culminating in an exodus of militants including many women who supported calls for change and renewal within the party. Furthermore, within all the major political parties there are relatively few women at leadership level. In 1986 only 7.8% of the representatives in the Cortes Generales and 5.9% in the Senado were women.[12] More recently, the 1996 elections saw an increase in the number of women in the Congreso to 22%, placing Spain in seventh place in the European Union. The political focus for radical-Marxist feminists was the Partido Feminista de España formed in 1979 by Lidia Falcón and legalised in 1981; this party, now disbanded, argued that women should be considered as a separate class.[13] Its radius of action was concentrated around Barcelona and its views publicised in the review *Poder y Libertad* (founded in June 1980), but as a party it had little social or political influence.

Joni Lovenduski in her discussion of women and politics in Europe (1986) distinguishes between the first and second waves of the women's movement fighting respectively for rights and liberation. In Spain these divisions correspond to the older, militant, anti-Franco feminists and younger feminists who had grown up in a more liberal Spain and tended not to be linked to political parties. The latter, known as *independientes* (independents), have on the whole rejected the formal political arena due to feelings of anger and disappointment with formal equality, an equality which seemed to exist more in theory than in practice.[14] As María Jesús Izquierdo was to state at the '20 years after "Women's Lib"' conference, held in Barcelona on 13-15 October 1988, double militancy had fomented:

> ...los derechos de las mujeres en tanto que individuos formalmente iguales ante la ley pero obscureciendo al mismo tiempo la existencia de condiciones

estructurales que impiden la integración de ambos sexos en las actividades públicas y domésticas en igualdad de condiciones.[15]

...the rights of women as individuals who are formally equal before the law but at the same time obscuring the existence of structural conditions which impede the integration under equal conditions of both sexes in public and domestic activities. (1988, 18)

The *independientes* set up short-lived groups which take part in campaigns and attend meetings but have no overall organisational strategy.[16] A feature which is perhaps particular to Spanish feminism is the tendency towards regional autonomy of groups and resistance to centralisation. This can be interpreted as a reaction to the extremely authoritarian and centralised nature of the Franco regime as it reflects the political situation in Spain as a whole. Reflecting a rejection of tight structures and authoritarian control groups have proliferated in an informal network. Despite their differences, the discourse of these groups tends to focus on the issue of female sexuality and the fight for reproductive rights. This reflects the influence, since the early 1980s, of Italian feminists such as Carla Lonzi and French theorists such as Luce Irigaray and Annie Leclerc on difference feminism in Spain. However, double militant feminists such as Carlota Bustelo, Isabel Alberdi, Justa Montero and Merché Comabella have argued that feminists need to participate in political institutions despite their hierarchical structure because of the importance that the decisions made in them have for women in society as a whole. They argue against what they perceive as the tyranny of a lack of structures in the Spanish feminist movement at present (Alberdi 1992, 62). The atomisation of the movement and resultant dispersal of energies would seem to have paralysed its capability for collective action. Nonetheless some coordinating bodies have evolved which form alliances or encourage solidarity around specific issues for example pro-abortion campaigners can mobilise large forces when necessary (Brooksbank Jones 1997, 30).

Despite this apparent proliferation of groups the period from 1982 onwards has seen the 'institutionalisation' or 'democratisation' of Spanish feminism; that is to say all the political parties now have either a spokesperson, caucus, or department for women's affairs. The Instituto de la Mujer was created in September 1983 and directed by a socialist feminist Carlota Bustelo who had previously been a leading figure in the feminist movement.[17] Its creation reflects a change in the perception of women's issues in that the personal is perceived as political. The aim of the Institute is to put into practice the principle of non-discrimination incorporated into the Constitution (1978) of 1978 and it has run various campaigns to improve women's status. Its main achievement has been seen as its success in awareness-raising and providing information (Fernández Poncela 1992, 31). It is to be noted, however, that its links to PSOE between 1983 and 1996 gave rise to the contention that it gave preferential treatment to projects which were in line with party policy.[18] Radical feminists have been amongst the Instituto's most vocal critics terming the women who work there *femócratas*. They reject the 'institutional channelling and promotion of feminist demands' as they maintain that institutions are inherently patriarchal in structure (Brooksbank Jones 1993).[19] Furthermore, they have criticised the Instituto de la Mujer for purporting to speak on behalf of women who do not share its priorities (Brooksbank Jones 1997, 44). An interesting development in the 1990s has been the increased devolution of power and responsibilities from the Instituto de la Mujer to regional and local government bodies. These are seen as being more accountable and accessible to grassroots organisations. Moreover due to underfunding they have worked more closely with NGOs and local pressure groups in both policy formation and implementation thereby encouraging the development of participative or direct, rather than representative, democracy (Brooksbank Jones 1997, 30-1).

In addition to the political institutionalisation of feminism various departments of Women's Studies have been created within universities; the first were set up in 1978 in the autonomous universities of Madrid and Barcelona. A feminist Athæneum was also set up in Madrid which holds lectures, exhibitions, and *tertulias*. This move within the academic system has been mirrored in the literary sector by the opening of feminist book shops, founding of several reviews, and women's publishing houses.[20] It is to be hoped that this 'institutionalisation' of feminism and the increasing interest in theoretical studies in centres such as the Seminario de la Mujer in the University of Granada, directed by Pilar Ballarín and the Instituto de Investigaciones Feministas in the Complutense University of Madrid, directed by Celia Amorós, may provide the basis for contesting the so-called 'invisible patriarchy' which is encoded within social relations and cultural practices.[21]

Until now, the achievements in the field of feminist theorising have been modest in comparison with empirical research. In the 1989 special edition of the *Cahiers du Grif*, devoted to the discussion of Feminist Studies, Cristina Borderías, in the entry for Spain, noted that during the 1980s many initiatives had been undertaken, notably in the form of *seminarios* (research groupings) outside the university curriculum. Due to the difficulty of obtaining financial and structural support much of the original research was empirical (Borderías 1989, 56-57).[22] However, that is not to say that important theoretical work is not currently being produced such as that published in the collection 'Pensamiento Crítico/Pensamiento Utópico' brought out by the editorial house Anthropos and more specifically the series within this collection sponsored by the Dirección General de la Mujer: 'Cultura y diferencia: Teorías feministas y cultura contemporánea'. The first volume in this series was published in 1993: *Breve historia de la literatura española (en lengua castellana) I. Teoría feminista: Discursos y diferencia. Enfoques feministas de la literatura española*, edited by Myriam Díaz Diocaretz and Iris Zavala.[23]

Despite the vigourous emergence and self-determination of Spanish feminisms, defining the boundaries of the current feminist movement in Spain is a problematic, and one might say futile, task. Relatively few Spanish women participate as active members of autonomous feminist groups. Although there were six hundred women's groups in Spain in 1985, only around 20% of these were of an overtly feminist nature and furthermore only 0.1% of Spanish women belonged to such groups (Davies 1991a, 213). As indicated above, at the 1988 conference entitled '20 Years after "Women's Lib"', held in Barcelona, speakers were to stress the disparity between past achievements and the present *desencanto*. The feminist movement as an organised whole was perceived to have collapsed.[24] In a discussion of the Spanish feminist movement during the 1980s and 1990s, María Moron, an *independiente*, stated that:

> El engaño que se produce de un estado de opinión generalizado que niega la existencia de discriminaciones, provoca un rechazo hacia el movimiento feminista tildándola de caduco.

The disillusion produced by a general state of opinion which denies the existence of discrimination, has provoked a rejection of the feminist movement by branding it as outmoded. (Cervera et al. 1992, 47)

This would seem to be the case for many young women who seem to perceive feminism as an outdated movement and take its gains for granted. Judith Astelarra, in an interesting two-part article on the future of feminism in Spain co-written with Antxon Pérez de Calleja, argues that it is too early to talk of postfeminism when the basic problems have not been resolved despite this institutional activity (1993, 33). One development of the 1980s was what Pilar Folguera termed *feminismo sectorial/profesional*, particularly in the legal and medical professions (1988c, 97). Furthermore, many women, whilst declaring themselves not to be feminist, seemed to ascribe to the ideals of the feminist movement as is attested by a survey carried out by the Instituto de la Mujer in 1987, the results of which were as follows:

ASSESSMENT OF THE EXISTENCE OF FEMINIST ORGANISATIONS (%)	
Very positive	9,3
Quite positive	34,8
So-so	26,3
Not very positive	9,3
Not/hardly positive at all	8,5
Don't know	10,8
No answer	1,0
	(1990b, 10)

Thus, 44.1% of the women in the survey considered the existence of feminist organisations as positive. Why then did they prefer not to describe themselves as feminist? The same women were asked what the term feminism meant for them:

OPINIONS ABOUT FEMINISM (%)	
It is a movement which vindicates and defends women	34
It is a non-traditional feminine way of life	14
The same as machismo, but by women	16
A way of changing the relationship between men and women	15
Don't agree with any of the above	2
Other definitions	2
Don't know, not sure	15
No answer	2
	(1990 b, 10)

This may reflect the ridicule of the feminist movement, particularly by some of the more *progre* (progressive) sections of the left in the 1970s (Oranich 1976, 70; Bustelo 1979, 221; Serrano 1979, 154) and the misconception, often propagated by the press, that feminism is a sort of *hembrismo* (female chauvinism) practised by aggressive, frustrated, intolerant, ugly lesbians (Astelarra 1986, 52-3; Col.lectiu de Dones Joves Desobedencia 1994, 223; Urruzola 1988, 17).[25] Perhaps, a more serious problem than such stereotypical representations of the feminist movement has been its failure to reach the mass of women in Spain. This may be explained by the perception of feminist theory by women outside the movement as being marginal, radical, intellectual and elitist (Synapse 1985).

This tendency to shy away from describing oneself as feminist is particularly prevalent among Spanish women writers, with the exception of those who are highly committed politically such as Lidia Falcón. A possible explanation may be that, as writing narrative is perceived as a traditionally masculine/public space, in order to accede to that space women choose to publicly renege feminism (Puleo 1994a, 28). Another would be that the above negative perceptions of the feminist movement cause writers to reject the feminist tag for fear that their writing would also be perceived as being written in a certain style for a limited readership (Davies 1994, 5). Lourdes Ortiz sums up the position of many women writers when she states that she is not a feminist in the sense of belonging to a militant group but 'si se entiende por feminista persona preocupada por el problema de la mujer y por los intereses de reivindicaciones, sí me considero como tal' (if one understands by the term feminist someone preoccupied by the problems faced by women and interested in vindicating women, then yes I do consider myself to be a feminist) (Porter 1990, 144).

Spanish Women's Narrative During the Transition and 1980s

In contrast with the relative paucity of published research on feminist issues in Spain during this period, mentioned above, there was an upsurge in fiction written and published by women. There was also increased recognition given to women writers by the literary establishment. In 1984 the Seminario de la Mujer of the Autónoma University of Madrid dedicated its annual 'Jornadas de Investigación Interdisciplinaria sobre la Mujer' to literature.[26] The philosopher María Zambrano became the first woman to win the prestigious Premio Cervantes in 1988 and in 1989 the publishing house Castalia launched a collection of women authors with the collaboration of the Instituto de la Mujer. In 1990 the Fifth International Feminist Book Fair was held in Barcelona and Drassanes. Literary commentators discussing narrative of the transitional period often refer to the boom of women's writing in Spain, this 'boom' consisting of a group of women writers who came to prominence during the late 1970s and early 1980s.[27] Rosa Montero has stated that 'en estos últimos cinco años el verdadero boom ha sido la literatura de mujeres; se hablará de una generación, a pesar de que no tenemos nada en común, por la coincidencia y por la fuerza que tenemos juntas. Creo que es un movimiento riquísimo que tiene muchas posibilidades' (in the last five years the real boom has been that of women's writing, we will be termed a generation despite the fact that we have nothing in common, because we coincide and are strong as a group. I think that it is a very rich movement with many possibilities) (Regazzoni 1984, 53).[28] Although these texts are diverse both in terms of style and theme, as several commentators such as Alborg (1987), Fuentes Molla (1991), Brown (1991a), and Davies (1991a) have pointed out, certain generalisations can be made about the period in question. Phyllis Zatlin (1987) traces the development of women's writing during the democratic period and broadly divides it into two prevalent tendencies: testimonial literature in the late 1970s and metafiction in the 1980s.

Novels published in the late 1970s tended to depict contemporary women's experience and thus fulfil a consciousness-raising function as such fiction reached a wider public than theoretical feminist texts. At the 1979 Feria del Libro, Jimena Alonso of the Madrid Librería de Mujeres, stated that the most common genre for fiction -in translation also- by women was testimonial (Carrasco 1979, 35). Romero et al. in their discussion of women's narrative and feminism in the 1970s see the narrative of this period as an autoanalytical literature (1987, 341).[29] It asks the questions 'Who am I?' 'What is my role?'. In its protest against the dominant parameters of patriarchal discourse it is 'una busquéda del yo, no con voz de autoridad, sino como algo en formación' (a search for the self, not with the voice of authority, but as something in the process of formation) (Rodríguez Iglesias 1993, 146). Female characters would seem to be confused in their search for a new identity in which they look to the past but lack role models as the women of previous generations, in particular mothers, would seem to represent the traditions they are trying to break free of.[30] As a result these women feel marginalised, different and frustrated. They are 'frontier women' (Regazzoni 1984, 15), in that they wish to transgress the roles imposed on them by society but are not quite capable of stepping out of the narrative framework they have been slotted into. Romero et al. interpret this as a consequence of 'una literatura fundamentalmente *testimonial*, basada en la *experiencia* y en la búsqueda de la propia *identidad* [...que] no ha dado el salto cualitativo hacia la imaginación por falta de capacidad para distanciarse' (a literature which is fundamentally *testimonial*, based on *experience* and on the search for *identity* of the self[...which] has not made the qualitative leap into the imaginary due to a lack of the capacity to distance itself) (1987, 355).

This narrative would seem to be describing the frustration felt by feminists at the gap between formal, legal equality and the damaging substructures still in place such as force of habit/the social fabric/the conservative influence of the church/husband's expectations (Costa 1991, 13). As Catherine Davies comments 'political and sexual liberation within existing structures lead nowhere' (1991b). It is important to note that whilst this has been a period of intense change, social transformation has not kept up with the pace of political transformation. As early as 1976, María Ángeles Durán had already noted that political involvement addressed specific problems rather than the wider causes of those problems (Durán Heras 1976, 110).[31] In the same year, the limitation of the effects of legal reform by social customs had been noted by the sociologist Julio Iglesias de Ussel who stressed the need to change the mentality and behaviour which constitute the 'invisible patriarchy' discussed below. In a premonitory statement he declared that 'Un decenio de bienintencionada legislación antidiscriminatoria -si la hubiera- quedaría barrido con uno solo de los habituales anuncios de Televisión Española' (A decade of well-intentioned antidiscriminatory legislation -were it to exist- would be wiped out with just one of the usual adverts on Spanish television.) (1976, 196).[32] Indeed, one of the objectives of the First *Plan para la igualdad de oportunidades de las mujeres (1988-1990)* was to promote non-sexist advertising; the Instituto de la Mujer instigated the Premio Casandra for adverts that treat men and women as equals (Peña-Marin & Frabetti 1990, 6-7). In an article on Rosa Montero's first novel, *Crónica del desamor* (1979), Cristina de la Torre notes that as the legal changes did not evolve from a National consensus but were effected from the top-down, they were 'more a promise of change than the reflection of an already existing reality' (1985, 1-2).[33] The *desencanto* felt by many, as Izquierdo stated above, is made evident in this novel in which the divisions between the personal and the affective are blurred. The disorientation felt by the women characters applies equally to their personal relationships with men as to their position in society, 'la lucha feminista tiene una dificultad especial [...] el oprimido [la oprimida?] y el opresor se hallan unidos por vínculos afectivos' (the feminist struggle has a particular difficulty [...] the oppressed and the oppressor are united by emotional ties) (Izquierdo 1988, 17).[34]

The early 1980s saw a switch to a more ludic fiction with metafictive tendencies coming to the fore.[35] In relation to the novels of Esther Tusquets, Nina Molinaro discusses the subversive potential of metafiction as women novelists question the binary oppositions of 'subject/object, reading/writing, fiction/reality' by calling attention to the 'narrative act (process) that informs the story being told (product) and problematises the relationship between fiction and reality' (1991, 24). She goes on to posit that this current in Spanish women's narrative has emerged 'from a position of difference, that of a female character (or characters) seeking to understand herself and the "stories" she has read and incorporated into her fictional reality' (1991, 24). Increasingly women's narrative set out to consciously undermine patriarchal myths and phallologocentric practices through self-conscious, alternative discourses. Female sexuality was also dealt with more openly in explicitly erotic and also lesbian narrative.[36] Within Spanish women's narrative of the 1980s the search for a feminine identity has involved the creation of an alternative female mythopoesis which has tended to emphasise the maternal in a utopic strand of current women's narrative (Ordóñez 1982 & 1988).[37] This phase of conquering creative freedom through the release of repressed fantasy and the creation of feminine myths corresponds to the present moment as described by Montero in 'Escribiendo en la luna' in which she traces four phases of which the last two roughly coincide with Zatlin's analysis, phase three being a testimonial, semi-autobiographical literature.[38]

The focus of Spanish women's writing was summed up in a similar fashion by Carme Riera in the round table held at the Feria del Libro of Madrid in 1983 as being twofold: it involved raising the awareness of Spanish women's marginal status whilst vindicating a new subversive language connected with the body (Ordóñez 1987, 46).[39] The emphasis would seem to be on the recuperation of a voice that has been silenced in a search for self-identity and a means of expressing it from the awareness of being a woman (Montero, unpublished paper on women writing in the West, 'Escribiendo en la luna', 8).[40] This 'búsqueda dolorosa' (painful search) is still that described in the introduction to Montserrat Roig's collection of feminist essays, *Tiempo de Mujer* in which she stated that women no longer know their 'identity' but are questioning that which has been imposed on them by patriarchy (1981a, 25). In an interview included in the press dossier drawn up to accompany the proceedings of the aforementioned 1988 conference in Barcelona, which questioned the achievements of the feminist movement in Spain, the ethics lecturer Victoria Camps notes once more the feelings of ideological uncertainty (1988, 4). Several articles by the philosopher Celia Amorós allude to the need to de(con)struct gender and the complexity of resignifying an identity for women (1980a, 1980b, 1987, 1989, 1992).[41] Perhaps this disorientation is to be expected in a practice grounded in difference and oscillation between often opposing positions. The difficulty lies partly in the intermediate stage of *desidentificación* and partly in the lack of an adequate conceptual framework within which to construct a new identity (Amorós 1992, 15). As Felicidad Orquín notes, it is much easier to reject or negate the feminine identity traditionally ascribed to women, than to invent models outside patriarchal culture (1984, 31).

A focal issue when speaking of a voice in women's writing is the feminine nature of that voice, in Spanish: *palabra de mujer*. Although embraced by some, such as Elena Gascón Vera (1987 & 1992) and Elizabeth Ordóñez (1987), the majority of Spanish women writers and critics would seem to reject the idea of a writing conditioned by the female body.[42] Instead, they posit that the specificity of women's writing may be due to the marginalisation and cultural silencing of women and vindicate a recuperation of discourse, a new mode of expression which would go beyond the opposition of masculine and feminine (Orquín 1984, 31; Cabanilles 1990, 17-19; Riera 1990, 32-5).

The Equality/Difference Debate

Equality and difference feminism would seem to be combined as writers search for a feminine identity. It must be stressed that the two tendencies are not fixed, mutually exclusive categories, nor are they necessarily antithetical. Indeed the rigid division of the feminist movement into two camps supporting equality and difference is problematic in itself in that it exemplifies the binary logic which has characterised dominant Western philosophical discourse. Paola Bono and Sandra Kemp in their introduction to *Italian Feminist Thought: A Reader* discuss the need to disrupt the symmetry of polarity and to contest definitions that are based on contraries and adopt Gilles Deleuze's politico-geographical metaphor for the functioning of the 'binary machine': if we take East and West as the poles of opposition then destabilising forces appear on the North-South axis. Subsequently they describe Italian feminism as coming from the South to contest the dichotomy drawn between French and Anglo-American feminism. Thus Italian feminists whilst investigating 'the symbolic structures which both express and shape reality' also accept the importance of considering socio-historical experience (Bono & Kemp 1991, 23).

Many Spanish feminists have also criticised the dichotomy drawn between equality and difference which led to the excision of the feminist movement (Valcárcel 1991, 52-53; Gil Ruiz 1996, 286-94).[43] Although the diversity of the movement, consisting of fragmented organizations which focus on different issues and espouse various ideologies, certainly does provide a platform for change in its challenge to patriarchy and is possibly its strength, such a pluralism should not be uncritical, as the extensive debate sparked by the publication of Annette Kolodny's polemical essay 'Dancing through the Minefield' in 1980 demonstrated.[44] In the specifically Spanish context, the potentially paralizing effect of relativism and the failure to articulate diversity within the Spanish feminist movement is discussed at length in the dossier on 'Feminismo: Entre la igualdad y la diferencia' in the March 1994 issue of *El Viejo Topo*. For Justa Montero of the Asamblea Feminista de Madrid, the failure to retain the momentum of the movement as an agent for socio-political change has probably proved its fundamental weakness. In order to progress from the crossroads that the movement found itself at, she proposed a shaking up of theory and practice to revitalize bandied about concepts such as gender, suggesting a shift to more open categories (1994, 44).

A move towards a synthesis of equality and difference feminism can also be traced in Spanish feminism of the 1990s. As regards the policy of the Instituto de la Mujer, this progression is evident if one compares the first *Plan para la igualdad de oportunidades de las mujeres, (1988-1990)* and the second *Plan para la igualdad de oportunidades de las mujeres, (1993-1995)*. Although the second plan published in 1990, like the first, proposes legal reforms designed to promote the equality of opportunities, it makes a clear distinction between legal and authentic equality (Brooksbank Jones 1993). This would seem to indicate the recognition by the Instituto of the need to go further than legal reform.[45] Indeed the second*Plan* affirms difference:

> El sujeto 'mujer' es una abstracción homogeneizadora detrás de la cual existen 'mujeres' con situaciones, perspectivas y demandas cada vez más diversas [...] Abordar esa realidad rica y compleja, sólo es posible desde el reconocimiento y la toma en consideración de esa creciente pluralidad.[46]

> The subject 'woman' is a homogenizing abstraction behind which exist women with increasingly different situations, perspectives and demands [...] Tackling this complex and rich reality is only possible if this growing plurality is recognised and taken into account. (1990a, 55)

The stress has shifted from quantitative to qualitative change. In the Instituto de la Mujer's blueprint of strategic objectives for the year 2000 the section of future aims, as well as proposing various legal changes and increased access to masculine spaces, stresses the need to change structures and attitudes in order to effectively transform society (Instituto de la Mujer 1995b, 107-12).

Ana Rubio Castro examines both sides of the equality/difference debate in a lucid article in which she argues for a complex equality (1990). Using Italian feminist writing as the basis for her argument she discusses the problematic strategy of searching for a feminine identity through striving for equality with men. She quotes Carla Lonzi's essay 'Let's Spit on Hegel' (1970):

> Equality [...] is the principle through which those with hegemonic power continue to control those without.
>
> The world of equality is the world of legalised oppression and one-dimensionality [...] Equality between the sexes is merely the mask with which woman's inferiority is disguised. (Bono & Kemp 1991, 41-2)[47]

Lonzi recognises the patriarchal ideology that lies behind the myth of equality, that is to say the ideology of the universal male subject or *arquetipo viril* (virile archetype) (Moreno Sardà 1986). The quest for equality with men can, therefore, only ultimately result in a sense of alienation for women because 'being like' will never be as good as 'being' (Bono & Kemp 1991, 15). In other words, neutrality of equality is put into question when it is conflated with identifying with the masculine (Dones en Lluita 1981, 8; Grupo Giulia Adinolfi 1992, 28-9). Indeed, paradoxically the promotion of equality may act to suppress diversity. Being equal does not by necessity imply homogeneity or being identical. In the November 1992 issue of *Isegoría*, in which the concepts of equality and difference are debated in a series of articles, Isabel Santa Cruz rejects an *igualitarismo* which serves to validate patriarchy because it assimilates the normative dominant model.[48] Such a concept of equality could be used to efface the history of oppression of women under the patriarchal system and minimise women's needs. She reformulates equality in terms similar to Italian *affidamento*: a reciprocal relationship of mutual acknowledgement between two autonomous subjects in which both have the capacity to exercise power (1992, 146-9).[49]

Difference feminist groups defend the autonomy of women, but, by rejecting political action it could be argued that they are isolationist and falling into the essentialist trap of seeking to define woman. One cannot pretend to ignore the other/oppressor and only transform oneself (Amorós 1989, 57).[50] Again, in the Spanish context, it is important to distinguish between difference and radical feminism such as the Colectivo Feminista de Madrid who criticise the adoption of the term 'natural difference', a term often used in anti-feminist discourse to signify the inferiority of women or their relegation to certain 'complementary' activities, and stress that humans are defined through their social relations with others (1979, 2-6).[51] Furthermore, as Paloma Saavedra of the Colectivo Feminista notes, one of the dangers of the difference approach is the confinement of women to the realm of sexuality and the home, as opposed to within the sphere of political power (Navajo 1978b, 31).[52] The rejection of difference feminism by many Spanish feminists may be explained with relation to the socio-political context from which the movement emerged. As Gisela Kaplan notes in her study of contemporary European feminism, the celebration by difference feminism of innate gender differences verges on fascist attitudes towards women and 'seems to surface only in countries which have not experienced fascism first hand' (1992, 30). In Spain a discourse stressing innate feminine qualities/attributes and celebrating the mystique of motherhood would seem all too familiar to women educated under Franco and subject to six months of obligatory social service with the Sección Femenina.[53]

The problematic aspects of vindicating difference between men and women were discussed by Empar Pineda, leader of the Movimiento Comunista de España, in her paper given at the 'Primeras Jornadas de Investigación Interdisciplinaria sobre la Mujer' held by the Seminario de Estudios de la Mujer in the Universidad Autónoma de Madrid, entitled 'El discurso de la diferencia. El discurso de la igualdad'. Pineda warned against the danger of the cult of the mother and exaltation of housework as these could tend to 'en última instancia, a glorificar por vía de la mitificación y de la autocomplacencia nuestras «miserias», aquellas a las que nos ha reducido la secular opresión' (in the final instance, glorify through mystification and self-complacency our 'miseries', those which secular oppression has reduced us to) (1982, 258). She argued against specifically masculine and feminine modes of knowledge stating that if women accept that their difference lies in a feminine mode of thought they might end up by voluntarily assuming a marginal role and fantasising in feminine ghettos instead of participating in the supposedly 'masculine' world (1982, 259-60). This marginal role is assumed by accepting, rather than questioning, the binary definition of the feminine in texts such as Victoria Sendón's proposal of a gynandry in which terms such as feminine mystery and paradox suggest a return to Freud's enigmatic Dark Continent (Sendón 1981, 229).[54] Pineda went on to affirm that apart from biological differences, differences between the sexes are socially constructed and what is needed is a transformation of both masculine and feminine roles.[55] Although Pineda recognised the value of the fight for legal equality, she affirmed that equality between the sexes would require a more profound transformation of the society in which we live.

As a Marxist feminist Pineda saw the first step in such a transformation to be the total incorporation of women in all areas of social production (1982, 263-4). In order for this to be possible the destruction of the patriarchal model of marriage and the family would be necessary. This view was also sustained by Cristina Alberdi in a paper given at the same conference (1982, 275). How could such a society be brought about and what would its culture be like? Pineda refused to speculate further than the affirmation that:

No podremos hablar para el futuro de una cultura femenina y una cultura masculina, esto es: de una división sexual de la cultura, sino que cada persona, mujer u hombre, podrá desarrollar libremente sus capacidades (racionales y sentimentales) y forjarse su propia personalidad en el seno de una sociedad de la que habrán desaparecido las relaciones de explotación y opresión.

In the future we will not be able to talk about a feminine culture and a masculine culture, that is to say a sexual division of culture, instead each person, woman or man, will be able to freely develop their capabilities (rational and emotional) and forge their own personality in the heart of a society in which relations based on exploitation and oppression will no longer exist. (1982, 269)

Pineda was arguing for nothing less than total revolution; a proposition she recognised as perhaps a utopic dream (1982, 271). Indeed, Gerard Imbert Martí, in the 1980 'masculine-feminine' edition of *El Viejo Topo* which also featured articles by Empar Pineda and Celia Amorós, posited identity itself as a ουτοπος, in another place beyond the sexes (1980, 43).

Rubio Castro also argues for the recognition of identity as constructed within a particular socio-historical moment but goes on to address the question of how women can participate in the political arena without compromising difference. Her argument is similar to that put forward by the philosopher Maite Larrauri (1993) who contends that although it is necessary to support women who occupy public posts and who have fought to accede to posts traditionally regarded as masculine, their presence in such posts is not sufficient and unfortunately may even serve to support the status quo. What is necessary, according to Larrauri, is to search for a feminine identity that has not been imposed by a patriarchal society in order to question the concept of power as it has been framed by that society. To do so Rubio proposes a dialectical relationship between feminist theory of difference and egalitarian practice using the ambivalence inherent in the feminine position to break down the barriers between the personal and the political.[56] In this she reflects the discussion of ambivalence by the Italian theorist, Maria Luisa Boccia in her essay 'The Gender of Representation' (1987):

By ambivalence I mean the determining of points of view and behaviour resulting from factors which would seem to be opposed or even irreconcilable... feminist ambivalence expresses itself, for example, in holding together alienation and participation in politics; in wanting to enact a presence and achieve a result which both tackles and involves the political system, while holding onto and indeed making plainly visible its position of eccentricity, of not being inscribed in the political order, given its own subjectivity and the sex-contradictions to which it refers. (Bono & Kemp 1991, 357)

What Boccia is arguing for is a practice that interrelates external political action with 'the internal'; by 'internal' she understands female subjectivity and the relations between women (Bono & Kemp 1991, 358). Boccia is no abstract theorist; indeed this essay forms part of the Italian Communist Women's Charter. A similar proposition was put forward by the Grupo de Mujeres Independientes de Madrid during the 'Jornadas «Diez años de lucha del Movimiento Feminista»' held in Barcelona on 1-3 November 1985:

> Buscábamos nuevas formas de debate, de estar, de trabajar entre mujeres... Los debates y discusiones no partían de algo ajeno a nosotras, y tratábamos de no hacer separaciones tajantes entre el mundo de lo público y de lo privado; para nosotras, lo privado también era político, público, y nos importaba como mujeres.

> We were looking for new forms of debate, of being, of working amongst women... The debates and discussions were not based on premises alien to ourselves and we tried not to make categorical divisions between the public and private world; for us the private was also political, public and important to us as women. (Rubio Castro 1990, 206)

The aim would seem to be to participate in politics whilst transforming political structures from within.

Despite apparent contradictions in their arguments, the conclusion drawn by both Pineda and Rubio Castro is basically the same: a valuation of difference. Pineda would seem to conclude by describing an *igualdad compleja* which is in fact a celebration of difference, albeit within the context of communist praxis:

> Más bien podremos hablar de un mundo de diversidad, de riqueza, en el que cada mujer no tenga tampoco que actuar o comportarse como las otras mujeres, ni cada hombre igual que otros hombres, sino que la individualidad de cada uno y cada una se desarrolle plenamente en armonía con los intereses colectivos.

> Rather we will be able to talk about a world of diversity, of richness, in which each woman would not have to act or behave like other women, nor each man

the same as other men, instead the individuality of each would develop fully in harmony with the collective interest. (1982, 271)

Rubio Castro clearly rejects the dichotomy drawn between the positions of equality and difference arguing for their integration. As noted above, this is a position sustained by many other Spanish theorists, particularly Celia Amorós in her expositions of the two-way trap of patriarchy for women: either they demand equality on the same terms as men or affirm difference but within the terms offered by patriarchal discourse (1980a, 32). As Amelia Valcárcel persuasively argues, in the study referred to in the introduction, it is necessary to reject both the generic man and woman which corset the individual person (1991, 116-18). If the causes of oppression are structural, then it cannot be simply overcome by increasing the number of 'exceptional' women who accede to traditionally masculine spaces nor by the increasing ghettoisation of the movement (Amorós 1980b, 118-19). In order to achieve authentic, as opposed to juridical, equality it is necessary to change the cultural paradigms which underpin society, to take an epistemological leap beyond binary polarisations (Sau Sánchez 1986b, 62; Sendón 1994, 69). In the words of Montero, to adopt 'el feminismo como teoría revolucionaría [...] en que se plantean las bases de la sociedad en que vivimos [porque] yo no quiero igualarme con el hombre en esta sociedad' (feminism as a revolutionary theory [...] in which the bases of the society in which we live are reconsidered [because] I don't want to be equal to men in this society) (Carrascal 1981, 13).

As Rubio Castro concludes, it is not sufficient to fight for legal equality without establishing another culture (1990, 207). This culture is not necessarily feminine in the essentialist sense attacked by Pineda, but it does involve the dismantling of androcentric interpretations of the world and universal paradigms based on the ideology of the universal male subject. One could argue that by proposing different perspectives or trajectories for culture and ideology, difference feminists are not aiming to enshrine some essential difference between men and woman, but to propose difference as a model for a non-patriarchal society.[57] In opposition to Pineda who gives primacy to social change over cultural change, Rubio Castro recognises the necessity of attempting to change the ideological framework of patriarchal society by proposing different ways of considering identity and culture in society at present. I would argue that it is this 'other culture' or contextual framework that Spanish women's narrative has set about constructing through the attempt to create a female discourse.

The Narrative of Rosa Montero

Evidently, the creation of such a discourse is a complex matter and the difficulty of working out the issues surrounding the search for identity positions for women will be evident from the discussion of historical and theoretical practice above. This difficulty is also manifest in the often contradictory writing of Montero herself, both in her journalistic and novelistic work. In interviews and articles, whilst on the one hand rejecting the ghettoisation of difference feminists and arguing against a mode of writing tied to women's corporeal experience, on the other she would seem to be accepting some of their tenets by embracing some sort of essential difference which limits and defines gender (1994a, 51). She admits to some confusion on the matter, 'No sé bien qué es ser mujer, de la misma manera que no sé qué es ser hombre. Sin duda, somos identidades en perpetua mutación, complejas y cambiantes' (I don't really know what it means to be a woman or a man. Without a doubt, we are identities in perpetual mutation, complex and changing) (1994a, 286).

This mutation is evident in the trajectory of Montero's narrative which broadly follows the outline traced by Zatlin whilst reflecting the debates within the Spanish feminist movement. *Crónica del desamor* (1979) and *La función delta* (1981) are both testimonial novels which deal with a wide range of feminist issues. It has been argued that *Crónica del desamor* in particular is a semi-autbiographical text (Davies 1991b, 109). They are also metafictive texts and so straddle the two tendencies posited by Zatlin for the late 1970s and early 1980s. With *Te trataré como a una reina* (1983) Montero moves away from novels depicting her social milieu. This is a consciousness-raising novel but not in socio-political terms. Rather it interrogates the 'invisible patriarchy' by questioning patriarchal texts and myths and deconstructing stereotypical portrayals of women. With *Amado Amo* (1988) Montero's narrative moves back, from the marginal world of *Te trataré como a una reina*, to depicting the professional classes, in order to deliver an incisive critique of the dynamics of power in a neocapitalist society. *Temblor* (1990) is markedly different from her prior novels, being a dystopic fantasy work set in a distant future. It is in this text that Montero most explicitly debates the various feminist positions discussed in this chapter. The fantastic quest for identity undertaken in *Temblor* is also followed in her first incursion into children's literature *El nido de los sueños* (1991). In her latest novels, *Bella y oscura* (1993) and *La hija del caníbal* (1997), she concentrates on how discourse can be appropriated to de/re-construct identity. The general trend in Montero's work is towards a greater emphasis on the personal rather than the political, from demands for equality to recognition of difference; although, as explained in the section above, the two positions are not mutually exclusive and are therefore combined in varying proportions throughout her often ambivalent narrative. Furthermore, there is a shift between the consideration of the differences between women as reflected in the multiple narrative viewpoint of *Crónica del desamor* to the consideration of the oscillation between different positions/identities adopted by women such as the main character Agua Fría of *Temblor*. The very title of the novel suggests the shifting ground of a *tembladal* (swamp), bringing to mind Teresa de Lauretis' description of feminism as 'a highly permeable terrain, [... which] shift[s] under one's feet and sometimes turns into a swamp' (1986, 7).

Montero's narrative develops from the 'realist' work *Crónica del desamor*, which examines contemporary socio-political issues of equality, criticising the social institution of motherhood, whilst tentatively celebrating difference, through the fantasy *Temblor* which interrogates the patriarchal socio-cultural order founded on binary oppositions whilst seemingly celebrating the potentiality of motherhood, to the increasing focus on the role of discourse in *Bella y oscura* and *La hija del caníbal*.[58] I would suggest that the evolution within Montero's narrative from socio-political analysis to theoretical debate, reflects the general trend in contemporary Spanish women's narrative away from realist consciousness-raising testimonial novels to affirmation of feminine identity and its difference in experimental fictional forms such as allegory, fantasy and pastiche.[59] Furthermore, this trend is analogous to the development of the Spanish feminist movement: from its dominance by double militancy feminists fighting for equal rights in the 1970s, to the proliferation of single militancy groups attempting to develop new conceptions of femininity through the exploration of difference in the 1990s; from political solutions to specific problems to critical explorations of the structural underpinnings of patriarchy itself.

[1] This quote is taken from the closing paragraph of Celia Amorós's 1980 article 'Feminismo: Discurso de la diferencia, discurso de la igualdad' (33).

[2] Her journalistic output also covers a wide range of issues related to sexual politics. This is particularly reflected in three of the sections of the collection *La vida desnuda* (1994) entitled: 'Nosotras', 'Amor y desamor' and 'Dolor del corazón'.

[3] For an analysis of social and political change affecting women see Durán & Gallego (1986), Roig Castellanos (1986), Scanlon (1986), SESM (1986), Folguera (1988b & 1988c), Pardo (1988a), Longhurst (1991), Kaplan (1992, chapter 6) and Benito (1993). For an account relating these changes to women's narrative during the twentieth century see Davies (1991a).

[4] Such groups include Las Brujas, Las Magas, La Lucha Antiautoritaria de Mujeres Antipatriarcales y Revolucionarias (LA MAR), and the lesbian caucus within the Instituto Lambda (a homosexual rights organisation).

[5] These groups included the Movimiento Democrático de Mujeres linked to the Partido Comunista de España, the Asociación Democrática de Mujeres connected with the Partido del Trabajo de España (a Maoist-oriented party); the Frente de la Liberación de la Mujer whose members ranged from moderate socialists to communists; smaller groups included the Unión de Mujeres Republicanas de Madrid, the anarchist group Mujeres Libres, and the Unión Popular de Mujeres which was a branch of the illegal group FRAP (Frente Revolucionaria Antifascista Patriótica). During the last years of the Franco regime there were at least ninety feminist groups and organisations, (Kaplan 1992, 198).

[6] Mª Ángeles Durán has noted that in the International Year more articles were written, colloquiums and press conferences held denouncing sex discrimination than in the previous ten years (Durán Heras 1976, 309). However, Natalie Ramos Vásquez criticised the ambiguity and superficiality of the mass media and the manipulative attempts by the government to assimilate the feminist movement and channel its demands (1975, 75). Similar criticisms were levelled in the round table section which prefaced the *Urogallo* special edition. It was also noted that the UN document was not translated in its entirety. Key sections on equality, NGOs, coeducation, family planning, improving prison conditions and stopping the 'white slave trade' were omitted.

[7] These divisions were an early indication of the subsequent polarisation of the movement.

[8] This opportunism was to continue after the elections. The UCD organised the 'Jornadas de la Condición Femenina', held on 14-16 September 1978. Many feminist groups refused to participate

due to the short notice they were given, ten days, whilst those that did walked out after a bitter polemic ensued opposing the categories *mujer* and *feminismo* (González 1978, 37).

[9] For a first-hand account of the achievements of and the reasons for the demise of *Vindicación Feminista* see Falcón (1988, 53-65).

[10] The split was already evident in 1975 according to the dossier on feminism drawn up in the July 1977 edition of *El Viejo Topo* by Palmes, Soria & Tuñón and a discussion by the Colectivo Feminista de Madrid on Spanish feminism in the 1970s (1977, 34).

[11] The 1978 constitution recognised the equality of men and women before the law with respect to civil rights and liberties. However, it has been criticised for not going far enough because it was a text born of consensus, a consensus from which women were excluded as none were involved in elaborating the first draft, and for actually being discriminatory in some aspects such as the privileging of male accession to the throne. See Navajo (1978a), Izquierdo (1979), Pardo & Comabella (1979) and Lucas Verdú (1981-2). For an account of the legal status of Spanish women see *Women of Europe*, Supplement #25 (1987, 108-11). In 1987 the Spanish government drew up a three year plan to bring Spain's equal opportunities policy in line with EC directives. See Lovenduski (1986, 282-85) and *Women of Europe*, #50, (15 March-15 July 1987, 30). A second plan was drawn up in 1990. See *Women of Europe*, #67, (December 1990-January 1991, 29).

[12] This placed Spain ninth in the EC. There were proportionately less women representatives in only the United Kingdom, France and Greece. See *Women of Europe*, Supplement #30 (December 1989, 14).

[13] The term 'radical feminist' as used within the Spanish context may give rise to some confusion. It is not used to refer to 'difference feminists' but specifically to indicate those who consider that women should be considered as a separate social class. See the booklet produced in 1979 by the Colectivo Feminista de Madrid, a radical group, which denounces the ludic strategies of 'difference feminists' and the celebration of an essential feminine identity.

[14] This rift was still apparent at the debate of Cristina Molina Petit's book, *Dialéctica de la ilustración* on 8 April 1994. Older women on the panel seemed confused by younger women in the audience arguing against equality and for postmodern theorising of difference.

[15] This reference is to one of many articles taken from the bibliography of Anny Brooksbank Jones paper on Spanish feminisms.

[16] Following the split at Granada the *independientes* set up their own 'Jornadas de Feministas Independientes'. An account of the reasons behind this decision and the direction taken by the *independientes* since was given in 1985 in the 'Terceras Jornadas Estatales: 10 años de lucha del

movimiento feminista' by the Asamblea de Feministas Independientes de Barcelona. For an account of the various 'jornadas' see Gil Ruiz (1996, 168-71).

[17] The Institute replaced the 'Subdirección General de la Mujer'created in 1978 by the UCD to promote new images of women and provide information on women's rights. It ran seminars and assisted various women's associations. In 1988 Carmen Martínez, a gynaecologist took over from Bustelo, she was replaced by Purificación Gutiérrez, a lawyer, in 1991 and the present director, the sociologist Martina Subirats assumed the post in 1993.

[18] See Pineda who also denounces the criticism of the radical vindications of the Movimiento Feminista by the Instituto de la Mujer (1988, 15).

[19] For a detailed account of the work of the Instituto de la Mujer and of arguments for and against it see Brooksbank Jones (1993).

[20] Reviews include *La Mujer Feminista, Langaiak, Tribuna Feminista, Mujeres*, and *Donas en Lluita*. Publishing houses include Feminae, Editorial Siglo XXI de España, and Horas y Horas. The publisher Cátedra is collaborating with the Instituto de le Mujer and the University of Valencia to bring out a range, entitled Colección Feminismos, of feminist theoretical works in translation.

[21] Within the Seminar in Granada courses are offered in feminist literary criticism by Carmen Martínez and on the equality/difference debate by Ana Rubio Castro. The Complutense Institute offers a course in feminist theory run by Celia Amorós and on sexuality and feminist criticism run by Alicia Puleo.

[22] See Durán Heras (1982a) for a detailed breakdown, by department and subject, of feminist research being carried out at that time.

[23] Unfortunately, whilst the stated aims within the prologue of the text -to use literature as a basis for epistemology and the construction of the subject, in order to examine questions of identity and identification- would seem to indicate an interest in the specifically Spanish social construction of the subject, this is not borne out by the rest of the text. Rossi's introduction does not take into account recent theorisation of gender and the main body of the text takes only a belated interest in culturally specific questions of identity and subjectivity.

[24] For an account of why this might have happened see Monica Threlfall's article on the aftermath of Granada where the lack of consensus and a certain *pasota* (politically apathetic) mentality was to put a brake on the mass expansion of the movement (1980, 127). Mª Jesús Izquierdo would later accuse the movement of complacency in a veiled attack on party feminists (1988, 21).

[25] Within *progre* circles the women-only nature of many branches of the feminist movement was seen as back-tracking to the sex-segregation of the Sección Femenina (Threlfall 1985, 47). In contrast, a measure of the conservative attitude might be gauged from an article by Carmen Bravo Villasante in which she branded the type of journalism written by Rosa Montero, Maruja Torres and Carmen Rigalt as shameless both in tone, theme and word, showing an adherence to an 'out-of-date' feminism and lacking in noble meditation (1988, 53)!

[26] There was a tendency in the papers given at the conference to privilege the sociological and 'images of women criticism' and relatively little work has been done until present in Spain on women as writers and readers. See Traba (1981), Riera (1982), De Fontcuberta (1987), Romero et al. (1987), Martín Gaite (1987), Molinaro (1991), Marimón (1992) and the introduction to Nichols (1992).

[27] However, as Zatlin notes, for many male critics women writers seem to have retained their 'traditional invisibility' (1987, 29). Santos Alonso in his review of the novel during the transition period includes around thirty novels but only one woman writer: Carmen Martín Gaite (1981). This lack of critical attention to contemporary Hispanic women writers was recently noted in the editorial of the special edition of *Quimera* (N° 123, 1994) dedicated to examining the work of twenty such writers. In an unpublished paper on women writers in Spain, Montero also denounces Spanish literary critics for their aggressive, sexist, derogatory, paternalistic attitude and the cultural establishment for omitting women from anthologies, encyclopaedias and academies ('Escribiendo en la luna', 13).

[28] In an interview with Javier Estrada in 1990, Montero stated that it was more of a sociological phenomenon than a literary boom (19).

[29] As does Dupláa (1982). Reader identification with these novels will be discussed in Chapter Two with reference to *Crónica del desamor* (Gándara 1981, 152 & Bachmann 1992).

[30] This confusion will be discussed further in Chapter Two with reference to the problematic relationship between mothers and daughters, in which the devaluation of the maternal model leads to lack of self-esteem and direction for the younger generation of women (Alberdi Alonso 1988, 22).

[31] In 1983, Carlota Bustelo -then head of the Instituto de la Mujer- stated the need to transform basic values (Instituto de la Mujer 1983, 183).

[32] The theme of sexism in advertising is particularly relevant to the novels *La función delta* and *Amado amo* in which the protagonists work for advertising agencies. For a more detailed analysis

of images of women in Spanish advertising see Montero (1977), Moreno (1983), Peña-Marín (1984 & 1986) and Peña-Marín & Frabetti (1990).

[33] P. Lucas Verdú points out that paragraph 2 of article 9 of the 1978 Constitution states that conditions should be promoted to ensure that equality is real and effective and obstacles that prevent this removed (1979, 27). Thus the text itself recognises that equality does not exist.

[34] Evidently this only applies to heterosexual relationships, the novel does not have any major lesbian characters. Further reference to this phenomenon of 'decepción, desencanto, desilusión, desamor' (deception, disenchantment, disillusion, unlove) is found in Consuelo de la Gándara's analysis of contemporary Spanish narrative written by women (1981, 150).

[35] For a theoretical discussion of metafiction in the context of Spanish literature during the transition see Spires (1984), Zatlin (1987) and Molinaro (1991).

[36] Examples of erotic narrative include *Un espacio erótico* (1983) by Marta Portal, *Las edades de Lulú* (1989) by Almudena Grandes, and *Artefactos eróticos* (1989) by Beatriz Pottecher. Esther Tusquets' 'trilogy' is an example of explicitly lesbian fiction.

[37] Works emphasising an alternative mythology include *Os habla Electra* (1975), *Argeo ha muerto, supongo* (1982) by Concha Alós; *Palabra de Mujer* (1980), *Una primavera para Doménico Guarani* (1981) by Carme Riera; *Urraca* (1982) by Lourdes Ortiz; *Otras mujeres y Fabia* (1982), *Los perros de Hécate* (1985) by Carmen Gómez Ojea, and *El rapto del Santo Grial* (1984) by Paloma Díaz-Mas.

[38] Phase one is the mimeticism of the masculine voice in pre-twentieth century writing and phase two the early twentieth century in which women writers were searching for a space in which to write as exemplified by Virginia Woolf's *A Room of One's Own*. These phases are, of course, arbitrary divisions describing general trends.

[39] On the silencing of women by the Franco regime see Rosario Sánchez López (1990, 57).

[40] For Aránzazu Usandizaga whilst this projection of such an identity may seem paradoxical and contradictory if one accepts the tenets of deconstructionism, it still makes sense to talk about identity in the case of a feminine culture which has been silenced and whose acknowledgement is still limited (1993, 11).

[41] A similar position is sustained by Carmen Marimón who discusses the crisis between signifier and signified (1992, 114).

[42] Whilst many writers rejected a discourse grounded in the corporeal experience of being a woman, narrative written in the 1970s and 1980s did set about reclaiming women's sexuality which will be discussed further in chapter two. See Bayón (1986) for the views of Adelaida García

Morales, Rosa Montero and Soledad Puértolas and the debate between women writers, entitled 'Sobre el sexo que tiene la literatura', held at the 1979 Fería del Libro (Carrasco 1979, 35). For Lidia Falcón the only *palabra de mujer* possible is a militant one (1990, 14); this is not a position shared by many women writers.

[43] See also Aubet et al (1981, 109) and the Tribuna de Debate in the first issue of *Dones en Lluita* (1981). Raquel Osborne discusses how such a dichotomy eliminates the subtleties of a complex issue (1985, 43).

[44] Kolodny's essay which advocated the adoption of a pluralist approach was criticised for not taking sufficient account of issues such as race, class and sexuality and for minimising the differences between feminists. See Kegan Gardiner et al. (1982), Marcus (1982) and Modleski (1986b). Elizabeth Meese noted the danger of concentrating on critique rather than construction in the field of theory (1986, 141-42). Kolodny, in the interchange subsequent to the original essay, acknowledged the problematic nature of the term 'pluralism' (1982, 667).

[45] To some extent this is also the case of the first plan which did pay attention to the importance of changing social structures and attitudes.

[46] This quote was originally picked out from Brooksbank Jones (1993).

[47] I am quoting the English translation.

[48] These issues were already being debated in the 1970s in Spain. See Serrano on the use of the term *equipararse* as opposed to *igualarse* (1979, 161). Celia Amorós prefers the terms *equipotencia* and *equifonía* to indicate equality of power and voice respectively (1994).

[49] See Valcárcel (1991) for further discussion of this concept of equality.

[50] Carmen Mestre makes a similar point in her defence of party feminism (1982, 101).

[51] See Pineda (1980) for a discussion of the use of the term 'difference' in anti-feminist discourse. For an example of such discourse see O'Shea (1976).

[52] Within sexuality there is the concomitant danger that such a standpoint may corset women in passivity with a new morality of good and bad girls (Osborne 1985, 49).

[53] Davies discusses the problematics of adopting postmodern theory or difference feminism because of their easy assimilation by reactionary right wing movements (1994, 180-2). Molina Petit sustains a similar position. Whilst acknowledging subjectivity as unstable, she attacks postmodern practise for hindering political activism and denying women agency (1994: 322-3).

[54] That is not to say that the concept of identity as paradox is not of value. Sendón's concept of life as representation and constant becoming (1981, 197) will be returned to in Chapter Three. In a 1994 article, in which she proposes a hologrammatic model for feminism, Sendón's position is

rather more complex. However, although she proposes a shift beyond binary oppositions, her own celebration of matriarchy would seem to reconfirm them. Can the hologram be interpreted as yet another masquerading posture: a three dimensional image of femininity that is not real?

[55] This is not to say that the notion of biological difference is not in itself problematic.

[56] Another radical feminist who has embraced the political arena is Lidia Falcón. As Brooksbank Jones (1993) notes, her attempts to synthesise Marxist and difference feminism, although problematic, also seek a way beyond the traditional dichotomy drawn between political activism and theoretical analysis, or between the social and the personal. However, as discussed above, her attempt to do so through the founding of a feminist political party met with little success.

[57] Not only sexual difference but also differences such as class, race, sexual orientation.

[58] In Chapter Two, the 'realist' nature of *Crónica del desamor* will be called into question.

[59] Davies relates this to the general movement that can be traced in European female-authored novels of the 1980s from realist fiction to fantasy, horror, gothic and the bizarre (1992, 302 & 1994, 175).

CHAPTER TWO

'WOMAN-WIFE-MOTHER': A SOCIAL CRITIQUE OF THE INSTITUTION OF MOTHERHOOD IN *CRÓNICA DEL DESAMOR*.[1]

> Esposa del Señor, Virgen, quizá Martir si tienes la suerte de encontrarte con un violador en la primera esquina... Y Madre. [...] Ser *Madre* como nos enseñaba la Madre X o como decían en la Sección Femenina: si «en el orden religioso» estaban las santas, las mártires y las vírgenes, «en el orden natural» estaba la *Madre*...
>
> Bride of the Lord, Virgin, perhaps Martyr if you are lucky enough to meet a rapist around the first corner... And Mother. [...] To be a *Mother* as we were taught by Mother X or as they used to say in the Sección Femenina: if 'in the religious order' you had the saints, the martyrs and the virgins, 'in the natural order' you had the *Mother*... (Roig 1981a, 69)

As concluded in Chapter One, the figure of woman is an ambivalent one that cannot be pinned down in essentialist definitions of her difference from man. Perhaps the most ambivalent female figure of all is that of the mother. Montero's narrative engages with the contradictions inherent in the figure of the mother by portraying a wide range of maternal figures through a number of divergent discourses ranging from the predominantly realist account of women's experience during the transitional period of *Crónica del desamor* to the fantastic interrogation of a matriarchal society in *Temblor*.[2] Both experience and myth are interrogated through narrative re-presentations of mothers and women through the process of re-writing which will be discussed further in Chapter Three. The use of such a wide variety of discourse by Montero in her narrative would seem to fit in to

Elizabeth Ordóñez's analysis of the 'maternal trope' for writing; that is the desire for an(other) discourse addressing the heterogeneity and multivocality of women (1991, 29). Ordóñez bases her 'maternal trope' on Domna Stanton's discussion of the possibilities of a practice grounded not in maternal metaphor but in maternal metonymy[3]. The trope of metonymy suggests contiguity and displacement, an indefinite exploration of female functions which remains context bound thus exposing specific cultural values, prejudices and limitations (Stanton 1986, 175). In this analysis she traces the emergence of divergent discourses in contemporary writing by Spanish women including the 'Gothic, myths, Arthurian romance, the fantastic and articulation of female corporeality' (Ordóñez 1991, 207).[4] Indeed, Montero's fiction not only subjects traditional myths and history to scrutiny but also their feminist inversions, as will be discussed in Chapter Six. In this chapter I will begin by examining the traditional historical representations of maternity in Spain, the social position of the mother and the change in that position during the transitional period as engaged with by Rosa Montero in the 'quasi-documentary' *Crónica del desamor* (Zatlin, 1992, 119).

Feminist Theorising of Maternity in Spain

According to Victoria Sau in her *Diccionario ideológico feminista*, *madre* is a word which 'expresa la relación entre una mujer y su hija o hijo biológico. Relación de origen natural, pero cultural en tanto que observada y nombrada como tal' (expresses the relationship between a woman and her biological daughter or son. A natural relationship which is cultural in that it is observed and named as such) (1990, 172). Whilst, Sau's definition recognises that to be a mother blurs the boundaries of the nature/culture divide, she falls into the trap of defining motherhood as a biological capacity. Where would adoptive or foster mothers fit in? Are mothers victims of a patriarchal society condemned to a life of hard work and no pay? Or is the figure of the mother one of overwhelming life-engendering power? Conformist or subversive? Or both?[5] During the 1970s and 1980s, motherhood increasingly became a point of focus for feminist writers in a broad spectrum of fields. Recognising the complexity of the issue, in 1984 the sociologist Sacramento Martí stated that maternity was the Achilles Heel of the Feminist Movement because it establishes 'una bifurcación entre la individualidad de las mujeres y las exigencias de la especie' (a divergence between the individuality of women and the demands of the species). Women's individuality has historically been set against their biological capacity (1984, 10) to give birth. Both Martí and Angel Pestaña, in an accompanying article, argue that maternity cannot be reduced to a question of biological instinct but involves a complex set of relations between biology and sociocultural order. In this they are following in the footsteps of the psychologist, Carlos Castilla del Pino who has argued, in various articles since 1970, against the biological fallacy of defining women through their reproductive capacity. Instead he defines maternity as a social function that should be examined in the context of the ideology of a particular society.[6] Similar conclusions are drawn by Aurora Longo, in a brief article on maternity, which considers anthropological and historical evidence that would also suggest that it is a historically and socially determined experience, influenced by factors such as family and social structure (1983, 18). In her epistemological analysis of maternity, Carmen Sáez Buenaventura goes some way to synthesising these approaches from disparate fields, considering both biological and historical evidence to elucidate issues such as the notions of 'maternal instinct' and 'maternal love' (1982). She argues that the biological fact of the capacity to reproduce -note that this account does not take into account the problematic status of infertile women- is interpreted according to the sociopolitical and economic needs of the dominant sex/class.[7] This constructionist view of maternity, in which motherhood is examined as a social experience, is that which is prevalent amongst both Marxist and radical feminism in Spain who have put forward arguments for dismantling the patriarchal model of marriage and the family (Alberdi 1982, Pineda 1982). As discussed in Chapter One, Spanish feminism has tended to resist a mystique of motherhood, due to the rebellion against models of behaviour promulgated by the Franco regime and perhaps the difficulty of configuring a practice grounded in the positing of maternal difference without entrapping women in the essentialist binary divisions of patriarchal discourse.[8] There is a corresponding paucity of theoretical writings revindicating the potentiality of maternity as positive for women as opposed to sociological analyses of motherhood.[9] An exception is the *Agora* group who argue for a superior ethics of maternity similar to Sarah Ruddick's 'maternal thinking' which they term *paidética* (Sendón de León et al 1994, 93-115). However, despite the attempt to make an epistemological jump beyond positions governed by the dichotomy of 'either/or' to the duality of 'both/and', this theory would seem to revert to essentialist claims and takes for granted the patriarchal familial model in which there are two parents and the mother takes sole responsibility for rearing the children.

As noted in Chapter One, Romero et al. in their discussion of women's narrative and feminism in the 1970s observed the difficulty women had in constructing a new identity for themselves due to the lack of role models; 'en la madre se busca el modelo, y como es imposible, se hallan con un presente desconcertante, sin identidad, y por consiguiente no pueden crecer' (they look to the mother as a role model and as this is impossible, they find themselves in an unsettling present and consequently cannot grow) (1987, 345). Characters reject their mothers as they represent authority, tradition and repression (1987, 353). In their mothers they see a past they have no wish to repeat and the possibility of a future they wish to avoid, 'la representación real de todas las desgracias que les pueden ocurrir' (the real life representation of all the misfortunes that could befall them) (1987, 353). Patrícia Gabancho, in her analysis, of Catalan women's writing during the same period, makes a similar point. Mothers and daughters are set against one another as keepers and breakers of tradition:

> La dona, prou ho expliquen les novelles era educada per ser dominada i tolerar el sofriment: guardar-se i obeir, parir i anullar-se. Les mares són els personatges que obligadament han d'encarnar aquesta actitud [...] i transmetre la disciplina viscuda a cops de frustració. Les filles són les que trenquen l'interminable successió de dones sotmeses al manament del sant matrimoni, si és que arriben a temps d'escapar del seu destí.

> Women, as the novels explain, were educated to be dominated and tolerate suffering: keep to oneself and obey, give birth and negate oneself. The mothers are the characters who are obliged to embody this stance [...] and transmit discipline which they have experienced through frustration. The daughters are those who break with the interminable succession of women subjected to the commandments of holy matrimony, that is if they manage to escape their destiny in time. (1982, 136)[10]

This literary panorama reflects that found in the sociological studies of the generational crisis of models for women's identity discussed above. A decade later, little seemed to have changed. In 1987, María Jesús de Miranda examines the generational crisis of models in a study of attitudes of younger women in Spain undertaken for the Instituto de la Mujer, the title of which reflects the continuing confusion and uncertainty surrounding identity: *Crónicas del desconcierto*. Miranda argues that the younger generation of women in Spain suffers from feelings of angst and insecurity towards the future because by rejecting their mothers as possible role models they have no past references/models to work from. Terms that interviewees use to describe their mothers included failures, unable and comfortable (Miranda, 1987, 118). Thus the younger generation attempts to construct their identity in opposition to those characteristics they consider typical of their mothers' generation (ibid). Likewise, in a study of the social integration of young women carried out in 1988, Inés Alberdi Alonso cites the problem of self-esteem among women faced with what they perceive to be a negative role model, the devaluation of the maternal model and the ensuing need to construct as yet unknown models (1988, 22). They are trying to break free of the mould which Geraldine Nichols refers to in her analysis of *Aloma* by Mercè Rodoreda (1936) and *La isla y los demonios* by Carmen Laforet (1970): 'Ha existido sólo un modelo de hacerse tal [mujer] en la España contemporánea: un único *Bildung* femenino para ser contado o vivido' (there has only been one model for becoming a woman in contemporary Spain: a unique feminine *Bildung* to be told or lived) (1992, 134). What was that model as put forward by the regime under which these novels were written? Marriage and motherhood.[11]

Francoist Ideology of Motherhood

Under the Franco regime, motherhood was idealised as a duty to the nation in order that Spain might recuperate her former glory and familialism was regarded as a moral crusade to combat the decadence of society supposedly caused by the Second Republic. In her analysis of pronatalist policies in Francoist Spain, Mary Nash states that motherhood was the key to the general ideological discourse on women of the Sección Femenina. This ideology can be traced back to the Obra

Nacional-Sindicalista de Protección a la Madre y al Niño, a section of the Falangist Auxilio Social:

> Necesitamos madres fuertes y prolíficas, que nos den hijos sanos y abundantes [...] La España Una, Grande y Libre, sólo será posible con hombres fuertes y numerosos, y para esto es preciso seguir atendiendo a la infancia a través de sus varios períodos, desde que se conciben hasta la madurez.
>
> We need strong and prolific mothers, who will give us healthy and abundant sons [...] The One, Great, Free Spain will only be possible with numerous strong men, and for this to occur it is necessary to carry on paying attention to infancy throughout its various stages, from conception to maturity. (Scanlon, 1986, 316)

Under the regime motherhood was regarded as women's 'biological and social destiny' (Nash, 1991, 160). This ideology was used to justify the exclusion of women from the workforce and women were trained for motherhood during their six months of social service with the Sección Femenina.[12] As the 1941 Abortion Law prohibited both abortion and contraception, women were denied access to birth control and defined by their reproductive capacity. Legislation revoking divorce and civil matrimony (for Catholics) was passed and the family declared 'a natural institution with specific prerogatives and rights which went beyond the boundaries of human law' (Nash, 1991, 170). Thus the family being advocated was the traditional Catholic patriarchal model in which the wife and mother was subordinated to her husband, head of the family. Franco received the open support of the Catholic Church in the form of National Catholicism. Mª Teresa Gallego Méndez quotes several members of the clergy in her analysis of Falangist and Francoist conceptions of the family: 'desde los medios religiosos las palabras más comúnmente dirigidas a la mujer eran de este tenor: «La mujer, en el sentido estricto de la palabra, es maternidad. Éste es el camino a seguir de la mujer y especialmente de la mujer cristiana»' (1983, 166), (the most common words aimed at women from religious circles were of this ilk: "Woman, in the strictest sense of the word, is maternity. This is the path that women must follow and especially Christian women."). Both the Sección Femenina and the Church set out to discredit feminism, and notions such as equality between the sexes, with speeches such as that given by the priest Delgado Capeáns in 1953:

Este feminismo moderno es símbolo de decadencia para muchos pueblos y de fatales ruinas para muchas almas. La mujer «suprarrealista» de hoy, de pelo corto, de falda corta, la mujer que juega, bebe, fuma y no se escandaliza de nada, es de tristes y dolorosas consecuencias para la humanidad... Pero esto aún le parece poco al feminismo moderno; quiere otras nuevas conquistas, quiere saborear los deliciosos éxtasis de la morfina, del opio, del éter y de todos los démas alcaloides, que llevan consigo salpicaduras de la muerte.

This modern feminism is a symbol of the decadence of many nations and the fatal ruin of many souls. The "superrealist" woman of today, with short hair, miniskirt, the woman who gambles, drinks, smokes and is not scandalised by anything, is of sad and painful consequences for humanity... But even this is not enough for modern feminism; it wants new conquests, it wants to taste of the delicious ecstasy of morphine, opium, ether and all the other alkaloids which carry with them splatterings of death. (Scanlon 1986, 330)

For Delgado Capeáns and many others in the Church the notion of equality between the sexes was an aberration. Biological difference was embraced as complementarity: the active man was destined to go out to work whilst the passive woman was destined to stay at home.[13] Thus a dichotomy was drawn up between men and women and their respective domains: public and private.

The Sección Femenina did set out to promote an image of a modern woman but this did not mean 'la «mujer modernista» que empieza por negar su femininidad, evitar la maternidad [... y] acaba por ser un simpático compañero del varón, comprometiendo la propia virilidad de él' (the "modern woman" who starts by negating her femininity, avoiding maternity [... and] ends up by being a pleasant companion of the man, compromising his virility) (Scanlon 1986, 324). However, nor did it mean that she should be 'intratable como madre, tormento como esposa y soporífera como compañera' (impossible as a mother, torture as a wife and soporific as a companion) (ibid). In a subtle twist of ideological rhetoric, the new woman of the regime was not inferior but different: she was educated enough to show interest in her husband's affairs, enjoyed motherhood and provided a *reposo del guerrero* (warrior's resting place).[14] In other words, she was confined to the private domain of domesticity. Various measures such as the obligatory six months of social service, grants for women who gave up work when they married, family allowances and concessions for large families were introduced to encourage women to accept marriage and motherhood as their primary social function.

However, Nash argues that these policies were largely unsuccessful in enforcing pronatalist practice among Spanish women due to the economic hardship suffered by many families during the post-war period (Nash, 1991, 174-5). Birth-rates were not to increase until the late fifties and sixties when the Spanish economy began to revive. Paradoxically the developing economy of the 1960s required a larger workforce and women were encouraged to work. As the country was becoming increasingly urbanised and consumerist in outlook, many women went out to work to supplement their husbands' incomes in order to purchase the consumer goods which were becoming available. Thus a contradictory figure emerges who is not covered by the Franco regime's ideological discourse: the working (and often single) mother who is portrayed in Montero's *Crónica del desamor* and will be discussed below.[15]

Beyond Generic Conventions, *Crónica del desamor*: Novel or feminist tract?

Crónica del desamor is set out as a documentary-style chronicle, set during the transition period, which interweaves the stories of several women all related in some manner to the principal protagonist, Ana. She works as a journalist, writing articles with a feminist slant, but what she would like to do is to write a book about the everyday life of her and her friends. As we progress through the novel we come to identify what we are reading as the book which Ana planned to write: a chronicle of women's everyday life which serves a clear consciousness-raising function touching on many major sociocultural issues. It is a historical novel in the sense that it is set in a specific time and place - Madrid in the immediate post-Franco years - and documents issues important to the women's movement in that context. It raises many questions and served to bring feminist issues and polemics of topical interest to the attention of a wide reading public. The novel discusses a panoply of issues including illegal abortion (abortion was not legalized until 1985 and then in a limited fashion), the (un)availability of contraceptives (legalised in 1978), domestic violence, marital rape, single mothers, inequality and sexual harassment in the workplace.[16] Through characters' discussions feminist debates on a variety of subjects such as difference, gender stereotyping, the dichotomy between reason and emotion traditionally ascribed to masculinity and femininity respectively, the inherent machismo of language -in this case colloquial Spanish- and Freud's account of the castration complex are included within the text.[17]

Indeed, the majority of critical reactions to the text point out its journalistic underpinning and the question has been raised as to whether it constitutes propaganda or art (Myers, 1988). As Phyllis Zatlin notes, it was groundbreaking for its content, particularly because it views sexual relationships from the perspective of the woman (1992, 115). It glosses many of the major traditional passages in a woman's life: menstruation, sexual education or lack of it, loss of virginity, the choice of whether or not to marry, the bearing and raising of children. In Biruté Ciplijauskaité's analysis of first-person narrative written by women it is classified as 'escritura rebelde' precisely for this reason (1988, 192). Furthermore, taboo subjects are dealt with in a frank manner. It could be argued that Montero is attempting to recuperate the everyday reality that is often divorced from such debates which, as is shown by Concha Cifrian et al. (1986, 5), are often cloaked in terms of abstract moral principles in a country with such a strong Catholic tradition. However, Zatlin, in her analysis of Montero's narrative production as experimental fiction, contests her own earlier view of *Crónica del desamor* as merely a 'collage of quasi-interviews' (1987, 30) pointing out that Montero's style and tone differs from that associated with feminist tracts (1992, 117). Although studies such as that by Concha Alborg (1988) focus on Montero's use of irony, they fail to focus on her use of wit and humour which is perhaps the most characteristic feature of her style and Zatlin gives various examples of comic distortion or exaggeration used in short scenes that seem almost like cinematic vignettes.[18] She cites the cinema of Pedro Almodóvar and its 'wildly comic and often erotic portrayals of contemporary Spanish life' staking a claim, in retrospect, for the reading of Montero's early novels as antecedents to films such as *¿Qué he hecho yo para merecer esto?* (1984) (1992, 118). Another parallel is the almost hysterical pace or 'vertiginous rhythm' noted on the dust-jacket of the 1993 pocket edition of *Crónica del desamor*.[19] Whilst many reviewers, both in Spain and abroad, have noted the Valle-Inclánesque nature of Montero's later novels, particularly *Te trataré como a una reina* (1983) and *Bella y oscura* (1993), they have tended not to recognise the traces of the grotesque in *Crónica* *del desamor*.[20] Humour allows Montero to broach taboo subjects whilst engaging readers, allowing them to identify with issues which were still polemical to talk about in public.

Eunice Myers, whilst admiring the bold new approach in the context of the historical moment in which it was written, censures Montero for allowing polemics to inhibit the action (1988, 112). Ultimately, perhaps the question to be asked is that which forms the basis of Emilio de Miguel Martínez's study: '¿Es o no una novela *Crónica del desamor*?' (1983, 11).[21] Should it be judged against the conventional generic limitations of the novel? Catherine Davies draws a useful analogy with nineteenth century realist narrative which also crossed the demarcations of genre, mixing fiction and documentary, to produce a fiction of debate (1994, 101). A prominent feature of such a fiction would be the replacement of the detailed delineation of character by the representation of issues such as the position of women within a patriarchal society. It would provide an effective forum for the debate of social and political topics such as the dichotomy drawn between equality and difference feminists, which led to rifts within the Spanish feminist movement.

Interestingly, in her analysis of the relationship between contemporary narrative practice in female-authored narrative (in English) and feminist theory, Paulina Palmer notes that the increasing fragmentation of the second wave of the feminist movement corresponded to an increased output of such fiction -an observation also applicable to the situation in Spain after 1979- which it could be argued provided some sense of cohesion for women bereft of the solidarity of a mass movement (1989, 5). Novels can be considered as performing supportive and informative functions, providing 'a valuable channel of communication and creating a forum for both airing and debating ideas' (Palmer 1989, 60). In a similar fashion, Martínez sees the potential of *Crónica del desamor* as a revitalizing variant within the panorama of Spanish fiction at the time, in which themes predominate over character and plot to leave a testimony of the way of life of thirtysomethings in 1978 (1983, 19). The effectiveness of this testimony is indicated by the fact that *Crónica del desamor* was an extremely successful best-seller which has been reprinted several times. It perhaps owes its success to its open treatment of many previously taboo subjects, especially women's sexuality.

It would seem that readers, particularly women of a similar age and professional position to Montero, identified with the novel. This is borne out in Consuelo de la Gándara's article on images of women in which she describes *Crónica del desamor* as:

> Una novela reportaje, escrita con rapidez y concisión, es el típico libro que se lee de un tirón en una noche, pero es también mucho más. Tengo algunos amigos de esa edad [entre 20 y 35 años] que me dicen verse reflejadas [sic] de pies a cabeza en algunas personajes de esa crónica.[22]

> A journalistic novel, written quickly and concisely, it's the typical book you read in one go in a night, but it's also much more. I have some friends of that age [between 20 and 35 years old] who tell me that they see themselves reflected from top to toe in some of the characters in that chronicle. (1982, 152)

Likewise, the director of the publishing house Debate, Jesús Lucía has cited this reader identification as one of the most important factors in the success of Montero's narrative, 'El éxito de Rosa Montero es muy singular. Se debe a lo querida que es entre sus lectores; ha enganchado con ellos por su forma de comprometerse con la realidad' (Rosa Montero's success is extraordinary. It is due to the affection her readers feel for her; she has hooked up with them because of the way in which she engages with reality) (Arco 1988, 160). Indeed, Montero told interviewer Sergio Vila San Juan (1981b) that this identification had reached the extent that readers of *Crónica del desamor* wrote asking her for advice as if she were some sort of agony aunt. Perhaps this identification can be related to the fact that *Crónica del desamor* is written in a predominantly realist mode. Several feminist critics including Palmer (1989), Felski (1989) and Greene (1991) discuss the value of the realist mode as a major literary form for oppressed groups in which problems of self and cultural identity are explored. In particular, Palmer stresses the strategic importance of the pleasure of reading such texts (1989, 7).

If reader identification is the key to the success of *Crónica del desamor*, and furthermore a specific affinity was felt with the characters by women in their thirties who were of the generation at the forefront of the feminist movement pushing for change in transitional Spain, this then begs the further question: Is

Crónica del desamor a feminist novel? Critics have been sharply divided over this question. Whilst almost all are in agreement -with the notable exception of Lidia Falcón (1981)- that it includes extensive sections of discourse on feminist issues, Montero's feminist stance has been widely debated. Whilst Davies interprets the novel as part of the general offensive by women for change (1994, 96), Roberto Manteiga interprets it as an indictment of the failures of the feminist movement claiming that the feminist posture -whatever that may be- is shown to be an assumed and unnatural charade through which, in their search for equality with men, women have lost their identity and consequently the ability to communicate and form meaningful relationships with men (1988, 115-17). He goes on to aver that Montero believes that true fulfillment lies in a happy heterosexual relationship and motherhood (1988, 119-20).[23] This is a rather strange claim to make about a writer who has never married nor had children. Certainly, Montero does question the push for equality but this does not mean that she accepts the tenets of difference feminism aligned by Manteiga with the reactionary position of woman as wife and mother. Instead, as we have seen above, she rejects a feminism based on a mimeticism of the traditional masculine position in order to question the roles both men and women play. Surely the solution to the ambivalence and uncertainty regarding identity during a period of radical changes in society, such as that captured in *Crónica del desamor*, is not for women to revert to their traditional position but for the very bases of patriarchal society to be called into question; for it is not only the younger generation in the novel who suffer from loneliness and frustration. What Manteiga fails to point out is that the older, 'happily married' women portrayed are also discontented with their situation.

Whilst academic critics have prevaricated over Montero's feminist stance, it was certainly foregrounded in interviews conducted by male Spanish critics who went so far as to dub her a member of a *mafia violeta* (Vila San Juan 1981a). Indeed, in an interview with Charo Nogueira in 1983, Montero notes the hostile reaction of male critics to her work. Ironically her work has also drawn the ire of Spanish feminists such as Lidia Falcón, perhaps due to statements such as that which gave the title to Nogueira's interview: 'Quiero hacer novelas lo mejor posible, no escribir panfletos feministas' (I like to write novels as well as I can, not write feminist pamphlets). In an article which gives a summary of the year's events for 1980-1981 from a feminist perspective, Falcón lambasts both Montero and Montserrat Roig for writing a narrative discourse in which women's economic and professional problems are mediated through sentimental preoccupations (1981, 23). She goes on to claim that their novels are not hard-hitting enough and that the men portrayed are 'de personalidades seguras, que ponen de relieve la insegura personalidad femenina que lucha para encontrar su huequecito en el lugar donde se dice que perdió su primera costilla Adán' (sure of themselves, which only emphasises the insecurity of the feminine character struggling to find her little niche in the space where Adam is said to have lost his first rib) (23). However, it would be fair to say that this insecurity is a reflection of the state of identity politics for women in Spain at that time. In 1978, Julia Arroyo described the transitional period, for women, as 'una época de crisis. No encajamos en los moldes antiguos, ni nos acomodamos a los nuevos' (an era of crisis. We don't fit with the old models, nor are we adapting to the new ones) (1978, 49). Similarly, in 1980 Ezequiel Ander-Egg noted the lack of a model for women searching for a new identity that breaks with the ideological, cultural and psychological conditioning of patriarchal society (1980, 85). As noted in Chapter One, the disorientation felt by the female characters in these novels is bound both to their position within society and their affective relationships, the personal and the political are inextricably meshed together. Furthermore not all the male characters are secure in this novel -many are liminal, marginal figures such as Cecilio, the homosexual friend of the main character Ana, and the bohemian regulars of the bar Toño- and the questioning of masculine identity becomes increasingly significant within Montero's novels, particularly in *Amado amo* in which the protagonist is male (1988).[24] Falcón whilst focusing on what she perceives to be the failure of these novels to provide role models, fails to follow through the implications of her recognition that these works of fiction do not only reflect 'real life' -indeed, as we have already seen, texts mediate socio-historical circumstances through particular discursive practices- but have been influenced by texts, particularly those regarded as popular culture such as radio soaps.

Furthermore, the refusal to provide a prescriptive model of what it means to be a woman can be placed in the context of contemporary academic debates about the problematic nature of the notion of a unified subject which fixes identity and experience. As discussed in Chapter One, women writers of this period often set out to deconstruct the previous, seemingly fixed role models put forward by patriarchal society by allowing women to assume their subjectivity as authors of their own life narratives in autobiographical (meta)fiction. In such novels, a hypostatic notion of identity constructed according to the patriarchal dichotomy drawn up between masculine and feminine, is brought into question as will be seen in Chapters Three and Four. In pointed contrast to Falcón, María Dolores de Asís was to retrospectively describe *Crónica del desamor* as an object of hope admirable for its freshness and spontaneity (1990, 258). Perhaps, its novelty lies in the ability to testify to the highly ambivalent state of identity politics for women in Spain at that time. Montero crosses the polemical divide between equality and difference by examining a variety of attitudes towards maternity; by providing the multiple perspectives of several female protagonists, Montero confronts the reader with a number of fluctuating identities and diverse experiences.

Crónica del desamor: Institution or Experience?

In *Crónica del desamor* (1979), Montero primarily examines motherhood as a social institution. Many of the characters are mothers or discuss motherhood. Their experiences are quite different from the model of motherhood promulgated by the Francoist regime: they almost all work to support themselves, they use contraception, various characters have aborted and the main protagonist, Ana, is a single mother who works as a journalist to support herself and her four year old son, rather appropriately named Curro (slang for work). As an autonomous, working single mother she falls outside the confines of the patriarchal family. Consuelo Escudero Álvaro, in a study of the family group, contrasts the triads *mujer-esposa-madre* (woman-wife-mother) and *hombre-esposo-padre* (man-husband-father) (1985). In the first triad the terms *mujer* and *esposa* are collapsed into one another, *mujer* being used to mean wife, thus causing 'una condensación y un desplazamiento que deja en oscuridad su lugar como sujeto' (a condensation and displacement which obscures her place as subject) (Escudero Álvaro 1985, 16). The central term of the triad is, however, *madre* and she goes on to discuss the difficult conjunction between the maternal function and the role of the working woman.[25] Note that in the 1981 census, almost 100% of married couples questioned as to who was the head of the household answered that it was the man. However, this is interpreted by the authors of a 1990 study of family structures in Spain to have been a culturally influenced perception because in many homes the responsibility of maintaining the family was shared or borne by the woman (Solsona & Treviña 1990, 84-6). Again as recently as 1993, Luz Mª Paz Benito, observes that although women are increasingly combining these two roles/functions, the androcentric perception of them as mutually exclusive, belonging to two different spheres -the private and the public- persists:

> La sociedad hace que, en la práctica, la realización de la mujer en la esfera tradicional de dominio masculina y en el ámbito doméstico de la maternidad sean muy difíciles de compaginar para obtener, en ambos a la vez, una sanción positiva de logro personal.
>
> In practice it is very difficult in society to combine the realisation of women in environments traditionally dominated by men and the domestic sphere of maternity to obtain, in both at the same time, a positive recognition of personal achievement. (1993, 720)

The difficulty is compounded for those who are single working mothers in Spain, as described by Mercedes Soriano, 'la madre soltera viene a ser una mano de obra superbarata a quien la necesidad obliga a aceptar trabajos duros y mal pagados' (the single mother becomes a supercheap source of labour as necessity obliges her to accept tough, badly-paid jobs) (1977, 53). Indeed, as *Crónica del desamor* comes to a conclusion, Ana is told yet again that she has been passed over for a fixed contract in favour of three men: 'Esto de ser madre soltera, reflexiona sonriendo con amargura, es verdaderamente una proeza, tienes todas las servidumbres del padre de familia y no se te reconocen los derechos' (This business of being a single mother, she reflected smiling bitterly, is really an exploit, you have all the responsibilities of being the father figure in the family but your rights as such are not recognised) (CD: 262).[26] Ultimately, Ana is not in a strong position in the workforce, she was fired from her earlier job at a bank because she was pregnant -and unmarried- and as a journalist she is used as the general dogsbody of the office. Although not under the control of a patriarchal head of a family, she is under the paternalistic control of her bosses who are all men.[27]

The novel is focalized predominantly through Ana, although other characters are also foregrounded such as Elena -a feminist academic, Cecilio -a middle-aged homosexual, Candela -Elena's sister who is a psychiatrist, and El Zorro -a marginal outcast. In this chapter I will concentrate on the three main female characters. Through the use of a narrative technique which presents the multiple perspectives of their actions, dialogues and thoughts -as well as those of the other female characters Ana María, La Pulga and Julita- Montero tackles several of the topical issues outlined above. Her narrative practice connects the personal and the political, interspersing events from Ana's life with those concerning a peripheral cast of characters portraying a diversity of women who share one feature in common: they are all living outside the traditional structure of marriage and struggling to do so in a patriarchal society. This collage of the daily life of a group of thirty-somethings is held together by the unifying thread of sexual politics in post-Franco transitional Spain. Many of the issues confronted by Montero in *Crónica del desamor* were still extremely politically sensitive at the time. Certainly, during the transitional period, much had changed in Spanish society. Attitudes were clearly more tolerant towards a more permissive sexuality, as can be measured by the wave of pornography which occurred in the media.[28] However, various articles of the time refer to the machismo of the supposedly progressive vanguard, known as *progres*, who promoted the *desmadre sexual* (period of sexual liberation) of the late 1970s and early 1980s.[29] Rather ironically, Laura Freixas refers to a consumerist notion of sex which for these men -often of a Marxist or socialist ideological background- consists in 'tirarse el máximo de tías al mes' (1979, 95). In conclusion, she argues that women must differentiate between *chicas liberadas* (liberated girls) -who never say no and expect nothing in exchange- and *mujeres libres* (free women) who make free choices about their sexuality (1979, 98). *Crónica del desamor* is full of jibes at these so-called progressive men who have reduced women's liberation to sexual permissiveness. Birth control was still controversial and abortion still illegal.[30] By presenting the problems of access to contraception and the consequences of aborting abroad or having an illegal abortion within Spain in a sympathetic light, Montero here evidently aligns herself with feminists campaigning for change.

In this novel, Montero clearly questions the supposed liberation of women through sex divorced from reproduction. This is evident in the episode in which

Ana, Elena and Candela go to the gynaecologist's together. He is middle-aged and apparently progressive, although appearances in this case would certainly seem to be deceptive: 'Como el ginecólogo va de progresista tiene la consulta en un barrio periférico, en una torre, eso sí, nueva y flamante que destaca del entorno de casitas baratas y aventejadas' (As the gynaecologist presumes himself to be progressive, his surgery is in a peripheral neighbourhood, in a tower, but of course, spanking brand-new which stands out from the surrounding cheap and crumbling houses) (CD: 19). He sits, behind the desk -probably handed down from his father- in this phallic tower, dispensing his wisdom in a patronising fashion. Instead of informing the women about various methods of contraception in an objective manner so that they can decide for themselves, he tries to convince them that the best method is an IUD or the pill despite Candela's objections that she does not want to carry on taking the pill and that she became pregnant after using an IUD, then suffered an almost fatal acute peritonitis after one was inserted in her womb too soon after an abortion (note that the reason for the infection is narrated previous to this episode when Candela and Elena are introduced to the reader through Ana's thoughts). He treats them as inferiors in need of his superior knowledge, dismissing Elena's experience of using a diaphragm in a vulgar fashion:

—¿cómo te lo pones? ¿Cortas al tipo y le dices que se espere?

(Hay algo común en muchos ginecólogos: ese desprecio por la persona, la grosería de grandes machos que-ven-y-curan-coños.)

"How do you put it in? Do you stop the guy and tell him to wait?"

(There is something that many gynaecologists have in common: that lack of respect for the individual, the crudeness of men in high places who-see-and-cure fannies.) (CD: 29)

When she produces her diaphragm out of her bag it becomes immediately apparent to the women that the doctor has never seen one before. He is thinking in terms of male pleasure and privilege, rather than what is safest or most appropriate for the women he treats. In articles published in 1981, both Montserrat Roig and Mª José Ragué accuse Spanish male gynaecologists of perpetuating the patriarchal order by upholding traditional sexual roles. In her essay 'Nosotras las mujeres', Roig asserts that their role is to uphold the patriarchal order in much the same way as priests did before:

> El médico entonces hace el papel de cura, y en lugar de orientar a la mujer, la abruma con su «moral» y la sumerge una vez más en la ignorancia utilizando el poder de su experiencia y sus conocimientos... De la misma manera que una noticia nunca es explicada de una manera imparcial, porque no existe en ningún terreno la neutralidad, tampoco ningún médico es neutral. Los médicos que humillan el cuerpo de la mujer en lugar de liberarla de los viejos tabúes, los médicos que no nos tratan como seres autónomos participan del poder de la sociedad patriarcal porque temen perderlo.
>
> The doctor then plays the role of priest, and instead of advising women, weighs them down with "morals" and submerges them in ignorance by using the power of his experience and knowledge... In the same way that an item of news is never explained in an impartial manner, because neutrality does not exist in any field, no doctor is neutral. The doctors who humiliate women's bodies instead of liberating them from old taboos, the doctors who don't treat us as autonomous beings, participate in patriarchal power because they are scared of losing it. (1981b, 71-2)

Likewise, the very title of the article by Ragué makes explicit the links between medical and religious discourse: 'Parirás con dolor... (Y Dios creó al ginecólogo)' (You will give birth in pain... (And God created the gynaecologist)). She cites various texts by gynaecologists in which they state that women are by definition frigid, fulfilled through maternity; ideally they should neither work nor be citizens but be good wives and mothers. In order to combat the effects of such attitudes gynaecological centres were set up by women who insisted on the dissassociation of sexuality and maternity and the need to inform women so that they could decide for themselves (Centro de Mujeres, 1979). Their approach was in clear opposition to the position of those male gynaecologists quoted by Ragué who used their privileged access to information to control women's sexuality by acting as a 'doctor-shaman-father-god' (Centro de Mujeres 1979, 497).[31] Already in 1979, Julio Iglesias de Ussel pointed out that contraception and abortion were the tip of the iceberg that includes sexuality, pleasure, relations between men and women and the patriarchal family (27). Four years later, in a sociological study of sexuality in Spain, he discussed texts written by gynaecologists and concluded that traditional texts prescribe not only what they consider biologically normal for women, as referred to by Mª José Ragué, but also normative sexual, familial and social behaviour (1983, 120). Themes which are absent from these texts or discussed as pathological behaviours are those which would indicate an autonomous female sexuality: masturbation, abortion, homosexuality, artificial insemination, contraception, sex education are some of the examples given.

Earlier, Candela -after the operation for the peritonitis- reflected that, for men, women's liberation can be reduced to its sexual aspect, to 'tener hembras más dispuestas, en olvidar el odiado condón, el coito interrumpido' (having more available women, forgetting the hated condom and coitus interruptus) (CD: 27).[32] The pill was supposedly liberating, although rather ironically, Candela muses 'Liberador de quién?' (Liberating for who?) (CD: 28). It had been proferred as the magic key to women's liberation, as if all that was needed to liberate them was to free them from being bound to reproduction without paying any attention to the underlying patriarchal ideology that pervades society. Thus male doctors prescribed the pill and inserted I.U.D.s as contraception was regarded as the responsibility of the woman if she did not wish to get pregnant. Furthermore, the 'copper fever', in which doctors prescribed IUDs, resulted very profitable as they cost 10,000 pesetas to have inserted. The narrator's sympathies with the women are patent both in the comments about the gynaecologist enclosed in parentheses and explicitly so in the commentary interspersed with rhetorical questions and interjections which follows this episode:

La píldora, el DIU, son problemas de la mujer. Es ella quien las toma, quien lo sufre. El diafragma, sin embargo, es algo más cercano a la pareja: ¿ha de interrumpir el varón sus acaloramientos previos para que ella pueda colocarse el disco de caucho? Qué horror. ¿Ha de utilizarse a veces crema espermicida? Qué desastre. Son tán cómodas las píldoras o el DIU, esos métodos que el hombre no padece...[33]

The pill, the IUD, are the woman's problem. She takes them, she suffers. Howver, the diaphragm is something which affects the couple: Does the man have to break off his foreplay so that she can insert the rubber disc? How awful. Does he sometimes have to use spermicide? What a disaster. The pill or IUD are so comfortable, those methods which men don't suffer... (CD: 30)

This commentary is followed by a discussion which takes place as the women return to their car. Their conversation which is included within the text, enclosed in quotation marks -as opposed to the standard linear separation of dialogue in Spanish, marked off with dashes- stylistically echoes the above passage with a similar use of alternating questions and exclamations:

Ana ríe, "resulta curioso que ahora se esté volviendo en todo el mundo al diafragma, cuando es uno de los métodos más antiguos", y Candela, "sí, sí, yo sé que mi madre lo ha usado, me contó que se lo traían de Francia, que entonces el aro exterior de la goma estaba articulado y que a veces al quitárselo se pegaba unos pellizcos terroríficos", "qué horror", dice Ana, "qué bárbaro", dice Elena, y añade, "¿mamá usaba eso?", "sí, sí, eso me dijo", "qué curioso", comenta Elena pensativa, "a mí nunca me ha contado nada".

Ana laughs, "it's odd that now everyone is using the diaphragm again, when it is one of the oldest methods", and Candela, "yes, yes, I know that my mother used it, she told me that they brought it from France, that in those days the exterior ring of the cap was articulated and sometimes when she took it out it pinched her terribly", "how awful", says Ana, "how barbaric, says Elena, and adds, "mum used that", "yes, yes, she told me so", "how odd", comments Elena thoughtfully, "she never told me anything". (CD: 30-1)

The taboos still surrounding women's sexuality are perhaps best exemplified in the issue of abortion rights. Parliament attempted to pass a bill permitting abortion in 1983. However, the opposition succeeded in challenging the abortion law through the Constitutional Tribunal and blocking it until 1985 when it was passed in a more restricted form than had been originally envisaged. Doctors' contracts included a clause allowing them to conscientiously object to perfoming abortions and even legal abortions were not covered by health insurance.[34] In 1986 alone, 11,935 Spanish women aborted in London, accounting for almost half the abortions performed on non-residents.[35] This would indicate that abortion was also a class issue as those who could afford it aborted outside of Spain (Iglesias de Ussel 1979, 49). In their study of the arguments for and against abortion, Cristina

Alberdi and Victoria Sendón criticised the social hypocrisy as regards abortion and analysed how class affects access to both contraception and abortion (1977). The taboo of abortion and the strong moral overtones of anti-abortion discourse are clearly related to the fear of women's autonomous sexuality.[36] In the episode at the gynaecologist's, Montero links the issues of birth control and abortion when we are introduced to the character of Candela who went to London after becoming pregnant despite the use of an IUD, 'Abortó higiénicamente, esterilizadamente, internacionalmente' (She aborted hygienically, in a sterilised fashion, internationally) (CD: 21). Ana contends that abortion is only illegal because men do not give birth and refers to the (mis)conception that it is a form of contraception for guilty women who have offended the genital order of a society controlled by men. She bitterly notes that politicians, and by implication those who can afford it, would not hesitate to send their daughters abroad for an abortion whilst women who cannot afford this option have to submit themselves to illegal Spanish butchers (ibid). She goes on to recall one such case: Teresa her ex-boyfriend's sister who had to be hospitalised after a backstreet abortion and face the callous treatment of a male doctor who threatens to denounce them.[37]

Several issues of importance are touched on here: the control of women's sexuality by men, the negative stereotyping of women who are sexually active, particularly those who are not in a long-term relationship with one man and sexuality as an integral component of social organisation. However, the novel does not only address these topical problems and issues which face women trying to live outside the confines of the patriarchal system. It also addresses the possibility of an empowering maternal mystique in an episode concerning the feminist academic, Elena, which has been used by critics such as Roberto Manteiga to interpret the novel as an indictment of feminism -a rather surprising conclusion if one considers episodes such as the one examined above. During her years as a Communist militant Elena regarded maternity as a product of traditional religious, cultural and social pressures as described above.

However as the novel progresses, her position has moved into line with that of many feminists who now recognise the positive aspects of maternity. As Mª Dolores Calvet argues, although the feminist movement has emphasised the right of women to control their own bodies through the vindication of contraception and abortion, 'no siempre se tiene en cuenta que utilizar el cuerpo como las mujeres desean quiere decir también proclamar el derecho de la mujer a ser madre' (it's not always taken into account that the right of women to use their bodies as they wish also includes proclaiming the right of women to be mothers) (1982, 201-3). There has been a shift from the right to choose not to get pregnant to the right to choose to have a child without moral, psychological or economic pressure (Martí 1984, 114). Empar Pineda exemplifies the Marxist feminist position, criticising those who would unquestioningly revindicate maternity without considering it in its sociohistorical context. She insists that it should be a voluntary option, 'una posibilidad para las mujeres y no como una obligación ni como el fin de la vida de la mujer' (a possibility for women, neither an obligation nor the ultimate purpose of life) (Pineda 1980, 23). Perhaps the most important point is that of choice, maternity as a possibility and not a myth to adore or hate (DAIA 1979).[38] Elena has come to regard maternity as an affirmation of the self thus recognising that feminine identity may after all lie in difference; in the biological possibility of giving birth as opposed to the experiential necessity of giving birth:

> No es que quiera tener un hijo, no. No siente ningún deseo de ser madre. Pero, ahora y esto sí es nuevo, ha empezado a considerar el embarazo como una opción real y propia. Quizá es que durante mucho tiempo ha confundido la liberación de la mujer con el desprecio hacia la mujer misma: la liberación pasaba por la mimetización con el sexo del poder, había que adoptar valores masculinos, copiar al hombre, repudiar la identidad de la hembra. Elena, ahora, ha descubierto en su cuerpo el orgullo de saber que puede parir, si quiere, y que esto no es una servidumbre. Ha descubierto el orgullo de reencontrarse como sexo.[39]

> It's not that she wants to have a child. No, she doesn't have any desire to be a mother. But now, and this is new, she has begun to consider pregnancy as a real option for herself. Perhaps it's that for a long time she has confused women's liberation with disdain for women: liberation required the mimeticisation of the sex in power, you had to adopt masculine values, copy men, deny female identity. Elena has now discovered the pride in knowing she

can give birth, if she wants to, and that this isn't an act of servitude. She has discovered the pride of finding herself again as a sex. (CD: 230-1)

She is aware of the need to revalue what has been traditionally devalued as 'feminine' both under patriarchy and by the initial wave of feminism. What Manteiga fails to note is that this is not an indictment of feminism per se, but an engagement with a feminism which recognises the positive aspects of motherhood.[40] In an interview with Vila San Juan in 1981 in which Montero reiterates her feminist position, she discusses how at the age of twenty as a *progre* she repudiated motherhood but now felt it to be an enriching option (1981b, 22). By critically examining the social experience of mothering whilst engaging with the possibilities for empowerment through a revaluation of the term 'maternity', Montero blurs the dichotomies which have often polarized the feminist movement in a similar fashion to Victoria Sau Sánchez in her essay 'Maternología' (1986b). Whilst criticising the sublimation of maternity by some feminists, Sau also criticises those who would renege their biological state altogether. Instead, she argues that it is necessary for women to recuperate maternity and maternal genealogy as sources of power.

Obviously the last sentence of the above quote from *Crónica del desamor* is rather problematic with its notion of 're-finding' one's sex as if there were some essential definition to discover. This concept of a coherent sexual identity linked to the biological capacity to give birth is as questionable as that of a fixed gender identity circumscribed by the terms masculine or feminine. Davies notes the lack of a clearly-defined differentiation between the terms equivalent to sex and gender in Spanish: *sexo* and *género* (1994, 180). Likewise Donna Haraway, in the introduction to her essay '"Gender" for a Marxist dictionary', notes that while the English and German words *gender* and *Geshlecht* adhere closely to concepts of sex, sexuality and sexual difference, the French *genre* and Spanish *género* seem not to carry these meanings so readily (1991, 130). In fact, in María Moliner's *Diccionario del uso del español* (1990) the definition of *género* includes no such references apart from in its fifth subcategory of grammatical gender. The terms masculine and feminine are defined both with relation to *sexo* (sex) -the biological category of being either *macho* (male) or *hembra* (female) and to characteristics ascribed to either men or women. In other words the biological and the sociocultural aspects of these terms are conflated. Rather disappointingly Victoria Sau's *Diccionario ideológico feminista* does not include the terms *sexo*, *femenino* or *masculino*. The entry for *género* does state that it is culturally derived from biological sex but then seems to conflate the two by characterising *género* as being a binary, antithetical, symmetrical relationship between the sexes (1990, 133-8). A similar confusion marks the conclusion of Sau's paper, 'La construcción del «yo» femenino: Hacerse a sí misma', given at the second Basque conference on 'Mujer y realidad social' in 1988, in which she discusses the concepts of *sexo* and *género*, Sau concludes by proposing new models of being for women outside those propagated by patriarchal society but would seem to posit some sort of essential feminine in her wish for the emergence of 'el *yo* femenino real' ('the real feminine "I"') in which women can 'verse de verdad' ('truly see themselves') (1988, 103). At the same conference, María Navarro recognises the existing confusion on the issue and the complexity of the concept of gender reiterating the questions posed by Jane Flax (1987) on the relationships between sex, sexuality, gender and individual identity (1988b, 31). How are these relationships constructed and how do they change over time? Within a Spanish context, Cristina Brullet Tenas (1996) has traced how sex and gender roles have been conflated in patriarchal society through the association of the female capacity to give birth with the social role of mothering. As Brullet Tenas indicates, changes in Spanish society such as the increasing use of family planning methods, improved education for women and their incorporation into the workforce have led to an opening up of attitudes towards maternity.

What then is this *sexo* that Elena has rediscovered? Perhaps the pull towards the notion of motherhood as a possible source of power is to be explained within the context of a culture in which mothers, whilst seemingly being in a position of social inequality, have been respected as strong figures within the family and communities of women in which there exists a sense of pride in oneself-as-woman. Whilst this fact may be due to such factors as a lack of economic opportunities for women and men's absence from the domestic arena, such networks may provide support and understanding (Chown 1983, 101). The simultaneous but contradictory pull towards both feminist autonomy and the feminine mystique exemplifies the difficulty in clearly drawing a dichotomy between the two poles of the feminist movement, reflecting the ambivalence felt by women relinquishing what has traditionally been a site of power.[41]

Maternal power?

As Linda Chown has noted in an article on narrative written by Spanish women between 1942 and 1980, the figure of the mother is often portrayed in an ambivalent fashion. This ambiguity of the mother figure as both a positive and negative figure is also examined by Biruté Ciplijauskaité in her analysis of 'novels of maternity'. Although mothers and older women are frequently described as perpetuating repressive values and inhibiting independence, they are also potential sources of positive power (Chown 1983, 104; Ciplijauskaité 1988, 64). Paradoxically, within patriarchal societies, the mother figure has simultaneously been portrayed as subordinated in social practice whilst being imbued with mythical live-giving power. Within the context of Spanish society, Chown contends that the mother in Hispanic society is not necessarily a sacrificial, self-abnegating figure. According to Elizabeth Ordóñez, in opposition to the ideal of the submissive wife, 'popular belief has often cast the Spanish mother into the role of domestic matriarch' (1987, 53). There would seem to be a disjuncture between the social experience of mothering as described in *Crónica del desamor* and the cultural myth of maternity. Many younger feminist women, as noted above, have rejected their mothers as role models without stopping to question how these women might have resisted the ideology that was imposed on them (Altable Vicario 1994, 104-5). For example, some secretly used contraception such as Candela and Elena's mother (CD: 30-1).

Candela is perhaps the most self-aware female character. She has to some extent broken free of the patriarchal mould by choosing to bring up her second child herself, leaving the father Vicente, who is already married to someone else. This decision is prompted by a confrontation with her mother, Antonia, in a feverish daydream in which her mother recounts the monotony and routine of her marriage (CD: 225-7). She would seem to have been the typical traditional wife and mother: she left her job when she got married, was faithful to her husband and became increasingly dependent on him as time wore on. However, we already know that she secretly used a diaphragm and in this vision discover that she has sexually liberated herself without the intervention of a man by having her first orgasm through masturbation after reading one of Elena's books about sexual initiation. Antonia sums up the tedium and humilliation of the traditional model of motherhood in the cautionary tale of the handkerchief, a drawn-out description of what seems a relatively simple act: washing a handkerchief. Throught the building up of detail, Montero reinforces the sense of the absurdity of such repetitive actions for so little gain:

> Esto es una mujer que coge un pañuelo sucio, prepara agua caliente en un barreño y echa detergente. Mete el pañuelo ahí durante largo rato. Luego tira el agua, pone otra limpia y frota bien el pañuelo con jabón. Cambia de nuevo el agua y echa unas gotas de lejía para que la tela quede bien blanca. Después lo aclara y lo mete con añil para que azulee de tan limpio. Más tarde le echa suavizador para que la tela quede rica de tocar, lo aclara, lo escurre bien y lo tiende en el patio, al sol, ¿eh?, para que termine de blanquear. Cuando ya está seco lo recoge, pone la mesa de la plancha, humedece ligeramente la superficie para poder quitarle todas las arrugas. Lo dobla con esmero y lo mete después en un armario, el de la ropa blanca, en donde antes ha puesto naftalina y unas bolsitas de hierbas para que den buen olor. Y ahí queda al fin el pañuelo, limpio, fragrante, dobladito... Entonces llega su marido del trabajo, da un beso distraído a la mujer, va al armario, coge el pañuelo, snrifffff, se suena las narices con gran ruido y lo tira arrugado al cesto de la ropa sucia. ¿A que es gracioso?

This is the story of a woman who takes a dirty hankie, fills a tub with water and adds washing powder. She soaks the hankie for a long time. Then she throws away the water, fills the tub with clean water and rubs it with soap. She changes the water again and adds a few drops of bleach so that the fabric goes really white. Then she rinses it and adds bluing so that it's a really clean blue-white. Later she adds fabric softener so that the fabric is really soft to the touch, she rinses it, wrings it out well and lays it out in the patio, in the sun, yeah?, to finish bleaching. When it's dry she gathers it up, sets up the ironing table and lightly dampens the surface so that she gets rid of all the creases. She folds it carefully and puts it in the wardrobe where she's already put mothballs and some pomanders so that everything smells nice. And finally there sits the hankie, clean, fragrant, folded up nice... Then the husband comes in from work, kisses his wife absent-mindedly, goes to the wardrobe, grabs the hankie, snrifffff, blows his nose resoundingly and throws it crumpled up into the linen basket. Funny, isn't it? (CD: 226)

It has taken nine sentences for the wife to clean the handkerchief and one for the husband to destroy all her efforts without so much as a second thought. Her hard work is made to seem irrelevant and without reward or appreciation. As Antonia concludes her tale she dissolves into fits of laughter and Candela resolves to try a different way of life freed from this absurd servitude to a man.[42] In this episode there would seem to be a two-way process of emancipation for both mother and daughter. Certainly, Montero's use of sharp and often black humour in passages such as this would seem to be liberating for, whilst the readers' first reaction may be to laugh, they empathise with the characters who are -as has been noted above- generally portrayed in a sympathetic light by the narrator.

In another comic episode, Candela not only confronts the experience of being a woman within a patriarchal society but also as a psychiatrist resists the scientific discourse of psychoanalysis which is used to justify women's supposed inferiority. Immediately prior to Elena's revaluation of the motherhood discussed above, a conversation is overheard between Curro, Ana's son, and Jara, Candela's daughter:

"Tú no tienes colita, tú no tienes", dice el Curro con todos los visos de estar enseñándola. "Pero cuando yo sea mayor tendré pechos y tú no", contesta la vocecita de Jara, "y además podré tener un niño en la barriga y tú no puedes".

"You don't have a willy, you don't have one", says Curro sounding as if he's showing her just what he's referring to. "But when I grow up I'll have breasts and you won't", pipes up Jara, "and besides I'll be able to have a baby in my belly and you won't". (CD: 229-30)

Candela, Ana and Elena laugh, coming to the conclusion that Freud invented the castration complex in order to disguise the complex men suffer at not being able to give birth. In an interview with Montero, she confirmed that this was her personal view and discussed the power of women through their capacity to give birth at length concluding that, 'En la base de las relaciones entre los hombres y las mujeres, en la base del patriarcado está el miedo del poder tremendo de la mujer, del poder procreador' (The basis of the relationship between men and women, the basis of patriarchy is the fear of the tremendous power of women, the power to procreate) (Knights 1994). This fear is clearly expressed by César, the male protagonist of *Amado amo*, who states:

La dictadura femenina de lo maternal: qué poder tan abusivo y repugnante. Ahí estaban ellas, decidiendo tiránicamente de quién querían parir y a quién condenarían a una esterilidad eterna. Mujeres: dueñas de la vida. Nunca podría perdonar a las mujeres su prepotencia de ser madres.

The feminine dictatorship of the maternal: what an abusive and repugnant power. There they were, deciding tyranically of whom they wished to give birth and who they would condemn to eternal sterility. Women: owners of life. He could never forgive women their arrrogance as mothers. (AA: 23)

In Elena's revaluation motherhood is not always oppressive and certainly the mother-child bond is, on the whole, portrayed in a positive light in the novel. It is not, however, as Ana ruefully reflects one which remains static. She recognises that despite her desire to keep Curro as a child in a relationship which 'algodona hoy la soledad, la engaña' (cushions solitude today, which tricks it) (CD: 202), he will eventually become a more independent, complex adult who will leave her. As the novel closes Ana has gained an increased sense of self-awareness of the roles she plays. Being a mother is only one of the positions that she takes up. The crucial episode for this moment of self-revelation is the final fling between Ana and her boss, Soto Amón whom she has fantasised about for a year. After spending the night with him, she recognises that he too is bound by clichés and stereotypical modes of behaviour. Whereas he mistakenly assumes that he knows what she wants, 'es como si te conociera desde hace mucho' (it's as if I've known you for a long time) (CD: 269), she recognises this as nothing more than an empty formula which she has already heard before. The layout of this section of narrative describing what happened back at Soto Amón's 'bachelor pad' -he has a wife and children- is particularly interesting. Only two lines of dialogue are marked off by linear separation, when they arrive Soto Amón comments:

—No mires mucho la casa: es horrorosa... en fin ya sabes.

"Don't look too closely at the house: it's awful... well you know what I mean." (CD: 270)

and when they leave Ana says:

—No me acompañes: voy a coger un taxi.

"Don't accompany me: I'll grab a cab." (CD: 271)

In the space of three paragraphs between these two parallel statements the long-awaited and all-too-brief affair with Soto Amón occurs. In the first paragraph, the flat is described by the narrator in a concise, matter-of-fact style with only one item of speech included in parenthesis: a comment made by Soto Amón, '(¿de verdad que tú no quieres?)' (Are you sure you don't want to?) (CD: 270), which could apply as much to their fling as to the glass of whisky he is proferring. In the second -which is entirely enclosed in parenthesis- Ana predicts Soto Amón's every word and move, ironically concluding that what they have done has not meant anything. Presumably it has not signified anything for Soto Amón, but for Ana it is a turning point. In the third paragraph, the narrator's description is punctuated by Ana's commentary in the form of rhetorical questions and interjections inserted parenthetically into the text, and Soto Amón's dialogue which has already been predicted by Ana:

Se desarrolla, pues, la pantomima con asombrosa semejanza a lo previsto (¿qué hago aquí con este extraño?), se hacen un amor callado y hueco (qué absurda situación, absurda, absurda), el aire se llena de silencios (es como si me contemplara a mí misma desde fuera, tan lejos de la realidad, de él, de todo), "lo siento, pero es tardísimo para mí, tenemos que marcharnos", dice él al fin (todo un año que se acaba con esto, si él supiera), "déjalo Ana, déjalo, ya lo recogerá la asistenta que viene cada día".

Well, the pantomime unfolds surprisingly much as she had predicted (what am I doing here with this stranger?), they make love silently without meaning (what an absurd situation, absurd, absurd), the air fills with silences (it's as if I were contemplating myself from outside, so far away from reality, from him, from everything), "I'm sorry but it's very late for me, we have to go", he says finally (a whole year ending up like this, if only he knew), "leave it Ana, leave it, the maid who comes every day will tidy it up". (CD: 271)

Ana is now narrating her own personal story, as her first-person commentary usurps the place of the third person narrator who has previously commented on characters' dialogue and actions within parenthesis, as in the scene at the gynaecologists discussed above. Not only does she challenge the narrator's authority to tell her story, but she manages to silence Soto Amón by not behaving as he would expect -refusing his offer to accompany her home, leaving him rather perplexed by her rebuff and her stifling her laughter- and it is this liberating step out of character which inspires her to write the 'crónica de desamor cotidiano' which is Montero's novel. But what is the source of this contemporary malaise? The loss of a stable identity in a society undergoing profound change. The solution? Not as Manteiga maintains for women to realise themselves through relationships with men, but to question defining categories such as 'woman-wife-mother' and rewrite them in new life narratives.

Crónica del desamor can indeed be classed as experimental fiction, as Zatlin argues, not only for its content but also its form. It combines the commitment to a seemingly referential, documentary fiction which raises important issues for women in a specific, cultural context -the transitional period in Spain- whilst sowing the seeds of a more self-conscious narrative through the use of techniques such as humour, narrative commentary and metafictional inflections. The use of such techniques perhaps allow a way forward that goes beyond Stanton's limited vision of a metonymic practice for female-authored fiction, discussed above, in which she takes up Roman Jakobson's view of the metonymic pole as characterising realistic narrative. Whilst this novel certainly is grounded in 'contextual, sociohistorical discourses' focusing on the 'imperfect past/present in which all processes of exploration are located and all discoveries must begin' (Stanton 1986, 176), it goes beyond immediate experience to go some way to exploring how this experience is mediated through discursive practice. By foregrounding the discursive nature of the text, Montero enters into negotiation with the realist mode, enlisting it as a valuable form for engaging in identity politics, whilst interrogating the premises of a representative fiction. The novel thus lies between Zatlin's categories, discussed in Chapter One, of a testimonial narrative of confession and self-discovery, and a more aesthetically self-conscious experimental writing. This feature of *Crónica del desamor* will be developed more clearly in *La función delta*, which as fictional autobiography calls the reader's attention to questions such as those of self-representation and referentiality.

---

[1] The term 'woman-wife-mother' (*mujer-esposa-madre*) is taken from Consuelo Escudero Álvaro (1985) and is discussed below.

[2] I use the term realist with some reservations, as *Crónica del desamor* contains elements of pastiche and there are several moments of humour which belie its documentary tone. However, in comparison with the works which follow, it can still broadly be classed as a realistic description of the society that it portrays.

[3] Stanton's article is a critical Anglo-American reading of the French theorists: Hélène Cixous, Luce Irigaray and Julia Kristeva.

[4] Several of these discourses will be discussed in further chapters.

[5] For the discussion of the ambivalence inherent in the figure of the mother, I am indebted to Marianne Hirsch's study of the mother-daughter bond in Anglo-American narrative (1989).

[6] The notion of maternity as a social function is also discussed by Concepción Fernández Villanueva (1982).

[7] Sáez Buenaventura draws heavily on the work of Elisabeth Badinter's historical review of different forms of maternal behaviour, which concludes that 'l'instinct maternel est un mythe. Nous n'avons rencontré aucune conduite universelle et necessaire de la mère. [...] Tout dépend de la mère, de son histoire et de l'Histoire' (Maternal instinct is a myth. We have not found any universal or obligatory form of conduct of the mother. [...] Everything depends upon the individual mother, on her history and History) (1980, 367). A similar argument is put forward by Iglesias de Ussel who rejects the concept of a 'natural' love for the child by the mother (1979, 30).

[8] See Navarro (1993) and Sendón (1981, 1994) for a celebration of the maternal.

[9] A notable exception is the essay 'Nosotras las mujeres' by Montserrat Roig (1981b).

[10] This translation was done with the aid of Teresa Perello Bestard.

[11] See Nuria Pompeia's cartoon collections *Maternasis* (1967) and *Mujercitas* (1975) for a graphic demistification of pregnancy and giving birth in the former and the social position of women in the latter. In the final cartoon of *Maternasis* the mother's identity is under threat of engulfment from a hugely magnified baby.

[12] Proof of having completed social service or having been exempted from it was necessary to obtain a degree/professional qualification, work in the public sector or politics, obtain a passport to travel abroad, obtain driving/hunting/fishing licence, belong to centres or associations covering many activities eg artistic, cultural, sporting, recreational (Scanlon, 1986, 327). Ironically, those working for the Sección Femenina had to be single. Gallego Méndez points out the apparent contradiction between theory and praxis of the hierarchy of the Sección Femenina (1983, 106).

[13] As stated by Andrés Romero, men and women are regarded as complementary because 'ha sido prevista y querida por Dios por disposición de la naturaleza' (1977, 287), (it has been preordained and desired by God through the disposition of nature).

[14] See Amando de Miguel for a discussion of *pseudo progresismo* whereby women acquired a 'varnish' of culture in order to adequately perform their orbital role as a support to their husbands (1974b, 84).

[15] Rey, Alonso & Walker (1985), in their study of maternity in Spain, note the lack of models for working mothers in particular.

[16] Although discrimination in the workplace on the grounds of gender had been outlawed by the constitutional reforms of 1978, the fact that it was still prevalent is demonstrated by the later incorporation of the principle of equal opportunities into the Worker's Statute of 1980. For a discussion of women's sociopolitical position in post-Franco Spain, see Longhurst (1991) and Schubert (1990).

[17] The revaluation of slang in which Candela suggests the replacement of the terms 'cojonudo' and 'coñazo' with 'ovarudo' and 'pollazo' (CD: 234) echoes Carme Riera's article on sexual language in which she examines the use of sexual insults which demonstrate 'una sobrevaloración del mundo macho y un modo de evidenciar el dominio masculino' (an overvaluation of the macho worls and a way of demonstrating masculine domination) (1981, 188-93). The Instituto de la Mujer produced a leaflet in 1995 which gives guidelines for the use of non-sexist language (Alario et al.).

[18] Other critics who have noted humour as a feature of Montero's narrative include Brown (1991b, 243), Amell (1994, 82-3), Davies (1993, 386 & 1994, 96-9) and Williams (1994).

[19] For Montero this pace is indicative of some of the changes occuring in Spanish society over the last twenty years (1993b &1996).

[20] Alma Amell places all of Montero's narrative in the tradition stretching back to writers such as Cervantes and Quevedo who used their wit to denounce the shortcomings of society (1994, 76).

[21] Initially, Montero was commissioned to write a book of feminist interviews but became bored by the project.

[22] She includes Rosa Montero and Esther Tusquets as the contemporary writers to complete her selective overview which includes both male and female writers from within and outside the canon from the Middle Ages to the present.

[23] Joan Brown makes a similar claim, emphasising the high value placed by Montero on heterosexual love and commitment (1991b, 244).

[24] The rather grotesquely humourous portrayal of the bar and its regulars in Chapter nine could be interpreted as a criticism of the *movida* and *progre* attitudes. Stylistically it is a clear precursor of *Te trataré como a una reina*.

[25] The supposed incompatibility of the two roles and the possible effect of trying to combine the two on women's health is discussed in Rey, Alonso & Walker (1985). For a detailed account of the situation of working mothers in Spain see *Women of Europe*, Supplement #31 (1989), 50-5.

[26] References to *Crónica del desamor* will be denoted herewith by CD and to *La función delta* by FD, followed by the relevant page numbers.

[27] Montero, herself, was in the same situation as Ana working for three or four years as a collaborator with *El País* before being offered a position on the permanent staff. (See *Vanidades* 1990, 17-18, 23-4.) For an account of women working in the press see Méndez (1996).

[28] However, it was not until 1986 that the *Ley General de Sanidad* provided for state-funded family planning services.

[29] Francisco Umbral criticises men for using the *progre* label as en excuse for sex with no strings attached (1973, 120-1). Josep-Vicent Marqués also discusses *progre* attitudes towards sex: it is divorced from affection, jealousy is labelled a *petit-bourgeois* emotion, women are told not to be tight and that virginity is a cancer that they should be vaccinated against (1987, 83).

[30] A report on the social situation of women in Spain by the Instituto de la Mujer in 1986 noted the general view that whilst contraception was now accepted by women, there was still a lack of information on the subject and limited accessibility (Astelarra 1988, 57).

[31] Carmen Díez de Ribera includes the government in her criticism of attitudes towards family planning in Spain, she censures the trilogy of doctor-priest-government (1977, 81).

[32] This view is echoed by Lucía in *La función delta* who argues that men regard contraception as the woman's problem, all they are interested in is finding 'amantes siempre dispuestas y sin complicaciones' (lovers who are always available without complications) (FD: 207).

33 Mª Luisa Maillard discusses the potential of contraceptives to liberate women through their sexuality, but concludes that in Spain those that have been liberated have been men (1978). Note that AIDS was not yet an issue at this time.

34 The difficulty of obtaining legal abortions in the public health sector was the focus of a recent dossier in *Ajoblanco* entitled 'Aborto: ¿Todavía es un crimen?' (1995).

35 At one point, charter flights were being organised to take women to London specifically to abort, see Peregrín (1985, 55). In 1972, Spanish gynaecologists were sent a letter from an English company organising such trips which reached the press (Ussel, 1979, 49).

36 See Marqués (1980) for a detailed discussion of the moralistic discourse used by anti-abortion campaigners. In fact in according to a survey carried out by the Centro de Vallecas in 1979-80, 69% of women who aborted were married (Parra 1986, 69). Among various reasons given by Peregrín for women aborting are pregnancy despite the placing of an IUD, being single/divorced or already having too many children (1985, 52).

37 In 1979, eleven women were put on trial in Bilbao for abortions carried out between 1966 and 1976. A petition containing four thousand signatures of women claiming that they too had aborted was collected in support for the women (Escario et al. 1996, 334-5).

38 No page reference is given as the proceedings the quote is taken from were not collated. They are held in the Biblioteca de Mujeres, Madrid.

39 Many feminist theorists draw on the work of Adrienne Rich which makes the distinction between maternity as a social institution and the positive potential of the experience of maternity, see Rich (1977).

40 Indeed, whilst Elena might be self-questioning, she is still politically active within small feminist groups which deal with issues on a local level.

41 Jane Flax relates the splits within the feminist movement to the conflict between nurturance and autonomy felt by women (1978).

42 The childhood books referred to by Elena and Ana, in which the female character Ana María is given the subtitle 'Giving' (CD: 107), would suggest that they have been educated through a similar logic of self-abnegation.

CHAPTER THREE

'THE NEVER-ENDING STORY': METAFICTION AND THE SEARCH FOR IDENTITY IN *CRÓNICA DEL DESAMOR* AND *LA FUNCIÓN DELTA*.[1]

> Autobiography is always a re-presentation, that is, a re-telling, since the life to which it supposedly refers is already a kind of narrative construct. Life is always, necessarily, a tale: we tell it to ourselves as subjects, through recollection; we hear it told or we read it when the life is not ours . (Molloy 1991, 5)

If *Crónica del desamor* goes some way to exploring how experience is mediated through discursive practice, in *La función delta* narrative is clearly posited as an ordering process which is part of the way we come to terms with experience. It has been argued -particularly by Phyllis Zatlin (1982) and Robert Spires (1984)- that a prevalent tendency in Spanish narrative of the post-Franco period has been towards metafiction, a self-reflexive and self-referential form of narrative in which the subject of writing is the process of writing itself.[2] By foregrounding the constructed nature of fiction and rejecting the mimetic function of the realist novel, metafictional texts raise many questions about the complex relationship between the 'real' and the 'fictional'. One of the insights of post-structuralist theory is the recognition that literary fiction cannot represent or mirror the 'real world', but can only '"represent" the *discourses* of that world' (Waugh 1984, 2). This follows on from Saussurean linguistics which contests the concept of language itself as simply representational. Instead, it is a functional signifying system for imposing meaning on the phenomenal world.[3] As the Spanish postmodern theorist Mª Carmen África Vidal points out, in the introduction to her study of the postmodern novel, reality is thereby not a given, but is supported by the shifting sands of partial and questionable testimonies (1990, 24).[4] Interpreting reality through the narrative process suggests that there are in fact as many realities as there are narrators/readers. Reality would thus become a web or network of interrelating multiple realities which may be open to change. However, this metaphor of interweaving realities suggests that reality cannot be completely relative to each subject, as it is mediated through language which has a social intersubjective function. As speaking subjects we must adopt the functioning system provided by the language of the society we are born into in order to communicate with others and be understood. (There can be no uniquely private language except in the case of psychosis.) Thus these multiple realities particular to each subject may be described as a network of lines which may run parallel, intersect, converge or diverge. Amongst the many varying perspectives of distinct subjects, there will be those which are adopted by groups within society or society as a whole as a narrative framework for what they perceive collectively to be reality.

Thus language plays an important role in the construction not only of fiction -the fictive world being an entirely verbal construct- but of reality too in that it shapes our perceptual world. Fiction performs a cognitive function as the narrative process is a 'central form of human comprehension, of imposition of meaning and formal coherence on the chaos of events' (Hutcheon 1990, 121).[5] It is a form of making human experience intelligible, of defining it and shaping it. Robert Alter describes the human being as:

> the language using animal [who] is quintessentially a teller of tales, and narration is his [or her] way of making experience or [...] of making non-verbal experience distinctly human. (1975, 64)

This image of the storyteller conjures up the traditional metaphors of the world as a stage or book recast in terms of contemporary literary theoretical currents such as poststructuralism and deconstruction. Indeed, as Zatlin reminds us, this recent metafictive trend can be placed into the context of a centuries-old Hispanic tradition, which can be traced back to the Quixote or even earlier, that sets out to 'juxtapose illusion and reality, self-consciously laying bare the creative process of the imagination' (1982, 73). Reality can thus be 'read' and metafiction provides a useful model to help understand how reality is written.

Both Zatlin and Spires note the quantity of examples and diversity of style and intent within the contemporary metafictional current. Whilst Zatlin's analysis of six novels published between 1975 and 1981 -three written by men and three by women- is of interest for its observations on individual texts, it fails to account for why the trend occurred at that particular historical moment. Spires accounts for the accentuated interest in metafiction in Spain after the death of Franco as a celebration of the creative process once censorship had been removed and freedom of expression regained (1984, 128).[6] He sees it as a restoration of polysemy to language and as a reaction against the illusion of absolutes as embodied in Francoist discourse.

I would argue that in the case of women writers, this reaction is not only against the discourse of the Franco regime, but also against hegemonic patriarchal discourse in which the masculine generic is conceived of as the agentive subject/producer of discourse invalidating alternative discursive practices. By focusing on the creative process in female-authored texts these writers subvert phallologocentric writing practices. Within Spanish feminist theory, the work of Amparo Moreno Sardà in particular sets out to contest the predominance of what she terms the virile archetype in patriarchal discourse and proposes an alternative non-androcentric reading (1986 & 1988).[7]

Testimony or Aesthetic Experiment?: Metafiction and the Search for Identity

Metafiction has been isolated by both Concha Alborg (1988) and Phyllis Zatlin (1987) as the most important unifying thread in Spanish women's fiction of the 1980s.[8] It can be placed within the larger context of post-Civil War women's fiction which has been described as intimate, auto-analytical and of autobiographical bent (Jones 1983). Rosa Montero's first three novels *Crónica del desamor* (1979), *La función delta* (1981) and *Te trataré como a una reina* (1983) have all been analysed as works of metafiction.[9] In this chapter I will be dealing with the first two novels, which deal with women's discourse and the construction of identity by women through textual means, as opposed to the later novel which deconstructs texts written and statements made by men, as read by both men and women.[10] Concha Alborg addresses the question of why Montero has adopted the metafictional mode, referring to the work of both Patricia Waugh and Robert

Spires. Waugh suggests that metafiction arises when a society is going through a period of change and that it is a form of exploring social and cultural conscience (1984, 3).[11] Previous social and cultural formations are shown to be of a constructed, rather than given, nature and narratives are written which try and make sense of the process of change. For Waugh the contemporary historical moment of the late Twentieth century is characterised by uncertainty, insecurity, self-questioning and cultural pluralism (1984, 6) This description is particularly applicable to Spain during the post-Franco period which has similarly been characterised by 'la incertidumbre, el escepticismo, la diseminación, las situaciones derivantes, la discontinuidad, la fragmentación, la crisis' (uncertainty, scepticism, dissemination, derivative situations, discontinuity, fragmentation, crisis) (Urdanibia 1991, 68-9). In a talk given in a cycle of talks on 'La Cultura Española en su Contexto Europeo' at the London Instituto Cervantes on 7 June 1993, Jo Labanyi described Spain as the postmodern culture par excellence in which an unstable cultural identity is constantly called into question. Spanish commentators have taken up the tag of postmodernity, although often in the mainstream press it is used glibly to refer to superficial, evanescent trends or to what is also termed 'la cultura *light*' (Tono Martínez 1991, Peiro 1991).[12] Montero, during a one-day conference at the University of Leeds entitled 'Aspects of Identity in Contemporary Spanish Narrative' (6 May 1995), referred explicitly to herself as a daughter of postmodernity when describing the new narrative being written in Spain. Refusing to define 'nueva narrativa', she referred, instead, to the plurality, or lack of a clear defining trend, which would reflect the apparent fragmentation of identity and subjectivity occuring in contemporary Spanish society.[13]

Texts which draw attention to the structures of fiction, can also point to the conventionality of the codes governing human behaviour (Greene 1991, 2). Thus, metafiction can perhaps facilitate a fruitful intersection between postmodern and feminist theory by providing a framework for fictions which set out to portray explicitly the constructed nature of society and acknowledge the potential for change in a society undergoing a transitional process, not only politically, but also socially and culturally.[14] As discussed in Chapter One, the transition period in Spain has certainly seen many significant changes in women's position in society and this is reflected in their narrative. Identity is shown to be constructed within a particular socio-historical moment and can therefore be deconstructed.[15] Consequently the crucial question asked in these first person narratives becomes not 'Who am I?' as discussed in Chapter One in relation to testimonial writing, but 'How am I represented?'. In other words identity is examined as not only grounded in experience, but also as discursive configuration. Furthermore, the deferral of narrative closure in these texts suggests that despite the often seemingly bleak or pessimistic endings there is a possibility for change; albeit a process of change that is both difficult and painful. Thus metafiction partakes in both the postmodern project of deconstructing fixed identities but also the feminist project of attempting to situate subjectivity through the encoding of change as a narrative process

The body of metafictional works by Spanish women writers demonstrates how language may be manipulated, particularly by the state apparatus and the mass media, as is evident in Montero's novels: in *Crónica del desamor* Ana is a journalist exploited by her editors; in *La función delta* Lucía directs commercials she finds personally objectionable; *Te trataré como a una reina* is framed by a piece of sensationalist reporting and *Amado Amo* revolves around the corruption of the world of advertising and the press. As Catherine Bellver argues in relation to Montserrat Roig, but equally applicable to Montero:

> Her involvement in the communication media has had an undeniable effect on her approach to fictional writing. It has shaped her voice, determined the construction of her novels and governed her use of vocabulary. (1988, 167)

Both Roig and Montero have used fiction to document Spanish society in the transitional process, concentrating primarily on the sociological, rather than the political, aspects of change. It should be noted that Montero's first novels have received mixed reviews due to the perception of her style and preoccupation with contemporary reality as journalistic. Perhaps rather predictably, Joan Brown's overview of Montero's narrative work -in a collection of essays on contemporary Spanish women writers- is entitled 'Rosa Montero: From Journalist to Novelist' (1991b).[16] Luis Suñen (1981), in particular, censures the attention accorded to theme over form in both *Crónica del desamor* and *La función delta* in an article which displays the derogatory, paternalistic tone that Montero has denounced in

Spanish male literary critics. Where Eunice Myers (1988) talks of polemics possibly obscuring artistry, Suñen accuses Montero of 'ciertos resabios como de marisabidilla' (certain bad habits of a know-it-all).[17]

It is of interest to note that many women writers gaining prominence in the 1980s are professionals in the tertiary sector and that a particularly high proportion are journalists, literary critics or university lecturers.[18] They are thus highly conscious of the use and influence of language. Whilst it is true that this period has seen an increasing number of women writers gaining both public and critical attention thus vindicating female creativity, Alborg argues that Montero is not necessarily using metafiction as a mode of literary experimentation. Indeed, Montero herself has stated that she regards her novels prior to *Amado Amo* as minor works and that they are less consciously elaborated than the latter (Glenn 1990a, 281-2; Talbot 1988, 95). However, one might argue that by making both the writers female in *Crónica del desamor* and *La función delta*, Montero does also question the notion of writing as phallocentric. The female protagonists assume their subjectivity as authors of their own life narratives. Furthermore, I will be taking up Phyllis Zatlin's convincing argument, already alluded to in Chapter Two, that all of Montero's texts may be classed as experimental fiction concerned with both genre and discourse (1992, 115). Whilst these texts do have features which lend themselves to the journalistic tag so often ascribed to these works, such as the use of vivid description and characterisation, they also question the relationship between fiction and reality. Furthermore, they emphasise the multiplicity of possible interpretations of any one representation of that reality. I would argue that these texts, in a manner similar to those written in English examined by Gayle Greene in an perspicacious study of metafiction by women, negotiate with realism to mediate between 'a narrative of self-confession and self-discovery and an aesthetically self-conscious experimental writing' which represents experience whilst redefining the very premises of that representation (1991, 21-2).

Why then does Montero adopt the metafictional mode? Alborg proposes that it is a way of emphasizing feminist issues such as gender stereotyping and the demythification of traditional feminine roles and norms imposed by patriarchal society (1988, 73). I would suggest that it is in part for all of these reasons that

Montero uses the metafictive mode not only to depict a society in the throes of change but, perhaps more significantly, to explore the individual's search for identity through discursive practice. Both Ana of *Crónica del desamor* and Lucía of *La función delta* attempt to define the female self through textual means which protest against the dominant parameters of patriarchal discourse. These novels appear to reflect a need, at that time in Spain, for women to question prevailing cultural paradigms. Indeed, as was the case with *Crónica del desamor*, in her review of *La función delta* for *Insula*, Milagros Sánchez Arnosi, again proposes reader identification as one of the reasons for the success of the novel (1981, 16).

Both Ana and Lucía have been consistently identified with Montero herself by critics. They are both professional women in their thirties: Ana is a journalist and Lucía's memoirs look back to the week when her first feature film was to be premiered. Montero herself has stated that in writing these novels she was working out her own problems and setting down her thoughts. In an interview with Lynn Talbot she declares,'todos los personajes son yo misma, y al mismo tiempo no soy ninguna' (I am all of the characters and at the same time none of them' (1988, 93). In answer to the question of whether these two novels are autobiographical, she prefers to term them a biographical cocktail in which real and imaginary ingredients are mixed together until they become indistinguishable from one another.[19] Her narrative:

> reproduce, imaginariamente y mezcladamente todo lo que ha pasado a mí y a mi gente, y a la gente y a mis amigos.
>
> reproduces, imaginatively and in a mixed fashion, everything which has happened to me and my crowd, to people and my friends. (Talbot 1988, 93)

For Montero fiction and reality cannot be clearly differentiated. According to Davies, integration of the personal and the social was a feature of women's writing in Spain in the late 1970s and early 1980s in a process in which the boundaries between fiction, history, biography, and autobiography were dissolved (1991a, 215).[20] Montero's novels would also fit into Waugh's category of metafictive texts which have assimilated the non-literary and the popular in order to undermine automatized convention (1984, 64). The use of a realist framework which appropriates features of popular genres thus allows for a wide readership of texts of polemical content, whilst the use of metafictive techniques gives the reader an active role in the construction of meaning.

A Multiplicity of Voices: *Crónica del desamor*

As discussed in Chapter Two, *Crónica del desamor* is an interwoven chronicle of the lives of several women all related in some manner to the principal protagonist, Ana, who writes articles with a feminist slant. However, what Ana would like to do is to write a book about the everyday life of her and her friends:

> Piensa Ana que estaría bien escribir un día algo. Sobre la vida de cada día, claro está. Sobre Juan y ella. Sobre Curro y ella. Sobre La Pulga y Elena. Sobre Ana María, que ha perdido el tren en alguna estación y ahora se consume calladamente en la agonía de saberse vieja e incapaz de hacerlo. Sobre Julita, muñeca rota tras separarse del marido. Sobre manos babosas, platos para lavar, reducciones de plantilla, orgasmos fingidos, llamadas de teléfono que nunca llegan, paternalismos laborales, diafragmas, caricaturas y ansiedades. Sería el libro de las Anas, de todas y ella misma, tan distinta y tan una.

> Ana thinks it would be good to write something one day. About everyday life, of course. About Juan and her. About Curro and her. About La Pulga and Elena. About Ana María who missed the train in some station and is now being eaten up silently by the agony of knowing she is old and unable to catch it. About Julita, a broken doll after splitting up from her husband. About slimy hands, dishes to wash, reductions in staff, fake orgasms, telephone calls which never happen, paternalism in the workplace, diaphragms, caricatures and worries. It would be the book of the Anas, of all of them and herself, so different and yet the same. (CD: 8-9)

As we progress through the novel we come to identify the book which we are reading with the book which Ana had thought about writing at the beginning of *Crónica del desamor*, had attempted to start whilst on holiday with her mother and son and finally feels ready to write by the close of the novel. The novel is a chronicle of women's everyday life, touching on many major sociocultural issues, some of which are detailed in the quote above, and glossing many of the major traditional passages in a woman's life. However, it does not, as the quote above might at first suggest, fall into the trap of biological determinism. Although at one point in the novel, as discussed in Chapter Two, Elena would seem to be renouncing feminism of equality in favour of feminism of difference, at no point is there the celebration of maternity and nature that would indicate a difference feminist perspective. Ana's desire to write is a political statement which is about both the predicament of women in general in a patriarchal society and their recognition as individuals, '...tan distinta y tan una'.[21] This 'una' or 'one' could be interpreted as a feminine essence, but I would prefer to interpret it as the collective experience or historical condition of women in a patriarchal society.[22]

Whilst there is obviously a tension between group and individual identity -especially when considering the breakdown of old oppositional models- there is a need for some sort of pragmatic 'we', as discussed in more general terms in the introduction to this study.[23] Why adopt a generic term? Perhaps the answer lies in the fact that Woman, whilst an unstable category to employ, is still regarded as a legitimate category within patriarchal society and, as the culturally dominant model, should therefore be engaged in the struggle for change.[24] In one of the few articles so far produced in Spanish which discuss the relationship between postmodern and feminist theory, Rosa María Rodríguez Magda posits the strategic need for a generic identity, 'Habrá, por tanto, al menos que admitir la necesidad de un «génerico operativo» que garantice el paso del «vosotras» definido desde el sujeto androcéntrico, hacia el «yo» y el «nosotras»' (It is necessary, therefore, to admit at least the necessity of an 'operative generic' which guarantees the move from a [feminine] "you" defined by the androcentric subject, to an "I" and [feminine] "we") (1992, 58). It would be an 'operative' rather than 'substantive' generic. Elsewhere Rodríguez Magda has proposed a transmodern feminism which combines the postmodern interrogation of fixed positions with an emancipatory, critical theory of agency (1994, 312).

Montero certainly shows an awareness of how the meaning of the sociocultural category of Woman affects the lives of individual women. Furthermore, some sort of collective identity would seem to be enabling, through the formation of communities of mutual support such as that which is formed by

Ana and her circle of friends who frequently meet up with each other to talk, offer advice and sympathy. The recognition of such a bond of commonality between women may function as a starting point for feminist consciousness (Braidotti 1994, 163). Paradoxically Ana decides not to write the proposed book at first for fear that it would be 'banal, estúpido e interminable, un diario de aburridas frustraciones' (banal, stupid and unending, a diary of boring frustrations) (CD: 12). The novel is indeed a tale of everyday occurrences that are often termed banal, but it is far from boring or stupid. When she begins to write down her memories during her holidays her young son, 'cruel y poderoso [...] comenta con tajante y sabio tono: "pues es una tontería"' (cruel and powerful [...] comments in a cutting and knowledgeable tone: "well it's daft"') (CD: 163). Curro is only a small boy but he speaks for patriarchy in condemning the female voice to silence. Time and time again women are silenced or fall silent in the company of men in this novel in a wide range of situations such as the following: Elena on her way to the chalet to have sex for the first time with Miguel Angel; Marisa who had been the life and soul of Julita's party becomes silent and inert when her husband arrives; Ana being sexually harassed during her interview with the 'sub-sub-sub-secretario' of the Ministry of Information and Tourism wishes she could be severe and icy but ends up helpless and speechless (CD: 51, 114-15, 156). At other times men fail to listen, for example the trade union activists who take over the march organised by the residents' association (CD:48) or Soto Amón who maintains a one-sided conversation with Ana as the novel closes:

Soto Amón es hombre acostumbrado a hablar y callar a los demás, y parece haber perdido la capacidad de escucha.

Soto Amón is a man used to talking and silencing the rest, and he seemed to have lost the capacity to listen. (CD: 267)

On the rare occasions when women reduce men to silence it is usually through humour or laughter which the men do not understand.

Notably Ana is ready to write just when she finally reduces her boss, Soto Amón, to silence. After the decidedly unromantic one-night stand with her boss who she has fantasized about for almost a year she concludes:

Sólo le duele que fuera el propio Soto Amón quien se quitó la corbata en un automático, bien ensayado, autosuficiente gesto. Un gesto cruel y poderoso que, quién sabe, recapacita ella con ácida sonrisa, puede ser un buen comienzo para ese libro que ahora está segura de escribir, que ya no sería el rencoroso libro de las Anas, sino un apunte, una **crónica del desamor cotidiano**, rubricada por la mediocricidad de ese nudo de seda deshecho por la rutina y el tedio.[25]

She was only pained by the fact that it was Soto Amón himself who undid his tie in an automatic, well-rehearsed, self-sufficient gesture. A cruel and powerful gesture which, who knows, she recapacitates with an acid smile, could be a good beginning for that book she is now sure she will write, which will no longer be the resentful book of the Anas, instead it will be a note, a **chronicle of daily unlove**, endorsed by the mediocrity of that silk knot undone by routine and tedium. (CD: 273)

As we have seen in Chapter Two, Soto Amón was not the interlocutor she was searching for: ultimately he fails to understand her. Ana's definition of the novel she plans to write as a chronicle echoes both the title of *Cronica del desamor* and Montero's comments on the dust-cover of the Debate edition of the novel:

¿Una novela? No, no considero que mi libro sea una novela. Creo que *Crónica del desamor* es precisamente eso, una crónica sin pretensiones, una mirada rápida al mundo que nos rodea, una aproximación a los problemas y afanes cotidianos de todos nosotros. Y me conformaría con que resultara mínimamente sugerente.[26]

A novel? No, I don't consider my book to be a novel. I think that *Crónica del desamor* is just that, a chronicle without pretensions, a rapid look at the world around us, an approximation to the everyday problems we all confront. And I would be happy if it turned out to be suggestive in the slightest.

The novel certainly is a chronicle of daily life which was inspiring in its historical moment in that it raised many questions and served to bring feminist issues and polemics of topical interest to the attention of a wide-reading public.[27] As noted in Chapter Two, *Crónica del desamor* has been an extremely successful best-seller which would seem to owe its success in part to its open treatment of many previously taboo subjects, especially women's sexuality, which engaged the interest and identification of a wide readership.

The novel can thus be seen to provide a model narrative for experiences which had hitherto remained unspoken. By interspersing the third person narrative of the chronicle with women's dialogue and interior monologue, Montero allows her characters to 'claim the authority to name and construct their own experience' (Frye 1986, 58). They attempt to break with conventional paradigms to construct their own narratives.[28] A multiplicity of voices is present, sometimes presenting a multifaceted view of the lives of this group of friends and acquaintances. These views do not necessarily coincide with each other. For example, La Pulga reflects sadly that Elena, not recognising her own privileged situation as a university educated woman, believes her to be more stupid than she feels she is (CD: 94). Elena and Ana would also seem to misjudge Julita as the typical abandoned wife -the former going so far as to designate her name as a denigrating diminutive, 'un nombre de ama de casa que lava con Persil y que lo recomienda a sus amigas' (the name of a housewife who washes with Persil and recommends it to her friends) (CD: 105)- who is incapable of doing anything for herself. However, Julita starts to go out with La Pulga, gets a job in the legal department of Elena's publishing house and begins a passionate new relationship with a young policeman who she sees on traffic duty at Legazpi on the way to work each morning. A plurality of voices/views are thus counterposed and juxtaposed in a dialogic mosaic.

A Multiple Voice: *La función delta*

Whilst in *Crónica del desamor* it is the act of narration itself which assumes priority, in *La función delta* it is the narrative process which is examined. To use a distinction drawn by Waugh on her sliding scale of metafictionality, in the first novel the emphasis is on the increasing consciousness of the narrator(s), whilst in the second the fictionality of the text is foregrounded (1984, 14).[29] In reference to her first novel Montero has said that she needed to speak out about issues which seemed to burn inside her, whereas in the second, 'lo que me interesaba no era el contar, en *La función delta* lo que me interesaba era el cómo' (what I was interested in wasn't the telling, in *La función delta* I was interested in how)

(Talbot 1988, 94-5). The narrative perspective has subsequently shifted from the blend of third person narrator, dialogue and interior monologue used in *Crónica del desamor*, to a first person narrator who clearly distinguishes between the narrating present and narrated past self.[30] Indeed, this desire to investigate the narrative process is evident in the structure of *La función delta*. The protagonist, Lucía, aged 60, is confined in hospital terminally ill with a cerebral tumour and to pass the time writes a diary situated in the present -the future for the reader at the time of the novel's publication because Lucía is writing in the year 2010- and her memoirs of a particularly important week in her life when she was thirty and the first (and last) film she directed was to be premiered.[31] The two narrative periods are differentiated in the text by means of the chapter headings: Lucía's memoirs are denoted by the seven days of the week from Monday to Sunday, whilst her diary is dated from the twelfth of September to the eleventh of December. However, the two texts are not completely discrete as is evident in the final lyrical chapter in which Lucía, by now extremely ill, confuses events and people from both temporal periods. Thus, in this text intimate confession and self-reflexivity merge in a text which both recounts experience and examines how that experience is mediated by language.

The metafictional text has been described as pre-empting the role of the critic because of its self-referentiality (Hutcheon 1984, xii). In *La función delta* there is a clear focus on the role of the reader, as the text includes an internal critic/reader in the shape of Ricardo, Lucía's friend who comes to visit her in hospital and reads her memoirs.[32] It is important to note that Ricardo is a male reader reading a woman-authored text. Female readers are implicitly invited to dispute his reading and interrogate his masculinist perspective. Ricardo questions Lucía's authorial perspective on a number of occasions, accusing her of falsifying the 'truth' and lacking verisimilitude:

Como novela está bien, pero como memorias es un fraude. Todo lo que cuentas es mentira, es una simple y llana distorsión de la realidad.

As a novel it's okay, but as a memoir it's a fraud. Everything you say is a lie, it's a plain and simple distortion of reality (FD: 51)

... está lleno de falsedades... lo elástico de tu memoria me tiene subyugado.

> ... it's full of lies... The elasticity of your memory has me enthralled. (FD: 93)

> Insisto en que rezuma falsedad... esta vez me estoy refiriendo a una falsedad absoluta. No se trata sólo de que aquello no fuera así, sino de que la vida NO es así. La vida no es blanca y negra.

> I insist that it oozes falseness... this time I'm referring to an absolute falsehood. It's not just that it didn't happen like that, but that life is NOT like that. Life is not black and white. (FD: 161)

Indeed life is not black and white. However, this would seem to negate Ricardo's point about the falsity of Lucía's memoirs. As noted above, for Spires (1984) the trend in Spain in the early 1980s towards metafictive texts which foreground the problematic relationship between fiction and reality can be interpreted as a reaction against the absolutist nature of Francoist discourse. In this novel Montero appears to ascribe to a postmodern contestation of absolute notions of truth and falsehood. If there is no absolute truth, the truth of one perspective does not necessarily entail the falsification of another, although one perspective may be valued as truer by society in general.[33] As we cannot unproblematically know, truth may therefore be interpreted as being historically and culturally specific. Subsequently, knowledge becomes a question of interpretation and the power to endorse -and indeed enforce- that interpretation.[34]

Ricardo refuses to accept the possiblity of a plurality of perspectives, preferring instead to assert that his is the one true reality: 'YO no recuerdo mal' (I do not remember incorrectly) (FD: 94). He is the unified patriarchal subject who believes his discourse cannot be contested and assumes his partial reality to be the whole story.[35] Whilst admitting that he was not always present at events related in the memoirs, and furthermore, that he lies to improve on the truth, he claims to know the *historia* (history/story) and revises 'herstory' to conform with his version. He challenges the account she gives of her lovers -Hipólito (a married man) and Miguel with whom she formed a relationship that lasted until his death- claiming that she has made Hipólito out to be completely perverse when the 'simple truth' of the matter is that he never loved her. Meanwhile, she has idealised her relationship with Miguel. He also disputes her representation of him, for he too figures in her memoirs; and he criticises her for the lack of social comment in what is essentially a personal diary.[36] This would rather depend on what is regarded as social comment, as the situation of women in contemporary Spanish society is addressed at some length. Furthermore, Montero's novel would seem to fit into Rita Felski's category of subjective realism in which testimonial novels by women focus on the feelings and responses of an experiencing subject rather than on the actual experiences, the central theme being the problematics of self-identity (1989, 82).

Lucía contests his criticism, asserting her authority, as both author and reader of her own text, to decide on its content and the validity of her interpretation. However, she would seem to be a contradictory figure. Whilst on the one hand she recognises the possibility that her memory may not be completely reliable, as evidenced by the faltering opening of her narrative which starts not with the affirmative 'recuerdo' (I remember) but the dubitative 'Creo recordar' (I seem to remember) (FD: 1), on the other she criticises Ricardo for his inability to tell the truth:

Me irritó su comentario. Yo no sé si estoy escribiendo un mundo de buenos y malos, tan sólo describo el mundo que viví. Hipólito fue así para mí, y yo lo sé mejor que nadie, y también así de dulce fue Miguel. Y además, para qué mentir, me tengo por una persona bastante justa, ecuánime. Por lo menos poseo capacidad autocrítica, cosa de la que Ricardo carece. El se cree perfecto, sin tacha, en perpetua posesión de la verdad. Es un tipo pretencioso e impertinente. ¿Cómo se atreve a decir que mis recuerdos son falsos? El, que miente tanto que cuando dice una verdad ruboriza...

His commentary irritated me. I don't know if I'm writing about a world of good and bad people, I'm just describing the world I lived in. Hipólito was like that for me, and I should know better than anybody, and Miguel was also that sweet. And furthermore, why lie, I think I'm quite a fair person, unbiased. At least I have the ability to criticise myself, something which Ricardo lacks. He thinks he's so perfect, without blemish, in perpetual possession of the truth. He's a pretentious, impertinent bloke. How dare he say that my memories are false? He, who lies so much that when he tells the truth he blushes... (FD: 161)

What Lucía has created is her own experiential narrative which may not necessarily coincide with those of the other protagonists of her memoirs, were they also to set down their memories. In writing an autobiographical text the narrator engages in a transformative process in which past events are invested with a meaning they may not necessarily have had at the time of their occurrence, as they are retrospectively recalled from the complex perspective of the present with all that this entails. As Montero has commented in an interview with Sigrid Bachmann:

> Como ya no somos lo que éramos, somos incapaces de ver el mundo como lo veíamos antes y por lo tanto, incapaces de reinterpretar la realidad como lo veíamos en ese momento, luego estamos reinterpretando lo que vivimos de lo que somos hoy. Hay una incapacidad de comprender lo que fuimos porque ya no lo somos.
>
> As we are no longer what we were, we are unable to see the world as we saw it before and therefore, we are unable to reinterpret reality as we saw it in that moment, we are reinterpreting what we lived from where we are today. There is an inability to understand what we were because we are no longer like that. (1992)

Thus memories are necessarily filtered through the perspective of subsequent experience and mediated through the structures of language. Furthermore, a selective process must be applied to the chaotic mass of memories that constitute a lifetime in order to construct a text. As Martín Gaite explains in her suggestive essay *El cuento de nunca acabar*:

> Todo es en definitiva, cuestión de ordenación, de una cierta disciplina sobre las intuiciones, de un resignarse a que se tengan que convertir en otra cosa, a trueque de salvarse de alguna manera [...] Balbuceo del ser al no ser. El texto tiene que ser mero trasunto de esa elaboración escondida. Sacar algo del caos es, claro, traicionar ese caos. La sangre hecha cuento. La oscuridad hecha luz. La vida hecha palabra.
>
> Everything is definitively a matter of order, of a certain amount of disciplining intuition, of a resignation that it must be converted into something else, in

exchange for saving it to a certain extent [...] A stirring from being into non-being. The text has to be a mere reflection of this hidden elaboration. Getting something out of chaos is, clearly, a betrayal of that same chaos. Darkness made light. Life made word. (1985, 26)

Autobiography is thus an act of auto-creation or self-invention through narrative process. In other words the construction, through language, of reality for a particular subject.

The analogy of telling a story can thus be used to describe the process of constructing agency for women, 'by piecing together our telling stories, by *emplotting* the events of our lives in narratives that have explanatory power' (Hartman 1991, 12). By writing her diary and memoirs, Lucía is attempting to validate her own personal experience and invest her identity with coherence and meaning through discourse. This identity however is inherently unstable and fragmentary because it is articulated through language. In *Crónica del desamor* Ana, as author, hints at the discontinuous nature of narratives of self, when she realises that the reams of pages that she has written whilst on holiday are filled with 'fragmentos inconexos del pasado' (disconnected fragments of the past) (CD: 148).

Inevitably, the narrator of an autobiographical text is to some extent unreliable in that the narration is not only influenced by present perceptions and articulation through language, but also by the wish to present oneself in a certain manner, more often than not as favourably as possible.[37] Any act of creation necessarily manifests the intertextual, ideological and cultural conditions of whoever is writing (Usandizaga 1993, 179). Moreover, as we have seen from the opening of the novel, memory is not infallible. Both Lucía and Ricardo question each other's version of events and whilst she tries to legitimate her point of view, on several occasions Lucía contradicts herself within her own text thus indicating that the author's interpretation of the text is not necessarily the only valid one. Kathleen Glenn argues that Lucía misreads the past and is suffering from figurative as well as literal myopia (1988, 89). She focuses on passages which illustrate on the one hand the discrepancy between how Lucía thinks she is and how her actions reveal her to be (demonstrating her to be self-centred, insensitive, jealous and touchy); and on the other the gap between how Lucía perceives these faults in others and fails to recognise them in herself. However, rather than being unreliable, Lucía could be described as writing a text in which identity clearly is not unitary, but fragmentary and shifting, despite her attempts to impose coherence on it. Indeed, Glenn recognises this, in the introduction to an article comparing *La función delta* with Ana María Matute's *Primera memoria* (1959), when she states that 'the idea that the self is a coherent, stable and unified whole, something given rather than than produced over time and constantly changing, is illusory', (1991a, 197). Surely then any autobiographical text, fictional or not, can be read more productively for its self-contradictions than by searching for coherence? Lucía herself comes to doubt the veracity of her memoirs:

> Qué poco segura me siento ahora de todo lo que he dicho a Ricardo: ¿yo he vivido, yo he compartido, yo he amado? ¿He sido yo, de verdad yo, yo misma? Mis recuerdos me parecen irreales, como vividos por otra persona. Pero fui yo.
>
> How unsure I feel now about everything I have told Ricardo: have I lived, have I shared, have I loved? Have I been me, really me, myself? My memories seem unreal, as if they had been lived by someone else. But it was me. (FD: 218)

Ricardo claims that Lucía wants to convince herself and make others believe that she is telling the truth (FD: 52). Perhaps, as Lucía is facing death, she wishes to cling on to her past loves who represent life itself. As she faces increasing confusion in the present due to the tumour, she turns to her narrative of the past to provide coherence. Yet increasingly, the tumour affects Lucía's memory, confusing her and at times preventing her from writing:

> Yo creía haber hecho una obra realista, una crónica, y ahora esto me parece no serlo. Hay escenas que no encajan en mi recuerdo, me siento confusa de repente, me cuesta seguir mis pensamientos, como si tuviera una niebla fría y espesa dentro de mí que me impediera razonar. Y, sin embargo, presiento que hay algo que se me escapa de la película, hay algo que equivoca y desconecta mi memoria.

> I thought I had created a realist work, a chronicle, and now this doesn't seem to be so. There are scenes which don't fit in with my memories, I feel confused suddenly, I have trouble following my thoughts, as if I had a cold and thick fog inside me which prevents me from reasoning. And nevertheless, I feel that there is something which escapes me about the film, something which disconnects my memory and makes it incorrect. (FD: 303)

Although as the novel closes, Lucía's confusion is due to the disturbing effects of the tumour, it could be argued that this is a more general comment on the nature of memory as evidenced by the hesitant first words of the novel. Lucía fears that she will die before she has finished setting down her version of her life and persists in continuing her narrative despite the difficulty she has in concentrating. Lucía has difficulty in concluding her text and expresses her wish to live longer that she might finish it. However, the only possible conclusion for her autobiographical narrative is death itself, the moment at which individual discourse ceases to be produced. Her struggle to continue writing her text is bound up with the struggle to carry on living. As the novel concludes, Lucía can no longer distinguish between people and intermingles the two temporal levels of the Sunday of her memoirs and the Sunday, the sixteenth of December, upon which she is writing her diary. She has lost the capacity to select and interpret through the imposition of narrative order and coherence. As she is losing her grip on her symbolic relationship with reality and is confronted with chaos, there can no longer be any meaning, only confusion.

Although Glenn reads the novel as an ironic portrayal of a self-denying character who is not to be emulated, she also acknowledges that Lucía is a multifaceted, finely-drawn character (1988, 95). Whilst I would agree in general terms with Glenn's discussion of irony, I would fully concur with Zatlin (1992, 123) that Lucía does not seem totally unaware of the image she is creating of herself through the narrative process. The fictionalised nature of her autobiography is evident in the allusions to the theatre and cinema throughout the text in which she, perhaps not surprisingly considering her career as a film director, describes herself and others as playing out scenes/roles:[38]

> Tomar el sol erguida en una silla, desdecía mucho de la imagen estival que me había hecho anteriormente (secuencia exterior, toma uno, joven sensual y

confortablemente instalada en magnífica terraza tostándose bajo un cielo verdaderamente esplendido).

Sunbathing rigid in a chair, didn't measure up to the summery image I had created for myself previously (outside scene, shot one, sensual young woman comfortably installed on a magnificent terrace bronzing below a truly splendid sky). (FD: 105-6)

Aunque no, quizá me estaba equivocando de película, quizá Hipólito estuviera en esos momentos arrullándose con alguna muchacha rubia-artificial-elástica capturada la víspera anterior en cualquier bar.

Although no, perhaps I was confusing films, perhaps Hipólito was at that moment whispering sweet nothings to some blonde-artificial-elastic girl picked up the night before in any old bar. (FD: 113)

Sobresalían de entre la masa de los invitados que estábamos tirados por los suelos como si estuvieran encaramados al escenario de un teatro.

They stood out amongst the mass of guests who were sprawled on the floor as if they were up on a theatre stage. (FD: 127)

Me parecía estar viendo la secuencia: yo esplendorosa en mi traje de gasa, con el pelo rizado y las mejillas enrojecidas de emoción, presentándoles en el vestíbulo del cine: «Hipólito, ¿conoces a Miguel?», todo dicho con aire muy casual, pero cargada de intenciones. O quizá esta otra escena, Miguel pasándome su brazo acogedor y suave por los hombros, yo felizmente estrechada contra él, estamos los dos en un rincón apartado del vestíbulo y nos decimos arrullos y lindezas. Y al fondo, zoom entre los corrillos formados por el público, Hipólito contemplando nuestro abrazo y nuestro mimo con rostro apagado, con el rictus gris y terso del perdedor.

I felt I was watching the scene: me, splendid in my chiffon dress, with curled hair, and cheeks rosy with emotion, introducing them in the foyer of the cinema: "Hipólito, do you know Miguel?" all said in a casual tone, but loaded with hidden meaning. Or perhaps this alternative scene, Miguel placing his warm and gentle arm around my shoulder, me happily squeezed up against him, the two of us in a corner isolated from the foyer whispering sweet-nothings to each other. And in the background, zoom through the small groups formed by the public, Hipólito contemplating our embrace and our cuddles with a subdued expression, with the grey and terse sneer of a loser. (FD: 299-300)

Indeed, Lucía is not the only character to construct her identity explicitly through language. In particular, Hipólito -a scriptwriter by profession- is fond of metaphorical language and is constantly recreating himself, taking on new roles/identities:

No me reconozco en ninguno de los papeles que debo representar. No me reconozco como padre, como esposo, como amante... Tengo demasiados personajes y me siento cansado de todos ellos. Hablaba bien Hipólito. Pensé que en realidad era todo palabras.

I don't recognise myself in any of the roles I have to play. I don't recognise myself as a father, as a husband, as alover... I have too many characters and I'm tired of all of them. Hipólito spoke well. In truth I thought he was all words. (FD: 21)

Cómo hubiera disfrutado exacerbando el equívoco y moviéndonos en su entorno como quien mueve a los personajes de una mala comedia americana.

How he would have enjoyed exacerbating the error and moving us about like someone manipulating the characters in a bad American soap. (FD: 111)

... ese tonillo literario repugnante, esa aparatosa sensiblería, esa mentira de novela rosa que rezumaban todas sus letras.

...in that repugnant literary tone of voice, that showy mawkishness, that deception straight from a romantic novel which all his writing exuded. (FD: 232)

Certainly, although both Ricardo and Lucía express a belief in the superiority of reality over fiction, they create themselves and are created through narrative. Indeed, identity here would seem to be a rhetorical construction which does not exist prior to its expression in language. Ironically Ricardo, who criticises Lucía for her lack of veracity, blends anecdotes and tall tales throughout the novel until both she and the reader have difficulty in distinguishing between them. In one particular episode, he recounts to Lucía that he has seen Hipólito, now wearing glasses and asthmatic, making a fool of himself trying to chat up a young woman. Lucía at first does not believe him and protests that he is lying. He convinces her otherwise and when she seems to believe him, questions her, '¿Y si te digo que todo lo que te he contado es mentira?' (And if I told you everything I have said is a lie?) (FD: 331). Why has he lied? In order to trap her into revealing the rancour she still harbours towards Hipólito. However, when she retorts that she knew all along that he was lying and does not understand why he makes up such absurd stories, he claims that the anecdote is absolutely true. He thus plays with the boundaries between fact and fiction, claiming to be lying when he is not and conversely lying when he purports to be telling the truth. For Ricardo lying is a philosophical option he has chosen in order to protect himself by not revealing everything he knows to others (FD: 52). He lies with the aim of maintaining power through the control of knowledge.

The most frequently occurring of Ricardo's somewhat absurdly embellished tales is that of the girl who drowns in the swamp.[39] Ricardo tells Lucía three increasingly dramatic variations of this tale and both she and the reader are left unsure as to which of the versions, if any, is 'true'. The first is a local legend about the swamp behind his house in the mountains in which it is said one of the village girls, Engracia, committed suicide after being spurned by the schoolmaster; in the second version Ricardo claims to have been in love with his sister (we are told that he has no sisters) who was the Engracia of the previous tale; and in the third he claims his first love at sixteen finished up by throwing herself in that same swamp. This tale then reappears in a modified form in Lucía's account of an interview she gave to promote her film. Her film is entitled *Crónica del desamor* in a clear intertextual reference to Montero's first novel; and as she begins to describe the plot the reader may recognise the plot of the novel. It is the story of a doomed love affair between a single mother, Ana Antón, who works as a journalist, and her editor, Soto Amón. However, radical changes have been made to the novel's plot, notably the inclusion of the mannequins with which Ricardo surrounded himself for company in his country house and the melodramatic reworking of the conclusion.[40] Ana does not leave Soto Amón's apartment inspired to write her book by the sheer mediocrity of their affair, but flees before they have a chance to make love and drowns in the swamp now transposed into the city. She is swallowed by the swamp just as the female characters in both *Crónica del desamor* and *La función delta* are constantly engulfed by male discourse, suffocated and silenced with words.

Lucía repeatedly keeps silent in the presence of her lovers, either because she is at a loss for words or as a defensive strategy. For example, during a particularly heated discussion with Ricardo about her relationship with Miguel, she tries using silence as a weapon to change the course of the conversation: 'Me callé intentando agotarle con mi silencio y forzarle a abandonar el tema' (I shut up trying to exhaust him with my silence to force him to abandon the subject) (FD: 215). However, Ricardo carries on relentlessly. His tales gradually take over Lucía's narrative and this is perhaps a comment on the stifling effect of relationships on women's creativity in both of these novels. Lucía, despite the success of her first film, does not direct another. She sacrifices her career to her relationship with Miguel. On moving in with Miguel she loses her room of her own, her creative space and indeed, prior to proposing that they should live together, she faints from a combination of desire and fear: 'Deseo de compartir y convivir, miedo a perder mi identidad, mi territorio, la frágil libertad que encierran estas cuatro paredes de mi casa' (Desire to share and live together, fear of losing my identity, my territory, the fragile freedom enclosed by the four walls of my house) (FD: 363).[41] Her creativity is duly repressed until after his death, when she takes up the pen whilst confined in hospital: confined yet paradoxically free. However this new-found freedom is soon constrained by the presence of her lover Ricardo and she struggles to maintain authorial control over her discourse in the face of his criticism. As opposed to the figure of the female muse for male writers, the physical presence of the male lover would seem to negate inspiration. That notwithstanding, it is important to note that the view we have of Ricardo is that written by Lucía, in both her memoirs and diary, as she is ostensibly the 'author' of the whole novel. As readers we depend on Lucía's depiction of Ricardo: he may be the implanted male perspective that must be questioned by a resisting rather than assenting reader.

After her interview, the narrating Lucía realises that she is perhaps confusing two different narratives in her description of the film. Indeed, she describes it as being about love and death, a statement made repeatedly by Montero and critics about *La función delta* (Monegal 1986, 8; Regazzoni 1984, 53; Vanidades 1990, 23). There would certainly seem to be a close relationship between the two novels. Most critics have pointed out various common themes such as the questioning of the masquerades of femininity and masculinity, criticism of *progre* attitudes, urban solitude, the need for love, frustrated relationships, misunderstandings and the development of self-awareness (Miguel Martínez 1983, 101-4; Davies 1994, 108). Miguel Martínez goes as far as to interpret *La función delta* as the possible projection of the future state of mind of the generational group depicted in *Crónica del desamor* (1983, 87). However, I would argue that the novel also focuses on the present moment. The device of using a first person narrator located in the future taking a retrospective view of the past, allows readers -in 1981- to distance themselves from their present which coincides with the narrator's past. By encouraging the reader to view the present critically as if it were the past, the fictive autobiography fosters heightened awareness in a manner similar to the techniques used in speculative fiction which will be discussed in Chapter Six.

Situating the novel historically, again there would seem to be a contradiction between achieving autonomous selfhood as a woman and entering into a relationship with a man without falling into the trap of dominant, patriarchal constructions. Catherine Davies's comment on another of the metafictional texts examined by Zatlin, *L'hora violeta* by Montserrat Roig (1980), seems apposite here:

> These women can envision a shift away from patriarchy itself, whether it be authoritarian or progressive, but they are held back by their cultural conditioning and social identity. They try to bridge the illusory gap between self and other, between the individual and society but they founder when it comes to personal relationships with men. (1994, 55)

Lucía notes the dilemma of the modern woman in Spain, seemingly liberated but still trapped by the weight of social convention:

> Yo, que también poseía objetivamente todo cuanto «ellos» poseían, era incapaz de contentarme con mi espacio, me asfixiaba, me sentía cercada de ausencias y estrecheces, embargada de urgencias sin motivos razonables. Como aplastada por siglos de educación femenil que hubieran robado mi integridad, mi paz, mi redondez. Era la maldición de la mujer-pareja, de la mujer-carente, de la mujer apoyo y apoyada. Es la maldición de la mujer amputada de sí misma.
>
> I, who also objectively possessed everything "they" did, was incapable of being happy with my space, I suffocated, I felt besieged by absences and lack of vision, overwhelmed by emergencies without reasonable cause. As if I were squashed by centuries of feminine education which had robbed me of my integrity, my peace, my well-roundedness. It was the curse of the woman-as-partner, woman-as-lack, woman-as-supporting and supported. The curse of the woman amputated from herself. (FD: 62)

Lucía would seem to be defining herself in relation to the masculine, as she chooses to write about a week in her life in which the most important players are her three lovers Hipólito, Miguel and Ricardo. Indeed, she appears to be shaped by their needs and desires. As noted above, to a certain extent Ricardo has the power to control and influence her discourse. There is a dialogic relationship between Lucía, the writer and Ricardo, the reader. After an exchange of particularly harsh words, Lucía fears that she may have driven away her only reader and without a reader her writing, and indeed her life, becomes pointless:[42]

> Yo no tengo nada, nada más que la rutina y un sosiego artificioso. Nada más que la memoria de aquellos años plenos, nada más que estos folios que voy rescatando del recuerdo y en los que juego a vivir. Pero si Ricardo no quiere leerlos, ¿qué me queda?.
>
> I have nothing, nothing more than routine and an artificial tranquility. Nothing more than the memory of those full years, nothing more than these sheets of paper I go about rescuing from my memory and in which I play at living. But if Ricardo doesn't want to read them, what's left for me? (FD: 89)

The paradox of the metafictictional text is that it is both 'narcissistically self-reflexive and yet focused outward, oriented toward the reader' (Hutcheon 1984, 7). It reflects upon its own creative process through the dialogue between the writer and the internal critic/reader in the text whilst inviting the actual reader to further reflect upon that process. Lucía not only writes her memoirs in order that they may be read by Ricardo, but also incorporates, consciously or unconsciously, his critical suggestions. After the discussion detailed above in which Ricardo challenged her portrayal of Hipólito, she casts doubts upon the sincerity of Hipólito's love for her. She denies that this is due to Ricardo's recommendations but his influence cannot be negated in the later stages of her narrative when she begins to incorporate his tales into her text. Furthermore, she changes her depiction of Ricardo as their relationship develops; after they make love in her hospital bed she writes the Saturday entry of her memoirs in which she refers to him as 'Ricardo, querido Ricardo mío, dulce Ricardo' (Ricardo, my dear Ricardo, sweet Ricardo) (FD: 285).[43]

In the passage cited above, Lucía, the writer-within-the-text, echoes one of Montero's concerns addressed within both her journalistic work and narrative: the problem of learning to live with solitude. In an interview with *La mujer feminista* Montero states that the fundamental task facing women is to free themselves sentimentally, that is to say from the obligation of having a man at one's side in order to feel a complete person:

A las mujeres se nos ha educado para ser medias personas, y es ¡tan profundo eso! Hay que trabajar tanto, tanto, tanto con una misma y con el entorno para llegar a ser una persona entera tú sola...

As women we have been educated to be half-people, and that's so deep rooted! You have to work so, so, so hard with both yourself and your surroundings to manage to be a whole person by yourself... (1985, 9)

This issue is also addressed in *Crónica del desamor* in which, as the novel opens, Ana feels the need to enter into a relationship as, despite her previous negative experience with Juan, she admits the difficulty of knowing oneself and living alone. However, as the novel closes, she becomes acutely aware of the pre-set roles played by both partners within relationships, be they one night stands, such as that with Gonzalo, or long-standing affairs, such as that with José María. She questions the validity of these roles and conventions which have trapped her in a series of unsatisfactory relationships culminating in the fling with Soto Amón:

> Ahora Ana intuye con melancolía que ha consumido media vida inventando amores inexistentes: y este Soto Amón de la treintena no es más que un nuevo y sofisticado artificio.
>
> Now Ana realises melancholically that she has spent half her life inventing nonexistent loves: and this Soto Amón of her thirties is no more than a new and sophisticated artifice. (CD: 216)

Ana comes to revalue the solitude and self-sufficiency she seemed to reject initially. However, whilst a sense of autonomy is important in the feminist project of agency for women, identity is necessarily a relational concept since the 'I' is mediated through others.[44] The problem lies perhaps in equating difference between the self and the other with gender difference. As is clearly evidenced in the final conversation between Ana and José María (CD: 253-9) and in Hipólito's failure to understand Lucía's letter (FD: 238), the men that Ana and Lucía love are far from ideal interlocutors. Indeed, a catalogue of misunderstandings, misreadings and lack of communication is the central theme of Montero's next novel *Te trataré como a una reina*. This theme of searching for and failing to find the perfect interlocutor is not unique to Montero. Emma Martinell Gifre, in her prologue to the Austral edition of Martín Gaite's study of women writers in Spain *Desde la ventana*, notes that the women portrayed:

> Nunca hallan en el hombre amado al interlocutor. En su soledad hacen de la carta o del diario su interlocutor que, si bien callado, acepta de buen grado el divagar de su mente, el vuelo de su fantasía, o el estallido de sus sentimientos contenidos.
>
> They never find the interlocutor in their beloved. In their solitude they make letters or their diary their interlocutor who, if silent, readily accepts the wandering of their minds, their flights of fantasy, or the explosion of their pent-up feelings. (1992, 9-10)

The Importance of Metafiction for the Feminist Reader

What, then, is the relevance of these texts for the female and indeed feminist reader? It could be argued that the self-reflexivity of contemporary women's narrative may serve only to reconfirm the primary exclusion of women from social discourse and the partition between the private and the public into feminine and masculine domains respectively. However, I would argue that metafiction can be used, as it is here by Montero, as a tool for the interrogation of cultural narratives and for the social critique of patriarchal substructures still in place in Spanish society, despite formal equality between the sexes. It is also a means of consciousness -raising through which an analogy can drawn between the process of writing and reading a narrative and the process of constructing the self. The reader is invited to decode the text, think about it and apply a similar deconstructive process to the cultural and social codes governing their own thoughts and behaviour. By identifying common ground between individual women's experiences and perceptions the novels serve to suggest possible new interpretive strategies for reading not only fiction but also lives. Furthermore, resistance against the fictions of dominant patriarchal discourse is encouraged by characters taking up the position of the writing subject and thus breaking out of the passive silence which would seem to trap women.[45]

Thus the novels fit into Riera's analysis of Spanish women's writing in the early 1980s, referred to in Chapter One, through their vindication of the recuperation of women's voices in the search for self-identity. While these are not strictly programmatic texts, for ultimately neither Ana nor Lucía achieves autonomous selfhood, the female 'I' of the text nevertheless encourages a complex interplay of distanciation, identification and interaction on the part of the female reader. I would thus concur with Aránzazu Usandizaga in her analysis of the recent crop of autobiographical novels by Spanish women in that 'su interés radica sobre todo en que reflejan las tensiones, paradojas y contradicciones inherentes a la proyección de la identidad femenina' (the interesting thing about them is above all that they reflect the tensions, paradoxes and contradictions inherent in the projection of feminine identity) (1993, 182). The notion of a fixed identity is questioned in particular in *La función delta* through the self-contradictory presentation of the narrator Lucía, despite the novel's supposed identification with both readers and Montero mentioned above. This is not surprising if one reconsiders the difficulty, alluded to in Chapter One, of resignifying an identity for women outside patriarchal cultural paradigms. Nonetheless, through a deconstructive critique of the subject, these novels recognize the validity of the diverse positions which may be assumed as feminine. Furthermore, both these texts engage with the complex interplay between the generic and the individual outlined in the introduction.

It would seem that women's metafiction can play a part in bringing about cultural and social change. But for change to occur self-knowledge, such as that which finally leads to Ana's decision to write the book of 'all the Anas', is necessary. Also necessary is an awareness of how feminine identity has been constructed in patriarchal discourse if women are to be able, like Ana, to write beyond the ending of a conventional plot. In *Crónica del desamor* Elena is in the process of writing a feminist polemic entitled 'Odds and evens' in which she examines gender stereotypes and the difficulties involved in defining difference. Pressurized by her editor to meet her deadline for publication she realises that: 'no lo acabaré [el libro] nunca, y lo que es aún peor, estoy a punto de acabarlo' (I'll never finish it [the book], and what's even worse, I'm almost finished) (CD: 149). She resists the closure imposed on her text by her male editor. The goal and conclusion of Ana's text are not a man and happy-ever-after marriage but the impulse to create and construct one's own identity. If this is a never-ending story, that is because the recognition that identity is multiple prevents narrative closure.

---

[1]This view of the discourse of reality as a never-ending narrative is taken from the title of Carmen Martín Gaite's 1985 essay collection, *El cuento de nunca acabar (apuntes sobre la narración, el amor y la mentira)*.

[2] The literature available on metafiction is extensive. For general works on metafiction I have consulted Waugh (1984), Hutcheon (1984), Chown (1986), África Vidal (1989) and Sánchez-Pardo González (1991). For theories of metafiction see Alter (1975), Christensen (1981), McCaffery (1982), Scholes (1979) and Spires (1984).

[3] Saussure demonstrated the link between words and the concepts they described to be arbitrary for example the words dog, *chien* and *perro* have the same meaning yet differ in configuration and pronunciation. The meaning given to words is dependent on social consensus and this consensus is

necessary for communication to take place. See Saussure's essay 'Nature of the Linguistic Sign' in Lodge (Saussure 1991).

4 This image will be returned to in chapter six when discussing *Temblor*.

5 The notion of order being imposed through language and law on a world that is actually ruled by chance is central to *Temblor*.

6 The stringent censorship laws of the old regime were revoked on the thirty-first of December, 1978.

7 Owens discusses how such a hegemonic discourse blocks or invalidates alternative representations in a particularly interesting article on the relationship between feminist and postmodernist theory (1985, 59). For a concise analysis of the discursive configuration of feminine identity in psychoanalytic terms see Tubert (1988) and Amorós (1990).

8 See also Tsuchiya (1990).

9 As a point of interest Montero has indicated Nabokov on a number of occasions as a novelist she feels an affinity with (Alba 1988, 92; Regazzoni 1984, 53). Nabokov's works are discussed in all the general works on metafiction I have listed above.

10 For comprehensive discussions of first person women's narrative see Jelinek (1980), Anderson (1986), Frye (1986), Smith (1987), Benstock (1988), Brée (1988), Brodzki & Schenk (1988) and Personal Narratives Group (1989). For a Hispanic perspective see Cipljauskaité (1983 & 1988) and Molloy (1991). For a woman author's perspective see Araújo (1985) and Gambaro (1985). For the theorising of autobiography which forms the basis for the approach I have taken, see *MLN* special edition (1978), De Man (1979), Gusdorf (1980), Lejeune (1980), Renza (1980), Jay (1982) and Olney (1978, 1980 & 1988).

11 Zatlin also bases her commentary on the metanovel primarily on Waugh (1984).

12 For a serious discussion of the reactionary potential and ambivalent politics of postmodernist theory, see Solé Puig (1988), Mardones (1991) and Usandizaga (1993).

13 Similar analyses are given by Solé Puig (1988) and Urdanibia (1991). África Vidal has also written a study of the postmodern novel which, whilst not exclusively on Hispanic texts, includes interesting insights on the work of Jorge Luis Borges (1990).

14 It is important to note again the problematic relationship between postmodernist and feminist theory. See Owens (1985), Flax (1987), Kaplan (1988), Scott (1988), Moi (1990), Pujal i Llombart (1992) and Molina Petit (1992 & 1994). As noted by Waugh (1989) and the Spanish theorist Concha Fagoaga (1989), women writers are rarely referenced by postmodern theorists.

[15] For discussions of the search for identity as a narrative process see Chown (1986), De Lauretis (1986) and Gunew (1992).

[16] An interesting contrast comes from the opening paragraph of Oscar Fontradona's 1995 interview with Montero for *Ajoblanco*, 'Narradora antes que periodista, Rosa Montero sorprendió en la Transición con su concepción literaria del reportaje' (Narrator rather than journalist, Rosa Montero surprised us in the Transition with her literary conception of reporting) (30).

[17] The definition of 'marisabidilla' from María Moliner's *Diccionario de uso del español* gives an idea of how patronising the term is: 'mujer de poca cultura, pedante o redicha que habla con presunción' (a woman of little culture, pedantic or affected, presumptuous when speaking). This is parodied in *La hija del caníbal* where the main character describes the fictional author Rosa Montero thus, 'la escritora de color originaria de la Guinea española: era un tanto marisabidilla y a veces una autoritaria y una chillona' (the coloured writer originating from Spanish Guinea: she was a bit know-it-all and sometimes bossy and shrill) (HC: 42).

[18] The journalists include Neus Aguado, Lidia Falcón, Cristina Fernández Cubas, Carmen Rico Godoy and Montserrat Roig; the literary critics Aurora de Albornoz, Carmen Martín Gaite, Marina Mayoral, Lourdes Ortiz, Rosa María Pereda and Soledad Puértolas and the lecturers Albornoz, Mayoral and Carme Riera.

[19] Women's writing is often criticised as being too autobiographical. The use of this label as a derogatory accusation by male critics in Spain when reviewing Montero's early novels is discussed by Montserrat Roig (1988, 28).

[20] This description could certainly be applied to perhaps the most studied work written by a woman during this period, the metafictive *El cuarto de atrás* by Carmen Martín Gaite in which the narrator, a writer identified closely with Martín Gaite, converses with a stranger dressed in black during the course of a stormy night. At the end of the evening when the man has gone, the narrator discovers a sheaf of paper which has been growing steadily throughout their conversation and bears the title *El cuarto de atrás*. Jean Chittenden's discussion of this novel as fictional autobiography (1986) is of particular interest.

[21] Although the novel is about 'all the Anas' it cannot strictly be taken to refer to all women. The women in *Crónica del desamor* and also *La función delta* are exclusively white, middle class and, in the majority, educated professionals. That notwithstanding the novels deal with many issues that are relevant to all women irrespective of race or class.

[22] As such it can be inserted into discussions of woman as positionality or nomadic subject in which identity is not independent of external situation but politically assumed and relative to

sociohistorical location. See Alcoff (1988), Lauretis (1990), Molina Petit (1992) and Braidotti (1994).

[23] See Valcárcel (1991).

[24] Denise Riley discusses the problems and ambiguities of using the term woman already referred to in the introduction to this thesis, recouching Sojourner Truth's famous question 'Ain't I a woman?' as 'Ain't I a fluctuating identity?' (1988, 1).

[25] Emphasis added is mine.

[26] The issue of whether or not *Crónica del desamor* is a novel has been discussed in Chapter Two.

[27] In this analysis I am following Lury who notes the importance of placing texts into the context in which they are produced and consumed 'not because they express a general, abstract notion of 'woman', or a particular, unique subjectivity, but because they are the product of a collective process of a specific group of social individuals' (1991, 103).

[28] This notion of speaking for oneself would seem to be originally quoted by Marta Traba from Bourdieu before becoming a catchphrase amongst Spanish theorists of 'literatura de mujer/literatura femenina' (Traba 1981, 11; Orquín 1984, 31; Riera 1982, 12 & 1990, 37).

[29] *Crónica del desamor* would be at the lowest point on Waugh's scale as a self-begetting novel.

[30] This is done within the first paragraph where Lucía states, 'Yo **por entonces** era tan alocadamente joven' (**At that time** I was so crazily young) (FD: 1), thus clearly distinguishing between herself as narrator and her younger narrated self (emphasis added is mine).

[31] For a discussion of women diarists see Blodgett (1988), Nolte Lensink (1987) and Simmons (1990).

[32] The text also has an implied reader for although the diary would seem to be an essentially private genre, its purpose in many cases is to be read.

[33] For a more detailed discussion of perspectivism see Clark (1990, ch.5) and Personal Narratives Group (1989, 268).

[34] Again this can be related to the question of hegemonic discourse and epistemology. In a Spanish context the non-neutrality of language and thought is discussed by Buxo Rey (1976) and Rebollo and Rodríguez (1980). For a cogent analysis of how questions of power enter into the production of meaning see Izquierdo (1989).

[35] In relation to the discourse of National Catholicism which was prevalent under the Franco regime, Fanny Rubio notes that it was presented as the only alternative thus stultifying social change (Tremosa & Roig 1977, 78).

[36] This is an unfair criticism as Lucía does include incidents that bear light on the sociopolitical situation in Spain at the time of writing her diary. One such incident is the murder of a youth wearing a communist badge by a group of ultras (FD: 176-8).

[37] This is particularly true in the case of the narrator of Montero's short story 'Paulo Pumilio' (1982).

[38] The cinematic nature of many of the scenes in *Crónica del desamor*, particularly the use of dialogue, has been noted in studies by Zatlin (1992, 118-19) and Davies (1994, 97). It is also a feaure of *Bella y oscura* where several key scenes are described in terms of either the theatre or cinema. Role playing also features on the lowest level of Waugh's metafictive scale (1984, 116).

[39] She allows herself to drown without resisting the pull of the swamp. This episode calls to mind the work *Self-Burial* by Keith Arnatt (1969) exhibited in the conceptual art section of the Tate Gallery, London. The work consists of a series of nine photographs of the artist gradually sinking into a swamp until he disappears.

[40] Lucía encounters the mannequins when she visits Ricardo (FD: 180-1).

[41] Similarly, in *Crónica del desamor*, Elena feels that her relationship with Javier robbed her of her space, 'irrumpió en su casa robándola el espacio, espacio en los armarios, en la mesa del trabajo, espacio en su existencia' (he burst into her house, robbing her of her space, space in the cupboards, on her desk, space in her existence) (CD: 58).

[42] Various women writers have stated the importance of the reader in the creative process: Carme Riera regards the reader as a confidant(e) (Guillaume 1988, 76-7), Esther Tusquets states that without a public (who condition what she writes) she wouldn't write (Regazzoni 1984, 13) and Rosa Montero herself affirms that she writes with specific readers in mind (Monegal 1986, 7).

[43] Similarly, Ana in *Crónica del desamor* reconstructs herself by playing out a series of roles in her telephone conversations with her male friends/lovers (CD: 9-11).

[44] This concept of subjectivity as not achieved necessarily through separation is central to the work of feminist object-relations theorists such as Nancy Chodorow, as will be discussed further in chapter five. To sum up the position, Patricia Waugh, in her study of postmodernism and gender, states that 'Women's sense of identity is more likely, for psychological and social reasons, to consist of a more diffuse sense of the boundaries of self and their notion of identity understood in relational and intersubjective terms' (1992, 135).

[45] The 'Plan de Educación de Adultas, 1990-95' as set out by the Instituto de la Mujer sets out to encourage the reading of women writers, especially those whose voices have previously been

silenced or who broach taboo subject areas, and furthermore, to motivate women to write in order to legitimize their creative protagonism (*Mujeres* 1994, 10).

CHAPTER FOUR

«NECESITO UN CORAZÓN QUE ME ACOMPAÑE...»: THE FUNCTION OF THE BOLERO IN *TE TRATARÉ COMO A UNA REINA*.

El bolero es un baile de seducción ritualizada, de juego, desafío, provocación, rico en inflexiones y complicidades... Elude sin tregua toda relación de seguridad, de verdad, todo discurso impositivo judicial (la familia, el matrimonio), los discursos de otro poder que no sea la seducción, con la promesa de un siempre.

The bolero is a ritualised dance of seduction, of play, challenge, provocation, rich in inflections and complicity... It relentlessly evades relations based on security and truth, all judicially imposed discourse (the family, matrimony), the discourses of any power other than seduction with the promise of forever after. (Zavala 1991, 40-1)

In contesting traditional narrative patterns, Montero engages in particular with the plot of the romance narrative or *novela rosa* whose conventions inform both *Crónica del desamor* and *La función delta*. An examination of these patriarchal intertexts is vital to the discussion of Montero's third novel *Te trataré como a una reina*, which is framed by pieces of sensationalist 'tabloid' journalism and the boleros which give the novel its title. *Te trataré como a una reina* may be regarded as the key text in Montero's novelistic production to date, marking a turning point in her style whilst continuing to engage with many of the issues tackled in the first two novels which are generally described as being more realist and even journalistic in form and content.[1] The focus of action in this novel has shifted from a setting readily recognisable as that of Montero's own professional ambience to a world of marginal characters in an indefinite city, reminiscent at times of a twentieth century *esperpento* vision of Madrid. Robert Saladrigas, critic for *La Vanguardia*, described the novel as being influenced by *costumbrismo*, melodrama, the *novela rosa* (romantic novel), the gutter press, Puig, the nineteenth century *folletín* and Valle-Inclán's *esperpento* (1983).[2] Indeed, the novel would seem to confound generic classification having been variously termed 'a pink tragedy' (Villán 1983b, 32), 'black farse (Olba 1983) and 'intimate story' (Martín Maestro 1984, 162).

All three of these classifications are of interest, especially when making apparent the links between this novel and the first two. Both *Crónica del desamor* and *La función delta* engage with the genre of the *novela rosa* particularly in the descriptions of the affair between Ana and Soto Amón and Lucía's idealisation of her lovers and her nurse María del Día's fantasy of living happily for ever after. If they both break with convention by having characters, to borrow Rachel Blau du Plessis's phrase, who write beyond the ending, in *Te trataré como una reina* the characters are tragically trapped by the ending in a text which engages directly with the genre which Rafael Castillo Zapata has termed the Hispanic 'ars amatoria' par excellence: the bolero (1990, 27-31).

However, the novel not only engages with the romantic genre but also another popular form: that of the *novela negra* (detective novel). On several occasions, Montero has expressed her admiration for writers such as Chandler and Hammett.[3] For both Samuel Amell (1986) and Francie Cate Arries (1990) the return to popularity of this genre, particularly the works of Vázquez Montalbán, was a product of the *desencanto*. It had the scope for ironic critique of socio-historical reality whilst being attractive to a mass readership, incorporating as it does the signifying systems of popular culture which the post-war generations have been brought up on. *Te trataré como a una reina* is not a detective novel since the crime and its perpetrator are identified on the first page of the novel and therefore the central question becomes not who did it but why she did it. Rather than adopt the typical plot, Montero has taken the ambience of the *novela negra* and it is the reader who is invited to solve the strange case of the smoking murderess set before them by the sensationalist piece of journalism that opens the narrative and which will be discussed in Chapter Five.[4]

The assimilation of popular genres into the collage of the various discourses juxtaposed in this hyperrealist novel is a feature of both metafictive and postmodern texts.[5] This technique allows the reader some level of familiarity with which to identify whilst simultaneously undermining convention. Thus *Te trataré como a una reina* can be taken as a mid-point in Montero's trajectory, following on from the clearly metafictive nature of her first two novels and pre-empting the intertextuality of *Temblor*. Yet as well as signalling the increasingly experimental use of various stylistic registers in Montero's writing, this novel can also be regarded as an intimate story, in that it examines the relationship between collective culture and individual desire in the construction of identity. There is also an increased emphasis on sexual fantasy and the expression of desire which will be discussed in more detail in Chapter Five.

Several articles have briefly examined the use Montero makes of boleros in this novel: Alborg (1988, 71-2); Brown (1991b, 249-50); Davies (1991a, 218), Glenn (1987, 199 & 1990b, 427); Jiménez (1995, 165-7); Zatlin (1987, 38-9). Each of these articles discusses the use of the bolero as a metafictive device which provides an ironic commentary within the text through its juxtaposition with the lived experience of the characters. Alborg points out the assimilation of popular culture into the psychology of the protagonists, particularly that of Bella the bolero singer. Both Brown and Zatlin interpret the bolero as a representation of the women's dreams providing an illusion of escape from the sordid reality which surrounds them. However, as Davies observes: 'the women are destroyed partly by a macho society, partly by their own romantic fantasies of dependence on heroic redeemers, a patriarchal construction in itself, propagated by pop-culture (bolero songs, etc.)' (1991a, 218). Both of the articles by Glenn emphasize the role of the male characters as writers/speakers and the female characters as readers/listeners of male-produced texts: 'Bella's reading appears limited to the words of the boleros she croons, sentimental songs that glorify love and engender impossible expectations' (1990b, 427). Indeed Glenn sees the boleros as 'male-produced lyrics' which help maintain male power (1987, 199 & 1990b, 427). Whilst broadly agreeing with the propositions put forward in these articles, I would contest the broad dichotomy drawn between male producers and female consumers of the bolero and argue that the interpretation of romantic fantasy, as expressed in popular culture, as a patriarchal construct which oppresses women, does not take into account the possibilities for resistance offered to women by the bolero form. The articles cited fail to engage with the issue of whether popular culture is regressive, liberating or a complex amalgam of both.[6]

The term entertainment is derived from the French 'entretenir': to keep/maintain/foster/feed. Its etymology suggests a discursive phenomenon: 'Let me entertain you'='Let me hold your interest', 'Let me create a bond between you and me'. Thus forms of entertainment may indeed serve to shape collective identities. However, the French and Spanish term currently in use, 'divertir', suggest a diversion or distraction rather than a rapprochement.[7] Is popular culture a drug which performs the function Marx had ascribed to religion: that of an opiate lulling the masses to sleep by bribing them with pleasurable dreams? It may indeed provide an escape or scenario for 'wish-fulfilment' of needs and desires by temporarily addressing inadequacies of the society being escaped but perhaps without offering models for change. It is this rather negative view of popular culture which would seem to have been adopted by the majority of critics who have analysed the use Montero makes of the bolero.

Pleasure, Escapism and Identity Politics

According to Iris Zavala, the Cuban bolero speaks the language of desire, of its absence and presence, of illusion and disillusionment (1991).[8] It is not about love or pleasure but about a desire which by definition is impossible to realise: the pursuit of the unattainable other.[9] For Manuel Delgado Ruiz the bolero expresses modern theories of desire in its tension between absence and desire for presence:

> Es como si inopinadamente, los Lara, Domínguez, Machín, etcétera, hubieran intuido, en clave músico-sentimental, las actuales teorías del deseo.[10]

> It's as if unexpectedly, Lara, Domínguez, Machín, etc., had intuited, in an emotional-musical code, current theories of desire. (1991, 95)

When Rosa Montero was asked why she used the bolero as the background music to *Te trataré como a una reina* she replied:

El bolero, lo escogí porque es un tipo de música, de letra sobre todo, evidentemente mentirosa. [...] Pertenece a un mundo romántico en un sentido completamente disparatado, o sea que no tiene nada que ver con la realidad. Cuando tú dices el bolero que me inventé yo y que es el título de la novela *Te trataré como a una reina*, cuando tú dices 'te trataré como a una reina' a alguien, hoy es obvio que no le vas a poder tratar como a una reina, pues eso es un deseo de un tipo de felicidad que es imposible ¿no? [...] O sea que es obvio que no puede ser; es un deseo de sentimentalidad extrema que ya está siendo traicionada en su enunciamiento.

I picked the bolero because it is a type of music, above all of lyrics, which is clearly false. [...] It belongs to a completely ridiculous romantic world which has nothing to do with reality. When you repeat the bolero that I invented which gives its title to the novel, *Te trataré como a una reina*, when you say 'I'll treat you like a queen' to someone, nowadays it's obvious that you're not going to be able to treat her like a queen as this is a desire for an impossible type of happiness, isn't it? [...] In other words it's obvious that it can't be so; it's an extremely sentimental desire which is already being betrayed as it is expressed. (Knights 1993)

For Montero then the most important feature of the bolero is that it is a discourse which essentially enunciates a desire which cannot be fulfilled. It expresses the tragic nature of the human condition which Montero has often spoken about, 'esa inquietud, esa insatisfacción, ese agujero que nunca se llena' (this preoccupation, this insatisfaction, this hole which is never filled) (Knights 1994).

For Montero the bolero eludes truth and certainly in that sense it could be said to have nothing to do with reality. However, contemporary cultural studies have shown the role of pleasure, fantasy and desire in the process of 'the cultural construction of subjects, identities and practices' (Franklin, Lury & Stacey 1991, 6). One of the features of the bolero is certainly that of enjoyment derived from the recognition of a form which tends to repeat tropes and have relatively simple catchy melodies and lyrics. For William Rowe and Vivian Schelling in their study of popular culture in Latin America, popular music forms such as the bolero supply the soundtrack to everyday life, shaping collective memory, identity and individual desire (1994, 233). They briefly discuss the use of the bolero in novels by Manuel Puig and Mario Vargas Llosa, but concentrate particularly on the novel *La importancia de llamarse Daniel Santos* by Luis Rafael Sánchez (1989) in which they argue the bolero becomes a cultural model displaying 'irreverence (in voice), transgression and retaliatory laughter, qualities which are the resources of the poor who are the majority' (1994, 233).[11] Similarly, Rafael Castillo Zapata, in his phenomenology of the bolero, describes it as the collective catharsis alleviating urban reality (1991, 37). I would argue that in Montero the bolero serves a similar function.

The novel revolves around the lives of a set of characters from the margins of society; it explores their relationships and why these ultimately fail. The principal players are Antonio Ortiz, a perfume tester, and his former childhood sweetheart, Isabel López, known as Bella, a bolero singer in a seedy club rather ironically called the Desiré.[12] Much of the action in the novel is related directly to the Desiré, a former pick-up joint, now owned by Vicente Menéndez who spends his time reading pornographic novels hidden behind a copy of *The Three Musketeers*. The only other member of staff, apart from Bella, is a mysterious character known as el Poco who acts as a doorman of sorts and composes boleros. He flirts both with Bella and a regular customer of the Desiré, Vanessa. Vanessa, real name Juana Castillo, is an eighteen year old vamp who works as a cleaning lady while dreaming of being a star in 'Jolibud' [sic] (TT: 136). Antonio and his friend, Inspector García are also regulars at the Desiré along with a young delinquent who talks with Bella. Completing the cast we have Antonio's devoted, spinster sister Antonia, her lover, Damián the simple, slightly cross-eyed nephew of the concierge of the house in which they live and Benigno Martí, Antonio's assistant who is secretly in love with Antonia. The novel has been likened to a bolero in which couples frequently change partners: Antonio and Bella, Bella and Poco, Poco and Vanessa, Antonio and Julia, Vanessa and Antonio, Antonia and Damián, Bella and the spiv (Alborg 1988, 72).

Boleros are sung throughout the novel, either in performance by Bella, hummed to herself or in her thoughts, as her world view is informed by the boleros she sings which would seem to express a better reality than that in which she lives. The world of the bolero is a dream or fantasy image of the other. In the case of the bolero as sung by Bella the setting of her dreams is Cuba, portrayed as an exotic dream world in which personal relationships, usually situated in a natural setting, are of prime importance: 'Lo nuestro es vida, espasio [sic] y tiempo, un sol que brilla y un firmamento, un río que canta, es mar y es playa, es brisa y viento' (Our [love] is life, space and time, the sun that shines and the stars above, a river which sings, it is sea and beach, it is breeze and wind) (TT: 29). In her analysis of postwar relationships, Martín Gaite describes the bolero as 'sensuous, warm and tropical' (1994, 142). Indeed, Poco presents Cuba as a tropical paradise of sandy beaches:

> Hay playas de arena blanca como azúcar, y palmeras tan altas como casas. Las mujeres son como de madera barnizada, y van vestidas siempre de blanco, blanca la ropa y las carnes como de caramelo. Y cómo andan...Todo en Cuba es blanco, y verde, y azul. [...] Me levantaba muy tarde y desayunaba los zumos de unas frutas que ni siquiera conoces. Después me iba al Tropicana. El mejor cabaret del mundo, Bella, y yo trabajaba allí y no me daba cuenta, ¿qué te parece? El Tropicana es un jardín, es como el paraíso, todo lujo, lleno de plantas que ni siquiera conoces, y una pista que se sube y que se baja, y allí sólo actúan los mejores, y los camareros son tan elegantes que parecen duques...
>
> There are beaches which are white as sugar and palm trees as tall as houses. The women look as if they were made of varnished wood and always wear white, white clothes and flesh like caramel. And how they walk... Everything in Cuba is white and green and blue. [...] I used to get up very late and have juice for breakfast made from fruits you've never even heard of. Afterwards I would go to the Tropicana. The best cabaret in the world Bella, and I worked there and didn't realise, what do you think of that? The Tropicana is a garden, it's like paradise, total luxury, full of plants that you've never even heard of, and a dance floor which goes up and down, only the best play there and the waiters are so elegant that they look like dukes... (TT: 84)

This fantastic otherness of the tropical colony, described by Poco, denies the true otherness of Cuba which is that of Castro's Cuba. The revolution of 1959 sparked off an exodus of singers which was only stemmed when exit visa control was tightened, as many singers who left Cuba to go on tour never returned. Indeed, the singer that Bella refers to on several occasions, Olga Guillot, left Cuba in 1961 to settle in Mexico (Rico Salazar 1988, 256). Those singers and composers who left were no longer mentioned in the Cuban media. Although the cabarets were kept open, bureaucrats rather than musical directors decided on the music to be performed, as state control of the music industry meant that music had to conform to moral standards and be pro-revolutionary (Diaz Ayala 1991, 273). In his study of the origin and development of Cuban music, Argeliers Léon, then head of the Department of Music of the Casa de las Américas, denounces the music of popular urban culture such as the bolero as being exploitative of the lower classes and rails against its lack of authenticity as it has increasingly assimilated the Latin American ballad tradition (1984, 31). It is interesting to note that the majority of boleros written during the 1960s that express nostalgia for Cuba, similar to that felt by Poco, were not written by Cubans (Rico Salazar 1988, 55). Bella points out that Cuba has undergone a revolution since Poco was there but he insists that the Tropicana has not changed.

The Cuba which Poco describes is that of the 1940s and 1950s, known as the golden age of the bolero, when cabarets such as the Tropicana had their heyday. Bella and Poco's dreams of going to Cuba are dreams of the impossible as their desire by definition cannot be fulfilled. It is a desire to go to a place which no longer exists, for whilst the Tropicana is still open in Havana as a tourist attraction, it is no longer the legendary club of the 1950s which drew international stars. When Poco shows Vanessa the letter from his friend Trompeta inviting them to Cuba and asks her to go with them, she turns on him in a rage but her words spoken in anger have a ring of truth about them. She does not want to go to Cuba with Poco and Bella because she sees them as old losers. Instead she has a more contemporary, if equally impossible, dream: to go to Hollywood to be a film star. Bella, herself, recognises that the bolero is an anachronistic genre:

> ¿Qué pintaba ella allí, por qué seguía Menéndez contratándola? Cantante de boleros en un mundo en el que ya no se llevaban los boleros. Ni ella ni el Desiré tenía futuro.

> What was she doing there? Why did Menéndez keep renewing her contract? A bolero singer in a world which no longer cared for boleros. Neither she nor the Desiré had a future. (TT: 33)

The bolero is anachronistic not only because of the vision of Cuba that it propounds, but also because by the early 1980s it was no longer a popular style of music. Its heyday in Spain was in the 1950s when the Franco regime encouraged a culture of evasion (Carr & Fusi 1981, 106). Whilst such a culture offered the popular classes a form of escape from the reality of the poverty and political repression of the post-War period, it was tolerated by the regime as it was regarded as devoid of political and intellectual content. This is, of course, highly debatable.[13] However, it can be argued that this culture which included films, radio soaps, kiosk literature and radio songs created an artificial silence because it avoided all reference to the present situation in Spain or the immediate past (Carr & Fusi 1981, 121). Nonetheless, despite the apparent anachronism of a bolero singer in a Madrid club in the 1980s, it is interesting to note that in the same year that *Te trataré como a una reina* was published the director Pedro Almodóvar used the bolero 'Encadenados' sung by Lucho Gatica for one of the key scenes of the film *Entre tinieblas*. Andrés Amorós in his analysis of the romantic songs of Raphael noted that the increasing popularity of such songs, in the 1970s, coincided with a sense of disillusion with reality (1974, 73). In a time of economic crisis, when people's life-style expectations had been raised through increasing urbanisation and the growth of a consumer culture in Spain, culture of evasion could again provide an escape valve for collective, frustrated illusions.[14] As the characters in the novel are marginalized by society and with the exception of Antonio, fairly poor, dreaming in terms of romantic songs or Hollywood films allows them a temporary escape from their sordid reality.

Indeed as economic crisis returned to Spain in 1993, so too did the bolero, both in the release of several compilation albums which have enjoyed great success and as sung by contemporary singers such as Agustín Pantoja, Gloria Estefan and particularly the Mexican pop star Luis Miguel, whose albums 'Romance' and 'Segundo romance' of remakes of classis boleros made him the biggest selling Hispanic artist of 1994. In his discussion of Spanish popular music of the last forty years, Jesús Ordovás points out that although the genres of the *canción española* and the bolero had not been popular during the early 1980s, largely due to their association with the *género nacional franquista*, they have undergone a renaissance with records entering the charts, articles appearing in the press, appearances by singers on television and the use of this music by popular film directors such as Almodóvar (1990, 351-2). In an article occasioned by the opening of the Cuban musical *La antología del bolero* in Madrid, Manuel Domínguez noted that it would seem that 'en tiempos de crisis se impone un giro hacia el romántico' (in times of crisis a switch to romance imposes itself) (1993, 80).

It could be argued then that the bolero, and other forms of popular culture, have served a double function in post-war Spain: to encourage a consumer culture and to provide an escape valve through what Montero has described as 'sweet lies' (Knights 1994) for collective frustrations when people's illusions created by that culture are not fulfilled.[15] Andrés Amorós, in his study of *subliteraturas* of the 1970s, suggested, paraphrasing the poet Antonio Machado, that it was time for Spain to wake up (1974, 70). Ten years later, through the ironic contrast of the bolero with the sordid reality of the characters' experience in the novel Montero, too, would seem to be suggesting that they need to stop dreaming and take action in order to change the situation in which they seem to be trapped.

Singing with «Feeling»: The Bolero as Camp Performance

The bolero was the most popular romantic rhythm of the 1950s both in Cuba and Spain where it was popularized by the singer Antonio Machín.[16] Women singers such as Olga Guillot, who was voted 'Queen' of Cuban National Radio in 1951, were particularly popular. Guillot and Elena Burke, also mentioned in the novel and known to her fans as 'her majesty' (Mora 1989, 107), were two of the main exponents of 'el movimiento del «feeling»' which consisted of singing with a greater expressiveness by varying the tempo and stress (Rico Salazar 1988, 52).[17] It was popularised by singers, who like Bella in the novel, were of humble extraction (Caravaca 1995, 76-87; Orovio 1981, 140-1 & 1995, 130-1; Núñez & Guntin 1992, 39-40). For the Cuban musicologist Natalio Galán, «feeling» was the equivalent of a camp sensibility associated with popular singers who performed in an accentuatedly dramatic, gestural manner (1983, 296-9).[18]

Voice and lyrics predominate over instrumentation and melody in the bolero: 'La voz es el vehículo de expresión, una lírica melosa y almibarada en instrumentación lenta' (The voice is the vehicle for expression, schmaltzy lyrics soaked in the syrup of a slow instrumentation) (Zavala 1991, 28). This voice may be seductive, offering images of the ideal other and promises of eternal love. Bella copies Guillot's style and also pronounces 'c' and 'z' in the Spanish American sibilant fashion so that the boleros sound more exotic and chic. This is indicated in the text by substituting the letter 's' for these letters in transcriptions of the boleros that she sings:

—Que me acompañe hasta el final de nuestra vida original y que me quiera de **verdá**, que me quiera como yo también lo quiera, que dé su vida por mi vida entera, que llene de **carisias** mi ternura, que diga que me quiere con locura, yo quiero un **corasón** que me acompañe, que **meá-compañeeeeeee**.

"Let him stay with me until the end of our original lives and truly love me, love me as I love him, give his life for mine, fill my tenderness with caresses, tell me he loves me madly, I want a heart that will stay with me, stay with meeeeeee. (TT: 40)

The 'portamento' or lengthening of a syllable at the end of a phrase is another characteristic feature of Guillot's style. Bella is appropriating the speech of a tropical other in her performance. By adopting the 'feeling' style of performance, she would seem to fit in with Sontag's description of camp as 'a love of the exaggerated, [...] of things-being-what-they-are not' (1994, 279). Indeed, Andrew Ross traces the etymological origin of the term 'camp' to the French 'se camper' meaning self-conscious posturing (1989, 157). Life is thus theatricalised through camp performance and Bella plays out a role in a similar fashion to the characters in *La función delta*. Unlike the singers she emulates, however, there is little likelihood of Bella ever being treated like a queen as she is from a small village in Castille and, unlike the typical rags to riches romance plot, ends up in a fairly seedy area of an inner city.[19]

Indeed, the Desiré club is run down and filthy: the light bulbs are broken, the carpets threadbare and covered with vomit stains, the ladies' toilet has been blocked for years. The descriptions of Cuba in the boleros are consistently contrasted with descriptions of the interior of the club. Instead of beaches of white sand, Bella sings the bolero «Luna en La Habana, milisiana» against the backdrop of a cardboard beach covered with the addresses and telephone numbers of the prostitutes who used to be based in the Desiré before Vicente took it over. Whilst she sings she looks out onto her audience: Inspector García, a pair of solitary drunks, an old woman who comes every night clutching a bag of saltwort and two couples busy feeling each other up (TT: 87). In an example of the grotesque humour which is a feature of this *esperpento* novel, as the bolero finishes a cat, which has had its tail doused in petrol and set alight, runs into the Desiré. It runs around the club, driven mad with the pain, screeching in agony as the flames consume its body. When it finally comes to rest Poco hits it with a hammer until he is sure that it is dead. One of the boys has fainted, a girl screams hysterically and a drunk throws up discreetly on the carpet (TT: 89). As well as contrasting the idealized, exotic setting of the bolero with that of the Desiré, Montero counterposes lines from boleros with the sordid discourse of male customers. Bella's rendition of Guillot's bolero 'Lo nuestro es amor' is followed by an obscene remark from a drunken customer and juxtaposed with her recollection of a brute she would rather forget who compared the vaccination mark on her arm to a cattle brand: 'Es la marca de la ganadería, todas las terneras tenéis que llevar hierro para que cuando os escapéis no se os confundáis' (It's the sign of livestock, all cows have to be branded so that when you escape you can be recognised) (TT: 28). As Bella notes, the boat pictured in this cardboard backdrop floats 'atrapada en un horizonte de mentira' (trapped in a horizon of lies), suggesting that escape is possible, whereas by the close of the novel the reader becomes aware that, at least for these characters, it is not (TT: 62).[20]

Yet, perhaps this is another defining feature of both camp performance and the bolero. Both are adopted by alienated and excluded groups. Andrew Ross examines the adoption of camp in particular by gay culture (1989, 157), whilst Mª Antonia García de Léon & Teresa Maldonado, in their analysis of the use of the bolero in Almodóvar, see it as a genre enjoyed especially by the lower classes, particularly women in the home (1989, 54).[21] The bolero forms an integral part of the fabric of these characters' lives. As well as configuring an alternative escapist fantasy world in contrast with their frustrating everyday life, it is a paradigm for their behaviour, shaping their desires and the discourse with which they express themselves.[22] Yet ultimately, although it offers temporary respite from the sordid existence of these characters on the margins of society, it does not provide a solution to their problems as it does not offer a viable alternative to their lived experience of solitude, failure and *desamor*. Both the women, and to some extent the men too, fail to recognise the difference between their material circumstances and their romantic dreams.[23] There is a seemingly unbreachable gap between these characters and the models they hope to follow in that when they attempt to interpret their reality in the terms offered to them by popular culture, tragic consequences ensue. José Diez Borque, in his analysis of romance and various other 'subliterary' genres, questions their escapism, noting that whilst they may indeed perform a cathartic function and provide gratification, there is the concommitant danger that they may increase frustration when external reality fails to match up to the romantic myth (1972, 181-2).[24] Again, I would argue that myth and reality perhaps cannot be separated so easily in that these songs form part of the collective memory. As Martín Gaite notes in her study of courtship in the post-War period, the most important feature of the bolero was its lyrics: 'recordar la letra era como hacer propio, al recordarlo el gran amor que se evocaba en ellos' (remembering the words were like making them yours, on remembering the one great love evoked in them) (1987, 154).

And They All Lived Happily Ever After...

However, absolute love is only possible in the discourse of the bolero; it exists in 'el reino maravilloso de ensueño que no es la realidad pero que debería serlo' (the marvellous daydream kingdom which isn't reality but should be) (Amorós 1974, 73). Each of the female characters dreams of escape in terms offered to them by popular culture. Bella's dreams are couched in the language of the bolero, whereas Antonia and Vanessa's revolve around films. When Antonia is first kissed by Damián, she thinks 'me están besando como besan en las películas' (I'm being kissed like they do in the movies) (TT: 119) and Vanessa compares Poco unfavourably to Robert Redford and Julio Iglesias (TT: 54). The bolero performs a function analogous to that of romantic fiction for women: it expresses their dreams of an absolute love. However, this one great love which gives meaning to their lives denies that meaning when it is shown to be no more than an illusion. This is particularly true of the promise encapsulated in the bolero which gives the novel its title; suggestive of a happy ending, it is shown to be no more than an empty promise. Antonio says to Inspector García in reference to his affairs with the wives of absent airline pilots: 'Hay que tratarlas como si fueran reinas. Son muy románticas, las mujeres' (You have to treat them like queens. They're very romantic, women are) (TT: 100). How does Antonio treat these women like queens? He deceives the women and deserts them when their husbands are due to return. In this particular case he was recounting his affair with Julia who had actually left her husband for him. Not all the women, however, are taken in by this promise. After Poco composes this particular bolero for Vanessa he stands by impassively as two pimps try to drag her off with them (TT: 178). When he later tries to persuade Vanessa to come away with him by saying 'Te trataré como a una reina' (I'll treat you like a queen) , she replies 'Oh, sí, la reina de las pulgas, la emperatriz de las escobas' (Oh yeah, the queen of the fleas, the empress of the brooms) (TT: 207). She has confronted Poco with the reality behind his promise. What he is offering is to turn her into a 'reina del hogar', the Spanish equivalent for 'angel of the house'. It is at this point that he flies into an uncontrollable rage and beats her savagely.

This is one of a series of incidents, drawing the novel to its climactic close, in which fantasy is brutally brought into contact with the scant possibilities these characters have for fulfilling their desires: Poco's realization that Vanessa is to marry Antonio and has spurned his offer to accompany them to Cuba; Bella's discovery that Poco has been deceiving her all along, as the letter inviting them to Cuba is shown to be from September 1954, prior to the revolution; Antonia's loss of Damián due to the interference of her brother. Whilst Antonia reacts by dissolving into tears, Poco and Bella react to their loss of discourse violently. Both have been frustrated when their dreams are shown to be incompatible with reality and lacking words to express this extreme sense of frustration they turn to acts of physical violence.[25] Believing Vanessa to be dead, Poco has no reason to go on living, for he has effectively killed his own nostalgic desire to return to a romanticised past. As Bella only discovers Poco's deception after he has committed suicide, she cannot take out her revenge on him; instead, she transfers her anger onto Antonio because he has also deprived his sister of her dream.

It is important to note that not all the boleros sung in the novel offer promises of love: some deal with deception and disillusionment. Indeed, Olga Guillot was famous for singing about deceived women who had had enough:

Ya lo decía Olga Guillot en esa canción tan preciosa, acabé por darme cuenta de que tu amor no es bueno, que hay en ti de la serpiente todo su veneno, acabé por convencerme que jamássssss [sic] podrás quererme, porque en tus venas corre arsénico en lugar de sangre, y la Guillot debía tener razón, porque todos los hombres a los que Bella había amado le habían hecho daño, todos tenían la sangre emponzoñada.

As Olga Guillot used to say in that beautiful song, I finally realised that your love is no good, that you have in you all the venom of the snake, I finally convinced myself that you would never be able to love me because arsenic instead of blood runs through your veins, and Guillot must have been right because all the men that Bella had loved had hurt her, they all had poisoned blood. (TT: 80)

The LP cover of Guillot's featured in the centre pages of Zavala (1991) features the suggestive titles 'Ya me liberé' (I finally freed myself) and 'Te voy a matar' (I'm going to kill you) which would seem particularly pertinent to Bella's actions at the close of the novel. Another exponent of feeling, la Lupe, is described as vindicating 'la contestación femenina al machismo reinante' (the feminine riposte to the predominant machismo) with songs such as 'La tirana' (The tyrant (female)), 'Carcajada' (Roar of laughter) and 'Puro teatro' (Pure theatre) (Caravaca 1995, 87). As well as female performers, there were various, famous women writers of boleros such as Consuelo Velásquez and Tina Polak.[26] Thus not all boleros are 'male-produced', as Glenn suggests, nor do they all 'glorify love and engender impossible expectations' (1990b, 427). Indeed, many boleros portray the flipside of romantic love: jealousy/abandonment/betrayal.[27] For Domínguez this is a defining trait of the bolero genre, the 'regusto acre del dolor' (bitter aftertaste of pain) which accompanies the passion (1993, 80). Whilst the bolero sung by Guillot above would seem to recognise the treacherous nature of romantic love, perhaps another bolero 'Miénteme' (Lie to me), also made famous by Guillot, is more pertinent not only to Bella's situation but as a description of the function of the bolero. In this bolero, although the singer acknowledges that her lover is deceiving her, she does not leave him because the lies he tells reflect the falsity of life itself and provide comfort:

> ¿Y qué mas da?
> La vida es una mentira
> Miénteme más
> que me hace tu maldad feliz.

> And so what?
> Life is a lie
> Lie to me more
> As your cruelty makes me happy. (Rico Salazar 1988, 257)[28]

Bella also seems to actively choose to escape from her material circumstances through the bolero. Thus although she has had enough of being deceived by men, deciding that it is better to live alone than 'mal acompañada', this does not stop her dreaming about a romance with Poco as she feels that the world is not meant for women on their own (TT: 31).

Bella has converted Poco into a hero who could have been lifted from the pages of a romantic novel:

> Se sentaba junto a la barra y le contaba cosas del Tropicana, o de África, asuntos íntimos, historias de tierras lejanas y de tiempos pasados. En ocasiones le brillaban los ojos como si quisiera llorar, aunque el Poco, claro, no lloraba: y acariciaba la mejilla de Bella, o le rozaba el pelo suavemente. En esos momentos Bella tenía la certeza de que el Poco la quería. Pero después el hombre se apagaba, como si se le secase algo por dentro, y parecía estar tan lejos de ella como sus recuerdos africanos.

> He would sit next to the bar and tell her about the tropicana, or Africa, intimate affairs, stories of faraway places and past times. Now and then his eyes would shine as if he wanted to cry, but Poco of course, didn't cry: and he would caress Bella's cheek, or stroke her hair gently. In those instances Bella was sure that Poco loved her. But afterwards the man would shut down, as if something had dried up inside and he seemed as distant from her as his memories of Africa. (TT: 114)

Zavala suggests that the bolero 'permite tocar el otro/la otra a distancia sin tenerlo/la' (allows you to touch the other from a distance without possessing him/her) (1991, 59) and Bella is attracted to Poco because he is mysterious and sometimes distant. She believes that she is the woman he has chosen to confide in and her ultimate dream is to go away with him to Cuba which would be akin to marriage, the goal of all heroines in modern, romantic fiction:

> Quería llevarla a Cuba. Con él. Quería llevarla a Cuba y unirse a ella atravesando un océano, que era cosa que sacramentaba más que un cura.

> He wanted to take her to Cuba. With him. He wanted to take her to Cuba and bind himself to her by crossing an ocean, more of a sacrament than any that a priest could perform. (TT: 114)

Poco is the author of Bella's fantasies, penning many of the boleros that she sings and believes to be addressed to her. However, as the listener is inscribed as a participant in the text of the bolero through its address to an indeterminate 'tú' ('you'), each bolero can have many meanings depending on who is singing and who is listening. In the bolero, it is not only the 'yo' ('I') but also the 'tú' ('you') which functions as a shifter. It can be argued that shifters play a crucial role in popular music inviting the emotional involvement and participation of the listener (Middleton 1990, 167). The addressee is made to feel both special and unique, a feature of the bolero noted by Domínguez 'al ser cantado cada uno lo sienta como suyo' (on being sung you feel as if it is yours) (1993, 82), and also identifies with an implicit community of others who share the same desires and frustrations (Durant 1984, 202-4). Certainly, in the novel there would seem to be a degree of commonality drawn between the experiences of the various women or 'reinas'.

Bella mistakenly believes Poco to be in love with her when in fact he has been composing the boleros for Vanessa. Ironically one of the songs she sings after listening to Poco recount his adventures in the Sahara refers to 'tu comedia de cariño calculado' (TT: 126). She only realizes that she has mistaken his friendship for love when, after listening to the bolero from which the novel's title is taken, she blurts out her feelings, thanking him for writing a bolero which expressed exactly what she felt:

Las gracias le salieron automáticamente, sin pensarlo. Porque el bolero era suyo. Tenía que ser suyo. Tenía que referirse a ella. ¿Por qué, si no, el Poco le acompañaba cada noche? ¿Por qué se lo había dado a leer, por qué la llamaba mujer, por qué la miraba de ese modo? Pero, ¿y si no era? De pronto a Bella le entró miedo, temió haberse puesta en evidencia. El Poco la estaba escudriñando con una expresión impenetrable. Después hizo una mueca rara, como si le hubiera paralizado la sonrisa.

–Bueno, Bella si de verdad te gusta tanto el bolero, te lo regalo... Para ti.

The thank you came out automatically, without thinking, Because the bolero was hers. It had to be hers. It had to refer to her. Otherwise why did Poco walk her home each night? Why had he given it to her to look at, why was he calling her woman, why was he looking at her like that? But what if she was wrong? Suddenly Bella felt afraid, she was scared of having shown herself up. Poco was scrutinising her with an impenetrable expression. Then he pulled a funny face, as if his smile had been paralised.

"Well Bella, if you really like the bolero that much, I'll give it to you... Just for you." (TT: 178)

As we have already seen in Chapter Two, identity is relational but as Zavala points out, 'el otro/a puede mentir y el sujeto jamás podrá estar totalmente seguro/a de sus propias señas de identidad' (the other can lie and the subject can never be sure of his/her identity) (1991, 85). Bella feels ridiculous and is angry with herself for having misunderstood. Earlier she had wished that Poco had not said anything about Cuba because 'se sufre menos sin deseos' (you suffer less without desires) (TT: 115). He has built up her hopes of a romance and a new life only to destroy them. However, this is perhaps to be expected as Poco expresses himself primarily through bolero lyrics which often talk of illusion and deception (Aristizabal 1987, 148).

The male characters in *Te trataré como a una reina*, despite the idealization of them by the women, are the antithesis of the hero of the romantic novel: they are weak and not particularly attractive either physically nor in personality. Antonio has dandruff, prostrate problems and, despite his boasting of his sexual prowess, is terrified of being unable to satisfy Vanessa. He cruelly mistreats his assistant Benigno, berates his sister, carries on affairs with the wives of absent airline pilots and decides to marry Vanessa because she will make a good trophy that can be moulded to his desires. Poco is stocky, dirty, with tattooed arms and a rough, red face. He lies about his past to Bella claiming that the love of his life left him to become a whore when in fact he abandoned his wife and child. As noted above, he stands by when two pimps attempt to drag off Vanessa and beats her unconscious when he realises she is to marry Antonio. Damián stammers and is cross-eyed. He leaves Antonia when threatened by Antonio. The young 'chulo' helps Bella home then demands money for having sex with her. Despite all this the women tend to idealize their respective lovers because they, like Bella, see romance as a way out of the situation they find themselves in.

'Sola, sola, sola': Dependency or Solitude?[29]

Romero et al., in their thematic analysis of women's writing in Spain in the 1970s, stress the importance of the theme of romantic love (1987, 349-50). The subtitle of this section of their analysis is 'Solamente una vez amé en la vida' ('I only loved once in my life'), the title of a famous bolero composed by Agustín Lara which expresses the ideal of one great love:

Una vez nada más en mi huerto
brilló la esperanza, la esperanza
que alumbra el camino de mi soledad.

Only once in my orchard
did hope shine, the hope
which lights up the path of my solitude. (Rico Salazar 1988, 435)

This one great love, then, is no longer directed to a 'príncipe azul con quien casarse y fundar un hogar feliz lleno de hijos sino un ser inalcanzable, idealizado que llene su vacío existencial' (Prince Charming who you get married to and found a happy household full of children but an unreachable, idealised being who fills her existential emptiness) (Romero et al. 1987, 349). As women gained new rights under the 1978 constitution and various pieces of legislation designed to promote equality were introduced, the traditional role models for women propagated by the Franco regime of mother and housewife were challenged, as we have seen in Chapter Two. However, as noted in both Chapters One and Two, in the narrative written by women in the 1970s, female characters seem to lack a sense of identity compounded by a lack of role models, as the figure of the mother is often representative of oppressive tradition. In *Te trataré como a una reina* this mother figure is represented by Antonia's mother, who was a dutiful wife despite her husband's gambling and visits to prostitutes. Confused, these female characters turn to a romantic love, divorced from the frustration of their experience, as they search for some sense of identity or meaning to their lives. This idea, that love can fill an existential void, is encapsulated in the bolero, appropriately titled 'Vacío' (Emptiness) by José de Jesús Morales:

Vacío... eso es mi vida...
y eso será si no vienes a darme
la luz de tu amor...

Emptiness... that's my life...
and it will continue to be so if you don't give me
the light of your love... (Rico Salazar 1988, 442)

As the object of desire in the bolero is some ideal other who by definition is out of reach, in practice relationships fail to live up to the expectations that women have of them. That is to say, relationships with men fail to give their lives meaning because they are searching for an unattainable, ideal other who could somehow transform their frustrating existence by treating them like a queen. As we have seen above, in the novel this promise is consistently shown to be worthless. Romero et al. suggest that these dreams of romantic love are an impossibility and consequently these frustrated and often marginalised women seem condemned to either accept solitude as a condition of independence or self-destruction through madness or death (1987, 350). The characters' dreams of stardom, true love and a new life are shattered in *Te trataré como a una reina*. As it ends Bella is in jail branded a mad murderess by the press; Antonia, who dreams of starting a new life by jumping on the first train she sees, ends up getting on the train to her birthplace; and Vanessa is in intensive care.

Indeed, the women's lives in this novel are conditioned by solitude: Bella has decided that she prefers to be alone after being mistreated by a succession of men; Antonia is the typical middle class spinster whose life revolves around looking after her brother; Poco composes a bolero for Vanessa that suggests that she too will end up alone and Bella wryly reflects that her youth and beauty will soon be gone (TT: 51). The following bolero is emblematic of the novel:

«Te pierdes en la noche, tan bonita.
sin saber los peligros que te acechan.
Te pierdes en la noche tan solita,
sin saber todavía que estás sola.
Si yo pudiera explicarte
que la noche no está hecha para niñas.
Si yo pudiera contarte
toda mi vida, para que tú supieras.
Ahora piensas que cambiarás el mundo
y será el mundo el que te cambiará.
Ahora eres alegre y joven pero en lo profundo
ya llevas la semilla de tu soledad»

"You get lost in the night, my pretty one
without realising the dangers that lie ahead.
You get lost in the night, so alone
without realising yet that you are alone.
If I could only explain to you
that the night is not made for girls.
If I could only tell you
the story of my life, so you would know.
For now you think that you will change the world
and it's the world that will change you.
For now you are happy and young but deep within
you already hold the seeds of your solitude." (TT: 59)

It describes the solitude that all these women face and the impossibility of escape from their situation as they are bound by social conventions. Even when the women enter into a relationship they are still in some sense alone due to a lack of communication and true affection. Clearly, for the characters in *Te trataré como a una reina* the way out of this condition of solitude does not lie in a relationship with a man. Indeed, it is these very relationships which precipitate the tragic chain of events which unfold as the novel reaches its conclusion. As discussed in Chapter Three with relation to Ana and Lucía of *Crónica del desamor* and *La función delta,* Montero has said that one of the basic problems for women in discovering and assuming their identity is learning to live alone. In the interview, already cited, with *La mujer feminista*, she stated her belief that romantic love is an alienating trap which women must fight against:

> El amor es alienante, un amor que aleja el centro de tu vida de tí misma, y que lo coloca en otra persona. Un amor totalizador, de modo que la otra persona tiene que serlo todo en tu vida... cosa, adémas, imposible.

> Love is alienating, a love which removes the centre of your life from yourself and places it in someone else. A totalising love, which means that the other person has to be everything in your life... something which is impossible anyway. (1985, 9)

Similarly Martín Gaite expresses her admiration for the independent 'chicas raras' (odd girls) of postwar Spanish literature, such as Andrea in Carmen Laforet's *Nada* (1945), who recognised that love as portrayed in the *novela rosa* does not exist (1992, 122). It is a patriarchal discursive construct.

Romantic texts portray the search for more than what is on offer but they also play out a drama of dependency in which women clearly depend on men. The bolero which Bella sings most often deals with the need for someone who will love her for life, someone who feels as she feels and will keep her company. This is the bolero 'Necesito un corazón' (I need a heart) cited above.[30] Bella sings it as she is about to leave the club to walk home. Once outside she is afraid because of threatening noises coming from the red-light district (TT: 35). Poco offers to walk her home and she takes this as proof of his love for her. Yet as we have already seen she is mistaken as to the nature of his feelings towards her.[31] Nonetheless, although Bella is given to romantic dreaming she is the least dependent of the women in the novel. She takes home men such as the cooked meats salesman because she believes that the body needs physical satisfaction from time to time.

She knows that she is only a passing affair for him and therefore does not feel deceived by him. Furthermore, through singing she can also actively express sexual desire. Central to the bolero is a certain amount of gender fluidity, allowing male and female performers to perform the same song. Indeed, a possible political aspect of the bolero and camp is the destabilisation of gender identities and sexual roles.[32] Both Zavala (1991, 87) and Ellen Koskoff (1987, 10) note that music allows the expression of sexual needs and anger by women. However, it would seem to be a sanctioned outlet which does not necessarily challenge basic social arrangements.[33] Vanessa is attacked by two pimps because she is actively sexual. A strong woman like Bella who rescues Vanessa from the two pimps whilst Poco and Vicente look on, and attacks Antonio in revenge for his treatment of his sister, does not fit into the mould of a subservient woman and must therefore be punished. She is deemed mad and imprisoned. Indeed, all of the women would seem to be punished by society for trying to step outside the roles allotted to them in the patriarchal order: Bella for becoming the active perpetrator of an act of violence instead of the passive victim, Antonia for having a relationship with a man young enough to be her son and the disreputable Vanessa for attempting to improve her social status through marriage to a supposedly decent man.[34]

Romance: Escape or Resistance?

According to Tania Modleski, romantic fiction embodies a contradiction in that 'whilst appearing to be merely escapist, such art simultaneously challenges and reaffirms traditional values, behaviour and attitudes' (1982, 112-13). The bolero is a particularly complex romantic form, as will be evident from the discussion above. Whilst on the one hand it would seem to embody some of the more conservative values of romantic fiction, on the other it does not simply shore up patriarchal ideology. The primacy of white, male, bourgeois values are questioned in boleros with a strong female voice, by singers of humble extraction and lyrics which deal with questions of race such as those of 'Angelitos negros', made famous by Antonio Machín who was the first Afro-Cuban singer to perform with the Orquesta del Casino Nacional de la Habana (Caravaca 1995, 55). Romantic texts such as the bolero clearly do not only function to reinforce patriarchy. Their meaning varies according to the context in which they are listened to, how they are performed and their reception by the listener/reader.[35] Furthermore, such romantic discourses can act as fictions of resistance, providing a temporary escape from a 'present reality that occasionally becomes too onerous to bear' (Radway 1983, 39). They can afford strength, hope and pleasure to women who feel trapped and underappreciated in their present condition by providing an outlet for women's anxiety, frustration and dissatisfaction with male-female relationships. However, they tend to fail to question the primacy of these relationships as a route to fulfilment.

Montero subverts the romantic genre, as described above, through both the ironic contrast between the romantic ideals of the bolero and the sordid reality of the characters' daily lives, and the celebration of a strong female voice made possible through the confusion of the masculine and feminine inherent in the bolero form. The use of the bolero in ironic juxtaposition to a degraded reality serves to debunk the patriarchal myths and male-generated scripts that women often try to follow. They must not allow themselves to be seduced by men's promises such as 'te trataré como a una reina'. Indeed, Bella and Vanessa see through this particular promise and Antonia attempts to have a relationship which does not adhere to social parameters. In this novel, there is a shift from the previous emphasis on women writing identity -although as noted some of the boleros are penned by women- to women 'reading' and negotiating popular cultural texts.[36] These texts may indeed be interpreted in such a way as to provide solace and strength to the female characters. However, role models are not presented for change, instead popular cultural forms would seem to provide a method of negotiating the present.

As well as a realisation by women of the necessity for change, for a transformation of society to occur that goes beyond legal and juridicial change, this will require a shift in the behaviour and attitudes of men, who are also to some extent victims trapped by, as well as colluding with, patriarchal ideology.[37] Indeed, the novel's pessimistic conclusion points to the difficulty faced by women when they attempt to step out of the roles imposed on them by the present patriarchal order: Bella and Vanessa have their futures cut off and Antonia is condemned to return to the past. Readers are encouraged to empathise with these characters, particularly through the use of pathos and humour, as they may also identify closely with the popular cultural forms incorporated into the novel which have configured the identity of the post-war generation in Spain. Whilst the conclusion may indeed seem closed for the main female characters, it may serve to jolt the reader, who feels a sense of outrage at how they are treated, into questioning the sociocultural circumstances which trap these characters.[38]

---

[1] The actual turning point in Montero's style would seem to be the short story 'Paulo Pumilio' (1982) set in a similar seedy ambience of a nightclub in which the performers are marginal outcasts who seem somewhat larger than life. See Davies (1994, 120-23) for a discussion of this short story.

[2] In an interview with Phoebe Porter, Montero expressed her admiration for the writing of Valle-Inclán (1989). Comparisons with the work of Puig, whose novels have also been described as literary boleros (Muñoz 1990), are of obvious interest and merit further investigation but lie outside the scope of this study. A comparative study of the use of the bolero in Guillermo Cabrera Infante's *Tres tristes tigres* and *Te trataré como a una reina* has been carried out by Dona M. Kercher (manuscript supplied by Rosa Montero).

[3] Over dinner in Cambridge on 21 October 1993 she particularly expressed admiration for their creation of ambience.

[4] The links between this genre and the male oedipal crisis will be discussed in the next chapter, as will the dialogic between the framing male-authored text and the corrective main body of the novel which implicitly invites the reader to resist the interpretation of events by the main male characters.

[5] Hyperrealist is the term adopted by Montero to describe this novel in interviews with both Sol Fuertes (1982) and Antonio Monegal (1985).

[6] See Modleski (1986a) for a concise introduction to the debate between the two directions studies of mass culture have tended to follow.

[7] This discussion of the etymology of the term entertainment has been adapted from Dyer (1981).

[8] The bolero is a duple metre dance/song, similar in rhythm to the *danzón* but slightly slower. It is characterised by expressive melodies and romantic lyrics. See Galán (1983, ch.10); Léon (1982, 243-5); Orovio (1981, 50-2 & 1995, 126-8); Pérez Sanjurjo (1986, 332-3) and Sadie (1980, 870-1).

[9] Other definitions talk about the promise of pleasure (Evora 1993, i); illusion as its substance (Castillo Zapata 1990, 91); a romantic lament comprised of melancholy, frustration and solitude

(Saladriga 1983). Its simultaneous expression of dichotomies forms the basis of both Rafael Castillo Zapata (1990) and Iris Zavala's (1991) book length studies.

[10] Delgado Ruiz is referring to perhaps the most famous Mexican composer of boleros, Agustín Lara, who wrote 'Solamente una vez', 'Noche de Ronda' and 'Piensa en mí' among many others; Domínguez could refer to Frank Domínguez who wrote 'Tú me acostumbraste' which was a hit for both Lucho Gatica and Olga Guillot or to Alberto Domínguez Borras of the Hermanos Domínguez who wrote 'Perfidia' and 'Frenesí'; Antonio Machín was one of the most successful singers to base himself in Spain, his first big hit being 'Angelitos negros' in 1947.

[11] These are also qualities which would seem to apply to *Te trataré como a una reina* in which transgressive humour features strongly and could indeed form the basis of a full length study of Montero's work. Briefly it allows the author to address taboo subjects which will be further discussed in Chapter Five, it is adopted as a survival strategy by these marginal characters and through bathetic means encourages the reader to sympathise with them.

[12] Dona M. Kercher claims that the character of Antonio was inspired by Patrick Süskind's *Perfume*. However, *Perfume* was first published in 1985.

[13] Martín Gaite, in particular, discusses the liberating potential of portrayals of women in Hollywood films and television series from the U.S.A. which the Catholic Church objected to (1994). See also Graham & Labanyi's Spanish Cultural Studies reader which engages with the complex issue of the Francoist project of cultural hegemony (1995).

[14] *Te trataré como a una reina* deals with characters who have moved to the city from rural communities. In a talk entitled 'Transición política y democracia cultural 1975-1992', given as part of the cycle 'La Cultura Española en su Contexto Europeo' at the Instituto Cervantes, London on 19 April 1993, Rosa Montero described urbanisation as the major sociological change to have affected Spain in the past twenty years.

[15] Drinkwater argues for a similar function for Montero's narrative. Such bestsellers not only bridge the gap between 'high' and 'low' culture but also paradoxically take issue with the very economics of consumer capitalism they participate in (1995b, 155-59).

[16] Antonio Machín left Cuba in 1934 and settled in Spain in 1939. He remained based in Spain until his death in 1977. For Evora, Machín and the bolero became synonymous in Spain (1993, iv).

[17] For biographies of Guillot and Burke see Caravaca (ch.11), Martínez (1994, 123-31), Rico Salazar (1988, 256) and Orovio (1981, 69-70). Guillot and many other artistes who chose to leave Cuba are not featured in the 1981 edition Orovio's otherwise excellent reference work (they have

been incorporated into the 1992 edition). Note that for Léon, manneristic styles of delivery such as 'feeling' would disappear in a classless society (1984, 31). What place would there be for Bella in Cuba?

[18]Note that in Sontag's canon of camp in her classic 1964 essay, 'Notes on "Camp"', another key exponent of «feeling» is included, La Lupe (1994, 278). A recent example of such a performance would be that of Marisa Paredes as Becky, lip-synching Luz Casal singing the classic Agustín Lara bolero 'Piensa en mí', in Almodóvar's *Tacones Lejanos* (1991).

[19] Bella, could also be compared to the Spanish *cupletistas*. Singers of this passionate-sentimental genre of song were originally linked to prostitution. They led often turbulent lives, with exotic love affairs and rags-to-riches careers. See Salaün (1995).

[20] See the cover of the 1990 Seix Barral edition of the novel which contrasts a black and white photo of a seedy neighbourhood, reminiscent of those featured in the 'film noir' whose ambience is reflected in the novel, with the bright neon of the Tropicana sign. Furthermore, within the novel, inside the Desiré there is a Tropicana sign which serves to underline the artificiality of the escape offered by the bolero. Bella would seem trapped in the sordid world of the Desiré as opposed to the glamourous Tropicana in which both Guillot and Burke performed.

[21] Note in Almodóvar's 1984 film *¿Qué he hecho yo para merecer esto?*, the grandmother who has emigrated from a village to the city, played by Chus Lampreave, identifies with the sentimental songs of her youth.

[22] Ezquerro (1991) and Pellón (1983) give interesting analyses of this phenomenon in Puig's *El beso de la mujer araña*.

[23] Campos notes that the bolero often inverts the traditional patriarchal male-female relationship by positioning the male voice as the vulnerable victim (1991, 638). In fact, with the notable exception of Caravaca, several of the studies I have come across concentrate on male reception of the bolero without considering the position of women as performers and listeners.

[24] Furthermore, Richard Dyer, in his essay on utopia in entertainment, notes that only certain aspirations are admitted (1981, 184).

[25] Some critics question the eruption of violence into the world of the bolero (Saladrigas 1983 & Kercher) but it is not as unusual as they make out. Agustín Lara, for example, bore a knife scar down his cheek from a jealous woman and began his career in a brothel. The violent reactions of Poco and Bella would seem to echo those of the murderers in the novels of Patricia Highsmith, as analysed by Montero in her introduction to the 1993 Spanish edition of *The Glass Cell*. These

characters attempt to negate that which harms them and are usually pushed to commit murder due to their broken dreams for happiness within a relationship.

[26] See Caravaca, ch.11.

[27] For example the bolero 'Flores negras' sung by Elvira Ríos:

> Me hacen daño tus ojos
> Me hacen daño tus manos
> Me hacen daño tus labios
> Que saben fingir
>
> Your eyes hurt me
> Your hands hurt me
> Your lips hurt me
> Because they all know how to pretend

[28] Lyrics for boleros not cited in the novel have been taken from Rico Salazar's excellent compendium.

[29] This is how Antonia sums up her situation in the final chapter of the novel (TT: 241).

[30] This bolero is cited on pages 30, 35 and 152.

[31] In this scene Dona M. Kercher notes the evocation of the bolero 'Media vuelta' whose first and last line 'Te vas porque yo quiero que te vayas' (You're going because I want you to) suggests the play of wills in a relationship. However, in this case Bella almost wishes Poco had stayed.

[32] For example in the lyrics of the bolero 'Sabor a mí' which Bella sings. This bolero expresses how both lovers cannot escape the effects of love.

[33] This is also a feature of romantic fiction as noted by Modleski (1982, 25) in that elements of protest and resistance may subsist beneath highly orthodox plots.

[34] Several acts of brutality by men against women are referred to in the novel: Bella recounts the story of a prostitute who was raped by the man who had cut the throat of her pimp/lover (TT: 78); two pimps try to drag Vanessa away and one of them reminds Bella of the brute who hit her and broke her tooth (TT: 180).

[35] A particularly interesting analysis of the dialogic between historical discourse and the bolero is that by Arnaldo Cruz Malave (1988) of the novel *Sólo cenizas hallarás* by Pedro Vergés.

[36] Whilst Antonia does write letters to her mother which are incorporated into the text, these letters are designed to conceal rather than reveal her relationship with Damián. She repeatedly states 'Estoy segura de que a usted le gustaría' (I'm sure you would like him), like a child seeking parental approval (TT: 63-4). The many errors of syntax and semantics in her letters would suggest that Antonia is not a skilled manipulator of discourse.

[37] This issue is examined further in *Amado amo*.

---

[38] In an interview with Sigrid Bachmann (1992) Montero decribes this novel as having a closed ending in contrast with those which follow. This sense of outrage was palpable in group discussions I had with a class of third year university students at the University of Newcastle who studied this novel as part of a course on gender, language and sexuality (1995-1996).

CHAPTER FIVE

'EL EXTRAÑO CASO': CROSSING SUBJECT/OBJECT BOUNDARIES IN *TE TRATARÉ COMO A UNA REINA*

El sujeto es plural, fragmentado, un tejido abigarrado de individuaciones, de momentos, de instantes de libertad y de momentos de placer.

The subject is plural, fragmented, a multicoloured tapestry of individualisms, of moments, of instances of freedom and moments of pleasure. (Elejabeitia 1980, 204-5)

As we have seen in Chapter Four, pleasure and desire, in this case mediated through popular culture, play an important role in the construction of identity. However, romantic fantasies based on the texts of the bolero and Hollywood cinema do not provide the only instances of pleasure in *Te trataré como a una reina*. Explicit sexual fantasies which also afford pleasure, whilst questioning fixed object-subject boundaries. Two articles by Kathleen Glenn examine the link between sexuality and textual authority in *Te trataré como a una reina* but do not explicitly address the role of fantasy, as opposed to textual discourse, in the construction of identity (1987, 1990b). I would argue that an understanding of fantasy is crucial in order to analyse how it is that these seemingly passive female characters negotiate their sexuality and assume subject positions in episodes which break down established binary divisions such as active-passive/subject-object. The liberating ambivalence of these erotic episodes in *Te trataré como a una reina* can be contrasted with the perceived conservatism of the recent erotic boom in women's writing in Spain.

Commentators writing about recent developments in contemporary Spanish narrative have noted the increasing number of erotic novels and short stories by women writers (Barriuso 1989. Drinkwater 1995a). Judith Drinkwater moves on from Zatlin's analysis of trends in contemporary Spanish narrative written by women, discussed in Chapter One, to examine whether or not what has been termed the erotic 'boom' of the 1980s and early 1990s actually empowers women. She notes that the erotic may represent 'an exploration of female sexuality, a celebration of the male as object, a desire to shock and transgress norms or sheer fantasy' (1995a, 98). However, she concludes that despite the claims often made by women writers for the ground-breaking impact of their work, the majority of these writers - who include Almudena Grandes, Mercedes Abad, Ana Rossetti, Emma Cohen, Susana Constante and Clara Janés - would seem to have internalized the 'male' paradigms of established erotica, and quotes Fanny Rubio on the subject in a recent debate in *Ajoblanco* on the state of contemporary Spanish literature -'¿Y ahora de qué vamos?'- in support of her argument:

> Vamos a hablar de qué tipo de literatura erótica han vendido mujeres, y no quiero citar ninguna, que han sido simples productos fáciles porque el erotismo que se estaba reflejando en estas páginas era un erotismo pendiente. Un erotismo masculino pero con firma femenina. Un erotismo absolutamente anacrónico.[1]

> Let's talk about the type of erotic literature that women have sold, and I don't want to name any names, which have been simple, easy products because the eroticism being reflected in their pages was an unresolved eroticism. A masculine eroticism with a feminine signature. An absolutely anachronistic eroticism. (Ribas et al. 1993, 45)

However, Drinkwater excludes earlier texts by authors such as Montero, Tusquets and Roig from this condemnation as for her they 'deal with eroticism as a necessary adjunct to the process of female self-discovery' (1995a, 97). Such texts address the issue of agency for women through the depiction of women as sexual subjects. In this respect *Te trataré como a una reina* follows on from *Crónica del desamor*, with its transgressive portrayal of sexuality from a woman's point of view, covering taboo topics such as masturbation. It would seem to fall into the category of texts which Fernando Valls, in his discussion of erotic literature published in Spain between 1975 and 1990, describes as falling outside the classification of erotic literature, but in which eroticism may serve as a vehicle for social critique (1991, 30). In this case, it could be argued that the critique is of the sexual objectification of women by men.

In various episodes in the novel the women are regarded by the men as objects of desire and appear to be denied their subjectivity by the objectifying male gaze. Their status is that of an object to be looked at. This is made clear not only in various voyeuristic scenes which will be discussed below, but also by Bella's job as a singer in a seedy club, the Desiré.[2] She makes herself up and changes into stage-clothes in order to attract the attention of the clientele. Her body is put on display, it is for show as the majority of the customers of the Desiré are men. Although it could be argued that dressing up has the potential to give one a sense of empowerment and control of one's body and appearance, this is not the case with Bella. Upon looking at herself in the mirror she feels old and ridiculous. Yet it is perhaps her 'making a spectacle of herself' so overtly that makes her a threatening figure for the men in the novel who seem unsettled by a strong, overtly sexual woman.[3]

Of all the women Vanessa would seem to be most subject to the process of objectification by male characters. Antonio decides to ask her to marry him because she will make a good trophy he can show off and exhibit. However, this image of beauty he so values is destroyed by the violent actions of Poco who confuses Vanessa with a woman he once knew. He transfers his hatred of the real woman to the image and beats her until she is 'hecha un ovillo, irreconocible ya' (curled up into a ball, unrecognisable) (TT: 209). She loses her identity when the image of beauty or object of desire is destroyed. Poco obliterates her in an act of violence which serves to temporarily bolster his sense of masculine identity in which masculinity is identified with power and control.[4] By possessing her as an object through violence, Poco denies her her subjectivity and identity, whilst also denying his dependency upon her. However, because he negates her completely, she cannot give him the recognition he desires as a subject and he too is thus negated. Unable to bear this lack of recognition he obliterates himself by commiting suicide.

Whilst the text does portray violence against women, as discussed in Chapter Four, it also examines men's fears of women's sexuality particularly through the connections made between orgasm and death. Furthermore, clichés regarding women's sexuality are overturned and undermined in episodes in which binary oppositions such as object and subject are deconstructed. Thus, through examining sexuality, cultural constructions of identity may be destabilised. Carmen Saez Buenaventura, in her discussion of feminism and psychoanalysis presented to the second Basque conference on 'Mujer y realidad social', examines how women have not only been the agents of social change -as described in the testimonial novels of the 1970s and early 1980s- but also of a rethinking of theoretical paradigms about sexuality. In this novel, Rosa Montero would seem to move from the discussion of women's legal rights regarding their sexuality present in *Crónica del desamor*, to an examination of the role of fantasy within sexuality.

Thus the novel goes beyond a critique of patriarchal structures which objectify women, in order to examine the possibility of agency for women. In Chapter Four the question arose of whether Bella and the other women were passive consumers of popular culture or actively chose what to consume and how to interpret it. Similarly, this chapter will examine the crossing of binary categories, such as active/passive and subject/object, through sexual fantasy. This will be done with particular reference to the framing male gaze and the use that Montero makes of voyeuristic scenes in which the mastery of the male gaze is broken, as women escape the category of object that the gaze attempts to fix them in. The text addresses the question of whether it is possible for women to gain pleasure through exhibitionism and voyeurism. In order to examine these particular issues various theoretical perspectives will be drawn upon including Anglo-American film theory; predominantly, although not exclusively, French psychoanalytic theory; and Spanish theorisation of sexuality. Before discussing the possible subversive strategies offered by sexual fantasy, I will begin by examining the various portrayals of women according to traditional gender stereotypes by the male characters in accounts which deny the women a voice. Despite this the women seem to escape easy categorisation and paradoxically, the images of dangerous and monstruous women can be reappropriated to signify their active agency against the patriarchal structures which attempt to confine them as feminine objects within the phallocentric sexual order.

El extraño caso: Inclusion of the Male Perspective

The title of the novel seems to indicate a romantic text. However, the reader's expectations are confounded when the novel actually begins with a *caso*, that is a case of murder published in a sensationalist crime magazine: *El Criminal*. This contrast between the title and opening pages of the novel may serve to place the reader on their guard about discourse which sets out deliberately to mislead. What we are initially presented with is an extract from the article published in the magazine in which the reader is given a glimpse of what happened, much as in the cinema or on the television a viewer is shown a trailer in order to arouse their interest. The article sets itself up as an authoritative text, since it is both dated and signed by a reporter named as Paco Mancebo.[5] In order to encourage identification on the part of the reader, more specifically on the part of the male reader, Mancebo consistently uses the pronoun 'us' and the first person plural verb form:

... nos ha sido imposible localizar [Juana/Vanessa]
Poco sabemos de los primeros momentos...
... nos confió doña MPG, quien no quiere que publiquemos su nombre
... nos encontramos con una energúmena como La Bella
... nos dijo doña MPG

... we have been unable to find [Juana/Vanessa]
We know little about those initial moments...
... we were confided in by Mrs MPG, who doesn't want us to publish her name
... we find ourselves with a raving lunatic like the Bella
... we were told by Mrs MPG (TT: 9-10)

As I shall demonstrate, the case is presented explicitly from the perspective of the men involved and is full of clichés about masculinity and femininity. Yet, paradoxically, the obvious bias in Mancebo's presentation of the facts may cause the reader to resist his interpretation of them. He depicts Antonio in terms which clearly portray him as an innocent victim who could not have possibly have provoked this vicious attack. Antonio is described as a quiet, educated man, almost priest-like and about to marry a beautiful and honourable young woman whom Mancebo has been unable to locate. As we have seen in Chapter Four, these character descriptions are not accurate. In retrospect, after reading the rest of the novel, it seems strange that Mancebo, an investigative journalist was unable to trace Juana/Vanessa as she was in intensive care after Poco's vicious attack. What is evident, even on first reading, is that Mancebo's portrayal of Bella is extremely one-sided: she is foul-mouthed, bloodthirsty, without pity or morals and capable of all manner of barbarous acts. He uses pejorative forms of the word *mujer* ('woman') -*mujerona* and *mujerzuela*- to reinforce this description.

The word *caso* can also be translated as 'event' and indeed the rest of the novel leads up to this particular event: Bella's attack upon Antonio in which she destroys his property, empties perfume bottles over his face, blows smoke into it and concludes by throwing him out of the window of his fourth floor apartment. In opposition to Mancebo's hack account, the main body of the rest of the novel could be construed as the case or evidence presented by the defence for Bella's actions. The case for the prosecution, as made by the article written by Paco Mancebo, is constructed from the statements he gathered from three men involved in the case: Antonio, Vicente and Benigno -four months after the event in the case of Antonio. Apart from Antonio, the witnesses are relatively secondary characters who are only indirectly involved in the actual case in question. Moreover, their accounts, which are incorporated into the text as transcripts, show them to be unreliable witnesses. The first transcription incorporated is that of Vicente who seems highly defensive and is primarily preoccupied with preserving his own reputation and that of his club. It is positioned after Chapter Nine by which time we know something of both Vicente and Bella's characters. He reads pornographic novels behind the respectable cover of *The Three Musketeers* and she muses that she would have probably been better off as the whore he suspects her to be and in his statement accuses her of being (TT: 32). In contrast Benigno, in his account following Chapter Twenty-three, idealises Antonia as an angel and speaks no ill of Antonio despite Antonio's appalling treatment of him in Chapters Four and Fifteen. Again, the positioning of this account is significant because the supposedly angelic Antonia is arrested in the preceeding chapter for public indecency. Lastly, like Vicente, Antonio characterises Bella as a whore using the terms which are incorporated into Mancebo's account 'beast, 'monster and 'raving lunatic' adding 'daughter of a bitch' (TT: 237-9). He is likewise convinced that the motive for the attack was jealousy. Yet Montero again undermines this account by placing it directly after Chapter Twenty-seven, in which Bella discovers that Poco has deceived her and that Antonio has ruined his sister's relationship with Damián.[6] Indeed, the possible alternative versions of Isabel, Antonia and Juana/Vanessa are suppressed by Mancebo and so what purports to be an objective presentation of the facts is in fact a one-sided view of the events.[7] The only female witness quoted in the opening article, doña MPG, was an eyewitness to the crime. However she refuses to be named, preferring to remain anonymous she does not speak for herself. Consequently the woman's voice is silenced and we are presented with the male perspective as set down by Paco Mancebo. Doña MPG plays a role akin to that of a spectator at the cinema in that she watches what is taking place without she herself being observed. She acts as a voyeur as does the reader when reading the sensationalist account presented by Mancebo.

The polarised images of woman as madwoman/whore/monster and angel/virgin/mother, which are set up in the opening article and subsequent transcriptions, are what rest of the text sets out to subvert through complex characterisation involving the use of dialogue, indirect monologue, free indirect speech and examples of the characters' own writing within a third person narration. As noted in Chapter Four, this is a reworking of the popular detective genre in which the reader discovers not who did it, as this is obvious from the opening of the novel, but instead why. Tania Modleski has interpreted the detective genre as in general masculine, portraying the male voice in a generic quest for identity in which the Freudian Oedipal complex is reenacted (1982, 12).[8] Thus the male detective often disables the evil femme fatale to assert his masculine superiority. Here Mancebo, the investigative journalist in the role of detective, provides the male voice which attempts to disable the apparently monstruous hetairic Bella. Montero sets out to expose this bias not through a direct confrontation with Mancebo's account, but by undermining it by providing a more complete perspective in the rest of the novel.[9] Furthermore, she also vitiates his authority by removing his voice from the transcriptions incorporated into the text (Glenn 1987, 193).

These purportedly male-authored sections of the novel have not only been the focus of the two aforementioned articles by Glenn (1987 & 1990b), but were also singled out by various reviewers of the novel, particularly Rafael Conte (1983, 5) and Luis Suñén (1984, 5). Both reviewers criticised these particular sections of the narrative, Conté interpreting them as superfluous and Suñén as too objective. Glenn suggests that this is because Suñén is 'reading like a man', in other words identifying with the male characters and not questioning their accounts; and argues that these fictional documents are crucial because they dramatise the possible distortions of male readings of the motivation behind women's actions (1987, 197). Obviously, it is problematic to suggest that all male readers will interpret these sections in the same manner, or that there is a specifically gendered way of reading. However, they do demonstrate the public credence given to the version of events presented by the male characters. The point of including these transcripts within the text would seem to be to show how interpretations or depictions of the same event may vary according to who is doing the telling, to whom and for what reason. Indeed these documents are central to the novel because they address the issue of constructions of identity through representation and self-representation which were discussed in Chapter Three with regard to *Crónica del desamor* and *La función delta*.

The Weaker Sex?: Subverting Gender Stereotypes

Whilst the transcripts are full of clichéd descriptions of the various women characters and Bella would seem to be categorised as a mad whore, she conforms to neither masculine nor feminine stereotypes. Returning to the 'extraño caso', it is described as strange by the author Mancebo precisely because the characters presented do not fit in with expected gender stereotypes. Bella is no reassuring female figure who follows expected patterns of behaviour. His description of her would seem to fit in with Encarna Sanahuja's analysis of the portrayal in patriarchal discourse of the Amazons, '¿Acaso las mujeres que luchan por arrancar el poder a los varones no son tachadas de locas, histéricas, excéntricas y frustradas?' (Have not women who fight to wrench power off men been branded madwomen, hysterical, eccentric, frustrated?) (1982, 89). Bella is ascribed the 'masculine' attribute of physical strength, yet her savagery does not lead Mancebo to identify her as masculine, but as mad and sexually frustrated.[10] In the article he infers that she may have been a prostitute because the bar where she worked is near the red-light district.[11] He also makes it clear to the reader that gender roles have been confused due to the reversal of the patriarchal norms of dominance and submission, when he states, 'no siempre el sexo débil es el sexo débil' (the weaker sex is not always the weaker sex) (TT: 10). Bella, rather than being a passive, weak, 'feminine' woman, is portrayed as a powerful figure to whom Antonio can offer no resistance; indeed he is completely overwhelmed by her strength and seems unable to defend himself at all. Thus the conventions of the crime thriller have again been reversed: the victim is a weak man who cries as he is unable to defend himself, whilst the perpetrator of the attack is a tall and corpulent woman who has no trouble in overwhelming him. To Mancebo, Bella therefore appears to be unrepresentative of her sex, an aberration; her behaviour is described as 'truly abnormal' (TT: 11). Indeed he indulges in character assassination labelling her a monster, madwoman, murderess and transforming the usual shortened form of her name into a supposedly criminal alias.

In the opening article Bella is referred to as both an assassin and a murderess. However, towards the end of the novel it transpires that she has not killed Antonio as his is one of the statements gathered by Mancebo. He has in fact been left lame from his fall. Yet worst of all, due to the plastic surgery he has undergone, he has lost his sense of smell. As a perfume tester this is tantamount to castration for Antonio:

> Es una mutilación ¿Entiende? Es una castración, es muchísimo peor que la cojera.
>
> It's a mutilation. Do you understand? It's a castration, it's much worse than the limp. (TT: 239)

For Antonio, his nose is his source of power and prestige and now that he has been symbolically castrated, he has difficulty in expressing himself and believes that the reporter will not understand him. He is placed in the position of the castrated woman, as described by Hélène Cixous in her essay 'Castration or Decapitation?' (1981) in which she equates women's 'castration' with their silencing, the removal of their tongues.[12] Parallels can also be found with Cixous' earlier work, *Souffles* (1975) in which she identifies the censoring of women's bodies with the censoring of speech and breath. Antonio, having lost the power which he held, not only has difficulties speaking clearly, but also experiences the choking sensations which have long plagued his repressed sister Antonia.[13] The doctors have made it clear to Antonio that this is not a physical effect of his injuries, rather it is due to the psychic shock sustained. I would suggest that what is shocking is that a woman, Bella, has been capable of symbolically castrating him. Antonio himself realizes that, 'Sin mi nariz no soy nada, no soy nadie...' (Without my nose I'm nobody, I'm nothing...) (TT: 239). He has lost his masculine identity and assumed the traditional feminine position of absence and lack.

The castration of Antonio is thus a moment of rupture in which the male gaze's mastery is broken as the gaze of the male voyeur, Paco Mancebo, has failed to ascribe lack to Bella, despite depriving her of her voice, and has instead disavowed her castration whilst Antonio's symbolic castration is carried out before our very eyes. This may account for the vitriolic tone of Mancebo's verbal attack on Bella through which he attempts to affirm his own position of power and authority as male writer. The anxiety generated by this castration for the male reader and indeed, the male writer Mancebo, is partially resolved by the capture of Bella by the police. She is punished for her crime against an 'innocent victim' by imprisonment. However, the main body of the text acts as a corrective to this view; it is Bella and the other women portrayed who are the victims.of abuse of power by men.

Gorgons, Vampires and Don Juan: Castrated or Castrating?

The novel, however, whilst setting up men as figures of authority within patriarchal society, undermines that authority by depicting some of the deep-rooted fears that these same men have about women. These fears revolve around sexuality and the mother figure. Indeed, the fear of castration alluded to earlier in Antonio's statement to Mancebo is brought out in the sexual relations conducted by both brother and sister. Antonia's only sexual relationship is with Damián who is young enough to be her son and furthermore is an orphan. She constantly refers to him as her child and her feelings for him have strong maternal overtones, as do her actions such as when she tucks him in when he is asleep and brings him lunch at boot camp. He is embarrassed when she appears and tells the other recruits that she is his mother. The joke runs around that, 'Damianín [...] quiere tomar teta' (Little Damián [...] wants to breastfeed) (TT: 168). Damián would seem to be still at the oral stage being suckled by his 'mother'. Indeed it would seem that he has not fully separated from her in order to enter the realm of the Symbolic, as he constantly stutters and searches for words.[14] His sexuality is fixed at an infantile level in which he submits to Antonia whilst fearing that she will overwhelm him.

> Me deshago, me pierdo, es como si me chuparas todo, me das miedo.
>
> I'm undone, I lose myself, it's as if you were sucking everything out, you scare me. (TT: 193)

Damián suffers the fear of merging completely into the other and feels as if he is losing control because his identity is no longer discrete. It is as if through penetrative sex he re-enters the body left at birth. There is thus a metonymical slippage between the vagina and the womb in which the love-object becomes a surrogate for the lost maternal body. This is a frightening process because although the womb provides protection and security, it does so at the cost of the separation upon which masculine identity is traditionally founded. Thus it is not the unknown here which is frightening, but that which is known of old, yet forgotten or repressed. Antonia's naked body exposes the threat of castration. Furthermore, the castrated female in turn becomes the castrating woman and this would perhaps explain Damián's fear of being sucked dry by Antonia, the devouring mother.[15] This fear of the womb may be related to the primitive castration fantasy of the 'vagina dentata' which can be traced back to the Greek origin myths of Ouranous, Kronos and Zeus. All of these underpin a male view of female sexuality as darkness, chaos, annihilation and dissolution.[16]

Antonio, despite his apparent confidence, suffers from similar fears to Damián. Whilst describing one of his affairs to his friend Inspector García he thinks of his lover, Julia, in terms of a series of horrific similes which reinforce each other through the repetition of the initial word 'como':

> Como un náufrago de sed insaciable. Como un pozo sin fondo en el que uno puede caerse. Como un abismo. Como un vampiro. Gorgona de cabellera asfixiante.

Like an unsatiably thirsty castaway. Like a bottomless pit into which you might fall. Like an abyss. Like a vampire. Gorgon of smothering hair. (TT: 102)

In this episode, through the direct appearance of his thoughts on the page, Antonio's underlying fear and hostility towards women is revealed. The use of the images of the suffocating Gorgon and vampire woman could again be interpreted as castrating.[17] He copes with this anxiety by poeticizing his affairs in a written file on indexed cards. His written description of Julia on these cards is in marked contrast to the thoughts quoted above. The similes used here are clichés drawn from romantic poetry which like the boleros discussed in Chapter Four afford pleasure:

Julia tiene la piel tostada como el pan... Llevaba Dioressence. Demasiado típico... Aún hoy recuerdo su fragancia y me sabe su piel entre los dientes, pero mi Julia se ha ido para siempre, reposa en lo imposible como una joya reposa en terciopelo.

Julia had skin toasted like bread... She wore Dioressence. Too common... Even now I remember her fragrance and I can taste her skin between my teeth, but my Julia has gone forever, she's resting in the realms of the impossible as a jewel rests on velvet. (TT: 74)

Julia is thus rendered non-threatening for Antonio through writing, she is reduced to a fragrance and described in terms of an inanimate object that can be put away. He thus limits women in his text by converting his lovers into objects of discourse which he can control and manipulate in his 'historias de amor perfectas' (perfect love stories) (TT: 187). His actual recounting of events to a public audience, Inspector García, differs yet again, in that it is crude, reducing Julia to a sexual object consisting of fragmented body parts much as a pornographic account would:

[ANTONIO] — [...] El pecho pequeño y la cintura pequeña y las caderas grandes y un culo, bueno, el culo es de campeonato, respingón, redondito, una maravilla. [...]

[INSPECTOR GARCÍA] —Y qué, ¿es de las fogosas? ¿De las que se mueven y dicen cosas? ¿De las guarronas? A mí las que me gustan son las guarronas.

[ANTONIO] — La primera vez se quedó muy quieta. Pero después, bueno... De todo. No veas. Hacía de todo. Putísima. Como un volcán.

[ANTONIO] "[...] Small breasts and a small waist, and big hips, and her bum, a champion bum, firm, nicely rounded, marvellous [...]"

[INSPECTOR GARCÍA] "And, is she horny? Does she move and say things? Does she talk dirty? I like the ones who talk dirty."

[ANTONIO] "The first time she was very still. But from then on, well... All sorts. You can't imagine. She did all sorts. What a tart! Like a volcano." (TT: 101-2)

This section, in which Antonio describes Julia as the fantasy available woman, is immediately followed by his fears aroused by her sexuality. Through this juxtaposition Montero, by exposing Antonio's words -written and spoken- and thoughts to public scrutiny, shows up the inherent contradictions in his attitude towards women. He attempts to portray himself, both to himself and to other men such as Inspector García, as a don Juan figure who has seemingly unlimited access to a pool of sexually available women. Indeed, as both Raquel Osborne and Lourdes Ortiz have demonstrated, the key to understanding the don Juan figure may be found not in his conquest of women, but his necessity of the admiration of other men (Marqués & Osborne 1991, 254-5):

La hombría se mide así por la cantidad y la abundancia y ese alarde del Don Juan es un espejo cóncavo en el que se reconoce el hombre de Occidente, fanfarrón, prepotente, agresivo [...] y acumulativo. Don Juan no busca el goce [...] porque representa la esencia misma de una masculinidad que sólo se siente realizada en la multiplicidad y el acoso, en la contienda con el otro a través de un tercero que es la mujer.

Manliness is measured in quantity and abundance and this boasting of being a Don Juan is a concave mirror in which Western man recognises himself, show-off, arrogant, aggressive [...] and accumulative. Don Juan isn't looking for pleasure [...] because he represents the very essence of a masculinity which is only realised in multiplicity, in pursuit, in competition with another through a third party in other words the woman. (Ortiz 1990, 143)

In the case of Antonio he has a captive audience in Inspector García. However, Antonio would also fit into Ortiz's analysis of the post-sexual liberation society in Spain in which men are fearful of women's sexual demands (1990, 146-50).[18] He is privately terrified of not being able to satisfy what he perceives to be the various women's sexual needs, particularly those of his fiancée, the youthful Vanessa, who disorients him by not seeming to care about his sexual performance.

Watcher/Watched, Pleasurer/Pleasured: The Obscure Logic of Masturbatory Fantasy

Whilst initially Bella may seem to be the female character who most evidently troubles gender stereotypes, the character of Antonia is particularly interesting in this respect. She is perhaps the woman who is most clearly portrayed as a victim of male authority. In many respects, she is a child-woman who submits completely to the authority of her brother as she previously had to that of her father, also named Antonio.[19] Antonia is positioned as the castrated, passive feminine object although, as has been made apparent, this positioning is not fixed and subject to change. That notwithstanding, at the beginning of the novel, she is in a state of total dependence upon Antonio and has no defined sense of identity, even her name is his name. Thus Antonia exists not in/for herself but to serve her brother in a self-sacrificing manner. She would seem to be the stereotypical spinster discussed in various Spanish sociological studies of the 1970s (de Miguel 1974b, Abril & Miranda 1978, Verdú Maciá 1978). Indeed, the three main female characters in this novel are all single women who have never been married. Both Bella and Antonia are older women who, having grown up under a regime which idealised the position of wife and mother, are deemed in some way to have failed because they are not married. The studies cited above not only discuss the sense of personal failure felt by women, but also the social view that such women were 'gente rara' (Verdú Maciá 1978, 22). Furthermore, they suggest that the women's sense of frustration may lead to aggressive behaviour which is interpreted as attempting to display masculine qualities such as Bella's attack upon Antonio.

Alternatively, they may become excessively passive and resigned, like Antonia, a behaviour pattern which is also deemed pathologically abnormal (Abril & Miranda 1978, 125). Both of these behaviour patterns are often classed as hysterical, an accusation which is levelled at both Bella, in the opening article by Mancebo, and Antonia, by Antonio when she dissolves into tears after he has treated her particularly harshly (TT: 75).[20]

Various studies on the mental health of housewives have examined the issue of dependency (López, Pintor & Buceta 1975). Antonio certainly behaves towards his sister as if she were a minor, incapable of looking after herself.[21] Furthermore, her social role as a housewife is to negate herself, as María Durán Heras states in her analysis of the position of housewives in Spanish society:

> El papel social de la mujer y sobre todo del ama de casa consiste en darse a los demás, en atender a sus necesidades físicas y afectivas [...] Su ser personal es el ser de los otros y han sabido llegar al desprendimiento absoluto. Su afirmación personal consiste precisamente en negarse.[22]

> The social role of women and above all housewives consist of giving oneself to others, attending to their physical and emotional needs [...] Their personal existence is being for others and they have managed to achieve total detachment from themselves. Their personal affirmation consists precisely in negating themselves. (1978, 90)

However, this lack of a separate sense of identity may also be explained with reference to the pyschoanalytic object-relations theories of Nancy Chodorow (1974 & 1978). Antonia identifies with their mother whereas Antonio has been able to separate himself absolutely from her. He feels repulsion towards his mother and admiration towards his father. Chodorow points out that in the traditional patriarchal family -such as that promoted under Franco- as it is women who 'mother', girls perceive themselves as contiguous with their mother, unlike boys who are able to differentiate themselves from the mother and thus establish their gender identity.[23] Consequently the feminine sense of identity would seem to be relational rather than discrete. Certainly, Antonia would seem dependent, firstly on her brother, then on her lover Damián, for her self-worth.

However, as noted above, in Damián's fantasies she is positioned as both castrated object and castrating subject. Antonia's position is therefore ambivalent: she is both passive object of male desire and powerful subject controlling her own sexual experience. This is particularly evident in the voyeuristic scene depicting the starting point of the relationship between Antonia and Damián. In this episode Damián, unobserved, watches Antonia masturbate with a soft toy through a window. This scenario calls to mind a pornographic peep show in which male voyeurs watch women performing sexual acts behind windows and Damián watches Antonia much as he might a pornographic film for masturbatory purposes. One of the most common heterosexual male fantasy scenarios, as illustrated by the discussion between Antonio and Inspector García cited above, is that of the available woman who desires to be pleasured. In this scenario the woman's body comes to be a sign of desire which signifies possible sexual satisfaction It represents the object which satisfies or gives pleasure.[24] Thus this scene can be linked to the later taunting of Damián by his fellow recruits as desiring his mother's breast, the breast being the infantile object of desire which is succeeded by the genitals.[25] Antonia would seem to be depicted as the object of desire, the castrated, passive feminine object alluded to above. It remains for Damián to step into the scenario to complete Antonia's apparent lack. He later does this but is initially content to maintain his separate identity and climax through masturbation.[26]

His male gaze intrudes into her private fantasy world. Indeed the eye may be equated with the penis in as much as it is an agent of penetration and possession:

> …this gaze gone hard…tends toward a certain violence, a will to penetrate, to pierce, to fix in order to discover the permanent under the changing appearances which implies a certain anxiety in the relation between spectator and object seen. (Caws 1986, 270)

Whilst Antonia fantasizes being raped, Damián penetrates her fantasy scene with his vision. She is the object of his scopophilia, watched without her consent and when she realizes that she has been watched she is ashamed and hides from his look.[27] However, his eyes pursue her in her dreams intruding into her fantasy world. Although initially ashamed of having been seen, Antonia becomes aroused by the eyes watching her in her fantasy and replaces the fantasy of being raped with the fantasy of being watched. This scene would seem to be making the point that sexual arousal is not a purely physical but also a psychical relation. Laplanche and Pontalis argue that sexuality in fact is not simply a biological instinct, but arises only with the emergence of fantasy (1986). In other words sexuality is characterized as the desire for the repetition of pleasurable sensations, the desire for a 'wished-for-satisfaction' rather than for an actual object.

Antonia's desire to be looked at is a passive form of scopophilia in that there is a certain eroticism in being exposed to the other's gaze. This would place her in the role of a desiring object actively desiring the subject's gaze and brings up the question of feminine subjectivity. Following phallocentric logic Damián would be described as the active subject looking at an object and Antonia as the exhibitionist object of his male gaze. However, it is Antonia who purposefully sets out to attract his gaze for her own sexual satisfaction. Thus this episode would seem to suggest that is possible to blur the boundaries between active subject and passive object. Anne McClintock discusses the obscure logic of the masturbatory fantasy in which:

I am the watcher/the watched; I am the pleasurer/the pleasured. (1992, 125)

Indeed, a general feature of fantasy is a certain amount of slippage between the positions of subject and object as demonstrated by Laplanche and Pontalis:

In fantasy the subject does not pursue the object or its sign: [s]he appears caught up [her]self in the sequence of images. [S]he forms no representation of the desired object, but is [her]self represented as participating in the scene although, in the earliest forms of fantasy, [s]he cannot be assigned any fixed place in it [...] As a result, the subject, although always present in the fantasy, may be so in a desubjectivized form... (1986, 26)[28]

Damián's initial look/gaze seems to transform Antonia, from a subject controlling her own sexual experience through masturbation, to an object of his desire and induces feelings of shame and humiliation in her. However, on discovering Damián's embarrassment on meeting her, Antonia realizes that there is not only power in the look, but that she can turn her 'to-be-looked-at-ness' to her advantage.[29] In her new fantasy she climaxes because she is being watched.

Rather than remain in the realms of fantasy she uses her vital power to attract Damián's gaze and entices him to watch in order to bring about her own pleasure and not necessarily to fulfil his desires. It is significant that when Antonia and Damián meet face to face it is Damián who is the more embarrassed of the two. The objectifying look is returned by Antonia and the male gaze's mastery is again broken, as it was in the opening sequence of the novel. Who is object and who is subject? The positions would seem to be interchangeable.

For Antonia, as the initial rape fantasy would indicate, her sexuality is simultaneously an area of pleasure and danger.[30] However, her fears are the product of a repressive Catholic education which seeks to inculcate what Freud termed the three dams on sexual development, as discussed in his 'Three Essays on Sexuality': disgust, shame and morality (Strachey 1981, v.VII, 125-248). The Pauline tradition regards sex as sinful outside marriage and even within matrimony, it is deemed to be for the purpose of procreation not pleasure. In what Josep-Anton Marqués terms the clerical-repressive model of sexuality, actions such as masturbation would therefore be regarded as a perversion (1987, 76). In Chapter Two we have seen how in Spain such attitudes permeated gynaecological as well as clerical discourse. A survey on women's sexuality carried out by *Vindicación Feminista* in 1979 noted the repressive effects of education in this respect (1979, 31). More recently, many of the women interviewed in Madrid by Alicia Puleo for her study of sexuality and feminine identity, noted the negative influence of the church on their sexual development through the prohibition of desire and pleasure (1994b, 171). It is recognised that prohibition may trigger a retreat into fantasy and indeed Antonia has fantasized about sex since her youth.[31] She deals with the guilt created by her fantasies by confessing her sinful thoughts to a deaf priest and can thus content herself with keeping to the letter if not the spirit of her religion.[32]

Perhaps the most obvious form of danger is the extreme instance of sexual violence that is the act of rape. It is, however, a fairly common fantasy scenario despite the fact that:

> Such accounts [of fantasies] offend the rational mind as well as moral norms, for how can women desire rape when it is the most extreme instance of male domination and violence against them? But precisely because of this it can be

used, in fantasy, to represent the most extreme of sexual desire, projected onto the active other whose very violence and insistent demand are but an inverse representation of the subject's own desire to be pleasured. (Cowie 1992, 142)

As Linda Williams argues, the rape fantasy permits the woman to preserve a facade of integrity and morality in the face of orgasms she can claim not to have willed. It allows her to deny her own sexual agency and may be interpreted as a ruse to obtain pleasure, particularly in a society which denies women that capacity.[33] If society regards women's bodies as objects then for women 'el lenguaje del deseo se transformará en fantasías o en imágenes más poderosas que lo real' (the language of desire will be transformed into fantasies or images which are more powerful than the real) (Altable Vicario 1986, 40). Paradoxically the rape fantasy is a fantasy in which passivity is pleasurable but also demanding. Indeed the rape fantasy can be understood as a fantasy which, much as in the scene of voyeurism/exhibitionism described above, allows the interchangeability of the active/passive role. Antonia projects the active role in the scene -that of watcher/rapist- onto the Other. However, this does not make her a merely passive participant because through fantasy she is seeking to control the actions of an other. Furthermore, by assuming her desire and deriving pleasure through auto-eroticism she is situating herself as a subject. There is again a breaking down of the dichotomies of active/passive, subject/object, as in Montserrat Roig's ideal sexual scenario: 'en un fecundo diálogo erótico, cada uno es sujeto y objeto a la vez. Ser pasivo y activo. Donde los papeles se reparten hacia el infinito' (in a fertile erotic dialogue , each is both subject and object at the same time. Both passive and active. The roles are shared out infinitely) (1981a, 118).

In the Name of the Father: The Assertion of Patriarchal Law

However, this ideal scenario, in which binary dichotomies are broken down, cannot be allowed to continue in a patriarchal society. Deviant women, such as Bella and Antonia cannot go unpunished. Antonia is separated from her lover by two figures of patriarchal authority: her brother, Antonio and the police inspector, García. This enforced separation is deemed necessary because the couple do not fit into the traditional bourgeois model of a relationship in which the male is always ready for sex whilst the woman is chaste (Marqués 1987, 78-9). Furthermore, their relationship would seem to pose a threat to society because of the difference in their ages (Antonia is twenty three years older than Damián).[34] Antonio is patently disgusted when he discovers their relationship, telling Damián that Antonia is old enough to be his mother. Yet he fails to make the obvious comparison with his own relationship with Vanessa which also crosses the generation gap. However, it would seem more culturally acceptable for the daughter to continue to desire the father than for the son to continue to desire the mother. Antonio plays the role of the Father in the Oedipal scenario in that he prohibits Damián from continuing his relationship with Antonia. The Child -Antonia refers to the orphaned Damián as her child or infant- is separated from the Mother by the Law of the Father.

The relationship between Antonia and Damián is discovered in a voyeuristic scene which is in clear contrast to the episode which led to their relationship. Inspector García encounters Antonia and Damián making love in the park during his nightly beat and arrests them for public indecency. In this scene the male gaze's mastery is partially affirmed because of García's acknowledged position of power within society as an upholder of the law. However, he needs the couple because he is also a scopophiliac who derives pleasure from voyeuristically observing young couples.[35] Both lovers are converted into an object to satisfy his own desire. Antonia, in particular, is seen by García as flesh, a body. Her body is fragmented, much as Julia's was in Antonio's description, as García concentrates on parts of it rather than the whole: 'un seno tembloroso y colosal, en las carnes abundantes medio desnudas de una mujer tremenda, qué abundancia de muslos, de vientre, de repliegues' (a trembling colossal breast, part of the abundant, half-naked flesh of an enormous woman, what an abundance of thighs, stomach, folds) (TT: 199). As noted above, this fragmentation is a common feature of pornographic cinematographic technique, and indeed García, like Damián in the episode examined previously, regards the scene he is surveying much as he would a pornographic film, using it for his own sexual arousal. Inspector García identifies to a certain extent with the males in each couple, by purveying the scene from their point of view. This is typical of the male voyeur watching a film in which the female character, in this scenario Antonia, is transformed into a fetishistic object for his consumption. Furthermore, unlike the earlier scene between Antonia and Damián, there is no mutuality here between observer and observed. García is a sadistic voyeur whose objective is to punish the couples for performing a sexual act which is not acceptable to society, and thereby ascertain his control over them by sundering the fusion of their bodies. He is able to do this because he is an agent of the law: not only juridical, but also patriarchal, as he is clearly portrayed as a father through the references to his own teenage daughters in this episode. His arrest of the couple could be interpreted as a means of reasserting his mastery which had temporarily been lost through his need for another to satisfy his desire. It also serves to soothe his conscience, which is pricked by the memory of his daughters, and reaffirm his dignity. Although his voyeuristic masturbation might itself be described as a perversion, particularly as the couple have not consented to be watched, Garciá defers his shame by vilifying the couple as 'guarros' and labelling Antonia as a whore. It could be posited that his pejorative treatment of her stems from his guilt at deriving pleasure from watching her and indeed from needing her in order to procure that pleasure. This is demonstrated through the interjection of his thoughts into the third person narration at this point:

> García regó el chopo y se ensució los pantalones. Peor era la suciedad de su conciencia, una blanca vergüenza pegajosa. No había sido un papel muy airoso el suyo, cascársela así detrás de un árbol. Eran unos provocadores, esos tipos. Un peligro público, realmente... Afortunadamente era el que les había pillado pero podía haberles visto cualquier otra persona menos preparada... Había que actuar con decisión.

> García sprayed the poplar and dirtied his trousers. Worse though was the filth of his conscience, a white, sticky shame. His role hadn't been a very distinguished one, wanking like that behind a tree. Those people were prickteasers. A public menace, really... Luckily he had come across them, but someone less well-trained might have seen them... He had to act decisively.
> (TT: 200)

Thus whilst this final voyeuristic scene -unlike those previously examined- would seem to assert the mastery of the male gaze, this is undermined by García's need for an object of vision to satisfy his desire. He is dependent on the couple, just as Poco was dependent on Vanessa's recognition of his subjectivity.

I would suggest that it is the following action of forcible separation of the couple by Antonio which is the most important contributing factor to Bella's attack upon him, as immediately prior to it, Antonia goes to see Bella and tells her what Antonio has done. Both Bella and Antonia are corpulent spinsters whose only sexual relationships are with younger men. Through the descriptions of these affairs they can be interpreted as maternal figures and so Bella enacts revenge in the place of Antonia and castrates the Father for having separated the Mother and Child. In contrast to Bella who would therefore seem to attempt to break out of the patriarchal mould, Antonia's final actions appear to illustrate the fatalism of the feminine woman whose adoption of the nurturant role of the Mother stunts her capacity for independent action. Antonia on being liberated from the tyranny of her brother/father returns to her mother as the novel concludes. She would seem to be bound up in a symbiotic relationship with her mother which she cannot escape.[36]

Nonetheless, both Antonia and Bella resist their allotted role as feminine object to a certain extent. Through their actions and fantasies they seem to cross subject-object boundaries, questioning clear-cut divisions between notions such as active and passive in the various voyeuristic scenes in the text which have been shown to disavow the mastery of the male gaze. Not only are gender stereotypes deconstructed in the text, but women's right to sexual desire and pleasure is also advocated through the sympathetic treatment of the female characters. However, in a patriarchal society female psychosexual identity remains problematic, as the inclusion of Mancebo's journalistic piece and the transcriptions of the three interviews would seem to indicate. The women's transgressions of social order do not go unpunished: Antonia's relationship with Damián is terminated by Antonio and Inspector García, and Bella is imprisoned. Within the hyperrealist framework of *Te trataré como a una reina*, which portrays a grotesque world but one which could plausibly exist, popular culture and sexual fantasy are thus used effectively to blur the binary divisions which polarise masculine and feminine. However, in order to deconstruct radically these divisions and propose new models for identity, a different narrative mode which departs from exisiting patriarchal social and cultural constructs would perhaps be necessary.

[1] Drinkwater also notes the possible commercialism of writers cashing in on a perceived boom in consumer demand for highbrow erotic literature (1995a, 98).

[2] The name of the club is ironic because the novel illustrates that desires canot be satisfied and may ultimately be destructive. That which is desired is precisely what one can never have. Desire is thus self-generating because its truest object remains always lost.

[3] This concept of 'making a spectacle of oneself' is taken from Mary Russo's discussion of carnival in relation to feminist theory (1986, 212).

[4] For a discussion of rational violence and its relation to the Hegelian master-slave dialectic see Jessica Benjamin (1980, 41-70 & 1990). Lynne Segal (1990) discusses the possible causes of masculine violence; a scenario which would be particularly applicable to Poco is that of the man frustrated by the disjuncture between a relatively powerless life -working in the Desiré- and images of masculinity as power -fantasisation of his past as a Legionnaire.

[5] The word 'mancebo' is an interesting example of masculine bias in language as whilst 'mancebo' signifies bachelor, in its feminine form 'manceba' it signifies concubine.

[6] For further discussion of the importance of the placing of these statements within the novel, see Glenn (1987, 194-6) and Davies (1994, 125-7).

[7] Much as women are excluded from Freudian discourse or consigned to the category of enigma (Anabitarte & Lorenzo 1978, 45), Mancebo also excludes their voices from his discourse leaving the reader to ask why.

[8] For the male child to resolve the complex -as set out by Freud- he must repress his desire for the mother by identifying with the father's authority. The boy's superego is defined through separation from the mother and he becomes a subject within the patriarchal order. A deeper identification between mother and daughter may make this separation problematic, thus complicating female access to subjectivity. The implications of this are explored in object-relations theory. See Chodorow (1974, 43-66; 1978).

[9] For Brown this satirization of sensationalist journalism is another use of Montero's own journalistic skill (1991b, 250).

[10] See Studlar (1990, 229-49). In this essay Studlar examines the importance of the concept of masochism in interpreting voyeurism and the masquerade in cinema. She looks at three mothering imagos: the primitive pre-uterine mother, the Oedipal mother and the good oral mother. The portrayal of Bella would correspond to the first of these.

[11] This inference is drawn from the statements made by Antonio and Vicente (TT: 94-5, 227).

[12] The basis for this piece is 'Medusa's Head' by Freud (Strachey, v.XVIII (1920-2), 273-4) in which decapitation is equated to castration. See also Cixous (1976).

[13] The sensation of choking is a symptom of hysteria, a condition traditionally ascribed to women but also suffered by men who feel impotent.

[14] The oral stage is taken from Freud's account of pre-oedipal sexuality whereas the passage from the imaginary to the Symbolic belongs to Lacan's account. This ambivalence towards the good/bad breast could also be interpreted as an example of the Kleinean paranoid-schizoid position.

[15] Within mythological discourse there are various examples of the terrifying, devouring and insatiable mother figure. For example, Ishtar, Cibeles and Lilith bind together Eros and Thanatos (Calvera 1982, 123; Sau 1980, 21).

[16] Ouranous is the original father who attempted to maintain his authority by confining his children in their mother's womb. Kronos, his son, castrated him with a sickle provided by his mother Gaia and took over his place of authority. The oracle warned Kronos that he too would be displaced in turn by his son. To avoid this he ate his own children. However, his wife Rhea in league with Gaia fed him a stone instead of Zeus who was taken away to the island of Crete. There he grew up in safety until he was old enough to overthrow Kronos. Zeus avoided the fate of his father and grandfather by devouring his wife Metis whole. He then produced his daughter Athene from his own head thus obliterating female genealogy.

[17] See Ortiz (1990, 149) for a discussion of the female vampire who is active, seductive and terrifying.

[18] This would also fit in with Marqués' capitalist permissive model of sexuality which Antonio would seem to follow through his obsession with his impotence and making women reach orgasm (1987, 80-1). Montserrat Calvo Artes discusses this obsession with what she terms the 'stereophonic orgasm' in various essays (1985 & 1986).

[19] The name-of-the-father in Lacanian terms represents the symbolic father who is identified with authority and the Law. For a feminist discussion of the name-of-the-father see Grosz (1991, 67-72).

[20] Emilce Dio Bleichmar (1991) has examined the category of hysteria as a possible form of spontaneous feminism in which the patriarchal valuation of gender may be overturned through women breaking out of the paradigms set up by systems of masculine representation. However, as a strategy for resistance it is ambiguous as to whether hysteria is ultimately emancipatory or disempowering due to its traditional association with femininity and marginalisation.

[21] Verdú Maciá examines the notion of marriage as entry into adult life (1978, 23).

[22] This sense of isolation is compounded for women originally from rural areas. As we have seen in Chapter Four, one form of escape is through romantic fantasy, listening to the radio or television whilst carrying out household chores. For Durán Heras another form of escaping the monotony of housework is through 'afectivizar cualquier expresión de su trabajo cotidiano' (giving an emotional connotation to any aspect of their daily work) (1978, 91). Antonia does this through her collection of objects.

[23] Whitford (1992) gives a useful summary of the significance of object-relations theory for feminist accounts but also points out the limitations of this approach. The most far-reaching critique is that of Marianne Hirsch (1989) who argues that women must move beyond the phallocentric parameters of male theorists and invent a new theoretical framework.

[24] For an extended psychoanalytic discussion of pornography, fantasy and desire see Cowie (1992, 132-52).

[25] 'For the baby, the 'breast' becomes the object of desire -as giving the experience of satisfaction- but is not so as itself but as a signifier of the *lost* object which is the *satisfaction* derived from suckling the breast, but comes to be desired in its *absence*.' (Cowie 1992, 135). Thus the breast and genitals are signifiers of possible satisfaction.

[26] It is interesting to note that in the majority of pornographic films the male orgasm is portrayed in the 'cum-shot' in which the male withdraws and ejaculates upon the female. There is thus no threatening merger of either bodies or identities.

[27] Scopophilia is the drive to look in order to gain sexual satisfaction. Active scopophilia entails the subject looking at an object of desire whereas in the case of passive scopophilia the subject desires to be looked upon by another subject.

[28] In accordance with Lauretis in her use of this quote (1991, 233), I have changed the pronominal gender used.

[29] See Mulvey (1989). Mulvey's essay 'Visual Pleasure and Narrative Cinema' is the point of departure for the majority of essays on voyeurism in the cinema. Writers have since contested Mulvey's equation of the gaze as masculine and the image as feminine. See Doane (1982 & 1991), and Gamman & Marshment (1988).

[30] This opposition between restriction/repression/danger on the one hand and exploration/pleasure/agency on the other is examined in a collection of essays entitled *Pleasure and Danger* edited by Carole Vance (1984a).

[31] It is essential to recognise that there is no straightforward connection between the rape fantasy and the material act of rape. The importance of fantasy for female sexuality is discussed by Vance (1984b), Ellis, O'Dair & Talmer (1990), Williams (1990), and Rodgerson & Williams (1991).

[32] The role of the confessional in controlling and regulating women's sexual behaviour within Catholic society is discussed by Zaretsky (1986).

[33] This fantasy can be related to the hero in romantic fiction whose violence provokes both fear and admiration (Cranny Francis 1990, 182-3). Through fantasy it is possible to flirt with danger and what is prohibited (Osborne 1989, 157).

[34] They are near the bottom of Gayle Rubin's hierachical system of sex value as their relationship crosses the generation gap (1984, 267-319).

[35] Mulvey divides male spectators into sadistic voyeurs and scopophiliacs. I would suggest that these categories are not mutually exclusive.

[36] Antonia fails to make the separation from the mother defined above as a prerequisite condition for subjectivity.

CHAPTER SIX

'BEYOND REALITY': ANTI-HEROES AND HEROINES IN *AMADO AMO, TEMBLOR* AND *EL NIDO DE LOS SUEÑOS*

Lo único cierto es la incertidumbre, el flujo, el cambio continuo. La ordenación perfecta y jerárquica del universo se disuelve; lo que prevalece es el azar.

The only certainty is uncertainty, flux, continuous change. The perfect, hierarchical ordering of the universe is dissolved; what prevails is chance. (África Vidal 1989, 56)

As we have seen in the preceding chapters, the exploration of constructions of identity in the narrative of Rosa Montero would suggest that identity is fragmentary and escapes categorisation. It consists of shifting networks of discursive practices including those of pleasure and fantasy. The novels clearly engage with a variety of such discursive practices, yet up to *Te trataré como a una reina* they do so within the 'realist' framework of a recognisable patriarchal society. As discussed in Chapter One, many Spanish feminist theorists in the 1970s and early 1980s noted the apparent difficulty in presenting alternatives to the patriarchal socio-cultural model and the identity imposed on women by that model. Women novelists of the time seem to be *'cronistas* cómplices de una época sin fantasía suficiente para descubrir otro mundo, ni confianza en su propia capacidad para crear' (complicitous chroniclers of an era lacking sufficient imagination to discover another world, without enough confidence in their creative capacity) (Romero et al. 1987, 357). Whilst they clearly reject the role ascribed to them by society, they would seem to find it difficult to construct another which would involve challenging the invisible patriarchy encoded within social relations and cultural practices (Regazzoni 1984, 15).

As much of the narrative produced by women in Spain in the late 1970s and early 1980s is testimonial in nature, it is particularly concerned with the crisis in identity politics and general values that occurred during the transitional period. It has been argued that this crisis was notably marked for those who had been involved in oppositional politics under the Franco regime (Davies 1991, 109). For women such as Elena and Ana depicted in *Crónica del desamor*, the disillusion or *desencanto* they feel towards Marxist discourse is reflected in the disillusion they experience in their love affairs thus blurring the dichotomy between the political and the personal. Whilst characters such as Ana of *Crónica del desamor* (1979) and Lucía of *La función delta* (1981) do attempt to construct their own identity through scripting their own life narratives, they are limited in that they chronicle existing patriarchal structures. In order to reconstruct a feminine identity outside the paradigms which constrain Ana and Lucía, it is necessary to take the leap of imagination into fantasy put forward by Romero et al. (1987).[1] As Patricia Gabancho states, in her study of contemporary Catalan women writers, it is time to move on from recording external experience, 'convenció, descoberta del cos, maternitat, violació [...] Ja comença a ser l'hora de superar l'evidencia' (convention, discovery of the body, maternity, rape [...] It's time now to go past the obvious) (1982, 137). Indeed, Elizabeth Ordóñez, in her 1991 study of contemporary Spanish women writers, traces the shift in the 1980s from the quest for voice and self-definition, through the rewriting of history, to the deconstruction of revered traditions:

> Patriarchal plots are turned on their heads, expected texts are inverted, subverted and ultimately displaced with an(other) discourse, a multiplicity of women's voices that refuse to be easily pinned down. (149)[2]

Such a leap of imagination is taken by Montero in her fifth novel, *Temblor* (1990). In the trajectory of Montero's narrative production, there is a sense of development from mimetic novels based on experience -*Crónica del desamor* in particular has been interpreted as semi-autobiographical (Davies 1991, 109)- to an exploration of the possibilities of fantasy for identity politics. As noted in Chapter Four, the turning point in Montero's fiction is the short story 'Paulo Pumilio', published in the anthology *Doce relatos de mujeres* (Navajo 1982). It represents a clear shift both in subject matter and style. Paulo Pumilio, a character from the margins of society, recounts his life-story as he sits in a prison cell, condemned for murder and about to commit suicide. This story is written in a black, humorous style. In an interview with Antonio Monegal, Montero said that this story allowed her to distance her writing from her immediate experience and thus to write her third novel, *Te trataré como a una reina* (1983), which also deals with characters from the margins of society in a similar style. She describes this style as a grotesque melodrama derived from the bolero song form which is the central motif of the novel (Monegal 1986, 10-11). However, as we have seen in Chapter Four, the bolero is more than a stylistic device in the novel. Through the performance of the songs and by working through their influence on those who listen to them, Montero interrogates the use of popular culture in the construction of identity.

La sustancia de la vida es temblor (The substance of life is fear) (AA: 144)[3]

Although Montero's fourth novel, *Amado amo* (1988), also employs grotesque humour, it shifts back to the professional milieu of *Crónica del desamor* and *La función delta* to deliver an incisive critique of postmodern, neocapitalist society.[4] The protagonist of the novel, César, works in the postindustrial field of advertising and lives in a world preoccupied with material success. His job consists in encouraging a consumer lifestyle by appealing to people's insecurities about their identity. However, César himself, along with his co-workers, is put under pressure to measure up to the expectations of a multinational company and as the novel progresses he seems to be increasingly unable to cope as he gradually loses the prestige he once had and observes how ruthless young executives such as Nacho consolidate their own position at the expense of others. He suffers from a form of insomnia known as delayed sleep onset which would seem to parallel the fact that he is out of step with how the company functions. César is a modern anti-hero in an absurd world where humans have been reduced to cogs in the transnational corporate machine, ultimately expendable and replaceable by a more efficient part.[5] He typifies post-modern man as described by the Spanish theorist Carlota Solé Puig. He fatalistically accepts the present, combining a lack of will to change with a lack of interest in the social (1988, 96).

Amado amo stands out within the narrative of Rosa Montero because it is the only novel to have a male protagonist. It is interesting to compare it with *Temblor*, written two years later, which depicts a female heroine, Agua Fría, who sets out on a quest for her identity with all the dangers entailed in that process. In contrast, César fails to construct a narrative of self and a dissolution of his identity would seem to take place (Drinkwater 1995b, 164-5). His personal narrative of self is subsumed by the alien norms imposed from the U.S.A. by the company Golden Line. These could perhaps be encapsulated in the axiom 'Survival of the Fittest' described in the novel as 'el modelo colectivo de la colectividad depredadora' (the collective model of the predatory collectivity) (AA: 195) and illustrated in Chapter Nine through Clara's recounting of the Oklahoma land run of 1889 in which tens of thousands of starving settlers fought each other brutally in the scramble to obtain land. In such an environment only the most selfish and inhumane can triumph. This is taken as the model for Western corporate systems in which individual identities are eroded as corporate paradigms are imposed. These are to be assumed and reproduced without criticism in a highly competitive milieu. César becomes increasingly insecure and even paranoid as the novel progresses. Like Antonio after Bella's attack in *Te trataré como a una reina*, César suffers from sensations of choking usually ascribed to women deemed hysterical. In a piece of verbal cross-dressing he refers to himself as 'la loca de la casa' (the madwoman of the house) (AA: 38). He also suffers from migraines which disturb his speech, thought, vision and induce nausea. These sensations are captured in the text through the use of parallelisms and repetitive structures. Although the narration is ostensibly in the third person, it is focalised through César and blends free indirect style with stream of consciousness. Unlike Montero's previous novels it fails to include substantial sections of dialogue as César does not form part of a supportive community. He is unable to express himself freely and unlike Ana and Lucía fails to piece together the events of his life in an explanatory narrative. This fragmentary narrative echoes the disintegration of César's daily routine and the disintegration of his social identity. He fantasises about returning to a pastoral, idyllic past in which identity is unproblematic. This would be a place where it is possible to 'dormir el sueño sin sueño de los justos, el sueño fácil y profundo de los que saben quienes son' (sleep the sleep without dreams of the just, the easy, deep sleep of those who know who they are) (AA: 167).

Carol Pearson and Katherine Pope, in the introduction to their analysis of the female hero in Anglo-American literature, contrast the metaphysics of much contemporary literature (in which the male central characters are 'anti-hero[es] in a hopeless and meaningless world; they view themselves and all humanity as powerless victims of metaphysical nothingness and technological, bureaucratic society') with novels, mostly, but not all, written by women, in which the female central character develops from a victim to a hero who is able to transform society (1981, 13).[6] In a similar fashion, Francisca González Rodríguez notes the appearance of the anti-hero in Spanish novels (1990). The hero no longer knows what he wants, whilst the heroine is neither passive nor submissive. This sense of tension or instability surrounding masculine identity echoes the findings of sociological surveys such as that carried out by the Instituto de la Mujer in 1988 (*Los hombres españoles, Spanish Men*). Persisting traditional representations of gender, particularly in the mass media, coincide with the 'igualitarismo' promoted by the state and exisiting to an increasing extent in personal relationships. Ortega et al. propose the concept of a floating identity due to their perception that 'cada persona está coexistiendo con múltiples y contradictorias imágenes acerca de lo que es' (each person coexists with multiple and contradictory images of who they are) (1993, 10). This is felt to be particularly acute for Spanish men and consequently masculine identity would seem to enter into crisis due to the lack of a clear interpretative framework. César is clearly threatened by women such as Paula who challenge the traditional masculine power hierarchy. Her subversive desire has the potential to bring the patriarchal house down by exposing company policy to the scrutiny of the press. However, the patriarchal ranks close to exclude her and even César, her lover, is called upon to betray her which he does thereby joining the ranks of the powerful from which he too has been previously routinely excluded.[7] This can be related to the social phenomenon of backlash against feminism in the 1990s despite continued inequality (Moreno 1988, 59).[8] As Montero stated in a 1995 interview:

> El hombre se ha encontrado sin sitio y se ha sentido perdido. Y le ha salido un impulso de ofensa, de reaccionarismo, de atrincheramiento. Se sienten débiles y piensan que la mujer les está robando el lugar.

> Men have found themselves without a niche and feel lost. And an impulse to attack, be reactionary, entrench themselves has emerged. They feel weak and think that woman are robbing them of their position. (Fontradona 1995, 34)

Indeed, women are again effectively silenced throughout *Amado amo* as they were in both *Crónica del desamor* and *La función delta* (Ciplijauskaité 1989, 73 & 1993, 3; Arribas 1991, 349-51). This occurs both at a public and private level. Within his personal relationships César prefers women who remain silent: for example his fondest memories of his ex-girlfriend Clara are of her sleeping and he drugs the young media student he beds to produce the same effect. On more than one occasion he silences Paula whose complaints he fails to take seriously as he selfishly regards them as inconsequential in comparison to his own needs:

> Quizá Paula tuviera razón, y además César se apresuraba a concedérsela para calmar sus ánimos; pero de algún modo pensaba en su interior que el drama que él vivía ella jamás podría entenderlo. Porque el que Paula no fuera ascendida a fin de cuentas no era una injusticia tan enorme. Las mujeres carecían de ambición.

> Maybe Paula was right, and besides César pushed himself to agree with her to calm her down; but somehow he thought to himself that she would never be able to understandthe drama he was going through. After all if Paula hadn't been promoted it wasn't such a great injustice. Women lacked ambition. (AA: 68)

He even goes as far as pretending that the telephone is cut off when she calls him to complain that two new members of staff have been promoted over her (AA: 96). César's egotism would refute one of the possible interpretations of the novel's title: 'being loved I love', as he seems incapable of intimacy with his lovers. From César's point of view women are objectified and reduced to an essential appendage, preferably blonde, for ambitious executives. The only woman with whom César seems to have a particularly close bond is his mother. However, this is a complex and contradictory relationship. Whilst she provides him with a feeling of confidence and security, he also despises her throughout his adult life for her passive resignation to the family's hardship. Nonetheless, the early mother-child bond is reactivated on her deathbed where her unconditional love provides a magical space into which César can retreat.

Despite the apparently clear contrasts between the anti-hero César and the heroine Agua Fría, there are perhaps more similarities between *Amado amo* and *Temblor* than first seem apparent. Both novels engage with the issue of power and its manipulation within a highly regulated, hierarchical form of organisation. They engage with how power is produced and reinforced discursively. Semmingly innocuous words and phrases uttered by a superior are agonised over at length by César. The quote heading this section actually comes from *Amado amo* in which the protagonist lives in constant fear due to the instability provoked in his life by the imposing presence of *Poder* and *Deber*. It is power which is inextricably linked with desire:

El Poder poseía esa energía secreta, esa asombrosa alquimia: la capacidad de aparejar amor y sufrimiento. Y así, en todo subalterno parecía existir una pulsión de entrega hacia sus mandos. Como el perro que lame la mano que le azota, o el campesino bolchevique que llora tras haber degollado a su señor. Amado amo.

Power possessed that secret energy, that amazing alchemy: the capacity to join together love and suffering. And thus, in every subaltern there seemed to exist an urger to submit to those in authority. Like the dog that licks the hand that beats it, or the Bolshevik peasant who weeps after slitting his master's throat. Beloved master. (AA: 142-3)

The identity being promoted by Golden Line would seem to be that described by Michael Kimmel as 'marketplace man'(1994, 123) who exists in a ferociously aggressive and competitive homosocial environment in which being a man is associated with power and control which must be continuously demonstrated to other men. For those, like César, who fail to live up to this hegemonic model of masculinity, it generates acute anxiety, a heightened fear of failure and a fear of other, more successful, men such as Nacho and Morton. For Paula this attempt to maintain 'hombría' at all costs betrays a lack of dignity. Manliness is a fiction which these men have created for themselves thereby excluding women from positions reserved for those who conform to the model of masculinity being promoted, 'es un invento, una mentira, una convención que vosotros mismos habéis creado' (it's an invention, a lie, a convention that you have created yourselves) (AA: 47-8).

Temblor probes further into the crisis of values within a similarly hierarchical and discursively regulated world, addressing issues such as the relativity of truth, which was discussed in relation to the individual in Chapter Three, but is clearly a collective, social issue here. Both novels would seem to express Montero's existential concerns highlighted by Glenn, in her review of *Temblor*, as being present in all of her fiction whether realist or fantastic (1991b, 401). Montero's position in this regard, as evidenced by various interviews, would seem to be fundamentally self-contradictory. Whilst on the one hand, as in *Amado amo*, she would seem to consider life as inherently absurd and subject to the forces of chance, on the other, as in *Temblor*, she states her belief in the power of dreams and the imagination to effect change (Cantavella 1990; LID 1990; Piñol 1990). She describes herself as 'una hija de la náusea y del existencialismo' (a daughter of nausea and existentialism) (Cantavella 1990). She appears to subcribe to existential angst, whilst reiterating the Guevarist slogans daubed on the Sorbonne in 1968, 'Soyez réalistes, demandez l'impossible' (Be realists, demand the impossible) and 'L'imagination au pouvoir' (Imagination to power) (García 1977, 21-2). In a further nod to existentialist thought, towards the end of *Amado amo*, César describes himself as Sisyphus, a reference which brings to mind Camus' *Le Mythe de Sisyphe* which explores the metaphysics of absurdity (1942). Perhaps the most salient point of contact between Montero and Camus' position is the emphasis placed on the passion for life coexisting with the tragedy of being conscious of the absurdity of life.

Sisyphus cannot escape his tragic condition and as we have seen above, narrative based on experience cannot evade patriarchal, cultural paradigms. Indeed, the female characters in Montero's novels prior to *Temblor* are trapped: Ana of *Crónica del desamor* seems to have no hopes of promotion in her job despite her competence and expertise and all of the women in that novel fail to have fulfilling relationships with men; Lucía in *La función delta* is dying as the novel closes; the three main female characters in *Te trataré como a una reina* are all trapped in some way; *Amado amo* ends with César betraying his lover, Paula, to keep his job.[9] In contrast to these narratives of entrapment, *Temblor* is open-ended: the heroine Agua Fría decides to carry on travelling rather than join the new society created at the end of the novel or returning to the home of the (dead) father of her unborn child. Similarly, the children's story, *El nido de los sueños*, published the following year (1991), ends with Gabriela imagining what she will create next in her travels. Thus although, as we shall see below, both protagonists undertake circular journeys which return to their place of origin, there is no closure as each ends with a new beginning.[10]

The classical genre of the quest myth is reworked in both these novels.[11] Critics examining female hero journeys have discussed at length the limitations of the 'male heroic pattern' of separation, initiation and return for women in the quest for their identity (Pearson & Pope 1981, Pratt 1982, Pearson 1991). Whilst Joseph Campbell's classic study, *The Hero with a Thousand Faces* (1956), begins by saying that the hero may be male or female, he proceeds to set out a male heroic pattern in which women figure as mothers, goddesses and temptresses to be overcome. Pearson and Pope argue that the presupposition that the male is hero and subject obscures the true archetypal elements of the hero's journey by limiting it according to patriarchal sex-role assumptions in which the hero demonstrates power through the domination of others (1981, 4-5). Indeed, domination is a key word in *Amado amo*. César feels that it sums up his personal life story to the extent that when he looks up 'dominar' (to dominate) in the dictionary he identifies all fifty one meanings as 'un diario autobiográfico' (an autobiographical diary) (AA: 147). One must dominate or be dominated in César's world which is void of compassion for and solidarity with others. In *Temblor* and *El nido de los sueños* an alternative archetypal ideal is posited which is to master the world through understanding it, thus discovering both one's identity and purpose.[12] Both Agua Fría and Gabriela constantly question their surroundings and collaborate with others to achieve their goals of personal and social transformation.

Fantasy, from the Greek φανταστικος: that which is made visible, visionary, unreal (Jackson 1981, 13).

The patriarchal plot of the hero myth is therefore clearly subverted in both texts and an alternative vision set out. However, this is not the only leap of the imagination taken by Montero. Although the settings of *Temblor* and *El nido de los sueños* are quite different -the former is set in a post-nuclear future and the latter is a fantastic journey in a child's imagination- both can be termed fantastic works.[13] *El nido de los sueños* certainly fits into the rubric set down by Ruth Nadelman Lynn in her bibliographical guide to fantasy works for children:

> In fantasy, the impossible takes place; animals talk, magical events occur, the barriers of time dissolve, mythical creatures exist, and inanimate objects come to life. (1979, vii)

Like *Te trataré como a una reina*, *Temblor* would seem to be a hybrid text which blends genres and escapes easy classification. For Zatlin (1992 & 1993) it mixes science fiction with 'medieval' fantasy in a subversion of the Gothic genre, whereas Davies terms it a magical or marvellous romance (1994, 151).[14] Certainly elements are drawn from science fiction, especially the final explanation by the high priestess Océano of how the world came about. However, the work would seem to draw primarily on elements from popular fantastic works such as those of Ursula Le Guin -with whom Montero has expressed an affinity (Piñol 1990; Fajardo 1990)- and Michael Ende, whose *Die unendliche Geschichte* (*Never Ending Story*) was a phenomenal success in Spain (Pereda 1982).

The use of science fiction in the construction of identity is well documented. Although some may argue that the genre's origins may be traced back to the nineteenth century and indeed beyond, it emerged as a clearly separate genre in the 1920s with the crisis of capitalism. In 1927 Hugo Gernsback coined the term 'scientifiction' which became the easier to pronounce 'science fiction' (Ferreras 1972, 62; Barceló 1990, 43). Sociological studies of the genre stress the effect of the economic crisis and the ensuing depression in triggering a sociocultural questioning of values (Ferreras 1972, 61-6). The development of science fiction in Spain is clearly traced by Carlos Saiz Cidoncha (1988) and Miguel Barceló

(1990). During much of the Franco regime the anticommunist ideology of the Right permeated science fiction books and cartoons which exalted Spanishness and national-patriotic values. However, in the 1970s, in parallel with other moves towards democratisation, particularly in the cultural and social sphere, there was a switch back to the Left by science fiction writers who increasingly distanced themselves from the U.S.A. The progressive political tendencies of authors were perhaps more explicit after the death of Franco, but in the early 1980s there was a recession in the market for science fiction and fantasy, and the legendary fanzine *Nueva Dimensión* ceased to be published in 1982. Since then in the late 1980s, early 1990s there has been a resurgence in the genre with new collections appearing such as Ultramar, Orbis and in particular Ediciones B: Nova. All of these collections have placed an emphasis on publishing Spanish authors. Saiz Cidoncha concludes his study of Spanish science fiction by commenting on the ostensible depoliticization of the genre in the 1980s with the emergence of the slick new collections (1988, 510). I would argue that this is not the case with several women authors, both of science fiction and fantasy, who use the genres to examine identity politics.

Turning to women authors, first of all I would like to look at the figures for science fiction authorship in Spain. Saiz Cidoncha estimates that at any one time 5-6% of authors may have been women. Barceló in his guide to science fiction published in 1990, breaks down the composition of over 1000 works published in Spain: 50 are by Spanish authors and more than half of those by four authors. Only one is by a woman: *Sagrada*, a collection of short stories by Elia Barceló, published by Ediciones B: Nova in 1989. Barceló mentions only one other woman writer of science fiction, the Argentinian Angélica Gorodischer.[15] A pioneering corrective study has been carried out by Dolores Robles Moreno of the Biblioteca de Mujeres in Madrid. This is a general study of the genre which also gives a bibliographical breakdown of women writers in Latin America and Spain. Some of these writers have written works questioning patriarchal social and cultural structures. For example in Teresa Inglés' 1970 play, *Complemento: Un hombre*, the Earth is run by a fierce matriarchy. A space crew of women from Earth with their male cook arrive at a male dominated planet where they fight with the men and are all killed. The male cook is offered a chance to stay and possibly become chief of a tribe, but he chooses to return to Earth, as he cannot escape his cultural conditioning. Perhaps the most important woman writer of the genre, indeed some would argue the best writer of the genre at present in Spain, is Elia Barceló. Unlike many of her contemporaries, she writes only science fiction. Her narrative examines issues such as the questioning of patriarchal society and normative sexuality.[16]

In Ordóñez's study (1991), referred to above, she traces a move within contemporary Spanish women's writing from the testimonial narrative of the 1970s, through the rewriting of history, to the deconstruction of patriarchal myths and the assertion of an alternative female vision. Thus the narrative of the 1980s and 1990s consciously engages in dialogue with the past and future.[17] However, as opposed to the conservative implications of looking primarily for role models in the past -a process which as we have seen in Chapter Two is ultimately frustrating for Spanish women- fiction situated in the future may serve to 'combat the closing of the mind by the imaginative extension of possible futures which will open up the space for imaginative restructuring of the possibilities inherent in the present, and, hence of the actual character and definition of what the present in fact signifies' (King 1991, 72). For King and, indeed many Utopian/Science Fiction critics, the importance of these genres lies in the transformative possibilities of their orientation to a speculative future which may inform the present.[18] However, as the 1989 study undertaken by the staff of the Madrid Biblioteca de Mujeres shows, much of mainstream Science Fiction is blatantly sexist (4). This may explain the relative lack of interest in the genre by Spanish women writers. Nonetheless, feminist writers have used speculative projection into the future both to question the fixity of past history set down within patriarchal paradigms and to interrogate the present cultural order.

In common with many feminist fantasy/science fiction works, *Temblor* does not confront the technological advances known as 'novum', common in male-authored science fiction, but examines different forms of social organization and modes of thought (Biblioteca de Mujeres 1989, 5; Bonner 1992, 94). The central concept informing the majority of analyses of science fiction is Darko Suvin's famous definition of the genre as a 'literature of cognitive estrangement' (Suvin 1979, 4).[19] This concept of estrangement (based on Shklovsky's *ostranenie*) and its utility for the exploration of the construction of 'woman' on a social level is examined at length in Sarah Lefanu's discussion of feminism and Science Fiction (1988).[20] For Lefanu the concept explains how science fiction may be both subversive and open-ended through a two-way process. On the one hand, it serves to defamiliarize the familiar, whilst on the other it serves to familiarize the unfamiliar. Whilst the latter technique serves to expand our notion of what is possible, the former fosters heightened awareness by distancing the reader from conventions which they usually take for granted. Thus the possibility for change is opened up not only by suggesting alternative scenarios for the future but also by making the reader view their own society and its cultural codes critically. Science fiction therefore can offer a narrative framework for not only the deconstruction of a coherent self -femininity as constructed by patriarchal, hegemonic discourse- but also the construction of a female subject outside the space bounded by that discourse. The very power of such fiction to effect social change is bound up in the relationship between the fantastic and the real, and the readers recognition of the conditions of the world as they know it transposed into a world which at first seems radically discontinuous from it.[21] As Jacqueline Held argues with respect to science fiction written for children, 'Nos hace despegar de lo real para retrotraernos a él en última instancia, mediante la tangente de lo imaginario' (It makes us distance ourselves from reality only to bring us back to it in the final instance through the tangent of the imaginary) (1987, 118).

A similar argument can be made for the subversive function of fantasy and its relationality or symbiotic relation to the real. This forms the basis of Rosemary Jackson's analysis of the possible sociopolitical implications of fantastic literature (1981). She begins her study by discussing the difficulty of articulating 'fantasy' because of its resistance to definition (1981, 1).[22] Criticizing the structural analysis of Tzetvan Todorov (1975) for its failure to consider the conditions of production of the text, its cultural formation, and its glossing over the possibilities of psychoanalytic readings of the fantastic, Jackson goes on to state that fantasy may be articulated upon the 'struggle against the limits of [the social] context [...and] characteristically attempts to compensate for a lack resulting from cultural constraints: it is a literature of desire, which seeks that which is experienced as absence and loss' (1981, 3).[23] This attempt to articulate the fantastic as a transgressive space, in which absence is made present through the re-combination of the constitutive features of this world to produce something apparently unfamiliar, recalls the discussion above of feminist science fiction as opening a space in which the female subject may be inscribed. Yet many science fiction critics such as Suvin would seem to regard fantastic literature as somehow static and escapist. Nonetheless, the term of cognitive estrangement can also be applied to fantastic works in which the relationship between the individual, the social and the psychological may be explored.[24] As opposed to escapism, such works may facilitate an expansion of possibilities through the transformation of cultural myths and the exploration of what Montero has termed the shifting sands which lie below the appearance of normality (Gándara 1988, 30).[25] As Germán Gullón states with reference to the perceived trend towards the fantastic by Spanish authors in the 1980s:

> Parece una literatura de escape sin serlo, lo que pretende es encontrar o ampliar nuestro sistema de valores (éticos y perceptuales) más allá del que adoptamos para valernos en la vida cotidiana [...] Así pues esta generación intenta hacer dos cosas: reflejar la vida, el mundo, la España que les ha tocado vivir, mientras expanden sus fronteras vitales.

> It seems to be an escapist literature but isn't, what it aims is to find or expand our values (ethical and perceptual) beyond those which we adopt to get by in daily life [...] Thus this generation is trying to do two things: reflect life, the world, the Spain they live in, whilst they expand the frontiers of life. (1987, 61)

The fantastic is therefore not so much an escape from reality as an examination of different facets of reality or what Montero has termed the enigma of our daily lives:

> En la realidad están las cosas y su ausencia, la fantasía y el miedo, lo imaginario y lo que ni tan siquiera somos capaces de imaginar.

> In reality both things and their absence exist, fantasy and fear, the imaginary and that which we are unable to imagine as yet. (1994, 45)

Tembladal: terreno pantanoso, abundante en turba y cubierto de césped, que retiembla cuando se anda sobre él (swampland, plentiful in peat and covered in grass which shakes when you walk on it) (Moliner 1990, 1381).

In *Temblor* Montero uses the genre of fantasy to depict a future society in which contemporary debates regarding identity can be played out and their possible consequences explored. Indeed, the very title of the novel, translated into English as 'trembling' or 'tremor', suggests the questioning of stable, fixed notions. Constantino Bértolo concludes that 'toda la historia de la protagonista es la ilustración narrativa de que el único peligro insuperable reside en la fe en una verdad absoluta o en la creencia de que la vida es algo cerrado y rígido' (the protagonist's story in its entirety is the narrative illustration of the fact that the only insurmountable danger resides in the faith in an absolute truth or belief that life is something closed and rigid) (1990). Both the novel, and even more so the operatic adaptation of it by Marisa Manchado -*El cristal de Agua Fría* (*Agua Fría's Crystal* 1994)- question dogma and absolute notions of truth which maintain corrupt power structures through fear.[26] The opera is clearly postmodern in structure. According to the notes which accompany the libretto, Manchado used an eclectic method of composition which strives to fuse contradictory elements.[27] When interviewed, she described it as being both fantasy and reality, 'es el mundo fragmentado y desesperanzado en que vivimos' (it is the fragmented world without hope in which we live) (Piña 1994). Several articles have been written about *Temblor* which centre on the postmodern aspects of the text (Glenn 1991b, Zatlin 1992, Franz 1993). These articles concentrate in particular on the playfully intertextual nature of the text, also mentioned by Catherine Davies (1994) and Stephen Hart (1993). There are various implicit and explicit references to works drawn from both popular and high literary genres. These are listed by Thomas Franz in what is on the whole an interesting article, although some of the links seem rather tenuous and there is a rather simplistic application of Campbell which does not take into account the feminist reworkings of myth theory cited above.[28] All commentators note the eclectic range of references which include such disparate elements as films such as *The Wizard of Oz* and the *Star Wars* trilogy and references to Tibetan geography. The latter are evident both in the landscape

Agua Fría journeys through, and the naming of the fortress Talapot: the Dalai Lama's palace is called Potala.[29] As Hart notes:

> *Temblor* seems to delight in cannibalized allusions to cultural texts whether popular or philosophical, and effects a postmodernist levelling of canonical texts. (1993, 133)

However, the novel, whilst displaying postmodernist features, would seem to have as its object the construction, rather than the dispersal, of the identity of its protagonist. At the same time, it appears to set out to deconstruct the binary opposition of gender. During her quest, Agua Fría comes into contact with various forms of social organization and ideological frameworks governed by gender: her own society, centred on the city of Magenta and the fortress of Talapot, ruled by the tyrannical high priestesses who were originally able to seize power because of women's capacity to give birth; the capitalist world of Aural and the merchants' caravan also led by a woman, Diamante; the revolutionary, egalitarian community of Renacimiento whose leader is again a woman, Enigma, and the primitive hunter-gatherer society of the Uma ruled by men. Thus Montero examines societies in which women have power (Magenta and Aural); in which men and women are considered as equals, yet their leader is still a woman (Renacimiento); and in which men have power (the Uma). It is to be noted that when women have power it is fundamentally patriarchal in nature: Magenta and Aural are authoritarian, strictly hierarchical societies and although Renacimiento is egalitarian in principle it also has a clear leader. In the reversal of power structures typical of the novel, contrary to the case of the majority of Marxist organisations, its leader is not a man but a woman.

In an interview given to Jochen Heymann and Montserrat Mullor-Heymann, Montero explains why she inverted the dominant male power strucure in the novel:

> Como a mí el sexismo, es decir el hecho de que por ser hombres o ser mujeres se nos obligue a tener un comportamiento determinado me parece ridículo y bárbaro, como es una cosa que me preocupa -cuál es la supuesta identidad que ha de tener un hombre o una mujer [...]- pues he utilizado esa inversión de papeles, simplemente para resaltar el absurdo de una sociedad sexista. [...] Yo

creo que mediante esa inversión quizá se pueda analizar con más distancia el fenómeno sexista dentro de nuestra propia realidad.

> As sexism, that is to say the fact that, by dint of being a man or a woman, we are obliged to behave in a determined manner, seems ridiculous and barbarous to me personally, as it is something which worries me -what is the supposed identity a man or woman is meant to have [...]- I've therefore used this inversion of roles, simply in order to emphasise the absurdity of a sexist society. [...] I think that through this inversion, it is perhaps possible to analyse, from a more distanced position, the phenomena of sexism within our own reality. (Heymann & Mullor-Heymann 1991, 90)

The inversion of sex roles allows the reader to examine the social structures of patriarchy critically by distancing them from those structures as they know them, in other words by defamiliarising the familiar. However, simply reversing the dominant structure does not necessarily interrogate current gender categories. It is therefore important to note that the reversal is not as schematic as it may first appear: male characters can be violent, ambitious and lust for power -all traditionally masculine qualities- but they are denied power because they are ascribed the traditionally feminine qualities of irrationality and an inability to control their emotions or desires. Both masculine and feminine roles are brought into question.[30] Whilst the power structure depicted in *Temblor* is a matriarchy, it is far from the utopic solution often envisaged by feminist science fiction writers and critics. The women in power are cruel, violent and injust. Indeed, there are many ways in which the world depicted in *Temblor* would seem to be backward compared with the twentieth century.[31] Montero offers us a dystopic view of the future in which children are no longer being born and whole areas disappear as they are forgotten about, particularly when people die.[32]

For Franz, this is an indictment of difference feminism by Montero in favour of pluralism. He describes her position towards feminism as inconsistent because of her declarations that she is not a feminist writer while she clearly echoes feminist concerns in her work (1993, 274). However, Franz does not take into account the issues surrounding the problematic use of the term feminist by women writers in Spain which were examined in Chapter One. Furthermore, as discussed at various points in this study, what Montero is denying is that she is deliberately writing militant literature, not that her texts are influenced by her feminist stance nor that they may be interpreted as feminist texts. Franz's application of feminist theory is rather sketchy and he makes some sweeping statements such as describing Francoist society as a resentful matriarchy. That notwithstanding, in *Temblor* there is a clear critique of difference feminists who posit the innate superiority of women. As noted in Chapter One, such a feminism may serve to reconfirm the same binary dichotomies as traditional patriarchal structures of gender.[33] However, whilst there is an indictment of difference feminism taken to the extreme, there is also a celebration of the power of women to give birth. Indeed, one of the main motivations behind Agua Fría's journey is the desire to avenge her mother's death thus indicating the strength of the bond between mother and child.

A somewhat different approach is taken to the novel by Hart who interprets it not as an indictment of essentialism, but as a delineation of the potential harm wrought by what he terms gender trouble (1993, 137). Again, he questions Montero's feminist credentials by taking on board Manteiga's rather problematic opinions which were discussed in Chapter Two. Hart comes to the conclusion that *Temblor* is a conservative novel which projects heterosexual relationships as some sort of paradise. However, this can only be applied to a limited number of relationships, in the novel which would suggest that such transcendence is limited to fleeting moments and far from the norm. Hart extrapolates from these moments that the novel is the tale of a heterosexual protagonist waging war on strident (possibly lesbian) feminists.[34] For Hart, further evidence that the novel expresses a deep-seated fear of gender trouble is found in the depiction of the treacherous androgynous kalinin who provokes a reaction of horror in Agua Fría. It is commonplace in feminist science fiction criticism to assume that the androgyne is the perfect image of unity and harmony (Annas 1987, 146). However, this particular androgyne would seem to be a melding together of negative traits traditionally described as masculine or feminine. Rather than interpret this as anxiety towards the destabilisation of gender categories, it can be seen as a critique of a commonplace utopian scenario in speculative fiction. The alternative posited here would seem to lie neither in inverting the present patriarchal structure, nor in merging the two sides of the binary dichotomy drawn up between genders, but in somehow moving radically beyond present notions of masculinity and femininity to new, unfamiliar concepts.

The novel does clearly unsettle assumptions about gender, in that cultural constructions of gender are deconstructed.[35] This is evident in a conversation, early on in the novel, between Agua Fría and her male friend Pedernal. He questions the opportunities available to her because of her sex, leading her to retort that this is due to her capacity to give birth. An argument ensues in which Pedernal insists on the necessity of both sexes for the reproductive process. (Indeed, later in the novel Agua Fría needs to travel to the land of the Uma, a society dominated by men, in order to become pregnant.) He then points out the hypocrisy of the priestesses in claiming that it is men who are violent when it is they who order torture and cruel punishments. This is borne out later in the novel when Agua Fría takes up arms to hunt and kill. One of the main areas of difference between the sexes in the world depicted is that it is only women who have access to higher skills -such as hypnosis, telepathy and telekinesis- which they use to subdue physically stronger men. However, this fundamental difference is shown to be artificially created through the control of knowledge, as Pedernal learns to master these skills despite being male. Thus supposedly innate gender differences are shown to be culturally constructed and transmitted through a discourse grounded in laws and prohibitionsl aid down by the caste of ruling priestesses. For example, in parodic reference to *Star Wars*, the customary greeting in Magenta is 'Que la Ley nos acompañe' (May the Law be with us). Thus Montero would seem to be criticising modes of social organisation in which difference is codified as the basis of a hierarchical power structure whether patriarchal or matriarchal.

What, then, is the 'alternative cognitive map' depicted in *Temblor*?[36] The way forward suggested by Montero in this novel would seem analogous to that set out by anarcha-feminist theorists: the recognition of the 'personal as the political', the necessity of total revolution for liberation, and the realization of individual autonomy within a social context characterized by voluntary co-operation and mutual aid.[37] In considering anarchist theory it must be remembered that there is a strong feminist tradition within the Spanish anarchist movements and in the late 1930s the anarchist women's movement, *Mujeres Libres* (founded in 1936), insisted on the primacy of individual autonomy for women.[38] Indeed, communitarian anarcha-feminists argue that the individual must actively gain control of her own life and the ideal would seem to lie in a balance between individual and collective action.[39] This is coordinated through fluid forms of organization capable of spontaneous action which mirror the move within the Spanish feminist movement since 1975, away from authoritarian structures and organizations towards a looser network of informal groups in which the emphasis is on personal action and transformation with a view to coalition politics.

During her quest Agua Fría's identity develops and as the novel closes she returns to Talapot, no longer a trainee priestess, but an individual with the strength of purpose to confront the ruling high priestess, Océano. I would concur with Davies (1994, 154) that Glenn is incorrect in her conclusion that Agua Fría, unlike the archetypal hero, returns from her journey without the solution to the enigma of why her world is dying and how to save it (1991b, 401). She knows that to resolve the problem she must confront Océano. However, to kill Océano she needs the help of Dogal and the Uma warriors. In other words, collaboration is necessary between the sexes, as ultimately neither is shown to be more powerful than the other. Indeed, as Zatlin argues, it is possibly Zao's macho instincts -or belief in the superiority of his physical prowess- which get him killed when he rushes to Agua Fría's defence (1993, 122). In contrast, Agua Fría achieves her goal, not through the traditional heroic pattern of dominance, but through co-operation with those she met upon her journey. It is her friend from Renacimiento, the dwarf Torbellino, who blows up the crystals which are the repository of Talapot's collective consciousness after reading Agua Fría's mind. Thus Agua Fría, as an individual, is clearly instrumental in the collective action which makes a new society possible.

In an analysis of the possibilities for feminist utopia Ilda Elena Grau states:

> La literatura fantástica resulta muy conveniente para efectuar crítica social y hacerse preguntas sobre las bases de nuestra cultura actual debido a que se encuentra libre de interpretación y de la realidad. Lanza a la imaginación a soñar todas las posibilidades.

Fantastic literature is very useful to effectuate social criticism and ask oneself questions about the bases of our present culture due to its freedom of interpretation and from reality. It projects the imagination into dreaming all possibilities. (1988, 281)

As we have seen, gender stereotypes are questioned in *Temblor* as patriarchal structures and cultural myths are deconstructed through the various strategies of cognitive estrangement such as the reversal and inversion analysed above. There is also a sense of revisionist mythmaking in that taboo topics such as menstruation are positively valued.[40] One of the earliest events in the novel is Agua Fría's first period. This takes place as the sun sets and she decides that it is the memory with which she would name a future student should she in turn become an Anterior. Nevertheless, this is not a utopic feminist work and the maternal figures depicted are ambivalent. There seems to be genuine love between Agua Fría and her birth mother, and a close bond with her Anterior -spiritual guardian- Corcho Quemado.[41] However, this is not true of the high priestesses: Océano has her own daughter, Relámpago, put to death for leading the conspiracy against her and it is Rélampago's own daughter, Piel de Azúcar, who gives the final command in the execution. Océano's sister, Oxígeno, the wise woman who Agua Fría journeys to the North to see, not only cannot answer her questions, but was directly responsible for Agua Fría's mother's death. Being a dystopic work, *Temblor* often resembles a nightmare more than a dream. As the High Priestess, Océano says, 'la realidad aunque rebelde, termina por parecerse a nuestros sueños si estos se sueñan con la suficiente perseverancia [...] acaba por adaptarse a nuestros sueños ... y a veces también a nuestras pesadillas' (reality, although rebellious, finishes up by resembling our dreams if these are dreamt with sufficient perseverance [...] it ends up by adapting itself to our dreams... and sometimes also to our nightmares) (TT: 240). It would seem to depict a possible scenario for a future world if there is not a radical transformation of the concept of gender which goes beyond simple inversion of current categories.

North American science fiction critics and futurists tend to concentrate on Utopic fiction, placing positive emphasis on egalitarian and ecological practice. However, in the dystopic world of *Temblor* these practices are shown to be of little avail if damaging cultural substructures -represented by the crystals- are left in place. Nonetheless, like many dystopias *Temblor* has a hidden utopian streak in its seemingly pessimistic conclusion. As stated above, the anarcha-feminist ideal is the abolishment of the state and the patriarchy; in other words total revolution. In *Temblor* this is only partially achieved as, although the state is brought down, at the close of the novel a new order seems to be emerging which is virile, hard, and disciplined with El Negro as its natural leader. However, Agua Fría decides not to join that new order but to carry on travelling with her as yet unborn child -and apparently reincarnated dog- and continue her search for her identity. Thus the novel picks up two of the main themes from Montero's previous work: the bond between mother and child, and the notion of the construction of identity as a continual process. As Davies asserts, Montero would seem to be clearing a space between essentialist and non-essentialist positions (1994, 160). Both the conclusion of the novel and Agua Fría's identity remain open-ended:

> Todo cambiaba, todo latía, todo fluía. El futuro hacia el que ahora se encaminaba el planeta no estaba aun escrito; las sociedades que se construirían sobre las ruinas del imperio no habrían existido nunca antes. Era un nuevo y efervescente mundo en el que ella tendría que encontrar su propio espacio.

> Everything was changing, everything was beating, everything was flowing. The future towards which the planet was travelling had not yet been written; the societies which would be constructed upon the ruins of the empire would never have existed before. It was a new and effervescent world in which she would have to find her own space. (T: 250)

When interviewed, Montero stresses that one has to carry on and denies that the novel has a pessimistic conclusion: 'No es mala, no es pesimista. [...] Ella se va, puede ir a buscar a gente de Renacimiento, puede ir a buscar a gente que piense como ella, puede seguir a luchar por conseguir sus sueños' (It isn't bad, it isn't pessimistic. [...] She leaves, she can look for people from Renacimiento, she can search for people who think as she does, she can carry on fighting to realise her dreams) (Knights 1993). Agua Fría chooses not to reintegrate herself into society and rides off into the sunset, like the archetypal outsider in twentieth century popular culture: the cowboy.[42] Having journeyed to the North, the traditional site of knowledge, she continues her journey to the West, the traditional site of new frontiers to be broken. Perhaps this is the nature of utopia, a place always situated elsewhere. Whilst this notion has been used in science fiction criticism, it is perhap best explained using an anecdote recounted by Eduardo Galeano, when interviewed by *El Viejo Topo* in 1994. The film director, Fernando Birri was asked by one of his students at the University of Cartagena de Indias what the function of utopia was. According to Galeano, Birri replied:

> Yo también me lo pregunto siempre. Porque ella está en el horizonte. Y si yo camino dos pasos, ella se aleja dos pasos. Y si yo me acerco diez pasos, ella se coloca diez pasos más allá. ¿Para qué sirve la utopía? Para eso sirve, para caminar.
>
> I also ask myself continually. Because it is always on the horizon. And if I take two steps forward so does it. And if I take ten steps closer it gets ten steps further away. What is utopia for? For that, to move forward. (Galeano 1994, 55)

There is no elixir or quick fix to society's problems. Change will be a continual process and perhaps the key message of *Temblor* is the necessity for the survival of hope in the climate of *desencanto* which followed the Transition in Spain. As the anarcha-feminist Peggy Kornegger argues, in the admittedly somewhat different North American context, although there is no immediate solution or formula for transformation of today's society, women must not lose hope or 'we [will] have already lost' (1979, 247). The model for Agua Fría, and perhaps the reader too, would seem to be the determined caterpillar who, like her mother, grandmother and great-grandmother before her, travels steadfastly up the tree trunk (T: 128). Change is an ongoing struggle which requires 'the courage to continue to create what we dream is possible' (Kornegger 1979, 247). Through the use of the fantastic, Montero highlights the power of the imagination and the need to engage with cultural myths in order to change social structures at their deepest level.

Once upon a time...

In *El nido de los sueños*, Gabriela's quest differs from that of Agua Fría, in that there is no sick kingdom to heal. The story is one of the personal development of an individual child.[43] However, the importance of children's literature in the complex process of socialisation should not be underestimated. For Madonna Kolbenschlag fairy tales are the 'bedtime stories of collective unconsciousness' in that, both as children and adults, we use them to give meaning to experience and to resolve conflicts (1983, 3). This analysis is based on Bruno Bettelheim's classic study of fairy tales as 'representing in imaginative form the process of human development' (1976, 12). The essential message of the fairy tale is that the child can succeed in overcoming obstacles and emerge victorious if steadfast in this struggle. In this way separation anxiety is overcome and infantile dependency wishes are relinquished.[44] However, as feminist critics such as Kolbenschlag (1983) and Ellen Cronan Rose (1983) have pointed out, in traditional fairy tales there tend to be very different developmental paradigms for boys and girls. Female characters usually stay at home, are patient and self-sacrificing and are often picked on; if they do wander off they get lost and need rescuing. Inevitably a prince comes along and either rescues the heroine or wakes her from her sleep in order that they may be married and live happily ever after. Cronan Rose uses the image of the mirror from Snow White, a male voice internalized by the female character of the stepmother, to discuss the internalization of such texts by the female reader. She concludes her brief study by arguing that it is time for the mirror to be shattered and for women to reinvent myths and fairy-tales. Indeed, Cronan Rose does discuss revisionary texts such as *Transformations* by Anne Sexton (1971), *Beginning with O* by Olga Broumas (1977), and *The Bloody Chamber* by Angela Carter (1979). However, these texts, and others such as the Attic collection of Fairytales for Feminists, are not intended for children.

In an interview given to Heymann and Mullor-Heymann, the author and editor Esther Tusquets -who herself has written a children's book *La conejita Marcela*- talks of the importance of what chidren read (1991, 44). Recent studies have noted the trend since the 1960s towards emancipatory texts in which children are encouraged to critically examine their reality and to gain a sense of self-esteem (Orquín 1983, 14; Polanco 1993, 14-15).[45] However, various articles published in the educational journal *Cuadernos de Pedagogía* in the 1970s analysed children's stories and found that they conformed to traditional gender dichotomies to a large extent (Rodríguez 1977, Cañellas et al 1979). Despite the publication of series such as 'A favor de las niñas', which the editor Tusquets describes as militant and feminist (Heymann & Mullor Heymann 1991, 44), it would seem that little has changed in the 1990s.[46] A recent article, in a special issue of *Cuaderno de la Literatura Infantil y Juvenil* devoted to feminist writing for children, complains of the relative scarcity of 'girls of paper' in genres which have traditionally been perceived as unfeminine such as science fiction and action adventures (Mañà 1992, 46-7). In an earlier issue of the same journal, the specialist in children's literature, Ana Garralón, argued that children should be encouraged to read texts which break with gender stereotypes such as *Ana Banana y yo*. In this novel a little boy relates how he wishes to be like Ana Banana because of her bravery and initiative (1990, 29).[47]

El nido de los sueños would seem to break with gender stereotypes in a similar fashion. The reviewer for *Cuaderno de la Literatura Infantil y Juvenil* described it as 'una apasionante novela iniciática' (an impassioned novel of initiation) which features adventure, surprise and humour (*CLIJ* 1992, 60). Its heroine, Gabriela -known as Gabi- does not conform to the fairy-tale paradigm of female development described by Kolbenschlag and Cronan Rose.[48] She is quite unlike traditional, feminine figures lost in the woods, such as Snow White who becomes a housewife and surrogate mother to the dwarves or Sleeping Beauty who passively awaits her Prince who will come and rescue her. Rather she is an active adventurer who sets out on a journey to self-actualization. Indeed, in her guise as Balbalú, she is regarded as the best warrior by the little boy knight they meet. Balbalú is described as 'fuerte, intrépida, infatigable; recorría sin miedo los mundos más extraños, hacía siempre lo que le antojaba y todas las personas, todas sin excepción, la amaban y admiraban' (strong, intrepid, untiring; she journeyed without fear through the strangest of worlds, she always did whatever she wanted and everybody, without exception, loved and admired her) (NS: 14).[49] Whereas in the real world, Gabi is left in the woods after a picnic and has to be rescued by her parents, in her imaginary world -as Balbalú- she enters the wood in order to discover her self. Balbalú can be seen to represent Gabriela's inner self or unconscious desires and the object of the quest appears to be the integration of Gabi and Balbalú as they are both revealed to be incomplete through the magic magnifying glass of the sympathetic witch detective, Mencar. Unlike in *Alice in*

Wonderland, the central question here would seem to be not 'Where am I?' but 'Who am I?'.

Both Kolbenschlag, in her analysis of fairy tales, and Pearson, in her analysis of the hero myth, interpret such narratives as representations of initiation rites or *rites de passage*. Thus the central protagonist is a character in a transitional or liminal period of life in which one identity is in the process of being shed but a new identity has not yet been attained. For example, as *Temblor* opens, Agua Fría is entering puberty. Although Gabriela is not an adolescent like Agua Fría, she is also a transitional character in that she is the sixth child in a family of eleven children. She belongs to neither the older nor younger group of five, but is considered an outsider by her siblings. In her study of child protagonists in Spanish children's literature, Mercedes Gómez del Manzano notes that since the 1960s there has been a tendency for protagonists to be marginal within their family and consequently to embark on a search for their identity (1987, 64-5). Gabi certainly feels rejected by her family and to compensate creates an imaginary world by renaming her surroundings. Language is again pivotal in this novel, as it was for the Anteriors in *Temblor* who transmitted important memories to their students through the act of renaming them. In this case, when Gabi renames her everyday surroundings she creates an imaginary landscape.[50] In the journey which is related, she is plunged into the imaginary world she has created which turns out to be very unpleasant and frightening: 'los países que había inventado resultaban ser, vividos desde dentro francamente siniestros' (the countries she had invented turned out to be, once lived in, quite frankly, sinister) (NS: 73). The only escape from the dangerous situations Balbalú finds herself in is to rip up the pieces of paper on which the names of each place are written. When the word is destroyed, so is the reality created through it indicating the importance of examining how identity is constructed and can therefore be deconstructed through discursive means.[51]

Gabi's journey, like Agua Fría's, is circular, as is indicated by the structure of the text and the chapter numbering. It begins with two chapters, I and II, situated in the contemporary, real world. This is followed by the section located in Gabriela's imaginary landscape in which chapters are numbered 1 to 8 and then we return to a second Chapter 1. The novel finishes with Chapter III, again located in the contemporary, real world. In Chapters 1 to 8, she encounters many perils which she overcomes with the aid of her travelling companions -Bicho, a stray dog and doña Macu, a chair- and various allies -the knight in shining armour, Mencar and her husband Merlin, a rather inept apprentice sorcerer. Her final challenge comes in the second Chapter 1.[52] This is the *juego de la oca*, a board game which includes the square of death which Gabi is clearly terrified of landing on.[53] However, the giant goose controlling the game tells her that playing is not just a question of luck. In a similar statement to that made by Océano in *Temblor*, the goose states that if Gabi desires something enough she will achieve it; having realised her worst nightmares, she can also realise her dreams. Gabi recognises that what she desires is to return home to her family and furthermore, that she has created this imaginary world in which they are travelling. Therefore, if she has the power to create it, she also should have the power to convert it back into reality. As doña Macu points out, it is Gabi who controls the game, 'Eso [la solución] sólo lo puedes saber tú. Fuiste tú quien inventó este juego y tú eres la dueña de tu vida' (Only you can know [the solution]. You invented this game and you are the owner of your own life) (NS: 139). She takes control by recognising the power of her imagination and her identity as Gabriela. Previously she had questioned who she was, as she saw herself sitting in her bedroom whilst trapped on a train rushing headlong to destruction:

¿No había visto allí, desde el tren, a otra Gabi asomada a la ventana? Y, entonces, si Gabi estaba allá, en su dormitorio, en su casa, en el antiguo mundo, ¿quién era ella, en realidad? ¿Balbalú? ¿Y quién diantres era Balbalú?.

Hadn't she seen from the train another Gabi at the window? And therefore, if Gabi was there, in her bedroom, in her house, in the old world, who was she, in truth? Balbalú? And who on earth was Balbalú? (NS: 127)

Thus Gabriela returns home by writing out her complete name, that is Gabriela as opposed to Gabi or Balbalú, for the first time. In this way she integrates her previously multiple selves.

However, as we have seen above, Gabriela's journey does not end there as the quest for self-discovery is a lifelong one. As *El nido de los sueños* closes, she is imagining the next place she will create, 'la próxima vez que nombre un lugar me inventaré un océano' (the next time I name a place I will invent an ocean) (NS: 146). The novel clearly foregrounds the importance for children of imaginative, creative play for the development of the self. This, along with the stimulation of a critical capacity of thought through the encouragement of curiosity and independence, is deemed a central feature of fantastic literature for children by several critics (Rodari 1977, 29-31; Egoff 1981, 80; Bortolussi 1985, 127; Cervera 1991, 72-4).

As Davies has noted, there are features of the text which make a feminist reading problematic (1994, 166). As the novel closes the patriarchal family unit is reaffirmed; its destruction, even though only imaginary, has been a negative experience for the female child. Furthermore, many difference feminists would posit the imaginary as the site of femininity because it lies outside patriarchal symbolic relations:

> Arguably, it is precisely to the chaotic, fluid and variable world of the unconscious and the feminine libidinal economy that the girl should look to undermine phallocentric constraints. (Davies 1994, 166)

However, in *El nido de los sueños*, the imaginary is shown to be a terrifying, dangerous place which the girl wishes to escape from. As Valls argues, the real world would seem more pleasurable and secure (1995, 99). Gabriela has discovered that the ideal self she had fantasised about, her beautiful and popular classmate Reyes, is not as happy as she had seemed. In fact she is deeply envious of Gabriela's apparent freedom and independence. Yet whilst the real world appears to be safer for the protagonist -after all, as Davies notes, it is only within the signifying chain of language that Gabriela can avoid psychosis and death (1994, 166)-, she nevertheless wishes to carry on inventing.[54] Also, elements of her imaginary world seemed to have crossed over with her into the real world. In the distance she hears a sound which could be the whistle of a train, despite the fact that in the real world there are no tracks in the vicinity of her flat. Furthermore, she has altered the dynamics of her family life in the real world. Upon her return, her parents are more attentive than they previously had been and consent for her to keep Bicho whereas theretofore they had been against the idea. Also her rather ordinary desk chair has been transformed into one reminiscent of doña Macu, giving her an immediate sense of security when she sits down. Thus positive results have been achieved from what seems to be a painful, negative process. It is also important to point out, as noted above, that Gabriela breaks with traditional paradigms for female development by being an active adventurer.

A Never-Ending Journey

As we have seen, the heroines Agua Fría and Gabriela both undertake a quest for their identity which comes to an open-ended conclusion. How might these quests be used to confront the crisis in identity politics addressed at the beginning of this chapter? Both are situated outside patriarchal structures in a fantasy world. Thus readers can distance themselves from those structures in order to examine them critically. *El nido de los sueños* provides a developmental paradigm for girls which breaks out of the traditional patterns described by Cronan Rose and Kolbenschlag and *Temblor* is also an emblematic tale but for adults: the reader develops associations between the fantasy world of the text and their experience outside it. When interviewed, Montero stated:

> Y efectivamente lo que yo quería hacer era una historia que fuera un poco como los cuentos infantiles, la fuerza que tienen de representación emblemática los cuentos infantiles, los buenos... *Caperucita roja*, pasan siglos y siguen contándose. ¿Por qué? Porque representan el mundo, o sea estos cuentos son un aprendizaje para los niños. Está el bien, está el mal, está el miedo... Bueno, yo quería hacer algo parecido pero para adultos, es decir una especie de cuento básico para adultos, de representación básica del mundo, efectivamente.

> In effect, what I wanted to create was a story like children's fairy tales, the strength of emblematic represenation which those tales have, well the good ones do... *Little Red Riding Hood*, centuries go by and people still tell those stories. Why? Because they represent the world, in other words those stories are a learning process for children. Good and evil are there, fear is there... Well, I wanted to create something similar for adults, a kind of basic story for adults, in effect, a basic representation of the world. (Knights 1993)

However, the text does not simply represent our world. Through the combination and deconstruction of cultural texts, it demonstrates how society and culture are constructed through language. The deferral of closure in the novel is suggested by the three riddles Agua Fría, must solve on her journey: 'Las aguas de un mismo río son siempre distintas' (The waters of the same river are always different), in other words not only is there difference between the sexes and diversity between women, but also within each individual; 'No entres en el corazón de las tinieblas sin haber salido antes' (Don't enter into the heart of darkness without having gone outside first), in order to change society one must think through radical alternatives or experience different forms of social organisation; 'Te convertirás en Dios si no cierras los ojos de tu mente' (You will become God if you don't close the eyes of your mind), each person must take charge of their own destiny with an open mind (T: 126). As the renegade priestess she encounters explains, the third enigma is a way of life: the recognition that there are no absolute truths (T: 166-7). Thus whilst traditional gender categories are broken down, no clear alternative is posited. Neither heroine achieves a unified, coherent identity as a result of their quest. Instead the formation of identity is revealed to be a continual process in which discursive practices are crucial. Ultimately, the novels do not set up a fixed or basic interpretation, unless of course this is the assertion made by Montero to Fajardo that in *Temblor* there is no revelation, as at the end no-one knows anything (1990, 100). Perhaps this is the revelation: knowledge is necessarily limited and partial.

As we follow Agua Fría from adolescent to mother-to-be, common forms of social organisation from our world are depicted in a critical manner and it is for the reader to discover, like Agua Fría, that it is possible to break out of the socio-cultural and discursive constructs that bind us. Thus we may embark on the journey, albeit at times a difficult one, of the continual process of discovery of the self. As Michael Ende said, when asked to comment on the success of *Die unendliche Geschichte* in Spain, fantastic novels are not works of evasion but journeys, for the reader as well as the protagonist, 'del que se vuelve con la conciencia cambiada a la realidad cotidiana' (from which one returns to daily life with a changed conscience) (Pereda 1982, 39).

[1] This leap into fantasy has its parallel in the epistemological leap beyond binary polarisations discussed in Chapter One.

[2] This move into fantasy is not exclusive to women's writing. Gullón notes that, particularly for a group of writers from the North-West of Spain, there has been a movement beyond mimetic realism and metafiction, 'buscan los complejos signos de lo real en contextos semánticos y significativos de mayor latitud donde todavía cuenta lo inasible, en una realidad agotada' (they search for the complex indications of the real in semantic contexts of greater latitude where the unreachable still counts, in an exhausted reality) (1987, 63).

[3] References to *Amado amo* will be denoted by AA, to *Temblor* by T, and to *El nido de los sueños* by NS, followed by the relevant page numbers.

[4] See Drinkwater (1995b) on the critique of the tenets upon which consumer society is founded in *Amado amo*.

[5] Characters are dehumanised in this predatory world. They are often referred to as animals, most consistently as dogs. It is an actual dog which causes César's public humiliation by masturbating on his leg.

[6] Pearson & Pope use the term 'hero' in preference to the term 'heroine' because they consider the latter, a diminutive form, to suggest a more passive character, that is to say a female protagonist in a supporting role (1981, vii). However, I prefer to rescue the term heroine because, as Pearson herself points out, the term hero tends to suggest the warrior archetype, which although useful in the quest for identity, is a somewhat limiting view of the hero myth (1991, 7). For another account contrasting the modern male anti-hero and the female novel of development see Ferguson (1983).

[7] For a detailed analysis of César's relationships with women and the dynamics of power involved, see Arribas (1991).

[8] For evidence of continued inequalities in the workplace see Sallé & Casas (1986, 96); Calle Fuentes, González Romero & Núñez Triguero (1988, 113); Aguilar (1995); Cañas (1996).

[9] This sense of entrapment is heightened in *Amado amo* through the manipulation of physical space to encode power relations (Davies 1994, 146-7).

[10] Davies notes the circular structure of each novel and in the case of *Temblor* refers to Glenn's review of the novel which sees this as demonstrating a particular affinity with the work of Le Guin (1991b, 401), as do Bértolo (1990) and Piñol (1990).

[11] Indeed, as Davies notes, whilst *Temblor* does have a fantastic framework, it could be deemed less experimental in style than the earlier novels in that it follows an established narrative pattern (1994, 153).

[12] In an article directed to feminist critics who have rejected archetypal criticism as inherently flawed because of Jung's dualistic assumptions about the masculine and the feminine, Annis Pratt argues that the insights afforded into the workings of the human psyche should not be rejected out of hand. She concludes by arguing for a criticism which analyses both 'external-material and internal-psychic components of women's experience' as depicted in literature (1973, 14). Sadoff (1978) gives a useful brief overview of the dualistic assumptions relating to Jung's anima/animus and goes on to discuss how women can reappropriate and transform the landscape of mythology.

[13] Clear synopses of both texts are provided in Valls (1995) but there are some inaccuracies e.g. he does not seem to realise that the Uma world is also vanishing into the mist.

[14] Zatlin lists the various Gothic themes which are incorporated and subverted in *Temblor*: threatening space, entrapment in a looming building, nightmarish quality, an orphaned protagonist who is both victim and heroine and solves a mystery to protect others (1993, 119-22). The clearest subversion is of the ending in which Agua Fría does not gain a husband, family and home of her own. Her husband is killed and she carries on travelling, pregnant but alone.

[15] In general women writers are barely referred to in studies of the genre in Spain: J I Ferreras (1972): María Guera, L Núñez Ladavese (1976): none, C Saiz Cidoncha (1988): Guera and Araujo.

[16] See the stories 'Minnie', 'La Dama Dragón', 'Sagrada' and 'Piel'. Full references for these can be found in Robles Moreno's study.

[17] A similar trajectory has been traced by Pamela Annas in Anglo-American women-authored narrative in the 1960s and 1970s (1978). Montero has made the argument for a ten year time lag with respect to writing by Spanish women as opposed to their AngloAmerican counterparts due to their particular socio-political situation (Knights 1993).

[18] See Kress (1981), Eichler (1981), Kessler (1984), Green & Lefanu (1985), Bossert (1987), Fitting (1987), Pfaelzer (1988), King (1991), Bonner (1992).

[19] A similar concept was developed by Frabetti in Spain in 1976 to refer to the 'poder distanciador y desrutinizador' (power to destabilise and go beyond routine) of science fiction (Núñez Ladavese 1976, 127).

[20] See also Morgan (1978), Russ (1981) and Patai (1983).

[21] This analysis is based on Robert Scholes' notion of 'structural fabulation' as discussed by Bossert (1987, 142-4).

[22] This difficulty was evident at the one day conference on fantasy, science fiction and fiction of the unreal at which this chapter was first presented as a paper. Participants failed to agree on a working definition of the concept.

[23] This critique is taken up by Pérez (1986) and Risco (1982 & 1987).

[24] Indeed, Emilio Ortega, when discussing the value of fantastic literature for children, describes it as 'un contacto cogniscitivo con la realidad' (a cognitive contact with reality) (1989, 39).

[25] See Talbot (1989) on the fantastic works of Cristina Fernández Cubas and Davies (1992) on the fantastic in contemporary European fiction by women.

[26] Thomas Franz interprets the novel as specifically criticising monastic regimens and worn out theology based on an unprovable God (1993, 268 & 277). This would seem a rather narrow view.

[27] I am grateful to the composer Dr. Agustín Fernández of the Department of Music of the University of Newcastle for his elucidation of Marisa Manchado's notes to the libretto of the opera.

[28] Franz draws on Tolkien for example whilst Montero has stated explicitly that she does not have an interest in his works (Fajardo 1990, 100). Like Valls, he misreads the text at various junctures ignoring the importance of the destruction of the crystals through collaboration between Agua Fría and Torbellino and claiming that the victors in the final struggle are fanatical adherents of Agua Fría from the Uma. In fact they seem to be led by a character called El Negro and comprise people from throughout society.

[29] The sources listed by Franz (1993) are: *The Wizard of Oz, Star Wars, Die unendliche Geschichte, The Handmaid'sTale, The Heart of Darkness, Il nome della rosa, 1984*, Wagner's Ring Cycle, the philosophy of Thomas Aquinas, Dante, Milton, Falangist rhetoric and Tibetan geography. *The Wizard of Oz* is also cited, along with *Alice in Wonderland*, by García Padrino as a source for *El nido de los sueños* (1992, 563).

[30] For discussions of the possibilities and limitations of the most common forms of social organisation proposed by feminist science fiction writers, see Sargent (1975), Annas (1978), Eichler (1981), Russ (1981), Mellor (1982), Schweickart (1983), Kessler (1984), Somay (1984), Izquierdo & Borras (1984 & 1987), Stimpson (1991), Bonner (1992).

[31] For example electricity is no longer known. It is interesting to note that the future society depicted in *La función delta* was also dystopic.

[32] The relationship between memory and life is taken up in similar episodes in both *Te trataré como a una reina* and *Temblor*. In the former Bella attempts without success to remember the house of her childhood and realises that she has lost the past and cannot recuperate it, whilst in the

latter Agua Fría returns to her house after her mother has died only to realise that she cannot remember designs on the roof of the bedroom. Characters in *Temblor* struggle to preserve the world from the mists of oblivion by fixing reality with the aid of a technique known as the *mirar preservativa* (preservative look). According to the flyleaf of *Temblor*, the source for the novel was Montero's inability to remember the pattern of the floortiles upon which she played as a child, causing her to confront the Berkleyan dilemma of what would happen if the world only existed if someone was thinking about it. She mentions this incident in various interviews (Fajardo 1990, Méndez 1990, Piñol 1990).

[33] Davies notes the paradoxically phallic nature of Talapot (1994, 151).

[34] Montero does not tend to explore the possibilities of homosexual relationships in resignifying gender identity. Homosexual characters like Cecilio in *Crónica del desamor* fail in their relationships because the latter seem modelled on heterosexual patterns.

[35] This is recognised by Gascón Vera's problematic analysis of the novel (1992) which is self-contradictory, describing *Temblor* as pacifist, ecological, reclaiming nature and reproduction, whilst also emphasising the culturally constructed character of gender relations. It seems to be an attempt to align Montero with both radical difference feminism and socialist feminism. The point of reversing dominant structures would also seem to be misunderstood as an abandonment of difference through reappropriation to the masculine, rather than a parodic inversion.

[36] This term is taken from the futurist Dennis Livingston (1978, 163).

[37] For an account of anarcha-feminism see the following essays: Ehrlich (1979a & b), Kornegger (1979), Leighton (1979) and Tower Sargent (1983). Gascón Vera (1992), in her analysis of *Temblor*, relates anarchist social theory to chaos theory in science in which a small difference in a single parameter can cause a non-linear system to exhibit chaotic behaviour (Hofstadter 1981; Cvitanovic 1984).

[38] For further discussion of Mujeres Libres during the Civil War see Kaplan (1971 & 1977), Lamberet (1975), Nash (1975), Pino (1976), Ruiperes (1979) and Ackelsberg (1985).

[39] When Montero was asked whether she considered *Temblor* to be an anarchist work she replied that although she had not set out to write a specifically anarchist work, she did feel this blend of individualist tendencies and social action, albeit difficult, to be a basic preoccupation of hers (Knights 1993). It becomes central to the novel *La hija del caníbal* in which one of the main protagonists is an ageing anarchist.

[40] This also occurs in *Bella y oscura* when Airelai attempts to cast a curse through the power of Amanda's menstrual blood (BO: 128).

[41] Arribas examines the importance of the mother figure in *Amado amo* (1991, 351). During his childhood, César's mother seemed a magical figure capable of transforming his life through the stories she told.

[42] For Buiza the typical science fiction hero also tends not to integrate into society (1972, 51).

[43] Various commentators have noted the prevalence of the quest in modern children's literature (Gil 1984, 42; Cerrilo & García Padrino 1990, 75; García Padrino 1992, 553).

[44] For Davies, *El nido de los sueños* can be categorised as an uncanny tale in which unconscious anxieties are objectified (1994, 162).

[45] Other trends noted by Orquín include utopian and anti-authoritarian texts (1983, 14-15).

[46] This series is cited by González Rubio, in a review of children's literature for the feminist journal *Poder y Libertad*, as being one in which girls are also adventurous (1990, 22).

[47] A catalogue, entitled *Érase una vez una niña...*, has been brought out to list books in which girls are not identified with traditional feminine roles.

[48] Montero has since written two more novels explicitly commissioned for children by Alfaguay: *Las barbaridades de Bárbara* and *El viaje fantástico de Bárbara*. Bárbara is a similarly bold heroine. These texts are more simplistic and aimed at a younger reading public. However, they also focus on the potential deceptiveness of appearances and the power of dreams and imagination. In the first Bárbara comes to realise that if your desire is strong enough it will be fulfilled and in the second she travels through a parallel universe with her firends Tulipa and Borán. They are accompanied by a book, el señor Libro in a journey in which the boundaries between the real world and dreams are dissolved.

[49] Agua Fría also has two names, her birth name is Talika.

[50] Senabre (1992) interprets the novel as an allegory for verbal creation.

[51] Montero has stated the importance of naming as a form of imposing meaning. See 'Nomenclaturas' (1994a, 137-8). The power to name and unname is associated with the power to affirm the self.

[52] See Held (1987, 85) and López Tamés (1990, 54) on the animism of young children and the subsequent use of animals as ideal interlocutors for children in fantasy.

[53] This game, now converted into a television series, is one of chance with an unlimited number of players.

[54] This is a point stressed by Montero in her interview with Davies. She also notes that desires, as discussed in Chapter Four with relation to the bolero, cannot be realised (1993, 384).

EPILOGUE

WORDS CREATE WORLDS: NARRATIVES OF IDENTITY IN *BELLA Y OSCURA* AND *LA HIJA DEL CANÍBAL*[1]

La identidad, primero, son miles de identidades que nosotros cosemos para hacer el espejismo de una sola y no sólo no nos posee sino que nosotros creamos la identidad. [...] La identidad es lo que narramos de nosotros mismos.

Identity, first of all, consists of thousands of identities which we stitch together to create the illusion of a unique one and not only does it not possess us but we create identity. [...] Identity is what we narrate about ourselves. (Montero in Knights 1998)

In this epilogue, I would like to conclude by discussing briefly how Rosa Montero's most recent novels, *Bella y oscura* (1993) and *La hija del caníbal* (1997), would seem to synthesise many of the issues examined in previous chapters. In particular they explicitly focus on how identity or rather identities are constructed through a narrative process. Stylistically, both would seem to merge the hyperrealism of *Te trataré como a una reina* with the fantastic elements of *Temblor*. In *Bella y oscura*, the first person narrator, known only by her nickname Baba, recounts a period of her childhood when she lived in the marginal 'Barrio' -an urban neighbourhood populated by violent underworld characters- with her grandmother doña Bárbara, her uncle Segundo and aunt Amanda, her cousin Chico, and the Lilliputian dwarf Airelai.[2] This period comes to an abrupt end when Baba's father Máximo returns to reclaim money stolen from him by Segundo. In several interviews, Montero has stated that she has a preference for depicting marginal urban areas because in the 'mundo canalla' (underworld) reality seems more vivid and immediate, whilst fantasy is necessary to cope with the pain of existence (Frade 1993, López 1993, Plaza 1993, Ortega 1993, Rodríguez 1993, Villena 1997, 36).[3] Although fantasy is used as a coping mechanism, Montero denies that it is escapist, arguing that it helps us to reach a deeper understanding of reality. She criticises realist literature as limiting reality as the latter also incorporates fantasies and desires. In *Bella y oscura* the magical element is introduced into the text through the character of Airelai who tells stories of a mysterious past in the Orient and performs charms and curses. However, Montero has denied that her novel has anything to do with the 'magical realism' of Latin American authors such as Gabriel García Márquez or Isabel Allende (Davies 1993, 385).[4] This is a predominantly realist novel in that it is set in a time and location not unlike the present.[5] Furthermore, the magic is confined to Airelai's stories and the narrator's belief in them as the charms do not seem to have any effect on other characters. Alicia Giménez Bartlett, in her review of the novel for *El Mundo*, criticises the fact that it is only these two characters -and perhaps the grandmother with her strange habits such as celebrating her 'deathday'- who are touched by magic (1993, 11).[6] Yet this is perhaps to be expected, as Baba is a child for whom anything is possible and Airelai, one of the many dwarves who feature in Montero's novels. She is neither adult nor child but both. The magical elements of the novel would seem to underscore the point that truth is relative; reality is what we narrate and therefore open to a multiplicity of interpretations which prevent narrative closure. The narrator observes the appearance of her Lucky Star in the sky, as predicted by Airelai, and prepares to begin a new life. Here Montero again makes use of effective ironic juxtaposition of accounts, as in the previous chapter, we have learnt that this star was actually the bomb which exploded upon the aircraft carrying both Airelai and Máximo, the two people Baba loves most.[7] This final event encapsulates the beauty and horror of life referred to in the title of the novel which approximate to Montero's seemingly paradoxical existential concerns which are evident in all of her novels: instances of beauty such as the star demonstrate the capacity to dream a better future and the daily horrors of life in the Barrío reflect existential angst. There are multiple references to both beauty and horror in *La hija del caníbal* in which the octagenarian Félix comes to the optimistic conclusion that 'la belleza siempre existe, incluso en el horror' (beauty always exists even in horror) (HC: 318). In both novels fantasy becomes a tool which, along with romance, is used in an attempt to fill the existential void felt by the characters (Montero to Rodríguez, 1993).

La hija del caníbal, whilst clearly situated in the contemporary moment in a Spain rocked by scandals and corruptions, is again not a straightforward realist text. It would seem to be a hybrid novel in that reviewers have found it difficult to categorise. It has been described as 'un relato criminal con ribetes de fantaficción' (a crime story with elements of fanta-fiction) in the style of Baroja (Sanz Villanueva 1997, 12), 'novela negra' (detective novel) (Villena 1997, 36), 'entre thriller policiaco y la novela de iniciación [...] en la madurez' (between a crime thriller and novel of initiation into maturity) with Gothic touches (García Posada 1997, 17). Whilst there is a clear process of initiation, the protagonist is not an adolescent as in *Temblor* or reaching puberty as in *El nido de los sueños*. Lucía is facing a quite different *rites de passage* into her forties in which her beliefs about the life narrative that she has constructed for herself thus far are called into question. The novel begins with the disappearance of Lucía's husband, a seemingly exemplary civil servant, from the toilets in Barajas airport. He turns out to have been kidnapped and what follows is an often blackly comical account of Lucía's attempts to trace him with the help of two of her neighbours: Félix, an anarchist in his eighties who was part of Durruti's gang of anarchists who pulled off a series of daring bank raids in Latin America in the 1920s and the twentysomething Adrián with whom she ends up having an intense affair.[8] The present day action, narrated by Lucía, takes place mostly in Madrid but also other locations such as Amsterdam in which the three main protagonists meet a variety of marginal characters involved with criminal activities. Interwoven with the mystery of Ramón's kidnapping is the narration by Félix of his youth as an anarchist and bullfighter.[9] This is clearly based in historical fact as stated in the foreword to the novel and the decision to make Félix a bullfighter, like Montero's father, is partially due to her desire to rescue bullfighters like Teófilo Hidalgo and Primitivo Ruiz from oblivion. However, it also corresponds to a stylistic preference already evident in *Te trataré como a una reina* and *Bella y oscura*, Montero describes the life of a bullfighter in the 1930s as rough and marginal, without the genteel middle-class varnish of convention (Clos 1997). However, in various sections relating events involving anarchist activists, names have been changed and fact combined with fiction. Furthermore as Montero herself states, it is difficult to separate the two and 'la realidad es una materia vidriosa que se empeña en imitar la ficción' (reality is a glassy material which insists on imitating fiction) (1997a, 8). In a novel in which the main narrator, Lucía, deliberately lies to the reader and characters swap and conceal their identities it becomes increasingly difficult to decipher what is real. As in *Bella y oscura* reality is seen to incorporate dreams, desires, fantasies and the imagination (Montero in Polo 1997, 5). Both novels stress the importance of discourse as a tool for interpreting reality and the existence of an objective reality divorced from the narrative process is called into question (Montero in Polo 1997, 5).

The boundary between fiction and reality is blurred through the lack of distinction between the acts of remembering and inventing. In the opening sentence of *Bella y oscura* the first-person narrator, Baba, questions the reliability of her own memory about events which she witnessed:

> De lo que voy a contar yo fui testigo: de la traición de la enana, del asesinato de Segundo, de la llegada de la Estrella. Sucedió todo en una época de mi infancia que ahora ya no sé si rememoro o invento: porque para entonces para mí aún no se había despegado el cielo de la tierra y todo era posible.[10]

> Of what I am about to tell I was a witness: of the betrayal of the dwarf, the murder of Segundo, the arrival of the Star. It all happened in a period of my childhood which I no longer know whether I am remembering or inventing: because for me back then the sky hadn't come unstuck from the earth yet and everything was possible. (BO: 5)

When the reader reaches the final two sections of the novel which actually recount the events detailed in the opening sentence of the novel, they discover that the narrator was not actually present at all as a witness, but was told what had happened by her cousin Chico. Indeed, a variety of accounts is present throughout the novel, albeit focalised through the narration by Baba. As doña Bárbara explains to her, 'Cuando yo nací [...] empezó el mundo' (When I was born [...] the world began) (BO: 5). We later learn that this is more than just an explanation of the beginning of time to an inquisitive young child. Doña Bárbara believes that each person creates their own world through the language they use and that that particular world dies with them (BO: 73). This is reminiscent of the physical fading away of the world in *Temblor* which can only be prevented through the preserving look, discussed in Chapter Six. Doña Bárbara has her own particular form of preserving memory through naming her cats after the dead in the graveyard she visits. Not only does she create her own world through language but her memories keep her alive. When her mementoes are destroyed in the second fire started by Segundo, she physically shrinks in stature and eventually dies. Thus Montero returns in this novel to the themes of the ambiguity of memory, the recognition of the partiality of each person's perspective and the construction of life narratives as a means of imposing meaning on the experiential world.

Indeed, the creation of a particular world through language is a recurrent theme in *Bella y oscura* through the stories which Airelai recounts. Her first story, in which she recounts the downfall of the man who taught her the art of storytelling, illustrates both the power and danger of language. Not only do words create worlds, but they also create and recreate people:

Lo que nos diferencia de los criaturas inferiores es que nosotros somos capaces de contarnos, e incluso de inventarnos, nuestra propia existencia.

(What differentiates us from inferior creatures is that we are capable of telling ourselves, and even inventing for ourselves, our own existence) (BO: 22)

The textual nature of life as narrative is reflected in the use of theatrical and cinematic metaphors in this novel, as in previous novels. This is particularly true of two key scenes in the novel which are represented as performative acts: after Segundo's imposing re-appearance at the Barrio's 'verbena', the narrator matter-of-factly states, 'Fin de primer acto' (End of the first act) (BO:106); and the climactic ending to the story, in which Airelai shoots Segundo on the stage, resembles a film for the observing Chico (BO: 191). Words can also act as protective charms or destructive curses: Chico repeating the words 'Estoy dormido' (I am asleep) to block out the sound of his parents fighting; the narrator's name for herself, Baba, which comforts her in moments of need; Airelai's magic against el Portugués. Language is Airelai's magic, a power extraordinarily granted to her in the womb so that she was able to speak before she was born. However, her tales can be used to deceive and her magic is shown to be nothing more than an illusion just like the fake knives used in Segundo's stage act. Nevertheless, throughout the novel, as in the story of her elevation to the status of a 'katami', a child goddess, the question is addressed of what is actually more real: the narration of the event or the event itself (BO: 81-2)? The narrator notes the importance of Airelai's stories and states her conviction that life would adapt itself to them (BO: 52). In this text narration does not represent reality, rather it shapes and creates it. Consequently reality cannot be fixed due to the multiplicity of interpretations possible for every text.[11] Ultimately, as Airelai states, knowledge is relative and it is impossible to know everything (BO: 96). As the alternative paradise myth recounted by Airelai concludes, desire and a feeling of incompletion are fundamental to the human condition. In the origin myth recounted there were two categories of being who are not divided by gender. Couples consisted of giants who carried dwarves on their shoulders. These couples lived in perfect harmony in an eternal present with no need for language to understand each other until one day one of the dwarves felt the need to remember the moments of pleasure experienced with its giant and painted the scene on a piece of bark. From that moment on the dwarf began to feel increasingly dissatisfied as the present did not seem to match up to memories of the past. Consumed by desire and angst, language was created with the words, 'Quiero que me digas que me quieres' (I want you to tell me that you love me) (BO: 181). This first enunciation of language caused the expulsion from paradise characterised by a sense of loss, 'la palabra nos hizo desdichados y humanos' (the word made us miserable and human) (BO: 181).

The concept of identity as a narrative process which defies completion is explored in *La hija del caníbal*. In this clearly metafictional text there are two first person narrators, Lucía and Félix who both interject comments on the narrative process. Lucía is a highly self-conscious narrator, being a writer by profession, who at times displaces herself into the third person through which she perceives her identity as a performative act, 'a veces a Lucía Romero le parece estar contemplándose desde el exterior como si fuese la protagonista de una película o de un libro; y en esos momentos suele hablar de sí misma en tercera persona con el mayor descaro' (sometimes Lucía Romero feels as if she were contemplating herself from outside as if she were the protagonist of a film or a book; in those instances she tends to talk about herself in the third person with bare-faced cheek)

(HC: 21). Events are explicitly described in terms of performances or role playing: 'escena típica de película negra' (typical scene from a film noir) (HC: 52), 'llevábamos toda la novela así [...] mi piso era un escenario teatral en el que se representaba un vodevil, con personas entrando y saliendo todo el tiempo y cada uno diciendo un parlamento previamente acordado' (we had spent the whole novel like that [...] my flat was a theatre stage upon which a vaudeville was being played, with people coming and going all the time and each one saying previously agreed lines) (HC: 294). Lucía is highly self-aware and relates her thoughts about the narrative process to the search for her own identity which takes place in parallel to her search for her missing husband. She realises that whilst the construction of identity is a continual process, the never-ending story referred to previously in this study, identity itself is discontinuous despite our attempts to maintain a stable, coherent sense of self. For Lucía identity is 'un tejido discontinuo que zurcimos a fuerza de voluntad y de memoria' (a discontinuous fabric which we darn with the strength of our will and memory) (HC: 51). It is in perpetual mutation and the only thing which remains immutable is the determination to believe that our identity remains the same (HC: 52). However, Lucía, like her namesake in *La función delta*, expresses uncertainty about her memories and admits that occasionally she lacks the ability to distinguish between her memories, dreams, imagination and the memories of others who have told her their stories. These all blend together in an imaginary simulacra of life in which the past, present and future are disconnected in a state of ambiguity and insecurity:

> En realidad, yo no soy la que fui ni la que seré; como mucho, no soy más que este instante de conciencia en la negrura y ni siquiera estoy segura de ser eso, porque a menudo me veo a mí misma desdoblada.
>
> In reality, I am not the one I was nor the one I will be; at the most, I am no more than this instance of consciousness in the blackness and I'm not even sure that I'm that because I often see myself split into two. (HC: 52)

However, Lucía Romero, unlike Lucía Ramos who was angry at the imputation that she might be falsifying her memoirs, freely admits to further complicating this process by deliberately lying or embellishing the truth. The reader is placed on their guard on the first page of the second chapter when the narrator confesses that 'no he hecho nada más que empezar y ya he mentido' (I've only just begun and I've already lied) (HC: 17). She reiterates this point as the novel draws to its conclusion, 'He mentido. Llevo escritas cientos de páginas para este libro y he mentido en ellas casi tantas veces como en mi propia vida' (I've lied. I've written hundreds of pages for this book and I've lied almost as many times in them as I have in my own life) (HC: 310-1). On the one hand, lying, like fantasy, is a way of facing up to the existential void, 'Aquí estoy inventando verdades y recordando mentiras para no disolverme en la nada absoluta' (Here I am, inventing truths and remembering lies in order not to dissolve into the absolute nothingness) (HC: 316). On the other hand it is the basic human way of coming to terms with experience through a process of reordering and reinventing. At first Lucía uses it as a stylistic recourse to make her narrative more interesting, for example changing the date of her husband's disappearance from the 30th to the 28th December, the Day of the Innocents (the Spanish equivalent of April Fools Day), to heighten the irony when the reader finally discovers that the kidnapping is an elaborate hoax. However, she comes to realise that this creative process is a basic human activity, 'para poder ser, los humanos nos tenemos previamente que *contar*. La identidad no es más que el relato que nos hacemos de nostros mismos' (in order to be, as humans we have to *tell* ourselves beforehand. Identity is no more than the tale we tell ourselves about ourselves) (HC: 17).

This celebration of ambivalence is also evident in the treatment of gender issues in *Bella y oscura*. Carlos Otero (1993) criticises Montero for allowing her feminist beliefs to hang around the novel like a dead weight. His schematic description of the female characters as representing spirituality and the male characters as representing brutality, whilst reflecting various statements made in the novel, oversimplifies the issue. Several incidents in the novel contradict this traditional categorisation of gender difference. None of the characters are black or white, or rather, as the title indicates, they are both. Even the brutal Segundo, who abuses his wife and child, is vulnerable, probably due to the fact that his mother evidently preferred his older brother as is clearly indicated in their respective names: Segundo and Máximo. At one point Segundo bursts out crying when his son, Chico, refuses to sit with him and listen to a story. A further incident which belies the brutality of the male characters is the murder of Segundo. Máximo does not kill his brother, despite the fact that he has betrayed him and probably been responsible for the death of his wife. It is the supposedly spiritual Airelai who cold-bloodedly shoots the defenceless Segundo in the head.

Nonetheless, one episode which would seem to indicate the spirituality of not only women but children too, is the night when Segundo and doña Bárbara have temporarily left. Airelai and Amanda waken the children to dance and jump through the house, laughing and smiling. In contrast to the Barrio which is safe by day and dangerous by night, the house seems beautiful and comforting in the light of the moon. The atmosphere is dreamlike and according to Airelai this can only be appreciated by women and children, as male children forget who they are when they grow up (BO: 47). This would seem to indicate an equating of women with the imaginary and men with rationality, as would Baba's interest in Airelai's esoteric knowledge as opposed to Chico's streetwise knowledge of the rules of survival in the Barrio. It could be argued that in this episode the feminine is given a fairly traditional characterization as magical, associated with night-time and nature. However, as demonstrated in interviews, Montero's position in this regard problematises such neat distinctions. She revalues the traditional strengths of matriarchal figures whilst negating a return to the role of housewife (Knights 1994). It is doña Bárbara who defends the family from attack by the thugs, el Portugués and el Tiburón, and indeed Chico aspires to be like her when he grows up, rather than like his father or mother.[12] She is yet another example of an ambivalent mother figure, neither good nor bad, like Océano and Oxígeno in *Temblor*, she can be loving, cruel, powerful and weak.

Airelai actually supports the family through prostitution, not magic as Baba believed. It could be argued that this serves to approximate her to the body, and she does describe the difference between men and women in categories which suggest the binary dichotomy traditionally drawn between the genders in Western patriarchal societies:

> Hay un poder que poseen todas las mujeres aunque no lo sepan, que es el poder del tránsito a la vida y a la muerte, la sangre y de lo que carece de palabras; así como hay un poder que poseen todos los hombres incluso si lo ignoran, que es el poder del óxido y del hierro, de la causalidad y del territorio.

> There is a power which all women possess although they may not know it, it is the power of transition into life and death, blood and that which lacks words; just as there is a power which all men possess even if they ignore it, it is the power of rust and iron, causality and territory. (BO: 125-6)

This radical statement of difference which inscribes women in the realm of the body and the semiotic, would seem to be easily assimilable to a rather conservative complementarity. When interviewed, Montero stated that this comparison is a verbalisation of how the sexes are traditionally symbolised, rather than a description of how they should be perceived (Knights 1993). Certainly the characters in the novel cannot be categorised so easily in terms of clear-cut binaries. For example, it is evident that Airelai's power comes not from a lack of words, but precisely from the manipulation of discourse. It derives from language which is supposedly masculine. In contrast, this statement precedes an episode in which Amanda and Airelai try to bewitch Segundo by making him drink Amanda's menstrual blood. Airelai expounds upon the power of women's blood, subverting the traditional taboos surrounding menstruation which were discussed in *Crónica del desamor*, by reclaiming them as a source of strength for women. However, the charm fails to work and Airelai concedes that women have changed:

> — Es que las chicas de ahora sois distintas — reflexionaba la enana —. Ya no funcionan las antiguas costumbres, ya no sirven los conjuros tradicionales. Es curioso: tu sangre ya no marchita y ya no cura. Sois seres mutantes.
>
> "Girls today are different", reflected the dwarf, "The old ways don't work anymore, the traditional spells are no use. It's strange: your blood doesn't wither or cure anymore. You're mutant beings. (BO: 128)

She later states that Amanda has not only lost the traditional power that women had in the past, but that she does not know what she has gained. This would reflect the ambivalence felt towards feminism in a society in which women were traditionally cast in the role of domestic matriarch. In this role they were potentially a source of positive power both within the family and within communities in which there existed a sense of pride in being a woman. There would seem to be a lack of role models for Amanda, a young mother, to follow: Airelai does have a strong sense of self-worth and her own potential but by her own admission she is unable to have children; doña Bárbara may be strong in the face of physical danger but she is a cruel mother. Nonetheless, the possible positive value of the mother-child bond is suggested through the close relationship between Amanda and her son Chico. Indeed, with Baba, they are the only characters left alive at the end of the novel.

The issue of maternity is again central to *La hija del caníbal* as a focal part of Lucía's fortysomething crisis is the realisation that she is a daughter who will never be a mother. Early on in the novel she states that she is not fulfilling the biological imperative that all creatures have to procreate (HC: 20). However, the key familial relationship is between Lucía and her father. It is clearly Oedipal with Lucía describing her father throughout as the cannibal who does not allow her to develop until she confronts him at the close of the novel. She realises that the image she has constructed of her parents does not correspond to that recounted by her father and comes to realise that her notions of parenting are of a constructed nature and can therefore be deconstructed. Identity is shown to be both relational and contextually bound. By recognising the partiality of her interpretation of her parent's identity, she liberates herself from the 'mirada umbilical [de la] mentirosa memoria hijocentrista' (umbilical outlook of lying childcentric memory) (HC: 335). She thus becomes free to assume all aspects of her identity, unfettered by previously constructed paradigms, and accepts it as both confused and extraordinary (HC: 337).

Both of these texts clearly focus on discursive practice to examine how we come to terms with our identity through the narrative process. The multiple narratives recounted question the concept of reality by blurring distinctions between fantasy and the real, history and fiction to invoke the ambivalence and complexity of signifying identity which cannot be hypostatised in fixed paradigms.

---

[1] Montero stresses the creative power of words and the importance of naming in the three interviews included in the appendix. this was picked up on by Sanz Villanueva in his review of *la hija del caníbal*, referring to both *Bella y oscura* and *La hija del caníbal*, he says, 'las palabras crean mundos y el relato de un suceso es más real que la realidad' (words create worlds and the story of an event is more real than the reality) (1997, 12).

² Most reviewers would seem to think that the narrator is actually a child. This has led some to marvel at the tone achieved and others, most notably Senabre, to criticise the rich use of metaphors and similes that seem beyond a child's capability. However, the opening of the novel, with its references to the act of remembering and instances in the text when the narrator referes to herself as 'la niña', point to an adult narrator narrating through a child's perspective. This is borne out by Montero in an interview with José Plaza (1993, 53).

³ Only two of the Spanish reviewers seemed to feel that this mix was not successful: Alicia Giménez Bartlett and Carlos Otero.

⁴ The book jacket of the first Seix Barral edition of the novel features the painting 'The Street' by George Grosz. For Davies, this would seem to indicate a connection with 'magical realism' in that the term was coined by German expressionists (1994, 167).

⁵ There are differences with contemporary Spanish society in that for example prostitution is depicted as legal within licensed red-light areas.

⁶ Giménez Bartlett concludes that this is not a magical realist text and instead notes the similarities with the work of Valle Inclán and Martín Santos (1993, 11).

⁷ According to Montero the central themes of the novel are the beauty and horror of life, death, lost innocence and the force of words through which we construct our lives (Plaza 1993, 52). The moments of beauty, however, are few and fleeting. In this novel, as in *La función delta* and *Temblor*, they are linked to an instance of overwhelming love which causes characters to forget momentarily their basic condition of solitude. In *Amado amo* César experiences a similar sensation when he is with his dying mother and tries to capture it, but fails, through painting.

⁸For historical accounts of Durruti and los Errantes see Ferrer (1985), Elorza (1995), Paz (1996), Taibo (1998),

⁹ The decision to make Fortuna an anarchist is described by Montero in Knights (1997). Her affinity with anarchist ideology is described in an interview about *La hija del caníbal* in terms similar to those used when questioned about *Temblor* (Knights 1994), 'Sempre m'he sentit a prop de l'anarquism, comparteixo aquest cant a l'individualism, al criteri propi, al desenvolupament cultural, la critica radical al poder' (I've always felt close to anarchism, I share the hymn to individualism, to using your own judgement, cultural development, the radical critique of power' (Clos 1997).

¹⁰ References to *Bella y oscura* will be denoted by BO followed by the relevant page numbers.

¹¹ Montero herself has stated how readers have interpreted her novels in a wide variety of ways (J.C. 1993, 35).

[12] Echoing the Oedipal scenario, Chico fears that his father would kill him if he knew he wanted to be like him (BO: 137).

CONCLUSION

PARADOXICAL AND SHIFTING IDENTITIES

> La gente normalmente entiende por realidad, o por realismo en literatura sobre todo, algo que no es más que un torpe costumbrismo. Para mí, la realidad es algo muchísimo más complejo: la realidad es lo mensurable, lo tangible, lo exterior, pero también es los sueños, los miedos, los deseos. Es todas las dimensiones del ser. Las dimensiones del ser son enormes y plurales y paradójicas y además se dan a la vez lo que es y lo que no es. Entonces para mí, buscar vías fantásticas no es más que una manera más profunda, más compleja, menos limitadora de reflejar la realidad.
>
> **People normally understand by the term reality, or above all realism in literature, something which is nothing more than a clumsy *costumbrismo*. For me, reality is something much much more complex: reality is what can be measured, the tangible, the external, but it is also dreams, fears, desires. It is all these facets of being. The facets of being are vast and plural and paradoxical and besides at the same time what is and what is not coexist. Therefore for me, searching for fantastic paths is nothing more than a more profound, more complex, less limiting way of reflecting reality. (Montero in Knights 1994)**

Throughout this study a variety of discursive practices used within the narrative of Rosa Montero have been examined for their relevance to identity politics In Chapter One this narrative was set within the context of contemporary narrative written by Spanish women and the theorisation of identity by Spanish feminists. It was argued that the trend which can be perceived within Montero's work from realist to fantastic texts follows the general trend which can be traced within contemporary Spanish women-authored narrative from testimonial narrative to the parodic deconstruction of patriarchal plots. Furthermore, this trend is analogous to developments within the Spanish feminist movement, away from double militancy feminism, preoccupied with equal rights, to the proliferation of single militancy groups concerned with issues grounded in difference. However, despite the increasing emphasis on difference, complex theoretical work is being carried out on the problematic polemics of equality and difference which attempts to go beyond the antithesis of these two positions. The simultaneous, yet contradictory, pull towards the feminine mystique and feminist autonomy was examined in Chapter Two through the analysis of the social and cultural myths surrounding maternity in both the Franco and post-Franco periods. The ambivalent depiction of mothers as either potential sources of strength or perpetuators of repressive values was discussed with particular reference to the rejection of the mother as a role model by many younger Spanish feminists. There is an attempt in *Crónica del desamor* to engage with the possible positive aspects of maternity whilst criticising the social experience of mothering in a patriarchal society. Stylistically, the value of realist, testimonial narrative as a forum for exploring problems of self and cultural identity was also analysed with reference to *Crónica del desamor*, which whilst seemingly referential, goes beyond immediate experience to examine how that experience is mediated through discursive practice.

This focus on discursive practice continues in Chapter Three which examined the feminist potential of metafiction with reference to both *Crónica del desamor* and the more explicitly self-referential *La función delta*, in which narrative is clearly posited as a way of imposing meaning on experience. It is an attempt both to counter the silencing of women in patriarchal society and to deconstruct the notion of a fixed feminine identity through the use of a first-person narrator who articulates a multiple, self-contradictory self. The discourses of pleasure and desire were focused on in Chapters Four and Five which analyse the troubling of binary categories through romantic popular culture and explicit sexual fantasy, as depicted in *Te trataré como a una reina*. In Chapter Four, the shift in emphasis in this novel to women reading and negotiating texts, as opposed to writing, was also discussed. However, the change in emphasis is not only thematic, but also stylistic. With this novel, Montero moved away from characters and settings which could be directly related to her own immediate experience. She has described *Te trataré como a una reina* as being hyperrealist in its use of a grotesque ambience which at times tends towards the absurd. In Chapter Six, the rejection of mimesis in favour of fantastic discourse in *Temblor* and *El nido de los sueños* is examined.

There is thus a clear shift from the realism of the earlier novels grounded in experience to a realisation of the possibilities of fantasy for feminist practice. Nonetheless, certain themes are present throughout Montero's novels. In particular, her existential concerns are foregrounded in the contrasting narratives of heroic hope for a better future -as in *Temblor* and *El nido de los sueños*- and existential angst -as in *La función delta* and *Amado amo*. Montero's most recent novels *Bella y oscura* and *La hija del caníbal* combine both of these narratives in first-person narrations which again recognise the partiality of interpretative strategies and clearly focus on the use of discourse in the construction of identity through the characters of the storyteller Airelai and the narrators Lucía and Félix.

Constructions of Identity

In the later novels, Montero would seem to recognise that for the changes wished for in *Crónica del desamor* to be possible, a profound reorganisation of the social system -as criticised in *Amado amo*- is necessary. This will require the deconstruction of cultural myths -as in *Te trataré como a una reina*- and a radical transformation of gender identity which moves beyond the polemic between equality and difference. Montero argues that a re-evaluation of both terms is necessary (Knights 1993). In other words, she advocates a push for equality of possibilities combined with an acceptance of difference. There is an increasing awareness within her narrative of the value of ambivalence, multiplicity and ambiguity.

Such a fiction may be perceived as failing to provide clear role models for women. However, Montero has repeatedly declared that these are not militant, programmatic texts. Nonetheless, she has also stated that she writes from the position of being a woman and her narrative does attempt to work through the issues surrounding identity and subjectivity.[1] Throughout the novels examined, it is recognised that identity is constructed through a variety of discourses which can consequently be deconstructed, and that it is a shifting, fragmentary concept which cannot be fixed and defies completion.[2] Identity is described as a narrative process in a constant state of flux, a text for which the only closure is death. The fact that these are not prescriptive texts allows them to negotiate the complex boundaries between postmodern and feminist discourse. Despite the apparent postmodernity of this deconstruction of the unitary subject described above, Montero's novels are also feminist texts, in that they attempt to recuperate a sense of agency for women.[3] They address the complexity of attempting to radically resignify identity outside patriarchal paradigms and the difficulty of breaking down the binary dichotomies which shape social organisation and cultural myths. Within feminist debate, Montero's position appears ambivalent, oscillating between a practice grounded in equality and one grounded in difference. There is a sense of development in the synthesis of these two positions in the later novels, although it is also evident, albeit in an embryonic form, in *Crónica del desamor*. Both the categories of equality and difference were found to be present in this text which is both an emancipatory narrative, advocating equal rights, and a positive recognition of difference through the revaluation of maternity. Hence Montero's narrative trajectory is indicative of the trend in Spanish feminism, present since at least the late 1970s, to go beyond antithesis to merge these two categories.

Her narrative also reflects the attempt by feminists to change cultural practices through the recuperation of a *palabra de mujer* which attempts to go beyond the opposition of masculine and feminine. This breaking down of binary dichotomies is certainly present in Montero's novels which form part of the feminist project for changing the ideological framework of patriarchal society and the work of writers such as Montero can be seen as one of the strengths of the Spanish feminist movement. Her novels are bestsellers which bring issues concerning identity politics to the attention of a mass readership, thus breaking with the social marginalisation and cultural silencing of women. In a country where on the one hand, relatively few women belong to feminist organisations, but on the other, they seem to positively value the achievements of the movement, such a fiction may help to undermine the damaging substructures of patriarchy still in place despite the formal legal equality enshrined in the Spanish Constitution. The feminist struggle continues in Spain, despite the perceived collapse of the movement as an organised whole and the attempts by the media to portray it as no longer valid in a supposedly postfeminist age. Large numbers of women still attend the general meetings called by the movement and smaller networks of groups are flourishing. The general meeting of feminists in Madrid, held on the 4-6 December 1993, was attended by some three thousand women from groups as diverse as the Colectivo Transexualia and Mujeres Cristianas de Logroño. Their motto was appropriately enough 'Juntas y a por todas' (One for all and all for one) and their closing statement was, 'Ante la cacareada crisis del feminismo, queremos decir que no ha muerto' (In light of the crowing about the crisis in feminism, we would like to state that it is not dead) (Rivas 1993). Indeed, the Belgian delegate, Françoise Collin (founder of the journal *Cahiers du Grif*), was astounded by the strength of the movement in Spain as compared to other European countries.

The Spanish theorists of identity politics, cited in Chapter One, seemed to regard their project as utopic. Nonetheless, despite the illusory nature of such utopic fictions, they are necessary to enable social and cultural change. Through a complex process of deconstruction and construction, the work of such theorists and the narrative of writers like Montero serve to both interrogate existing paradigms and suggest alternative concepts of identity. This attempt to reconfigure an autonomous identity outside of patriarchal structures may be represented as an ongoing journey which is not without its difficulties, but upon which we may choose to follow the example of the heroines, Agua Fría and Gabriela, who keep on travelling and inventing.

---

[1] To some extent this point needs to be further clarified: she is writing from the position of an educated, white, urban, heterosexual professional who openly declares herself to be feminist. She therefore does not claim to speak for all women in Spain.

[2] This is particularly applicable to *Bella y oscura* in which binaries are constantly set up and deconstructed.

[3] They are also modernist, in that they posit some notion of transcendence in various moments of epiphany. In *La función delta*, *Temblor* and *Bella y oscura* they are linked to an instance of overwhelming love which causes characters to momentarily forget their basic condition of

solitude. In *Amado amo* César experiences a similar sensation when he is with his dying mother and tries unsuccessfully to recapture it through painting.

APPENDIX: INTERVIEWS WITH ROSA MONTERO

INTERVIEW ONE
(Cambridge, 22 October 1993)

— *¿Cómo te sientes, periodista o novelista?*
— Do you feel more of a journalist or novelist?
— Para mí, el periodismo me gusta mucho, me parece un trabajo fascinante que permite conocer otros mundos, y no hablo de otros mundos geográficos sino de otros mundos mentales. Permite conocer otras maneras de estar frente a la vida. Eso es muy enriquecedor y está muy bien. Me gusta mucho, pero para mí siempre ha sido un trabajo. Entonces siempre he mantenido con el periodismo una relación exterior. Una parte de mí está en el periodismo y nada más, mientras que la novela para mí es fundamental. La escritura narrativa es mi manera de vivir, es mi manera de estar frente al mundo. Vamos, yo puedo concebir la vida sin el periodismo, no es que lo quiera dejar, pero puedo concebir mi vida perfectamente sin el periodismo. Y si pienso en que me falte la novela, es que me dan sudores fríos. No sé como me las podría arreglar para vivir sin escribir. Vamos, a veces no sé como se las arregla la gente para vivir sin escribir, verdaderamente. Me da terror pensar que algún día se me acabe esta pasión porque no sabría vivir sin la escritura. Entonces lo que me he sentido es narradora siempre. Y de hecho creo que soy periodista porque antes escribía narración, no al revés. Lo que pasa es que la gente me ha conocido antes como periodista. Claro, he empezado como periodista con dieciocho años pero yo, antes de escribir periodismo, lo que hacía era escribir cuentos. O sea que sobre todo narradora, escritora.

— I like journalism a lot, it's a fascinating job which allows you to come into contact with other worlds, I'm talking about mental not geographical worlds. It enables you to encounter other ways of thinking about life. That is very enriching and worthwhile. I like it a lot but it's always been a job for me. So I've always had an external relationship with journalism. Part of me belongs to journalism and no more, whereas the novel is something fundamental to my being. Narrative is my way of life, it's my way of facing the world. Let's see, I can conceive of life without journalism, not that I want to give it up, but I can conceive living perfectly well without it. However, if I think for a minute that I couldn't write novels, I break out in a cold sweat. I don't know how I could bear to live without writing. Honestly, sometimes I don't know how people get by without writing. It terrifies me to think that some day this passion of mine might end because I wouldn't know how to live without writing. So I've always felt I was a narrator. In fact I think that I'm a journalist because I'm a narrator and not the other way round. What happened is that I became famous as a journalist first. Of course, I became a journalist when I was eighteen years old, but before writing as a journalist I wrote short stories. So above all I'm a narrator, a writer.

— *Empezaste la carrera de psicología, ¿qué temas te interesaban y por qué renunciaste para estudiar periodismo?*
— *You began a psychology degree. What interested you and why did you drop out to study journalism?*
— Empecé psicología porque me interesaba y me interesa, sobre todo, el género humano: las personas, lo que somos, lo que pasa por nuestras cabezas. Pero en cuarto de carrera vi que se aplicaba la psicología como si fuera una ciencia exacta, que no lo es; y que en nombre de esa ciencia se hacía muchas barbaridades. Por eso lo dejé.
— I began psychology because I was interested in, and still am, the human species: people, what we are, what goes through our minds. But in the fourth year of my degree I realised that psychology was being applied as if it were an exact science, which it isn't, and in the name of that science many barbaric acts were committed. That's why I dropped out.

— *Hay varios temas del psicoanálisis que aparecen en tus novelas, sobre todo el complejo de Edipo y la castración. ¿Crees que el psicoanálisis nos puede ser útil a las mujeres para indagar las relaciones con los hombres?*
— *There are various psychoanalytic themes which appear in your novels, above all the Oedipus and castration complex. Do you think that psychoanalysis can be useful for women in investigating their relationships with men?*
— No, no creo que el psicoanálisis nos sea especialmente útil a las mujeres. El análisis, analizante, digo, puede ser útil para hombres y mujeres, en determinados casos pero no como norma general. Por otra parte, en mis novelas yo no he aplicado en absoluto lo que aprendí en la carrera de psicología. Me interesan más los mitos básicos, como tales, que las fórmulas psicoanalíticas.

— No, I don't think that psychoanalysis can be especially useful for women. Analysis, as practised by analysts, may be useful for men and women in certain cases but not as a general norm. And what's more, in my novels I have not applied at all what I learnt in my psychology degree. I'm interested more in basic myths, as such, than psychoanalytic formulae.

— *¿Piensas que la literatura de mujeres puede crear su mundo propio con nuevos mitos y arquetipos?*
— Do you think that women's writing can create its own world with new myths and archetypes?
— Claro, evidentemente. Bueno, yo creo que es el reto que tenemos precisamente. O sea que no sólo que se puede, sino que se debe y además ese es el momento en el que estamos, obviamente ¿no? Justamente, eso es lo que ha creado la literatura femenina.
— Of course. In fact, I believe that that is precisely the challenge we face. In other words not only is it possible, we must do it and this is the moment in which it is happening, isn't it? That's exactly what feminine literature has created.

— *Sí, por ejemplo creo que* Temblor *es literatura feminista más bien por eso de los mitos.*
— Yes, for example I think that Temblor is feminist literature because of those myths.
— En este sentido sí. Es literatura de mujer. Me gustaría más porque no es que reniegue para nada del adjetivo feminista como persona, pero cuando se califica una literatura de feminista parece que se está calificando lo mismo que eso, de socialista, de pacifista, se le está calificando de militante... y a eso sí que me niego. Lo que sí es cierto es que es una literatura hecha desde el ser mujer como es lógico, como la literatura de los grandes hombres esta hecha por el ser hombre, y también en la búsqueda de nuestro propio panorama creativo. Como mujeres hay una parte común pero hay una parte que es propia. Entonces es la búsqueda de esa parte.
— In that sense it is. It's women's writing. I prefer that term, not because I'm rejecting the adjective feminist as a person, but when you qualify a literature as feminist you seem to be qualifying it as the same as for example socialist or pacifist, you're qualifying it as militant... and that it is not. What is certain is that

it is a literature written from a woman's point of view as is logical, just as the great literature written by men is written from a man's point of view, and also it's written in search of our own creative panorama. As women we have something in common but there is also a part which is particular. It is the search for that part.

— *¿Te ha influido algún escritor o personaje del panorama cultural en particular?*
— *Have you been influenced by any writer or cultural figure in particular?*
— Pues no soy consciente, todos seguramente. Date cuenta que una novela es todo lo que el escritor es; o sea todo lo que ha leído, todo lo que ha visto, todo lo que ha pensado o todo lo que ha soñado. Entonces, todo lo que he leído sin duda está en mis novelas; todo lo que me ha gustado y todo lo que no me ha gustado. Pero como empecé a escribir tan joven y empecé a escribir además públicamente en prensa, es decir, no con el prurito de hacer una obra, porque los escritores jovenes, incluso escritores que luego son magníficos, Cortázar por ejemplo, cuando empiezan a escribir, intentando hacer una obra literaria, pues suelen empezar a escribir "a la manera de"... Cortázar decía que tuvo una época, por ejemplo, de simbolista, escribía a la manera de los simbolistas. Pero, como cuando empecé a escribir era una cosa que no tenía una ambición así, sino algo de prensa y tal; entonces no tuve esa etapa de "a la manera de". Para tenerla tienes que tener una ambición de hacer una obra literaria, yo no la tenía. Por lo tanto, no soy consciente. Sin duda las influencias tienen que estar allí, pero no soy consciente de que en ningún momento haya querido escribir como éste o como ésta o de aquella manera conscientemente.
— Not consciously, all of them probably. You have to take into account that a novel is everything a writer is, in other words everything they have read, everything they have seen, everything they have thought and everything they have dreamed. Therefore, everything I have read is without a doubt in my novels; everything I have liked and everything I haven't liked. But as I began to write at such an early age and furthermore I began by writing for the press, that is to say not with the aim of producing a great work, because young writers, even writers who are later magnificent, such as Cortázar, when they start writing, trying to create a literary work, they usually start by writing "in the style of"... Cortázar said that he had a symbolist period, for example, he wrote in the style of the symbolists. But because when I started to write I lacked that ambition, it was just

the press; I didn't go through that stage of "in the style of". To go through it, you have to have the ambition to create a literary work and I didn't have it. At least not that I'm aware of. Without a doubt the influences are there but I'm not aware that at any moment I've wanted to write like anyone in particular at least not consciously.

— *He notado que en entrevistas te refieres mucho a Nabokov.*
— *I've seen that in interviews you refer quite often to Nabokov.*
— Cuando descubrí a Nabokov, yo ya estaba escribiendo en esa línea. A mí cuando me dio la locura por Nabokov fue cuando escribía *Te trataré como a una reina*. Ya me interesaba ese tipo de literatura. Entonces, lo que pasa es que en ese momento yo pensaba que él era todo lo que a mí me interesaba en la literatura llevado al máximo. Luego me he dado cuenta de que mi aventura personal de la escritura me ha llevado por otros lados. Ya te digo, ahora me ha llevado más por la parte fantástica que Nabokov no tiene. Y ahora me interesa más esto, no controlas, en alguna medida no lo controlas.
— When I discovered Nabokov, I was already writing in that vein. I became crazy about Nabokov when I was writing *Te trataré como a una reina*. I was already interested in that type of literature. Therefore at that time I thought that he represented everything that interested me about literature taken to the limit. Since then I've realised that my personal adventure as a writer has taken me down other paths. I tell you, now it's taken me more towards the fantastic which Nabokov doesn't do. Now I'm more interested in that, you don't control it, to some extent you're not in control.

— *En una entrevista con Antonio Monegal (en Harvard) dijiste que te gustaba mucho la obra de Patricia Highsmith. En* Amado amo *César lee y relee una página de Highsmith en la que un hombre asesina a una mujer. ¿Pensabas en alguna obra en particular?*
— *In an interview with Antonio Monegal (in Harvard) you said that you liked Patrica Highsmith's writing very much. In* Amado amo *César reads over and over again a page in Highsmith in which a man kills a woman. Were you thinking of a particular novel?*
— La obra de la Highsmith en la que estaba pensando era *Mar de fondo*.
— The work by Highsmith which I was thinking about was *Deep Sea*

— *Me interesó también la escena en* La función delta *cuando Lucía mira un dibujo de Escher. ¿Por qué escogiste a Escher?*

— *I'm also interested in the scene in* la función delta *in which Lucía is looking at a drawing by Escher. Why did you choose Escher?*

— Porque era un dibujante que me gustaba y me gusta mucho. Creo que lo que más me interesa de Escher es que hace posible lo imposible; que mezcla la realidad minuciosa con lo fantástico.

— Because he is an artist whom I liked and still like a lot. I think that what interests me most about Escher is that he makes the impossible possible; he mixes meticulous reality with the fantastic.

— *Has dicho a Antonio Monegal que en el momento de escribir* Te trataré como a una reina *te inspiró una visita a un cabaret de Sevilla. ¿Por qué escogiste el bolero como tipo de música?*

— *You have said to Antonio Monegal that when you wrote* Te trataré como a una reina *you were inspired by a visit to a cabaret in Seville. Why did you pick the bolero as the type of music?*

— El bolero lo escogí porque es un tipo de música, de letra sobre todo, evidentemente mentirosa. Dice cosas tan inocentes y tan ignorantes de la sentimentalidad de la vida real, pertenece a un mundo romántico en un sentido completamente disparatado; o sea, que no tiene nada que ver con la realidad. Cuando tú dices el bolero que me inventé yo, y que es el titulo de la novela *Te trataré como a una reina*, cuando tú dices "te trataré como a una reina" a alguien hoy, es obvio que no le vas a poder tratar como a una reina, pues eso es un deseo de un tipo de felicidad que es imposible, ¿no? Me gustaba esa sentimentalidad extrema y al mismo tiempo tan absolutamente falsa. O sea que es obvio que no puede ser; es un deseo de sentimentalidad extrema que ya está siendo traicionada en su enunciamiento. Entonces, me parecía muy conmovedor porque en *Te trataré como a una reina* está la distancia insalvable que hay entre los deseos de felicidad del ser humano y la posibilidad de cumplir estos deseos de felicidad. El ser humano desea absolutamente y con todas sus fuerzas una felicidad completa, total, pero no tiene ninguna capacidad para conseguirla ni para controlar su vida y está sometido al azar y no somos más que juguetitos del viento de la historia y de la vida. Entonces, el pobre ser humano manifiesta sus deseos de felicidad y al mismo tiempo su menudencia y su carencia para completarlos. Y bueno, eso me parece muy conmovedor, esta distancia entre el deseo de felicidad y la posibilidad de cumplirlo. Eso es de lo que se trata *Te trataré como a una reina* y eso es lo que está manifestado claramente en el bolero.

—I picked the bolero because it is a type of music, above all of lyrics, which is clearly false. It says things which are so innocent and so ignorant of sentimentality in the real world, it belongs to a completely ridiculous romantic world which has nothing to do with reality. When you repeat the bolero that I invented which gives its title to the novel, *Te trataré como a una reina*, when you say 'I'll treat you like a queen' to someone, nowadays it's obvious that you're not going to be able to treat her like a queen as this is a desire for an impossible type of happiness, isn't it? I liked this sentimentality which was extreme and at the same time so totally false. In other words it's obvious that it can't be so; it's an extremely sentimental desire which is already being betrayed as it is expressed. Therefore, it seemed very moving to me because in *Te trataré como a una reina* you have the unbridgeable distance between human beings' desire for happiness and the possibility of satisfying those desires. Human beings desire absolutely and with all their might a complete, absolute happiness but they neither have the ability to achieve it nor to control their lives. They are subordinated to chance, we are no more than the playthings of the winds of history and life. Therefore, the poor human being manifests desires for happiness and at the same time a loss or lack preventing their satisfaction. Well, this seems very moving to me, this distance between the desire for happiness and the possibilty of achieving it. This is what *Te trataré como a una reina* is about and what is clearly manifested in the bolero.

— *¿Escuchaste muchos boleros para poder crear los de <u>Te trataré como a una reina</u>?*

— Did you listen to a lot of boleros to create those in <u>Te trataré como a una reina</u>?

— Dentro de la cultura española se ha escuchado bastante bolero, antes sobre todo. Pero luego me fui a hablar además con Juan Madrid, que es un especialista en boleros -es un escritor, amigo mío- y él me dio bastantes discos. Digamos que escuché más y estudié más.

— Within Spanish culture we have listened to the bolero quite a bit, in the old days above all. But I also went to talk to Juan Madrid, a specialist in boleros -a writer, a friend of mine- and he gave me quite a few records. Let's say that I listened and studied more.

— *Phyllis Zatlin divide en dos períodos la narrativa femenina española desde la muerte de Franco: los años setenta cuando se escribieron obras testimoniales que servían para que las mujeres tomaran consciencia de su situación sociopolítica para poder actuar mejor, y los años ochenta, cuando se empezó a escribir una ficción más literaria que enfatizaba la búsqueda de una nueva palabra de mujer. ¿Qué te parece esta división?*

— *Phyllis Zatlin divides Spanish women's narrative since the death of Franco into two periods: the 70s when testimonial novels were written which acted as consciousness-raising novels, and the 80s, when women began to write a more literary fiction which emphasised the search for a new women's language. What do you think of this division?*

— Creo que la división de Zatlin no está mal, aunque toda generalización, claro, tiene sus fallos. Pero esas dos etapas son las mismas que se dieron en todo el mundo occidental, sólo que en años distintos: en Europa, en los sesenta, se hacía una literatura de mujer más testimonial. Yo creo que no haces testimonio para concienciar a las mujeres, sino porque, de algún modo, necesitas sacar eso fuera: nombrar cosas que antes no han sido nombradas, para poder liberarte de ellas.

— I think that Zatlin's division isn't bad, although like all generalisations it has its defects. But these are the same two stages that occurred in all of the western world, just in different years: in Europe, in the 60s, women's writing was more testimonial. I don't think you write testimony to raise other women's consciences, but because, in some way, you need purge something, name things that haven't been named before in order to liberate yourself from them.

— *Varios críticos han descrito sus libros como obras metafictivas. A mí me parecen obras de "re-visión" como diría Adrienne Rich. ¿Piensas que uno crea su propio mundo por el lenguaje que utiliza?*

— *Various critics have described your books as metafictive works. To me they seem "re-visionary" in the words of Adrienne Rich. Do you think that you create your own world through the language you use?*

— Todas esas etiquetas de metaficción y demás son eso, etiquetas de los estudiosos, que tienen poco que ver, desde mi punto de vista, con el proceso narrativo. Yo creo, en efecto, que al nombrar creas; y no es sólo una cuestión de lenguaje, sino también de imágenes. Pero sí, por supuesto: el lenguaje crea un mundo propio.

— All those labels like metafiction are just that, academic labels which have little to do, in my point of view, with the narrative process. I do believe that by naming you create and it's not just a question of language but images too. Of course language creates a particular world.

— *Me parece que en tus primeras obras te propones la deconstrucción de varios estereotipos de lo masculino y lo femenino, sobre todo en* Te trataré como a una reina. *¿Has leído teoría lingüística/literaria feminista?*

— *It seems to me that in your first novels you are deconstructing various stereotypes of the masculine and feminine, above all in* Te trataré como a una reina. *Have you read feminist linguistic or literary theory?*

— Odio en general la teoría lingüística/literaria feminista. Bueno ya te matizaré esto de odiar. No es que odio la crítica feminista por feminista. Es fundamental además para la correcta apreciación de la obra de las mujeres que haya más mujeres críticas, que haya más editoras mujeres, que haya más antólogas mujeres, que haya más profesoras mujeres. Eso es fundamental. Pero de lo que estoy en contra, y además me saca de quicio, me pone enferma y me parece ridículo, y me parece la antitesis de lo que es la creación y de lo que es incluso el feminismo, es esta estúpida crítica supuestamente radical feminista que desbarra, que no hace más que utilizar por otro lado también un mimetismo con el "name-dropping" del varón, que dice tonterías y fuerza las cosas hasta el extremo. Yo he recibido libros, trabajos sobre mis obras ridículos, verdaderamente ridículos, cogiendo las cosas y forzándolas para hacer una tésis feminista absurda. Es decir, primero tienen la tésis y luego da igual, adaptan el libro. Eso no, eso no es cientifico, eso no es feminista, eso no es inteligente y eso no es creativo. Eso me saca de quicio y de esas hay muchas. Y desde luego, los libros de teoría feminista y tal, con esto no se hace una novela. Esa es la antitesis, es la muerte de la creatividad. Las novelas salen de los sueños, de una necesidad interna y no de la lectura de un libro teórico. Esto sería la muerte de una novela.

— In general I hate feminist linguistic/literary theory. Well I'll qualify the word hate. I don't hate feminist criticism because it's feminist. What's more I think that for women's writing to be properly appreciated, it's fundamental that there are more women critics, women editors, women anthologists, women teachers. That's necessary. But what I'm against, and it drives me nuts, makes me sick and seems ridiculous, what seems the antithesis of creativity and even feminism itself, is the stupid supposedly radical feminist criticism which talks nonsense and what's more partakes mimetically of men's "name-dropping", it says ridiculous things and forces them in the extreme. I've received books, studies of my work which were ridiculous, truly ridiculous, taking things and forcing them in order to sustain an absurd feminist theory. That's to say first they have the theory and then it's all the same, they adapt the book. That isn't scientific, it isn't feminist, it isn't intelligent and it's not creative. It drives me mad and there's a lot of it. And of course you don't write a novel with books of feminist theory. That's the antithesis, the death of creativity. Novels emerge from dreams, from an interior need and not the reading of a theoretical text. That would be the death of a novel.

— *¿Qué opinas sobre el sexismo en el lenguaje?*
— *What do you think about sexism in language?*
— Pues efectivamente el lenguaje, todos los lenguajes están manchados, son sexistas, porque el lenguaje refleja el mundo del que manda. O sea que se conforma. Entonces, efectivamente son todos sexistas. Lo que pasa es que eso no es lo más importante, quiero decir que está claro que hay cosas muy evidentes, por ejemplo en español tú puedes hacer un esfuerzo, y yo hago un esfuerzo, jamás digo el hombre por el genérico, el hombre por el hombre y la mujer jamás, digo la persona o el ser humano. Intentas evadir, evitar este tipo de excesos o extremos pero, lo que no puedes hacer con un lenguaje es forzarlo tampoco como Monica Wittig o como gente así porque es ridículo. El lenguaje es una criatura viva, que va cambiando normas constantemente y que tiene su propia vitalidad. Entonces, esos intentos de crear un nuevo lenguaje que se han dado mucho a lo largo de la historia, o bien de este tipo feminista o yo qué sé... Juan Ramón Jiménez que intentaba también hacer otro lenguaje y otra ortografía. Mentira, eso no sirve para nada. No sirve absolutamente para nada. La única manera de cambiar el lenguaje es de cambiar la sociedad. A medida que la sociedad cambia, el lenguaje se va

adaptando a esa nueva sociedad, por esto hay cosas en el español que se están cayendo por su propio peso; y si no cambia la sociedad, el lenguaje tampoco va a cambiar. Por ejemplo, ahora ya casi nadie dice señorita en España, queda ridículo, acaba perdiendo su sentido. Pues eso se está yendo solo, se está muriendo solo. Y como eso todo. Otro ejemplo, que ya he dado, es decir persona o ser humano en vez de hombre por genérico, ya lo dice mucha gente. ¿Por qué? Porque hombre por hombre y mujer ya empieza a chirrear, a resultar desfasado con lo que ya es la sociedad de ahora. Esos son los cambios de verdad, cambios que se producen dentro del lenguaje en sí. Así que eso es lo de menos además. Creo que es mucho más importante dentro de la escritura tener el cuidado de no ser mimético de los mitos culturales, eso es más grave que el propio uso del lenguaje porque todo escritor ha de inventar su propio lenguaje. En ese sentido tu puedes manejarlo muy bien. Es más difícil escapar de la impronta cultural masculina que es la artística, que es la que hemos heredado; o sea hemos aprendido la literatura a través del mundo masculino literario. Y eso... ese marco de referencias, eso es lo más difícil de evitar y eso es lo que es más importante de evitar.

— Well in effect language, all languages are tainted, are sexist because language reflects the world of those in power. In other words it conforms. And therefore all languages are sexist. But that's not what is most important. What I mean is that of course there are clear examples such as in Spanish you can make an effort, and I make it, I never say man as a generic, man for man and woman never, I say person or human being. You try to avoid that type of excess or extreme but what you cannot do with a language is force it like Monique Wittig because it's ridiculous. Language is a living creature which constantly changes norms and has its own vitality. Therefore those attempts to create a new language which have occurred throughout history whether feminist or otherwise... Juan Ramón Jiménez also tried to create another language and spelling. Lies, it's of no use at all. No use whatsoever. The only way to change language is to change society. As society changes, language adapts to that new society, that's why there are expressions in Spanish which are falling under their own weight, and if society doesn't change then neither will language. For example, in Spain almost nobody says "señorita" (Miss) now, it sounds ridiculous, it's lost its meaning. Well that's happening by itself, it's dying off. And that's how it is. Another example which I've already given is that of saying person or human being instead of man as a generic, a lot of people are doing it. Why? Because man for man and woman grates, it's out of step without society nowadays. These are real changes, changes produced from within language itself. And that's the least of it. I think that it's much more important within writing to be careful not to reproduce cultural myths, that's more serious than the use of language because each writer has to invent their own language. In that sense you can manipulate it well. It's more difficult to escape the masculine cultural imprint which governs art, that which we have inherited as we have learned what literature is through the masculine literary world. And that... that frame of reference, is the most difficult, and yet most important, thing to avoid.

— *El movimiento feminista en España se ha fragmentado mucho desde 1975...*
— *The feminist movement in Spain has fragmented a lot since 1975...*
— Sí, en todas partes ¿no? Quiero decir que ahora mismo hay una crisis y no solamente feminista. Hay una crisis de militancia en todo el mundo. De militancia en los partidos, quiero decir, de militancia en los sindicatos. De militancia, por lo tanto también en los grupos feministas. Entonces, el movimiento feminista en todo el mundo está haciendo aguas, como está haciendo aguas la militancia partidaria. O sea que yo creo que eso es un fenómeno general que forma parte de otro fenómeno más amplio.
— It's the same all over, isn't it? I mean there's a crisis now which involves more than just feminism. There's a crisis of militancy the world over. Of militancy in parties, I mean, of militancy in trade unions. Of militancy, then in feminist groups too. Therefore the feminist movement all over the world is foundering, as is party militancy. In other words it's a general phenomenon which forms part of a wider phenomenon.

— *En una entrevista hablaste de "un sexo enfermo, en una sociedad enferma" (La mujer feminista nov-dic 1985). ¿Es ésta la sociedad de Te trataré como a una reina en la que Antonia tiene fantasías de ser violada?*
— *In an interview you talked about "sick sex in a sick society" (La mujer feminista Nov-Dec 1985). Is this the society in Te trataré como a una reina in which Antonia fantasises about being raped?*
— Sí, claro, efectivamente. Lo que pasa es que supongo que la entrevista debería hablar además de la pornografía o algo así. Yo estoy en contra de prohibir

la pornografía como algunas quieren; completamente en contra porque no puedes matar al mensajero. Eso existe, es decir, las fantasías existen, las fantasías de violación por parte de las mujeres, las fantasías de violar por parte de los hombres. Entonces, eso forma parte del marco de referencias de las relaciones también. Es como el lenguaje, emana de las relaciones que mantenemos, profundas, hombres y mujeres. A medida que eso no se cambie, y afortunadamente se va cambiando, el sexo no se convertirá en un bien. El sexo es como la radiografía más íntima de esos tipos de relaciones. Si las relaciones sexuales de la sociedad tal como están planteadas, las relaciones entre sexos, ya no sexuales sino entre sexos, no cambian; si las relaciones de poder no cambian; si el concepto de lo que es el cuerpo y de la relación con él no cambia, que va cambiando pero muy lentamente; bueno si todo eso no cambia, no van a cambiar tampoco las fantasías. Entonces, estas fantasías son importantes para la supervivencia y el equilibrio de las personas. Eso era a lo que me refería cuando dije que estoy totalmente en contra de esa cosa ridícula que es el fanatismo. Es que odio el fanatismo en todo, en el feminismo también. Ya no podemos soñar con cosas que no sean "politically correct"

— Yes, of course. I guess that in the interview we were also talking about pornography or something of that ilk. I'm against banning pornography unlike some women; completely against it because you can't kill the messenger. It exists, in other words, fantasies exist, fantasies about being raped for women, fantasies about raping for men. Therefore this forms part of the frame of reference for relationships too. It's like language, it emanates from the deep relationships we have, men and women. Unless this changes, and fortunately it is changing, sex will not become something positive. Sex is like the most intimate X-ray of relationships. If sexual relationships in society as they are conceived at present, if the relationships between the sexes, not sexual but between the sexes, don't change; if power relationships don't change; if the concept of what the body is and the relationship with it doesn't change, which is changing too but very slowly; well if all this doesn't change neither will fantasies. Therefore these fantasies are important for people's survival and balance. That's what I was referring to when I said I was totally against that ridiculous thing: fanaticism. I hate all types of fanaticism, in feminism too. We can no longer dream about things which aren't politically correct.

— En <u>Crónica del desamor</u> y <u>Amado amo</u> se describe un mundillo profesional parecido al tuyo. Estas obras parecen criticar este mundo bastante ¿no?

— In <u>Crónica del desamor</u> and <u>Amado amo</u> you describe a professional ambience like your own. Those works seem to criticise that world a fair bit, don't they?

— Sí, bueno eso sobre todo en *Amado amo*. *Crónica del desamor* como es tan testimonial y tal... Pero en *Amado amo* sí, hay una construcción allí de una mirada crítica sobre ese mundo. Vivo en él y me parece que verdaderamente es delirante. Se rompe el ser humano, ha perdido su lugar en el mundo, ya no sabe quién es él; la medida de su propia dignidad, de su propia percepción pasa por cosas tan ridículas como es el jefe, un jefe al que desprecia y, por otro lado, le sonríe por la mañana al llegar a la oficina... Entonces, eso aparte de ser ridículo, es una cosa dramática, lleva a la catástrofe personal. De allí resultan las catástrofes personales. Y eso es el mundo del neoliberalismo y del poscapitalismo de nuestra realidad. Me parece que es muy deshumanizado y que es muy absurdo y que es muy machacante para la persona. Eso es lo que quería contar en *Amado amo* concretamente.

— Yes, above all in *Amado amo*. As *Crónica del desamor* is testimonial... But in *Amado amo* there is the construction of a critical look at that world. I live in it and it truly seems delirious to me. Human beings are broken, they have lost their space in the world, they don't know who they are; the measure of their own dignity, their own perception is filtered through something as ridiculous as the boss, a boss who is despised and yet, on the other hand, smiled at in the morning whne they arrive at the office... This, apart from being ridculous, is dramatic, it leads to personal catastrophe. This is what causes personal catastrophes. And this is the world of neoliberalism and postcapitalism, of our reality. It seems very dehumanising to me and very absurd and very wearing. That's what I wanted to talk about specifically in *Amado amo*.

— También en <u>Crónica del desamor</u> y <u>Amado amo</u> utilizas varios términos anglo-americanos. ¿Qué te parece el uso de los anglicismos en la lengua castellana actual?

— You also use various Anglo-American terms in <u>Crónica del desamor</u> and <u>Amado amo</u>. What do you think about the current use of anglicisms in Spanish?

— Lo mismo que he dicho antes de la lengua. O sea, puede haber anglicismos que sean adoptados por la lengua porque los necesita. Yo no creo en la protección de la lengua como de una especie. Creo en el uso, y me encanta la lengua castellana. Quiero que haya Institutos Cervantes, quiero que se haga lo posible por extenderla y protegerla, vale. Pero la lengua tiene que tener vitalidad. Esa sociedad tiene que tener la vitalidad suficiente para mantener una lengua vital que sea capaz de crear nuevas palabras para los nuevos retos sociológicos. Entonces, si de repente hay una palabra, yo qué sé... "jetlag", no hemos inventado nada para el "jetlag" o el "stop"" estamos utilizando el "stop" en todo el mundo y es inglés. Bueno, vosotros también utilizáis la palabra "guerrilla", por ejemplo, y otras cosas... "patio", no sé... Pues esos son los triunfos de un lenguaje, encontrar una palabra, encontrar un concepto. Eso no me importa nada, no me importa absolutamente nada. Estoy hablando dentro de un nivel culto, no estoy hablando ya de los niños tontos que ven una película de televisión y que andan hablando mitad en inglés. Eso no cambia la lengua. O sea esas minorías estúpidas no cambian una lengua. La lengua es más compleja.

— The same as I said before about language. That is to say that there are anglicisms which are adopted because the language needs them. I don't believe in the protection of language as if it were a species. I believe in its use and I love the Spanish language. I want there to be Institutos Cervantes, I want them to do whatever is possible to spread it and protect it fair enough. But language needs vitality. This society has to have sufficient dynamism to sustain a dynamic language which is able to create new words for new sociological challenges. Therefore if there is a word, like... "jetlag", we haven't invented anything for "jetlag" or "stop", "stop" is used the world over and it's English. Well, you use the word "guerilla' for example and others such as "patio"... These are the successes of a language, finding a word, finding a concept. I don't mind that at all, not at all. I speaking of a certain educated level, I'm not talking about the daft kids who see a film on TV and wander about talking half in English. That doesn't change the language. Those stupid minorities don't change a language. Language is more complex.

— *En Amado amo aparecen mucho las palabras "Poder" y "Deber" y siempre empiezan con mayúscula...*

— In *Amado amo* the words "Power" and "Duty" appear frequently and always capitalised...

— Sí, los puse con mayúscula como fetiches, para indicar que eran fetiches de esa sociedad que estaba intentando... Eran casi dioses crueles para el protagonista. El poder y el deber eran cosas tiránicas, mandatos tiránicos para el protagonista. Por eso los puse con mayúsculas.

— Yes, I wrote them with a capital letter to indicates that they are fetiches for this society which is trying to... They are almost cruel gods for the protagonist. Power and duty are tyrannical things, tyrannical mandates for the protagonist. That's why they are capitalised.

— En *Amado amo* la compañía donde trabaja César se describe en términos que se refieren a la monarquía, a las fuerzas armadas y a la Iglesia. Estas tres siempre han sido el marco del poder tradicional en España ¿no?

— In *Amado amo* the company which César works for is described in terms which refer back to the monarchy, the armed forces and the Church. These three have always been the traditional framework for power in Spain, haven't they?

— Claro, evidentemente éste es el nuevo poder. Un poco en la novela me parece recordar que hay un momento en que dice además que es la nueva esclavitud. Creo que en un párrafo, no sé cual porque hace bastante que lo hice, pero creo que en este párrafo se habla de la nueva esclavitud del asalariado que es el esclavo de ahora como antes el siervo. Entonces, está bien observado eso; si antes el poder absoluto era el monarco absoluto, si antes el poder aterrador era el ejército dictatorial, pues ahora el poder que te destroza es un poder mucho más cotidiano y mucho más íntimo, es el jefe que llevas dentro ¿no? A eso me refería.

— Of course, evidently this is the new power. I seem to remember that what's more in the novel there's a passage where it says that it is the new slavery. I think that in a paragraph, I don't know where exactly because it's a long time since I wrote it, but in that paragraph it talks about the new slavery of the wage-earner who is as much of a slave as the serf before him. That's a sharp observation, if the terrifying power before was the dictator's army, the power that destroys you now is a much more everyday power and much more intimate, it's the boss you carry inside, isn't it? That's what I was referring to.

— También en <u>Amado amo</u> hay una frase que dice que el temblor es la sustancia de la vida. ¿De allí salió tu novela <u>Temblor</u>?

— There's also a sentence in <u>Amado amo</u> which says that fear is the substance of life. Was that the origin of your novel <u>Temblor</u>?

— Ya, sí, pues eso lo vi en tu fax y me parece muy curioso. Eso demuestra, efectivamente, que tienes una serie de ideas, de miradas sobre el mundo que se van repitiendo. No me acordaba yo que esto estuviera allí. Pero es exactamente igual, esa frase podía ser de *Temblor*.

— Right, I saw that in your fax and it's very interesting. In effect, it shows that you have a series of ideas, opinions about the world which repeat themselves. I didn't remember that that was there, But it's exactly the same, that sentence could be out of *Temblor*.

— <u>Temblor</u> es una historia muy emblemática; se parece a los mitos clásicos de búsqueda...

— <u>Temblor</u> is a very emblematic story; it's similar to classical quests...

— Sí, es una historia de iniciación, la iniciación de una niña en la vida adulta. Es mi novela más clásica creo yo, porque además es la única que se adapta claramente a un género. Las demás están en terrenos mucho más fronterizos. Y luego es un género que tiene unas normas muy rígidas, es decir, si quieres hacer una novela que tenga ecos épicos y ecos míticos pues tienes que tener una narrativa muy clásica, clásica de lenguaje, clásica de linealidad, cronológica, muy clásica porque no puedes hacer otra cosa. Ese género te obliga a adaptar y a adoptar, te obliga a seguir sus normas. Efectivamente, lo que yo quería hacer era una historia que fuera un poco como los cuentos infantiles, la fuerza que tienen de representación emblemática los cuentos infantiles, los buenos como *Caperucita roja*, pasan siglos y siguen contándose. ¿Por qué? Porque representan al mundo, o sea estos cuentos son un aprendizaje para los niños. Está el bien, está el mal, está el miedo... Bueno, yo quería hacer algo parecido pero para adultos, es decir una especie de cuento básico del mundo, efectivamente.

— Yes, it's a story about initiation, the initiation of a little girl into adult life. I thnk it's my most classical novel because it's the only one which clearly adapts itself to a specific genre. The others occupy much more borderline territories. What's more it's a genre with very rigid norms, that's to say if you want to write a novel which has epic echoes and mythical echoes then you have to maintain a very classical narrative, classical language, classical lineality, chronology, very classical because you can't do it any other way. This genre obliges you to adapt and adopt, it obliges you to follow ts rules. In effect, what I wanted to create was a story like children's fairy tales, the strength of emblematic representation which those tales have, well the good ones do... *Little Red Riding Hood*, centuries go by and people still tell those stories. Why? Because they represent the world, in other words those stories are a learning process for children. Good and evil are there, fear is there... Well, I wanted to create something similar for adults, a kind of basic story for adults, in effect, a basic representation of the world.

— *Tiene algunas cosas en común con El nido de los sueños que es un cuento para niños, ¿no?*
— It has things in common with El nido de los sueños which is a children's story doesn't it?
— Sí, supongo, pero no sé. ¿Qué tienen en común?
— I suppose so, like what?

— *La búsqueda de identidad del personaje central...*
— The search for identity of the central character...
— Sí, eso sí.
— Yes, that's right.

— ... *pero me parece más optimista la conclusión del cuento.*
— ... but the conclusion of the story seems more optimistic.
— Sí, el cuento es más optimista, es mucho menor. La otra es muy metafísica, ¿no? *Temblor* es mi primera novela cosmogónica, en el sentido de que es la primera novela en que me dije: bueno, voy a decir lo que pienso sobre el mundo. La primera vez que me senté y me dije: bueno, una novela de la mirada completa. Voy a hacer un modelo del mundo, un modelo de la existencia. Y en ese sentido es muy ambiciosa. Es una novela larguísima. Tiene cuatrocientos cincuenta folios en el original, más, casi quinientos folios. Lo que pasa es que se editó con un tipo diminuto. Luego, *Bella y oscura* es también una representación del mundo, las dos son representaciones completas del mundo. Lo que pasa es que *Temblor* es más verbalizada. O sea que está más debatido, pues eso... la metafísica, los pensamientos...

— Yes, the story is more optimistic, it's a minor work. The other is more metaphysical, isn't it? *Temblor* is my first cosmogonic novel in the sense that it's the first novel in which I said to myself, "Well, I'm going to say what I think about the world." The first time I sat down and said to myself, " A novel with a complete vision. I'm going to create a model of the world, a model of existence." In that sense it's very ambitious. It's a very long novel. The original had four hundre and fifty pages, more, almost five hundred. What happened is that it was printed with a very small typeface. Then *Bella y oscura* is also a representation of the world, both are complete representations of the world. But *Temblor* is more verbalised. It's more debated, you know…metaphysics, thought…

— *Describe varias formas de organización digamos sociopolítica: la sociedad de "Aural" que es capitalista, la sociedad de "Renacimiento" que está basada en la igualdad…*
— It depicts various forms of shall we say sociopolitical organisation: the capitalist society of Aural (Golden), the society based on equality of Renacimiento (Renaissance)…
— Sí, lo que pasa es que tampoco funciona del todo. Claro, es un "intento de" pero no es el paraíso. Falla también, que "Renacimiento" también falla.
— Yes, but it doesn't really work either. Of course, it's an attempt but it's not paradise. It fails too, Renaissance fails too.

— *Bueno, y la solución de <u>Temblor</u>, el fin…*
— Well, the solution of <u>Temblor</u>, the end…
— Sí, pues el final, es un final abierto, lo que indica es que tienes que seguir. No es mala, no es pesimista. Ella va va a tener un hijo, ha aprendido cosas. Además como dice el libro veinte veces las cosas no se repiten, cambian todo el rato. Entonces aunque parezca… no es que se vuelve a repetir. Ella se va, puede ir a buscar a gente de "Renacimiento", puede ir a buscar a gente que piense como ella, puede seguir luchando por conseguir sus sueños. Es un final abierto como la vida misma porque no hay finales felices pero tampoco finales del todo desgraciados.
— Yes, well the ending is an open ending, what it indicates is that you have to keep going. It isn't bad, it isn't pessimistic. She's going to have a baby, she's learnt things. Anyway as the book say twenty times over, things don't repeat

themselves, they change all the time. So although it seems... it doesn't repeat itself. She leaves, she can look for people from Renaissance, she can search for people who think as she does, she can carry on fighting to realise her dreams. It's an open ending like life itself because there aren't any happy endings but nor are there any totally unhappy ones.

— *La solución de <u>Temblor</u> me pareció anarquista.*
— *I felt that the solution prposed in <u>Temblor</u> was anarchist*
— ¿Sí? ¿Cómo?
— Really? Why?

— *Por ejemplo individuos como Torbellino o Agua Fría trabajan juntos para el bien de la sociedad pero cada uno trabaja por su parte.*
— *For example individuals such as Torbellino or Aguag Fría work together for the good of society but each works individually.*
— ¡Qué interesante! Pues, esto es una emanación de mi concepto también de la vida. Es decir, yo nunca he militado en ningún sitio, en nada, soy muy individualista. Al mismo tiempo, sin embargo, creo que tengo una gran percepción de lo social y una gran preocupación por lo social. Hay un conflicto siempre entre lo individual y lo social en todas las personas. Yo lo siento muy agudo porque, por un lado, soy muy individualista y por otro lado, creo que tengo mucha preocupación social. Entonces, está bien observado por tu parte. Y en *Temblor* está, son gente que trabaja por lo colectivo pero individualmente, es verdad, está bien pensado.

— How interesting! Well, that comes out of my theory of life. That's to say I've never been a militant of any sort ever, I'm very individualistic. Nevertheless, at the same time, I believe that I'm very perceptive about social issues and very preoccupied by them. There is always a conflict between the individual and the social in everybody. I feel it very sharply because, on the one hand, I'm very individualistic, and on the other, I think I'm very preoccupied by the social. That's a good observation of yours. In *Temblor* it's there, there are people who work for the collective but individually, it's true, that's well thought out.

— *Bueno, las anarca-feministas dicen que la primera cosa que tenemos que hacer es cambiar nuestra vida personal, cada persona tiene que transformarse a sí mismo...*

— *Anarcha-feminists say that the first thing we should do is change our own personal life, each person has to transform themself...*

— Sí, lo que pasa es que en esto yo soy un poco menos radical, en el sentido de creo que hay que hacerlo a la vez. O sea tú no puedes hacer tu transformación y que el mundo se hunda y que se muera. Porque además no se puede, tienes que intentar hacer las dos cosas.

— Yes but I'm a little less radical, in the sense that I think you have to do it all at once. You can't transform yourself and leave the world to sink and die. Because you can't, you have to try and do the two together.

— *En* Bella y oscura *Airelai compara lo femenino con la naturaleza y lo masculino con la cultura que es algo que hacen mucho las feministas radicales.*

— *In* Bella y oscura *Airelai compares the feminine to nature and the masculine to culture which is something that radical feminists do a lot.*

— ¿Sí? ¿Cuándo lo hace eso?

— Yes, when does that happen?

— *No sé, ahora no me acuerdo, está hablando con Amanda, creo...*

— *I can't remember exactly right now, I think she's talking to Amanda...*

— Sí, creo que es cuando le dice, pues el hombre es el hierro y no se , la mujer es... Es que creo que no es una comparación tan clara. Creo que no está tan, tan...

— Yes, I think it's when she says that man is iron and woman is... I don't think that the comparison is so...

— *¿Tajante?*

— *Cut and dry?*

— ...tan tajante. Lo que yo quería hacer con esa tirada era hablar de la separación de sexos, de la representación, de que cada uno tiene una parcela de simbolismo, de representación y de funcionalidad en el mundo completamente diversa y distinta, y darle a eso una verbalización un poco poética... la mujer es la sangre y el hombre es el hierro y el óxido. Entonces sí, es cierto que tradicionalmente son "grosso modo" los registros en que se nos ha metido. No quiero decir con esto que tengamos que quedarnos allí, ni que sea verdad radical que nosotras seamos aculturales y animales y que ellos sean toda cultura y nada de animalidad porque no es cierto. Pero es verdad que tradicionalmente son las dos esferas en las que nos han puesto.

— ...so cut and dry. What I wanted to do with that section was talk about the division of the sexes, about representation, that each has their own share of symbolism, of representation and function in the world which is completely diverse and distinct, and give that a slightly poetic verbalisation...woman is blood and man is iron and rust. Therefore yes, it's true that traditionally these are more or less the registers in which we have been placed. That's not to say that we have to stay there, nor that it is the whole truth, that we are acultural and animal and that they are all culture and no animal because that's not true. But it is tru that traditionally these are the two spheres in which we have been placed.

— *También Airelai le dice a Amanda que no sabe lo que ha ganado.*
— *Airelai also tells Amanda that she doesn't know what she has gained.*

— Sí, porque Amanda la pobre es una tía que es un desastre. Es una tía joven pero al mismo tiempo está llena de miedos, yo conozco algunas que son así... Entonces no sabe lo que ha ganado, es decir, ya no tiene que ser una esclava en alguna medida. Ha perdido la fuerza de las mujeres tradicionales. Esas eran las que sabían manejar, sabían llevar, tenían esa fuerza, esa resistencia... Es que las mujeres tradicionales eran como dioses, oye, lo digo en serio. Eran capaces de tener diez hijos, llevar la casa, trabajar en el campo, cuidar de los muertos con una entereza... bueno, eso lo hemos perdido las mujeres. Hemos ganado otras cosas claro, tenemos la cultura y no sé que... Amanda no lo sabe porque Amanda está tan desprotegida que no sabe lo que ha ganado. Entonces, está la pobre allí, perdida. No es nada, es la mutante, es la que esté en transición, es el símbolo de la mujer perdida completamente.

— Yes, because poor Amanda is a disaster case. She's a young woman but at the same time she's full of hangups, I know plenty like that...She doesn't know what she has gained, that she doesn't have to be a slave anymore. She has lost the strength of tradtional women. Those who knew how to manage, they had that strength, that resistance... Traditional women were like gods, I'm being serious. They were capable of having ten kids, running a household, working in the fields, looking after the dead with a fortitude... Well, that's what we've lost as women. We've won other things of course, we have culture... Amanda doesn't know that because Amanda is so vulnerable she doesn't know what she's won. The poor woman is there, lost. She's nothing, a mutant, the one in transition, she's a symbol of the totally lost woman.

— *¿Qué piensa de la polémica que ha habido en España entre el feminismo de la igualdad y el feminismo de la diferencia?*
— *What do you think about the polemics in Spain between equality and difference feminism?*
— Bueno yo creo que eso no es solamente una polémica en España sino que la había en todas partes. Yo creo que ya es evidente para el grueso del feminismo, salvo alguna loca atrasada que no se entera, que el feminismo de la igualdad, igualdad es absurdo. O sea quiero decir que fue un paso ¿no? El feminismo de la diferencia radical tampoco. Son los extremos de un movimiento. Esa gente que de repente empiezan a decir bueno, pues a lo mejor lo que tienen que hacer es volver a meterse en la casa y cuidar plantas y nada de trabajar y no sé qué porque somos distintas, eso... Pero el criterio de la sociedad de mujeres, ni siquiera te digo de las feministas militantes sino de la sociedad de mujeres cultas del mundo occidental, el criterio absolutamente mayoritario es que no queremos ser como los hombres. O sea que somos efectivamente distintas, que queremos un tipo de integración e incorporación al mundo de trabajo distinto, y lo que queremos es cambiar un poco las relaciones. Ahora bien, queremos incorporarnos al trabajo, queremos las mismas posibilidades, queremos las mismas leyes, las mismas capacidades para subir. Eso, sí, una igualdad de referencias y de marcos y de posibilidades. Luego no el mimetismo con el varón. Creo yo, que no hay duda, que la inmensa mayoría piensa esto ya.

— Well, I think that it's not a polemic which is unique to Spain. I think that it's now clear for the majority of the feminist movement, except for some out of date madwomen who haven't caught on, that total equality feminism is absurd. In other words it was a stage. Radical difference feminism isn't the way either. They are the extremes of a movement. Those people that suddenly say well, maybe we should return to our homes and look after plants and not work and whatever because we're different... But the criteria of women in society, and not even militant feminists but educated women of the Western world, the absolute majority are of the opinion that we don't want to be like men. We are different, we want a different type of integration and incorporation into the workforce and what we want is to change relationships a little.Now what we do want is to be able to incorporate ourselves into the workforce, we want the same opportunities, the same laws, the same possibilities for promotion. That we do want, equality of references, frameworks and opportunities. But not the mimeticism of men. I believe, without a doubt, that the immense majority think that way.

— *¿Qué te parece la literatura de la mujer ahora en España?*
— *What do you think about women's writing in Spain?*
— Después de la muerte de Franco hubo un fenómeno muy curioso y es que dentro del mundo de la nueva narrativa, uno de los rasgos más curiosos de ese fenómeno fue la explosión de mujeres escritoras. Aparecieron montones de mujeres ecritoras. Hubo unas cuantas antes pero como aisladas, se contaban, se podían contar, las podías nombrar. Ahora es que casi no las puedes ni nombrar, son muchísimas. Entonces, eso ha sido un fenómeno sociológico muy importante. He de decir de todas maneras que para mí es más grande el número que la calidad. Pero, también he de decirte que cada vez hay más calidad, cada vez aparece gente joven más importante. O sea que yo creo que es un fenómeno super-alentador y super-excitante también, muy importante de renovación de mujeres escritoras. Yo creo que está muy bien, un florecimiento de mujeres escritoras.

— After the death of Franco there was a very curious phenomenon, within the world of the "new narrative", one of the most unusual features of that phenomenon was the explosion of women writers. Loads of women writers appeared. There were a few before but isolated, they were counted, you could count them, you could name them. Now you can almost not even name them, there are so many. This has been a very important sociological phenomenon. I have to say that in my opinion the quantity is greater than the quality. But I must add that all the time the quality is improving, there are more and more importnat young writers. I think it's a very encouraging phenomenon and very exciting too, very important for the renovation of women's writing. I think it's great, a flowering of women writers.

— *Para terminar, ¿estás escribiendo otra novela?*
— *To finish off, are you writing another novel?*
— Pues no, nada de nada.
— No, not at all.

INTERVIEW TWO
(Madrid, 3 July 1994)

— *Quisiera que me explicaras un poco el proceso de coger una novela tan compleja, como es* Temblor, *para transformarla en una ópera.*

— *I'd like you to explain the process of taking a novel as complex as* Temblor *and transforming it into an opera.*

— Hay que hacer otra cosa. Es decir hay que olvidarse de la novela porque los libretos de una ópera son una simple excusa anecdótica sobre la que se apoya la música. Los libretos son cortísimos, para cantarlos necesitas que tengan poquísimo texto. De hecho el libreto de *Temblor*, de que se quería hacer además una ópera corta, tiene veinte folios. Entonces, lo que hice fue olvidarme de toda la parte metafísica y de toda la parte simbólica para dejarlo como un cuentecito de aventuras y potenciar la línea mágica y incluso un poco circense. O sea lo que tienes que hacer es olvidarte de la novela verdaderamente porque si no, es imposible.

— You have to do something completely different. In other words you have to forget the novel because the libretto in an opera is a simple anecdotal excuse which acts as a support for the music. Librettos are very short, to sing them they have to have very little text. In fact the libretto of *Temblor* from which they wanted to make a short opera, has twenty sides. So what I did was to miss out all the metaphysical side and the symbolic side to finish up with an adventure story in which the magical and even circus element is fostered. You really have to forget the novel completely, otherwise it's impossible.

— *Me interesan los cambios que has hecho. Por ejemplo toda la parte que se refiere al problema entre los sexos desaparece con la ausencia de personajes como Pedernal, Respy y Mo. También me interesa la mayor importancia que cobró Torbellino.*

— *I'm interested in the changes you made. For example the part which referes to the problems between the sexes disappears with the absence of characters such as Pedernal, Respy and Mo. I'm also interested in the increased importance given to Torbellino.*

— Claro, yo creo que concretamente en una ópera con el libreto tienes que ser obligatoriamente muy modesta. Porque el libreto, te digo, no creo que sea más que un soporte musical, y lo importante de una ópera es primero la música y después la puesta en escena, la dramaturgia escénica. Entonces, yo me puse al servicio de Marisa Manchado que es la compositora. Le hice un primer libreto, lo leyó y me dijo pues yo aquí necesitaría un cuarteto, aquí necesitaría un coro, aquí necesitaría una aría... Además como era la primera vez que hacía una obra tan importante, es una compositora muy joven que tiene treinta y siete/treinta y ocho años, estaba insegura, la cambió muchas veces. Por ejemplo, el final lo cambió como siete veces. El papel preponderante de Torbellino también tuvo razones escénicas. O sea que en alguna medida es un trabajo supeditado, subordinado a la música y la dramaturgia.

— Of course, I think that with the libretto of an opera you are obliged to be very modest. Because the libreto, as I said, is no more than a support for the music, the most important thing about an opera is the music and then the staging, the scene setting. Therefore, I placed myself at the service of Marisa Manchado, the composer. I wrote a first draft, she read it and told me here I need a quartet, there I need a chorus, here I need an aria... What's more as it was the first time that she had written such an important work, she's a very young composer who is thirty seven or thirty eight, she was very unsure of herself, she changed it a lot. For example she changed the ending something like seven times. The predominant role of Torbellino was also due to reasons of staging. To a certain extent it's a jod which depends on the requirements of the music and staging.

— *Sí, la ópera se parecía casi a un cuento de hadas. Torbellino, por su forma de vestir se pareció mucho a Campanilla de <u>Peter Pan</u>, ya no era enana.*

— *The opera seems almost like a fairy tale. Torbellino's costume resembles that of Tinkerbell in Peter Pan and she wasn't a dwarf.*

— No, hubo problemas para encontrar a una enana que cantara. Pero está muy bien observado lo del cuenticito de hadas. La idea era hacer esto, un cuenticito como de aventuras, mágico, circense, un anecdota digamos.

— No, we had problems finding a dwarf that could sing. But that's a good observation about the fairy tale. The idea was to do something that would be like a fairy tale, and adventure story, magical, circus-like, an anecdote let's say.

— *La producción teatral de <u>El nido de los sueños</u> ¿cómo fue?*
— *What was the theatre production of <u>El nido de los sueños</u> like?*

— Pues, en esa yo no interviné para nada. Era una producción de un grupo especializado en teatro para niños, que tiene un teatro estable de hecho, tiene un local que es suyo en propiedad. Entonces, cada año hacen una o dos obras y las mantienen y luego hacen repertorio. Es una gente muy maja y lo hicieron muy bien. Son producciones muchas más baratas sin comparación con la ópera, como puedes comprender. Es decir, la ópera tenía una subvención del estado. Como es privado está hecho mucho más como teatro 'amateur'. Son profesionales, pero está hecho más como ese tipo de teatro. A pesar de eso era muy gracioso, los dragones eran un aparato que daba vueltas y echaba fuego... Era bonito, estaba bien.

— Well, I had nothing to do with that. It was a production by a group which specialises in children's theatre, in fact they have a regular theatre, I mean their own locale. So each year they put on one or two plays and then do repertory with them. They're a great bunch and did it very well. Their productions are low budget, no comparison with the opera as you can understand. The opera had a government subsidy. As this was private it was much more like amateur dramatics. They are professionals but it's more like that type of theatre. Despite that it was very amusing, the dragons were an apparatus which swivelled round and threw flames... It was nice, it was well done.

— *¿Ha habido intentos para filmar tus novelas?*
— *Have there been attempts to film your novels?*

— Sí, varias veces me han propuesto hacer películas pero no te creas que estoy muy interesada relativamente. Quiero decir en primer lugar, yo desde luego no tengo ningún interés en hacer un guión de mis libros para nada, me aburriría muchísimo. Un guión cinematográfico es mucho más largo que un libreto de una ópera, necesita mucho más trabajo y no tengo ningunas ganas de meterme en ese trabajo. Y luego, lo único que puede interesarme de un paso al cine de mis libros, es que un director o directora que a mí me interese haga algo propio, suyo sobre mis libros. Ver lo que les haya inspirado, eso sí que me interesa. Para eso necesito primero que me interese el director o la directora. Ha habido a veces propuestas, conozco muy bien el medio cinematográfico que es un delirio. Ha habido varias propuestas que yo he rechazado y luego ha habido otras que si que he aceptado que luego... Por ejemplo hubo una propuesta hace muchos años de Josefina Molina, que es una directora española que me interesa mucho, para hacer *Crónica del desamor*. Se empezó, la pagaron y todo, y un poco antes de empezar a rodar quebró la productora. Hay una directora argentina joven que también me interesa, no me acuerdo de como se llama. He visto una película suya sobre un cuento de Bioy-Casares, estaba bien. Tomó una opción para *Te trataré como a una reina*, pero no se que pasó con ella. Así que ha habido algunas que me han interesado y les he dado opciones pero ninguna ha terminado ninguna película.

— Yes, I've had quite a few prpositions to make films but I'm not that interested really. In the first place, I'm not at all interested in converting my books into scripts, I'd get very bored. A cinematographic script is much longer than the libretto for an opera, it needs a lot more work and I really don't feel like getting involved in that line of work. The only aspect that might interest me about transferring my books to the cinema would be if a director I really liked did something that was their own with one of my books. To see what had inspired them, that would interest me. For that first you need to be interested in the director. I have had propositions, I know the cinematographic milieu which is crazy. There have been proposiiotns which I have rejected and others which I accepted but... For example many years ago Josefina Molina, a Spanish director I like a lot, suggested making *Crónica del desamor*. They started, they paid and everything but a little before shooting was due to start the production company went bankrupt. There was a young Argentinean director who I also like, her name escapes me. I'd seen a film of hers based on a short story by Bioy-Casares which was good. She took an option on *Te trataré como a una reina* but I don't know what happened. So there have been some which have interested me and I've given options but no film has ever been finished.

—*En la portada de* La vida desnuda *dice que tienes publicados libros de cuentos, yo pensaba que no...*

— *On the flyleaf of* La vida desnuda *it says that you have published books of short stories, I didn't think you had...*

—Pues, no. Se equivocan con eso. Piensan que *El nido de los sueños* es un libro de cuentos, no sé por que. Es un error que he visto en varios sitios. Luego, lo que sí que está es un libro colectivo *Doce relatos de mujer* editado por Ymelda Navajos donde hay un cuento mío.

— I haven't. They made a mistake. They thought that *El nido de los sueños* was a book of stories, I don't know why. It's a mistake I've seen in various places. What does exist is a collective book, *Doce relatos de mujer* edited by Ymelda Navajos which contains one of my stories.

— *Varios de los cuentos que has escrito tienen como protagonistas a hombres mientras que eso pasa en tan sólo una de tus novelas, <u>Amado amo</u>. ¿Por qué?*
— Several of your short stories have men as their protagonists but that only occurs in one of your novels, <u>Amado amo</u>. Why?
— Está bien pensado, muy bien mirado. Es curioso, sí. ¿Por qué? El cuento que estoy escribiendo ahora tiene por protagonista a una mujer pero de primero pensé hacerlo un hombre. Sabes, no lo sé, no me había parado a pensarlo... No creo que sea siempre así pero algo que puede influir en esto es que al ser un cuento hay una distancia tan corta. Si tu haces una novela, es un mundo tan complejo que puedes crear algo propio. Como ya me has oído decir hablando de eso, una cosa muy importante en la literatura es encontrar la distancia con el objeto narrado. En una novela no es que sea más fácil, sino que es un trabajo tan complejo que la distancia está metido ya dentro de ese trabajo. En un cuento que es brevísimo, yo he solido hacer cuentos muy breves además, encontrar la distancia con el objeto narrado quizá sea más difícil porque para eso necesitas una elaboración mayor. Quizá el hecho de que sea un hombre, el protagonista, favorece la creación de esa distancia. No lo sé, estoy pensando en él y pienso que puede ser uno de los ingredientes. Favorece la creación de esa distancia de una manera más rápida mientras que en una novela no necesitas eso.
— That's well thought out, well spotted. It's curious, isn't it? Why? The story I'm writing now has a woman as protagonist but initially I was going to make it a man. You know what? I don't know why, I've never thought about it... I don't think that this is always the reason but something that might influence this is that there is such a short distance in a story. If you write a novel, it's such a complex world that you can create something which belongs to you. As you've already heard me say, something very important in literature is finding the distance between you and the object narrated. In a novel it's not that it's easier, but it's such a complex piece of work that the distance is already embedded in it. In a very short story, and I do usually write very short stories, finding that distance is perhaps more difficult because for that you need a greater development. Perhaps having a man as protagonist favours the creation of that distance. I don't know, I'm thinking about it and that could be one of the ingredients. It favours the

creation of that distance in a more rapid manner whilst in a novel that's not necessary.

— *En todas las novelas aparece el problema de la comunicación entre hombres y mujeres, especialmente en* Te trataré como a una reina. *¿Por qué crees que tenemos ese problema?*

— *All of the novels feature the problem of communication between men and women especially in* Te trataré como a una reina. *Why do you think we have this problem?*

— Creo que hoy habría dos niveles, por un lado el problema básico de comunicación entre seres humanos al margen de los sexos que es, yo creo, lo que me preocupa por la sencilla razón de que refleja esa cosa metafísica y básica de la soledad individual. Es decir todos estamos solos, pero no solos físicamente sino frente a nuestra propia muerte o existencia. Entonces, esa falta de comunicación última con el entorno refleja y potenzia esa soledad metafísica básica. Me conmueve mucho la soledad externa, básica que es la soledad de tu propia muerte. Eso sería en cuanto a la comunicación general. Luego, específicamente habría otro nivel que es inferior, ese es más básico y engloba todo, que es el de la dificultad de entendernos hombres y mujeres. Creo por un lado que esa ansiedad, esa soledad metafísica de que he hablado antes que es la soledad de la propia muerte, queremos engañarla de una manera más fuerte con el amor. El amor, el deseo de amar, el espejismo del amor, el espejismo de la pasión hace que en esos momentos de amor apasionados no nos sintamos solos, sintamos la fusión. Es un espejismo, es mentira pero tendemos a creer en esos momentos que podemos comunicarnos, más que comunicarnos, fundirnos con el otro y no estar solos por lo tanto. Entonces, eso pone más en evidencia, cuando el espejismo se rompe, la distancia, el abismo insalvable que hay entre hombres y mujeres. Hemos creído que nos podemos entender pero no es más que un espejismo. Por otro lado además, hombres y mujeres somos muy distintos. ¿Por qué somos muy distintos? Es muy interesante, somos lo otro el uno del otro. Yo creo que simbólicamente, culturalmente, nuestras fantasías son muy distintas. A medida que voy creciendo más, me voy dando cuenta de lo distinto que somos y hasta cierto punto es excitante eso. Quiero decir, antes me desesperaba y ahora no me desespero. Ahora creo que eso es lo que crea la magia del espejismo, y es muy fascinante la dualidad que representamos. Hay una dificultad básica de comunicación pero porque hay una dificultad básica entre los seres humanos, y con los hombres, siendo mujeres, todavía estamos más lejos los unos de los otros pero, curiósamente y paradójicamente cuando nos enamoramos nos creemos que estamos más cercano.

— I think that nowadays there are two levels, on the one hand the basic problem of communication between people, leaving to one side the question of sex, which worries me for the simple reason that it reflects the metaphysical and basic thing which is individual solitude. That's to say we're all alone, but not only physically but in facing our own death or existence. Therefore, this ultimate lack of communication with our surroundings reflects and strengthens this basic metaphysical solitude. This basic external solitude, the solitude of your own death, moves me a lot. This would refer to general communication. Then there is another more specific inferior level which is basic and includes everything, the difficulty of understanding between men and women. I think that on the one hand this anxiety, this metaphysical solitude which I talked about which is the solitude of your own death, we want to outsmart it with something stronger, with love. Love, the desire to love, the illusion of love, the illusion of passion mean that in those moments of passionate love we don't feel alone, we feel fusion. It's an illusion, it's a lie but we tend to believe that in those instances we can communicate, more than communicate, we can merge with other and therefore not be alone. But this makes even clearer, when the illusion breaks, the distance, the unbreachable abyss between men and women. we think that we can understand each other but that's nothing more than an illusion. On the other hand, what's more, men and women are very different. Why are we different? It's very interesting, we are the other of each other. I think that symbolically, culturally, our fantasies are very different. As I get older, I realise just how different we are and to a certain extent that is exciting. I mean it used to make me despair but not anymore. Now I believe that it's what creates the magic of illusion and the duality we represent is fascinating. There is a basic difficulty in communicating but because there is a difficulty between human beings, and with men, as women, we're even further from one another but, strangely enough and paradoxically when we fall in love we think that we are closer.

— *Bueno en la respuesta salieron varios temas de las cuales quisiera hablar. Uno era la soledad, ¿es importante para ti?*

— *Well, in your reply there were various themes I wanted to talk more about. One was solitude. Is it important for you?*

— ¿La soledad cotidiana quieres decir? Claro, es fundamental para todos los seres humanos aprender a vivir solos. ¿Y qué significa aprender a vivir solos? Soportarse a sí mismos, no tener miedo de sí mismos, poder estar solos consigo mismos sin aterrarse y sin salir corriendo. Hay mucha gente que no rompe con una pareja solo por el miedo de estar solo aunque sea una relación asquerosa. Hay mucha gente que si se quedan solo una noche en casa empiezan a llamar a toda la agenda porque no lo soportan. Eso es ser esclavo de ti mismo. También la soledad me es importante. He vivido sola muchos años, como diez años. No es lo que más me gusta. Supongo que es mejor una vida compartida, rica si funciona, pero por otro lado necesito momentos de soledad. Para mí creo que lo ideal sería una vida en pareja pero que viajara mucho. [Se ríe mucho] O que viviera en otra ciudad y sólo nos viéramos los fines de semana. O sea la mezcla porque la soledad es muy importante, es muy creativa. Te permite reunirte contigo misma, te permite apartarte un poco del ruido exterior, te permite concentrar tus fuerzas. La creatividad necesita la soledad, no puedes ser creativo si no estás solo y te piensas el mundo. Por eso necesitas estar solo.

— Do you mean day to day solitude? Of course, it's fundamental for humans to learn to live alone. What does learning to live alone mean? Putting up with yourself, not being afraid of yourself, being able to be alone without being terrified or running out as fast as your legs can carry you. There are lots of people who don't split up with their partner just because they're frightened to be alone although the relationship is lousy. There are lots of people who if they're alone at home one night start to call everyone in their address book because they can't stand it. That's being a slave to yourself. Solitude is also important to me. I've lived alone many years, ten or so. It's not what I like most. I suppose a shared life is better, great if it works, but on the other hand I need time alone. For me the ideal would be living with a partner who travels a lot. [She laughs a lot] Or who lived in another city and we only saw each other weekends. A mix, because solitude is very importrnat, it's very creative. It allows you to meet up with yourself, set yourself aside from the noise outside, it allows you to concentrate your efforts. Creativity needs solitude, you can't be creative unless you're alone and think about the world. To do that you need to be alone.

— *Otro tema muy importante en tu obra es el amor.¿Para ti, cuál es la diferencia entre amor-pasión y amor-cómplice?*

— *Another important thene in your work is love. What is the difference for you between passionate love and the love of companionship?*

— Pues eso esa una reflexión que me hice cuando escribí *La función delta* y era un intento de gobernar el ingobernable. Hoy, no sé si eso existe tal cual pero con esa diferencia quería reflejar una dualidad que ha sido tratada en la literatura universal de toda la vida que es la dualidad entre el amor-pasión que en hombre es el amor-carnal y el amor-cotidiano que en hombre será el de la madre de tus hijos. La madre de mis hijos y la amante, esa ha sido una dualidad tradicional. Eso es lo que yo intentaba también ordenar u organizar o analizar o reflexionar sobre ello, porque hay un tipo de amor que es el de la pasión, que es el invento, que es emocionante, que es maravilloso, que te crees que te puedes unir con el otro, lo que hablábamos de la fusión, el éxtasis. Ese tipo de pasión enloquecida y maravillosa y brillante se apoye en el invento, o sea en el desconocimiento del otro. Por lo tanto, no hay complicidad porque desconoces al otro, no hay cariño cotidiano porque desconoces al otro. Eso es el tipo de amor que normalmente entendemos por amor. Luego, está el otro que es el del cariño cotidiano, conoces al otro y eres amigo de la otra persona. Es una complicidad amistosa más que nada pero, no existe la pasión. ¿Cómo se puede solucionar esto? Hay personas, hombres y mujeres, que sienten esa dualidad de una manera muy extrema y hay personas, hombres y mujeres, que son más afortunadas y no sienten esa dualidad de una manera tan extrema. Yo lo siento de una manera muy extrema, para mi desgracia porque dificulta mucha la vida.

— That was a reflection of mine when I wrote *La función delta* and it was an attempt to control the uncontrollable. Now I don't know whether it exists but with that distinction I wanted to reflect a duality which has been written about in all universal literture and that is the duality between the passionate love which for a man is carnal love and the veryday love which for a man would be that for the mother of his children. The mother of my children and my lover, has been a traditional dualism. That is what I was also trying to order or organise or analyse or reflect upon, because there is a type of love which is passion, which is make-believe, which is exciting, which is marvellous, which makes you think that you can unite with the other, the fusion we were talking about, ecstasy. This type of mad, marvellous, brilliant passion is based in make-believe, i.e. in ignorance about the other. Therefore there is no complicity because you don't know the other, there isn't the everyday tenderness because you don't know the other. This is what we usually understand by love. Then there is the other type of love which is everyday caring, you know the other person and are their friend. It is a friendly complicity more than anything but passion doesn't exist. How can you solve this? There are people, men and women, who feel this duality in a very extreme way and there are people, men and women, who are more fortunate and don't feel it in such an extreme fashion. I feel it in a very extreme way, unfortunately for me because it makes life very difficult.

— *¿Por qué crees que el bolero, el tipo de canción que utilizaste en <u>Te trataré como a una reina</u>, está recobrando popularidad aquí en España? Han sacado colecciones de varios cantantes que están funcionando muy bien como por ejemplo de Los Panchos y Lucho Gática.*

— *Why do you think the bolero, the type of song you incorporated into <u>Te trataré como a una reina</u>, is becoming popular again in Spain? Some very successful compilations have been released by various singers such as Los Panchos and Lucho Gática.*

— Pues, no lo sé. Siempre creo que hubo un público para el bolero. Es posible sí que haya un nuevo público. Son modas, entre otras cosas Almodóvar pone boleros en sus películas y crea una moda. Puede que esté unido con el auge de los culebrones y fotonovelas. Hay como una necesidad de lo sentimental y de las mentiras dulces. Quizás porque la vida cotidiana ha alejado mucho esa parte de lo sentimental. Quizás, no lo sé por que, pero es verdad que hay un cierto retorno.

— I don't know. I think there was always a market for boleros. It's possible that there is a new one. There are fashions, amongst other things Almodóvar includes boleros in his films and creates a trend. It could be linked to the rise of the soap operas and photoromances. There is a sort of need for sentimentality and sweet lies. Perhaps because daily life has distanced itself from its emotional component. Perhaps, I don't know why, but it's true that there has been a move back to it.

— *En el bolero se habla mucho del deseo, un deseo muchas veces frustrada. Se trata de un deseo que no se puede cumplir. En <u>Te trataré como a una reina</u> los deseos tampoco se cumplen.*

— *The bolero talks a lot about desire, a desire which is often frustrated. It's about a desire which cannot be satisfied. Also in* Te trataré como a una reina *desires cannot be satisfied.*

— Sí, los deseos nunca se cumplen. Desgraciado aquel que cumple sus deseos. El deseo siempre está fuera de nosotros, tan inalcanzable como el horizonte. Si cumples el deseo, el deseo se abrasa, el deseo se quema, deja de ser deseo. Entonces, eso es una de las condiciones básicas del ser humano, esa inquietud, esa insatisfacción, ese agujero que nunca se llena. Esa falta de completud, que nunca somos completos. Tenemos siempre algo fuera que es como la proyección de lo que nos sanaría, de lo que nos curaría, de lo que nos calmaría. Eso es una de las cosas que más me conmueve del ser humano, la evidente imposibilidad de cumplir los deseos. De eso trata fundamentalmente *Te trataré como a una reina*: la distancia enorme que hay entre el deseo de felicidad y la posibilidad de cumplirlo. El bolero especifica muy claramente esa contradicción y por eso lo escogí.

— Yes, desires are never satisfied. Miserable is he whose desires are satisfied. Desire is always outside us, as unreachable as the horizon. If you satisfy your desire, the desire is consumed, the desire burns up, it is no longer desire. This then is one of the basic conditions of the human being, this preoccupation, this insatisfaction, this hole which is never filled, we are never complete. We always have something outside us which is like the projection of that which would bring us back to health, cure us, pacify us. That is one of the things which moves me most about humans, the obvious impossibility of satisfying desires. That is what *Te trataré como a una reina* is basically about: the enormous distance between the desire for happiness and the possibility for being happy. The bolero clarifies this contradiction in particular and that's why I chose it.

— *¿Qué entiendes por los terminos realidad y fantasía?*
— *What do you understand by the terms fantasy and reality?*

— Pues mira, para mí la fantasía es parte de la realidad. Lo que pasa es que normalmente la gente entiende por realidad algo absolutamente limitador, algo absolutamente corto desde mi punto de vista. La gente normalmente entiende por realidad, o por realismo en literatura sobre todo, algo que no es más que un torpe costumbrismo. Para mí, la realidad es algo muchísimo más complejo, la realidad es lo mensurable, lo tangible, lo exterior pero, también es los sueños, los miedos, los deseos, es todas las dimensiones del ser. Las dimensiones del ser son enormes y plurales y paradójicas y además se dan a la vez lo que es y lo que no es. Entonces para mí, buscar vías fantásticas no es más que una manera más profunda, más compleja, menos limitadora de reflejar la realidad.

— Well look, for me fantasy is part of reality. But people normally understand by the term reality something completely limiting, insufficient from my point of view. People normally understand by the term reality, or above all realism in literature, something which is nothing more than a clumsy *costumbrismo*. For me, reality is something much much more complex: reality is what can be measured, the tangible, the external, but it is also dreams, fears, desires. It is all these facets of being. The facets of being are vast and plural and paradoxical and besides at the same time what is and what is not coexist. Therefore for me, searching for fantastic paths is nothing more than a more profound, more complex, less limiting way of reflecting reality.

— *Dijiste una vez que nombrar es una manera de construir...*
— *You said once that naming is a way of constructing...*

— Bueno, esto es complejísimo. [Se ríe] Quiero decir ¿qué es la palabra? Primero, la palabra es lo que nos hace humanos, la palabra es lo que nos saca de la animalidad. La palabra nos da el alma. Y con esa palabra, ¿qué conseguimos? Conseguimos ordenar el mundo. ¿Por qué ordenamos el mundo? Porque al nombrarlo le vamos dando una forma determinada. La palabra es una manera de codificar la realidad, detallar la realidad. La realidad es compleja y tiene muchísimas dimensiones. De hecho tu puedes escoger un tipo de vida u otro. Los budistas tibetanos viven una vida sensorial muy distinta de la tuya y de la mía. Pueden creer en el tercer ojo que ve el aura magnética, su visión del mundo es absolutamente distinta. O el indio yaqui del desierto de Sonora, cuando ve un águila está viendo a sus antepasados o a su totem y yo estoy viendo un águila. O sea que vemos cosas distintas. Todo eso se refleja en una ordenación verbal. El discurso que vas desarrollando es el que va dando forma al mundo, y cada vez que nombras estás escogiendo una de las posibilidades del mundo y haciendo que sea esa y no otra. Desde este punto de vista, también al nombrar estás poseyendo esa parte de la realidad. De hecho, estás creándola, por así decirlo. Las posibilidades de la realidad son infinitas y, al nombrar de una manera al mundo y no de otra, estás creando ese mundo concreto para ti, esa realidad concreta para ti. Y al crear lo que creas es tuyo, tu creación es hija tuya. Es para mí una explicación del mundo, de la realidad que vivimos. Por otro lado, te darás cuenta de que la escritura de una novela es un símbolo de esto. Al nombrar estás creando mundos concretos que son mundos narrativos. Al nombrar tienes el poder de la creación de esa historia que has hecho.

— Well, this is very complex. [She laughs] I mean, what is the word? Firstly, the word is what makes us human, the word is what differentiates us from animals. The word gives us soul. And with that word, what have we achieved? we have managed to order the world. Why do we order the world? Because by naming it we give it a certain shape. The word is a way of codifying reality, detailing it. Reality is complex and has very many dimensions. In fact you can choose one way of life over another. Tibetan buddhists live a very different sensory life to yours or mine. They believe in the third eye which sees the magnetic aura. Their vision of the world is completely different. Or the Yaqui Indian of the Sonora desert, when he sees an eagle he is seeing an ancestor or totem and I'm seeing an eagle. In other words we see different things. All of that is reflected in a verbal ordering. The discourse that you develop is what gives shape to the world and each time you name somehting you are choosing one of the possibilities of the world and ensuring that it is this one and not another. From this perspective, by naming you are also possessing part of reality. the possibilities of reality are infinite and by naming the world in one way and not another, you are creating a concrete world for yourself, a concrete reality for yourself. And by creating what you create is yours, your creation is your daughter. That is an explanation of the world for me, of the reality in which we live. By naming you are creating concrete worlds which are narrative worlds. By naming you have the power to create the story you have told.

— *Has utilizado una metáfora muy interesante para la creación, la de dar a luz...*

— *You have used a very interesting metaphor for creation, that of giving birth...*

— Espera un momentito, es simplemente para una cosa de lo de antes, lo del poder de las palabras. De ese poder mágico, ese poder creador de las palabras... el ser humano ha sido consciente desde siempre y, de hecho, en todas las religiones hay palabras mágicas. Los judíos no pueden decir el nombre de Dios. La cábala tiene números y palabras mágicas. Palabras mágicas ha habido siempre porque se tiene consciencia del poder creador; en los cuentos por ejemplo, en *Las mil y una noches* Alí Baba que llega y dice "Abre sésamo", las palabras parten montañas.

— Hang on a second, it's about something we were talking about before, the power of words. Of that magic power, that creative power of words... humans have always been conscious of it and in fact, in all religions there are magic words. Jew cannot say God's name. The kabbalah has magic numbers and words. Magic words have always existed because we are conscious of their creative power, in stories for example, in *The Thousand and One Nights* Ali Baba arrives and says "Open Sesame", words can split open mountains.

— Quería hablar un poco del miedo que tienen los hombres a las mujeres por ejemplo en <u>Te trataré como a una reina</u> o <u>Amado amo</u>. No sé si en la última instancia ese miedo se podría relacionar con la capacidad de la mujer de dar a luz.

— I'd like to talk a bit about the fear that men have of women for example in <u>Te trataré como a una reina</u> or <u>Amado amo</u>. I don't know if ultimately that fear can be realted to the capacity for women to give birth.

— Sí, creo que sí, completamente. De hecho, eso se dice un poco en *Temblor* cuando digo una tesis de la cual estoy completamente convencida que es: toda la estructura machista, la estructura patriarcal de la sociedad desde el principio de los tiempos se ha creado por el terror del hombre hacia el poder mágico de la mujer de dar vida. Imagínate en sociedades primitivas lo aterrador que debía ser esa capacidad, ese poder increíble de la mujer de dar vida. Es lo más importante que se puede pensar. Ante ese terror, seres físicamente más fuertes inventaron toda una estructura que mantuviera eso dominado de algún modo. El complejo de castración de Freud es alucinante porque el habla del complejo de castración de las mujeres, que nos falta la polla, y el tío no se para, como buen hombre con ese trauma metido dentro desde milenios, no se para a hacer una revisión en absoluto de lo que pueden sentir los hombres ante el hecho alucinante de la capacidad de la mujer de dar a luz y de crear vida. Entonces, yo creo que el complejo de castración es también una defensa del hombre ante su vacío, su esterilidad, su incapacidad creativa. En la base de las relaciones entre los hombres y las mujeres, en la base del patriarcado está el miedo del poder tremendo de la mujer, del poder procreador.

— I think so, absolutely. In fact that is expressed to some extent in *Temblor* when I put forward a theory I'm completely convinced of: all the machista structure, the patriarchal structure of society since the beginning of time has been created because of man's terror faced with woman's magical power to give birth. Imagine how terrifying that ability must have been in primitive societies, that incredible power women have to give life. It's the most importnat thing you can think of. Faced with that fear, physically stronger beings invented a whole structure which could dominate this in some way. Freud's castration complex is astonishing because he talks about women's castration complex, the fact that we haven't got dicks and he doesn't stop to think, like a typical man with that trauma which he has kept inside for millenia, he doesn't stop to consider for a momen what men might feel faced with the amazing ability of women to give birth and create life. Therefore I think that the castration complex is a male defense against emptiness, sterility, creative incapacity. At the heart of relationships between men and women, at the heart of patriarchy is the fear of women's tremendous power, the power to procreate.

— *Para terminar, ¿Estás escribiendo algo?*
— *To finish off, are you writing anything?*
— Sí, estoy escribiendo un cuento para *El País*, para las lecturas del verano pero, estoy bloqueada, desde que terminé *Bella y oscura* no he escrito nada. Me bloqueé otra vez, como sabes, después de *Te trataré como una reina*. Estuve cuatro años sin escribir, esta vez también me he bloqueado y yo creo que por las mismas razones posiblemente. En *Te trataré como una reina* me fui muy lejos de lo que hacía antes y yo creo que en *Bella y oscura* también ha habido un adelanto, un cambio fuerte, un salto. Entonces, cogí un cuento en *El País* a propósito para forzarme a escribir. Estoy contenta porque, aunque me está costando, he encontrado una historia que yo creo que es muy bonito y creo que me está quedando bien. Noto que estoy un poco oxidada pero la historia está y a lo mejor consigo salir del atasco. El cuento lo he terminado, ya está y yo creo además que es un buen cuento pero no sé si eso luego redundará en más cosas.

— Yes, I'm writing a short story for *El País*, for the summer reading but I have writer's block, since I finished *Bella y oscura* I haven't written a thing. I had a block before, as you know, after *Te trataré como a una reina*. I didn't write for four years, this time I've also got a block and it might be for the same reasons.

With *Te trataré como a una reina* I went much further than with what I had done before and I think that with *Bella y oscura* I have also taken a step forward, there has been a strong shift, a jump. That's why I decided to write a story for *El País*, to force myself to write. I'm happy because although it's proving difficult, I've found a story which I think is very attractive and I think it's turning out well. I can tell I'm a bit rusty but the story is there and maybe I'll get out of the rut. I've finished the story, it's done and I think that it's a good story but I don't know if it will lead to anything else.

INTERVIEW THREE
(Madrid, 23 July 1997)
This interview appears with the permission of Carfax Publishing Ltd

— *Leí el libro que hiciste para niños, <u>Las barbaridades de Bárbara</u>. ¿Por qué otro libro para niños?*
— *I read the book you wrote for children, <u>Las barbaridades de Bárbara</u>. Why another children's book?*

— Me lo propusieron y cometí un error. Me llamó el que llevaba Alfaguay que antes era Miguel Barrero. Me dijo que quería hacer libros para niños, que querían hacer un personaje que fuera realista para niños de diez años. Un encargo muy concreto, una chica, una niña. Yo me lo pensé y me dije, pues a lo mejor yo divido mi trabajo de escritura entre la escritura profesional, que me encanta hacerla lo mejor posible, y la escritura personal, las novelas. La escritura profesional con la que me gano la vida es el periodismo. Entonces pensé, pues podría diversificar, hacer también otras cosas como escritura profesional. A lo mejor hacer libros de niños que es como poner una huertecita, ¿no? Los libros de niños se venden por otro lado, se siguen vendiendo de una manera pequeña pero regular. Pues puede librarme un poco del periodismo porque llevo demasiados años ya como periodista. Entonces dije que sí y firmé un contrato por tres libros y me equivoqué porque ahora lo único que he hecho ha sido cargarme de demasiado trabajo porque al principio no te puedes librar de nada de lo otro. Lo único que tienes es más trabajo. It could free me a bit from journalism because I've been a journalist too long now.

Ya he entregado el segundo libro. Es mucho más fantasioso. Es fantástico porque me aburría volver a hacer otro libro como el primer Bárbara, tan realista.

He hecho un segundo Bárbara muchísimo más fantástico, con los mismos personajes pero les meto en otro mundo. Me he quedado con el otro tercero y estoy deseando terminarlo y acabar con el encargo.

— I was asked to do it and it was a mistake. I was called by the boss of Alfaguay, it used to be Miguel Barrero. He said that he wanted to do books for children, they wanted a realistic character for ten year olds. It was a very specific commission, a little girl. I though about it and said to myself, well why not divide my work between professional writing, which I like to do as well as possible, and personal writing, the novels. The professional writing I earn my living with is journalism. So I thought I could diversify, do other things too as part of my professional writing. Maybe writing children's books is like having a little orchard to fall back on. Children's books have a different market, they carry on selling slowly but surely. So I said yes and signed a contract for three books but it was a mistake because now all I've done is end up with too much work because at first you can't free yourself from anything. All you have is more work.

I've submitted the second book now. It's much more fantastic. It's fantastic because it would have bored me to write another book like the first Bárbara, so realist. I've created a second much more fantastic Bárbara, with the same characters but transported to another world. I'm still stuck with the third and I want to finish it and the commission.

— *El primero sí era realista, pero había dos ideas que ocurren a menudo en su obra: lo de que las cosas no son siempre como parecen y lo del truco del deseo.*

— *The first was realist but there were two ideas which reoccur in your work: things are never as they seem and the trick of desire.*

— Sí, al fin y al cabo soy la misma persona que escribe pero lo hice de una manera muy profesional. El segundo, me he divertido más haciéndolo. Me he enrollado más y es que no he hecho ni caso de lo que me pedían y es mejor.

— Yes, after all I'm the same person writing but I did it in a professional manner. With the second, I had more fun. I got more involved and didn't pay any attention to what they had asked for and it's much better.

— *¿Por qué lo hiciste en primera persona?*
— *Why did you write it in the first person?*

— Para darle simplemente más fuerza a ese tipo de libro. Un poco como un recurso estilístico para niños, ni siquiera niños muy lectores. Yo pensé que podía atraer más, una manera de entrada más fácil en la lectura para los niños.

— To give that type of book more impact. A kind of stylistic device for children, not even children who like reading a lot. I thought it might be more attractive, an easier way into reading for children.

— *La hija del caníbal* también está en primera persona...
— *La hija del caníbal* is also in the first person...

— Sí, eso sí que es una elección. Me apetecía porque yo nunca había hecho una novela en primera persona. Entonces me apetecía porque la primera persona tiene mucho encanto, tiene mucha fuerza y tiene una capacidad de escritura que me apetecía ensayar. Ya soy lo suficientemente madura, literaria y personalmente, para poder utilizar la primera persona sin miedo a que el ruido de tu propio entorno se meta en la novela porque esto es uno de los peligros de la literatura joven, ¿no? La primera persona vehicula mucho eso. Y ahora no. Yo sé que puedo utilizar la primera persona como recurso literario.

— Yes, that was a clear choice. I felt like it because I had never written a novel in the first person. So I felt like it because the first person is very attractive, it has a lot of impact and a capacity for writing which I wanted to try out. I'm now sufficiently mature, both literarily and personally, to be able to use the first person without being scared that the noise of my own life will interfere in the novel because that is one of the dangers of literature written when you're young, isn't it? But not now. I know that I can use the first person as a literary device.

— *Ha sido un éxito tremendo, ¿no?*
— *It has been a great success, hasn't it?*

— Bueno, la verdad es que además está pasando una cosa con este libro curiosísima y es que hasta ahora no he encontrado a nadie a que no le haya gustado. Más o menos, a todo el mundo, con todos mis libros... para nada, lo cual es lógico. Cuando vas por ejemplo a la feria del libro, allí llegan los lectores y te dicen «A mí este último...», *Bella y oscura*, por ejemplo, que es un libro que me gusta mucho, es un libro muy cercano y tengo un rollo con este libro muy especial. Pues es un libro que a mucha gente no le ha gustado. A muchos sí les ha gustado, pero a mucha gente no le gusta porque es duro, es raro. Entonces llegaban lectores y me decían «Me gusta este mucho pero *Bella y oscura*, pues...». Pues éste todavía no he encontrado a nadie que me ha dicho que no le ha gustado. Yo no sé si es porque tiene muchos niveles, a unos les gusta por la aventura, a otros les gusta por el humor...

— Well, the truth is that something very odd is happening with this book and that's that so far I haven't found anyone who doesn't like it. More or less everyone does, which isn't the case for all my books... not at all, which is only logical. When you go to the *feria del libro* readers come up to you and say. "Well this last one...", for example *Bella y oscura*, which is a book I like a lot, it's very close to me, I have a special relationship with that book. Well it's a book that a lot of people didn't like. A lot did but a lot didn't because it's hard, strange. So readers would come and tell me, "I like this one a lot but *Bella y oscura*, well...". Well I've yet to find anyone who's told me that they don't like this one. I don't know if it's because it has lots of different levels, some like it because of the adventure, others because of the humour.

— *Todas las reseñas que he leído han sido buenas...*
— *All of the reviews I have read have been good...*
— Incluso las de los enemigos, como por ejemplo en *ABC*. La hizo un tío que siempre me ha puesto a parir y no ha tenido más remedio que decir que está bien escrito, que es una buena narrativa. No ha tenido más remedio que no hacer una mala crítica y eso es la hostia. Está como tocado, el libro este, por la magia. Eso es curioso, es raro, es demasiado la unanimidad. Me da un poco de miedo.
— Even those by my enemies, like *ABC* for example. It was written by a guy who has always slagged me off and he had no choice but to say that it was well written, that it's a good narrative. He had no option other than to write a good review and that's amazing. It's as if this book has a magic touch. It's odd, it's strange, it's too unanimous. It scares me a little.

— *Para el próximo libro, ¿no?*
— *For the next book?*
— Pero el próximo no tiene por qué ser así, no tiene que gustar a todo el mundo. Vamos, lo normal es que no sea así. Estas cosas pasan, es pura casualidad.

— But the next doesn't have to be like that, it doesn't have to please everyone. After all, it would be more normal if it didn't. These things happen, it's pure chance.

— *En La hija del caníbal se observan ciertas preocupaciones que suelen repetirse en tus libros: la sensación de carencia, de pérdida de algo, acompañada, sin embargo, de una fe profunda en la vida. Sobre todo, hay en este libro, por una vez, un final feliz.*

— *In La hija del caníbal several of the anxieties which tend to reoccur in your books appear: the sense of lack, of loss of something, accompanied nevertheless by a deep faith in life. Above all, in this book, you have a happy ending for the first time.*

— Sí, es la primera vez que consigo hacer un final feliz y es una afirmación de la vida. Creo que quería, desde hacía tiempo, escribir un libro con un final feliz pero no conseguía creérmelo. En éste creo que hay un final coherente. No es idiota sino que es comprensible. Creo que lo necesitaba. Necesitaba, emocional y biográficamente, construir un libro que renovara la fe en la vida de algún modo. A mí me ha sentado bien escribir este libro.

— Yes, it's the first time I've managed to write a happy ending which is an affirmation of life. I think that I've wanted to write a book with a happy ending for a long time but I couldn't believe in it. In this one I think that the ending is coherent. It's understandable not stupid. I think I needed it. I needed, both emotionally and biographically, to construct a book which would renew my faith in life to some extent. It felt good to me to write this book.

— *Como el libro dice, merece la pena luchar, como las ancianitas en sus sillas de ruedas, ¿no?*

— *As the book says, it's worth the struggle, like the little old women in their wheel chairs.*

— Sí, siempre merece la pena.

— Yes, it's always worth fighting for.

— *El luchador más claro en este libro es Fortuna, anarquista y torero, ¿Cómo le salió este personaje?*

— *The clearest fighter in this book is Fortuna, anarchist and bullfighter. How did you create this character?*

— En seguida. Es una obra existencial sobre el crecimiento y las dificultades de la maduración, es una obra de iniciación, en definitiva, pero iniciación en la edad madura. Toda obra de iniciación necesita un maestro, y yo quería buscar a un viejo que tuviera una existencia ya entera mientras que ella tiene una vida por la mitad. Entonces estaba ya pensando en buscar a un viejo y de repente vi un recorte sobre las andanzas de Durruti por América en *El País* del 94/95. Ya estaba por poner a un viejo que le ayudara y dije «¡Joder, anarquista!», porque a mí siempre me han encantado y además siempre me he sentido como muy cercana, íntimamente... aunque nunca he estado en ningún grupo anarquista, me he sentido muy cercana al ideario anarquista. .Entonces me pareció fantástico y dije ya está, y salió anarquista. Luego, la parte de los toros porque mi padre fue torero. Entonces es lo que mi padre me ha contado, y también salió naturalmente porque el personaje empezó a crecer muchísimo y mientras iba pensando en la novela cada vez iba adquiriendo más espacio. De hecho, se convirtió en otro narrador. Yo, al principio, no pensaba que él contara su vida de esa manera, en primera persona, pero luego se convirtió en lo inevitable y tuve que empezar a leer y releer libros sobre el anarquismo porque el tío pedía más y más espacio como personaje. A mí lo que más me gusta de la novela es él.

— Straightaway. It's an existential work about growing older and the difficulties of maturity, it's a work of initiation, specifically, but initiation into old age. All works of initiation need a master and I wanted to find an old man who would already have an entire existence whilst she has a life half lived. So I was already thinking of looking for an old man when I saw a newspaper cutting about the travels of Durruti in America in *El País* in 94/95. I was already looking for an old man to help her and I said "Bloody hell, an anarchist", because I've always liked them and what's more I've always felt very closely, intimately... although I've never been in an anarchist group, I've always felt very close to anarchist ideology. So I thought this was great and said that's it and he came out an anarchist. Then the bullfighting bit is because my father was a bullfighter. It's what my father told me, and it came out naturally because the character started to grow a lot and whilst I was thinking about the novel he began to take up more and more space. In fact, he turned into another narrator. At first I didn't think that he would tell his life like that, in the first person, but it became inevitable and I had to read lots and lots of books on anarchism because the guy needed more and more space as a character. He's what I like most about the novel.

— *Has afirmado en una entrevista que el único personaje real en la novela es la perrafoca, pero en cierta manera Lucía se parece un poco a ti.*

— *You've said that the only real character in the novel is the 'sealdog', but to a certain extent Lucía is like you.*

— Pues, yo creo que no se parece a mí, fíjate. Lo que pasa es que yo no hubiera sabido escribir esa novela a los veinte años. Naturalmente es una novela entendida desde los cuarenta y algo, y trata de la crisis de los cuarenta. En ese sentido hay unas reflexiones que comparto con montones de personas. Pero Lucía es una tía debilísima, yo no me considero así para nada, es una tía tremendamente frustrada y yo no me considero así para nada. Al contrario, soy muy vitalista y creo, hasta ahora... bueno, me he equivocado, pero podría morirme ahora y decir pues he hecho lo que quería hacer. O sea, la antítesis de su manera de relacionarse con la vida. Es una tía que se quiere tan poco a sí misma que hasta el momento de la novela no ha sabido ni construirse amigos.

— You know, I don't think she's like me at all. The thing is that I wouldn't have been able to write this novel when I was twenty. Of course it's a novel from the point of view of being forty-something and it's about the crisis of the forties. In that sense there are thoughts I share with loads of people. But Lucía is a very weak woman, I don't think I'm like that at all, she's extremely frustrated and I'm not like that at all. On the contrary I'm very dynamic and I think that up to now... well, I've made mistakes, but I could die now and say that I've done what I wanted to. In other words, the antithesis of her way of dealing with life. She has so little love for herself that up to the point at which the novel occurs she hasn't even known how to make friends.

— *Lo digo más bien por la conclusión...*

— *I mean more because of the conclusion...*

— A la que llega al final sí. O sea la idea que se desprende del final del libro sí que es mía, pero el personaje no. Yo me siento más cerca quizá, o por lo menos tan cerca, desde luego, de Fortuna como de Lucía.

— That she reaches at the end, yes. In other words the idea that emerges at the end of the book is mine but not the character. I feel closer to perhaps, or at least as close to, of course, Fortuna as Lucía.

— *¿Y la definición que haces de Rosa Montero en la novela?*

— *And the definition of Rosa Montero in the novel?*
— Pues, ésa no soy yo. No es más que un juego con los límites de la identidad que cada vez me interesa más y más. Lo que yo quería hacer con eso es un juego con la realidad y la ficción. Es un pequeñísimo juego, simplemente de todo el juego de las cajas de espejos que es la novela, en donde no se sabe hasta qué punto los personajes se confunden unos con otros, las identidades se confunden unas con otras. Lucía es confundida... podía haber sido la autora del 'Patito Patachín', además podía haber sido la que ha robado el coche pero no lo ha robado, podría ser la Toñi, que va a ver al viejo que se está muriendo pero no es ella. O sea hay una serie de identidades. Por ejemplo, Fortuna que es también Félix, ha sido clandestino. Todo ese juego de las identidades y la irrealidad de la realidad me interesa mucho. Es un juego de espejos mareante. Y dentro de todo este espejo todo el mundo se ha fijado en una chorrada, es un jueguecito más. Lo puse al principio sólo para poder ponerlo al final. Como las novelas parten de la identificación del lector con los personajes, pues me apetecía mucho llegar al final y hacerle una putada al lector. Al final, en el momento en que ella empieza a preguntarse, bueno, qué es ser uno mismo, qué es la identidad. Yo ahora mismo podría ser la Toñi, a quien se le ha muerto el padre, podría ser la que ha robado el coche, incluso podría ser Félix, y ya que miento tanto, quién dice que no sea Rosa Montero y que esto me lo haya inventado todo. Y es la verdad, hasta allí literal. Y eso es una putada para el lector. A mí por lo menos me jode cuando estoy metida en un libro... Pero es que a mí me encanta. Hay que sacar al lector de la convención de la novela de alguna manera. Es un pequeño juego, pero inmediatamente entra la convención otra vez porque no soy negra, no soy guineana, no soy pobre. Vuelve a entrar la convención narrativa. Pero, por un momento, corta con la realidad, la desvela y la niega. Es un juego de la realidad de la imagen. Estoy empezando a pensar en una próxima novela histórica, de la época de Eleonora de Aquitania, de los caballeros, en donde haya al mismo tiempo referencias históricas y referencias completamente inventadas como si fueran históricas pero imposibles. La mezcla entonces resulta desconcertante porque todo está tratado al mismo nivel.

— Well, that's not me. It's no more than a game with the limits of identity which interest me more and more all the time. What I wanted to do with that was play with reality and fiction. It's a tiny little game, within the game of the boxes of mirrors which constitute the novel, in which you don't know to what extent the characters are confused with others. Lucía is confused... she could have been the author of 'Patito Patachín', what's more she could have been the one who stole the car but she didn't, she could be Toñi, who goes to see the old man but it's not her. In other words there is a series of identities. For example, Fortuna who is also Félix, has been clandestine. All this play on identities and the irreality of reality interests me a lot. It's a dizzying game of mirrors. And within this mirror everybody has picked up on a daft little thing, one more small game. I put it at the beginning to return to it at the end. As novels depend on the identification of the reader with the characters, I felt like getting to the end and playing a dirty trick on the reader. At the end when she begins to ask herself, well what is the self, what is identity? I could be Toñi whose father has died, I could be the one who stole the car, I could even be Félix, and as I lie so much, who says that I'm not Rosa Montero and I've made all this up. And it's the literal truth. And that's a dirty trick to play on the reader. At least it pisses me off if I'm immersed in a book... But I love it. You have to remove the reader from convention in some way. It's a little game, but immediately convention returns because I'm not black, I'm not Guinean, I'm not poor. Narrative convention returns. But for a moment, it breaks with reality, it unveils it and denies it. It's a game with the reality of the image. I'm thinking of writing a historical novel next, in the time of Eleanor of Aquitaine, about the knights, in which at the same time there are historical references and references which have been made up as if they were historical but impossible. The mix is therefore unsettling because it's all treated the same.

— *Lucía, en la novela, se escribe o se desdobla en tercera persona como si fuera protagonista de un libro.*

— *In the novel Lucía writes about herself or splits herself into a third person as if she were the protagonist of a book.*

— Sí, exacto, entra dentro del mismo juego de la identidad y de la ficción.

— Yes, that's right, it comes into the same game of identity and fiction.

— *Pasa también en otras novelas anteriores, como por ejemplo <u>La función delta</u>, donde los personajes se miran como si fueran protagonistas de una película o de una escena de teatro. ¿Piensa que es algo que hacemos en la vida cotidiana?*

— *It also happens in previous novels such as la función delta where the characters look at themselves as if they were the protagonists of a film or scene in the theatre. Do you think this is something we do in our daily life?*

— Creo que lo hacemos mucho y creo que forma parte de la disociación y de la multiplicidad de la identidad. Todos los seres humanos somos muchos. No somos dos como se decía en el siglo XIX, como el Doctor Jekyll y Mister Hyde. Eso ya es una banalidad. No somos dos, somos millones. Lo que pasa es que algunas personas tienen más clara esa percepción de la disociación y otras personas, menos. Los novelistas, lo mismo que los actores u otros profesionales así tenemos más clara la percepción de la disociación. En este sentido, quizás somos más tendentes a estos juegos, pero la experiencia de verse desde fuera es una experiencia básica del ser humano ¿Quién no se ha visto desde fuera en algún momento de su vida? Ahora que tenemos la referencia cultural del cine, pues lo puedes explicar así. Hay gente que no necesita verse como protagonista en una película pero que se ha visto desde fuera en un momento, que son conscientes de la mirada desde fuera de lo que uno está haciendo.

— I think we do it a lot and I think that it forms part of the disassociation and multiplicity of identity, All of us are many. We're not two as was said in the nineteenth century, like Dr Jekyll and Mr Hyde. That's banal. we're not two, we're millions. The thing is that some poeple have a clearer perception of this disassociation and others less so. Novelists, like actors or other professionals like that have a clearer perception of disassociation. In that sense, perhaps we have more of a tendency to play those games, but the experience of seeing oneself as if from outside is a basic human experience. Who hasn't seen themselves from outside at some point in their life? Now that we have the cultural referent of cinema, you can explain it that way. There are people who don't have to see themselves as the protagonist in a film but who have seen themselves from outside At some point, who are conscious of observing what you are doing from outside.

— *A mí me interesa mucho todo lo que relaciona esta novela y la identidad porque estoy trabajando en el análisis de la búsqueda de la identidad en tu narrativa. En esta novela se ve muy claramente que la identidad es algo discontinuo pero que nosotros queremos creer que es algo continuo.*

— *I'm very interested in the relationship between this novel and identity becuse I'm working on an analysis of the search for identity in your narrative. In this novel it's clear that identity is something discontinuous but that we want to believe is continuous.*

— ¡Y fiable! Algo que nos posee, algo que tiene una realidad natural por encima de nosotros y no es verdad. La identidad, primero, son miles de identidades que nosotros cosemos para hacer un espejismo de una sola y no sólo no nos posee sino que nosotros creamos la identidad. La poseemos y la creamos. La identidad es lo que narramos de nosotros mismos.

— And trustworthy! Something which possesses us, which has a natural reality despite us and that's not true. Identity, first of all, consists of thousands of identities which we stitch together to create the illusion of a unique one and not only does it not possess us but we create identity. We possess it and create it. Identity is what we narrate about ourselves.

— *Bueno, cambiemos de tema. En* Historias de mujeres *rescataste historias olvidadas. Dijiste en una entrevista que esas mujeres te escogieron.*

— Well, let's change subject. In Historias de mujeres you rescued forgottem stories. You said in an interview that those women chose you.

— Sí, había sido hecho por dos razones. Yo siempre he leído muchas biografías. Me gustan mucho. Entonces, puse sobre todo las historias que a mí me habían gustado y, luego, tuve otro criterio, que era no repetir el tipo de mujer. Pues si pones una mujer mártir como Zenobia Camprubí, la mujer de Juan Ramón Jiménez, pues no pones a otra mujer mártir como puede ser la mujer de Fitzgerald. Intenté no repetir en la tipología y, al margen de esto, pues poner historias de mujeres que me habían fascinado.

— Yes, I did it for two reasons. I've always read a lot of biographies. I like them a lot. So, above all I included all the stories I had enjoyed and then I had another criterion which was not to repeat the type of woman. So if you include a martyr type like Zenobia Camprubí, the wife of Juan Ramón Jiménez, you don't include another martyr like for example the wife of Fitzgerald. I tried not to repeat the typology and apart from that, I included stories of women who had fascinated me.

— *Se ha dicho que no son mujeres ejemplares pero tampoco hace falta que lo sean para que se pueda aprender de ellas...*

— It's been said that they're not exemplary women but there's no need for them to be exemplary to learn from them...

— Pero si yo creo que lo importante es que no sean ejemplares. ¡Basta ya de mujeres ejemplares! ¿Qué es esto? A lo que yo aspiro es a la humanidad como mujer, a la posibilidad de la humanidad total. Aspiro a poder ser asesina múltiple y santa también, pero todo.

— For me the important thing is that they're not exemplary. I've had enough of exemplary women! What is this? I aspire to humanity as a woman, the possibility of total humanity. I aspire to be a multiple assassin and saint too, but everything all at once.

— *De todas maneras son mujeres apasionadas.*

— In any case they are all passionate women.

— Eso sí. Son mujeres tremendamente fuertes o debilísimas, pero apasionadas.

— That's true. They're extremely strong or weak women but passionate.

— *Y ahora estás escribiendo una serie en <u>El País</u> sobre las pasiones.*

— And now you're writing a series in <u>El País</u> about passions.

— Sí, lo de las mujeres fue una idea mía y lo de las pasiones ha sido una idea de mi jefe, que lleva el suplemento, Alex Martínez Roig. Me pareció una idea preciosa. Entonces lo estoy escribiendo ahora y me lo estoy pasando bien.

— Yes, the one about women was my idea and this one about passions was the idea of my boss, in charge of the supplement, Alex Martínez Roig. It seemed a lovely idea. So I'm writing it now and having a good time.

— *Es un tema que sale en tus novelas por ejemplo en <u>La función delta</u>...*

— It's a theme which occurs in your novels for example in <u>La función delta</u>...

— Es verdad. Por eso me fascinan estas historias.

— It's true. That's why those stories fascinate me.

— *Parece que te interesa lo de la enajenación de la pasión.*

— You seem to be interested in the alienation of passion.

— Sí, la pasión como engaño, la pasión como mentira, la pasión como invento, la pasión enajenada, claro, siempre.

— Yes, passion as deceit, passion as lies, passion as make-believe, alienated passion, of course, always.

— *También hay la obsesión por el Otro, que preocupa tanto a Lucía en La hija del caníbal.*

— *There is also the obsession for the Other which preoccupies Lucía so much in La hija del caníbal.*

— Y a Félix con Manitas de Plata, que pierde la cabeza completamente. Se obsesiona de tal manera que se destruye. La obsesión por el Otro existe, la conozco, la he conocido, la he vivido. Sé lo que es la pasión. Soy una persona muy apasionada. La he vivido tantas veces como para desmontarla ya, como una bomba. Bueno, quizá ya no funciona igual porque la he desmontado ya. Pero cuando funciona te puede llevar a la destrucción o al éxtasis, pero normalmente a la destrucción.

— And Félix with Manitas de Plata, he loses his head completely. He gets so obsessed that he destroys himself. The obsession for the Other exists, I know it, I've known it, I've lived it. I know what passion is. I'm a very passionate person. I've lived it so many times that I could take it apart now, like a bomb. Well, perhaps it doesn't work the same any more because I have taken it apart. But when it works it can lead you to destruction or ecstasy, but normally to destruction.

— *Es algo que has comparado muchas veces con el proceso de la escritura, ¿no?*

— *It's something that you've compared many times with the process of writing, isn't it?*

— Sí, pero con mucha ventaja para la escritura. La escritura es constructiva mientras que la pasión es normalmente destructiva, o vaciadora por lo menos.

— Yes, but writing has the advantage. Writing is constructive whilst passion is normally destructive, or emptying at least.

PRIMARY SOURCES

Montero, Rosa, 1976. *España para ti para siempre*, Madrid: AQ ediciones

—, 1977. 'Las alegres chicas Bankinter', *Vindicación Feminista*, 9, 60

—, 1979. *Crónica del desamor*, Madrid: Debate

—, 1981. *La función delta*, Madrid: Debate

—, 1982a. *Cinco años de País*, Madrid: Debate

—, 1982b. 'Paulo Pumilio', in *Doce relatos de mujeres*, ed. by Ymelda Navajo, Madrid: Alianza, 67-93

—, 1983. *Te trataré como a una reina*, Barcelona: Seix Barral

—, 1986. 'La vida fácil', *Litoral: Revista de la Poesía y el Pensamiento*, special edn., 'Literatura escrita por mujeres en la España contemporánea', ed. and intro. by Lorenzo Saval & Juan García Gallego, 322-5

—, 1988. *Amado amo*, Madrid: Debate

—, 1990. *Temblor*, Barcelona: Seix Barral

—, 1991a. *Absent Love: A Chronicle*, tran. and intro. by Cristina de la Torre & Diana Glad, Lincoln: University of Nebraska Press

—, 1991b. *El nido de los sueños*, Madrid: Siruela

—, 1993a. *Bella y oscura*, Barcelona: Seix Barral

—, 1993b. 'Transición política y democracia cultural 1975-1992', unpublished seminar paper given as part of the cycle 'La cultura española en su contexto europeo' at the Instituto Cervantes, London, 19 April

—, 1993c. 'La aventura de escribir', unpublished seminar paper given at a Hispanic Research Seminar at the University of Cambridge, 21 October

—, 1994a. *La vida desnuda: Una mirada apasionada sobre nuestro mundo*, Madrid: El País, Aguilar, col. El Viaje Interior

—, 1994b. *El cristal de Agua Fría* , libretto for opera in one act, music composed by Marisa Manchado, Madrid: Instituto Nacional de las Artes Escénicas y la Música

—, 1994c. 'El puñal en la garganta', in *Relatos urbanos*, Madrid: Alfaguara Hispánica

—, 1995a. *Historias de mujeres*, Madrid: Alfaguara

—, 1995b. 'El camino de las palabras', unpublished seminar paper given at the day conference 'Aspects of Identity in Contemporary Spanish Narrative', held at the University of Leeds, 6 May

—, 1995c. 'España: Tierra de nadie', plenary at the annual ACIS conference, Queen's University of Belfast, 16 September

—, 1996b. *Las barbaridades de Bárbara*, Madrid: Alfaguay

—, 1996b. 'La revolución silenciosa', unpublished seminar paper given as part of the cycle 'La mujer española hoy' at the Instituto Cervantes, London, 16 May

—, 1997a. *La hija del caníbal*, Madrid: Espasa Calpe

—, 1997b. 'Pasiones: Amar el amor', *El País*, 20 April, 107-16

—, 1997c. *El viaje fantástico de Bárbara*, Madrid: Alfaguay

—, 1998. *Amantes y enemigos: Cuentos de pareja*, Madrid: Santillana

—, 'Escribiendo en la luna', unpublished paper provided by Rosa Montero [n.d.]

SECONDARY SOURCES

Abel, Elizabeth, Marianne Hirsch & Elizabeth Langland, eds., 1983. *The Voyage In: Fictions of Female Development*, London: University Press of New England

Abellán, José Luis, 1993. 'La cultura en la España de los ochenta', in Guerra & Tezanos (1993), 575-609

Abril, Mª Victoria & Mª Jésus Miranda, 1978. *La liberación posible*, Madrid: Akal

Ackelsberg, Martha A., 1985. '"Separate and Equal"? Mujeres Libres and Anarchist Strategy for Women's Emancipation', *Feminist Studies*, 11/1, 53-83

África Vidal, Mª Carmen, 1989. *¿Qué es el posmodernismo?*, Alicante: Secretariado de Publicaciones, Universidad de Alicante

—, 1990. *Hacia una patafísica de la esperanza: Reflexiones sobre la novela posmoderna*, Alicante: Secretariado de Publicaciones, Universidad de Alicante

Agra, María-Xosé, 1993. 'Feminismo y política', in *Teoría feminista: Identidad, género y política*, ed. by Arantza Campos & Lourdes Méndez, País Vasco: Instituo Vasco de la Mujer/Universidad del País Vasco, 13-28

Alario, Carmen, Bengoechea, Mercedes, Lledó, Eulalia & Ana Vargas, 1995. *NOMBRAR en femenino y en masculino: La representación del femenino y el masculino en el lenguaje*, Madrid: Ministerio de Trabajo y Asuntos Sociales & Instituto de la Mujer

Alba, Narciso, 1988. 'Entrevista con Rosa Montero', *Ventanal: Revista de Creación y Crítica*, 14, 81-100

Alberdi, Cristina & Victoria Sendón, 1977. *Aborto, sí o no*, Barcelona: Bruguera

Alberdi, Cristina, 1982. 'El discurso jurídico como superestructura ideológica: Crisis del patriarcado como ideología', in Durán (1982), 272-5

Alberdi, Inés, 1990. 'Las mujeres españolas y la familia', in Astelarra (1990), 67-82

—, 1996. 'Nuevos roles femeninos y cambio familiar', in García de León et al. (1996), 41-68

Alberdi, Isabel, 1992. 'Pactos desde la diversidad', in Forum de Política Feminista (1992), 60-4

Alberdi Alonso, Inés, 1988. 'Las mujeres jóvenes y su incorporación social', *Revista de Estudios de Juventud*, 29, 19-30

Alborg, Concha, 1987. 'Cuatro narradoras de la transición', in Landeira & González del Valle (1987), 11-27

—, 1988. 'Metaficción y feminismo en Rosa Montero', *REH*, 22, 67-76

Alcobendas Tirado, María Pilar, 1984. *The Employment of Women in Spain*, Luxembourg: Office for Official Publications of the European Communities

Alcoff, Linda, 1988. 'Cultural Feminism versus Poststructuralism: The Identity Crisis in Feminist Theory', *Signs: Journal of Women in Culture and Society*, 14.1, 196-203

Altable Vicario, Charo, 1986. 'Cuerpo de mujer o tierra de lo imaginario: Caminos en la construcción de una erótica femenina', *Desde el Feminismo*, 1 (Autumn), 40-5

—, 1994. 'Relaciones entre mujeres' in Federación de Organizaciones Feministas del Estado Español (1994), 103-9

Alter, Robert, 1975. *Partial Magic: The Novel as a Self-Conscious Genre*, Berkeley: University of California Press

Álvarez, Natividad et al., 1977. *Aportaciones a la cuestión feminista*, Madrid: Akal

Ambrosio Servodidio, Mirella d' & Marcia L. Welles, eds., 1982. *From Fiction to Metafiction: Essays in Honour of Carmen Martín Gaite*, Lincoln, Nebraska: Society of Spanish and Spanish American Studies

Amell, Alma, 1994. *Rosa Montero's Odyssey*, Lanham, Maryland: University Press of America

Amell, Samuel, 1986. 'La novela negra y los narradores españoles actuales', *REH*, 20/1, 91-102

Amorós, Andrés, 1974. *Subliteraturas*, Esplugues de Llobregat, Barcelona: Ariel

—, 1977. *Sociología de una novela rosa*, Madrid: Cuadernos Taurus

—, 1980. 'La literatura española ante los ochenta', in *El año literario español, 1980*, ed. by Andrés Amorós, Madrid: Castalia, 7-13

Amorós, Celia, 1980a. 'Feminismo: Discurso de la diferencia, discurso de la igualdad', *El Viejo Topo*, extra 10, 30-3

—,1980b. 'El feminismo entre la autonomía y los partidos', *Zona Abierta* (Madrid), 23, 118-25

—, 1987. 'Espacio de los iguales, espacio de las idénticas: Notas sobre el poder y el principio de individuación', *Arbor*, 504, 123-5

—, 1989. 'Del feminismo al feminismo', *Debats*, 27, 52-60

—, 1990. 'Violencia contra las mujeres y pactos patriarcales', in Maquieira & Sánchez (1990), 1-15

—, 1992. 'El feminismo como axis emancipatoria', *Canelobre*, 23-4, 15-27

—, 1994. 'Igualdad e identidad', in *El concepto de la identidad*, ed. by Amelia Valcárcel (1994), Madrid: Pablo Iglesias, 29-48

Anabitarte, Hector & Ricardo Lorenzo, 1978. 'Freud y la femininidad', *El Viejo Topo* (Barcelona), 20, 45-7

Ander-Egg, Ezequiel, 1980. *La mujer irrumpe en la historia*, Madrid: Marsiega,

Anderson, Linda, 1986. 'At the Threshold of the Self: Women and Autobiography', in *Women's Writing: A Challenge to Theory*, ed. by Moira Monteith, Brighton: Harvester Press, 54-71

Annas, Pamela J., 1978. 'New Worlds, New Words: Androgyny in Feminist Science Fiction', *Science Fiction Studies*, 5/2, 143-56

Araújo, Helena, 1981. '¿Escritura femenina?', *Escandalar*, 4/3, 32-6

—, 1985. 'Yo escribo, yo me escribo...', *RI*, 132-3, 457-60

Arco, Miguel Angel del, 1988. 'Así se fabrica un best seller: Los cazatalentos de las editoras dan con un filón de novelistas rentables', *Tiempo*, 316, 156-63

Aristizabal, Alonso, 1987. 'La América del bolero y el tango', *Cahiers du Monde Hispanique et Luso-Brésilien,* 48, 145-8

Arranz Lozano, Fátima, 1995. 'Reflexión a própósito del origen y mantenimiento de la subordinación femenina: De la «explotación» a la igualdad formal en el sistema de géneros', in Brullet Tenas & Carrasquer Oto (1995), 217-25

Arribas, Inés, 1991. 'Poder y feminismo en *Amado amo* de Rosa Montero', *RLA*, 3, 348-53

Arroyo, Julia, 1978. *¿Qué hacemos las mujeres ante una sociedad en cambio?*, Madrid: Ediciones S.M.

Asamblea de Feministas Independientes de Barcelona, 1985. 'El movimiento de feministas independientes: Del placer de la diversidad al goce de la autonomía', in *III Jornadas Feministas Estatales: 10 años de lucha del movimiento feminista*, collection of papers held at the Biblioteca de Mujeres (Madrid)

Asís, Mª Dolores de, 1990. *Última hora de la novela en España*, Madrid: Eudema Universidad, Textos de apoyo

Astelarra, Judith, 1984. 'El feminismo como perspectiva teórica y como práctica política', in *Teoría feminista (Selección de textos)*, ed. by CIPAF, Santo Domingo: Ediciones Populares Feministas, Colección Teoría, 39-68

—, 1986. *Las mujeres podemos: Otra visión política*, Barcelona: Icaria

—, 1988. 'El patriarcado como realidad social', in Navarro (1988a), 39-59

—, ed., 1990, *Participación política de las mujeres*, Madrid: Centro de Investigaciones Sociológicas

Astelarra, Judith, & Antxon Pérez de Calleja, 1993. 'Feminismo: ¿crisis o renovación?', *Emakunde*, 11, 30-3

Aubet, Mª José et al., 1981. 'Reflexiones en torno a la lucha feminista', *Mientras Tanto*, 6, 109-16

Bachmann, Sigrid, Madrid, 23 March 1992. Unpublished interview with Rosa Montero (transcript provided by Rosa Montero)

Badinter, Elisabeth, 1980. *L'Amour en Plus: Histoire de l'amour maternel (XVIIe-XXe siècle)*, Paris: Flammarion

—, 1994. *XY: La identidad masculina* (trans. of *XY: L'identité masculin*), Barcelona: Círculo de Lectores

Ballarín, Pilar & Teresa Ortiz, eds., 1990. *La mujer en Andalucía: Actas del Primer Encuentro Interdisciplinario de Estudios de la Mujer*, Granada: Seminario de Estudios de la Mujer, Feminae

Bannet, Tanor Eve, 1992. 'The Feminist Logic of Both/And', *Genders: Art Literature Film History*, 15, 1-20

Barceló, Elia, 1994. *Consecuencias naturales*, Madrid: Miraguano

Barceló, Miguel, 1990. *Ciencia ficción: Guía de lectura*, Barcelona: Ediciones B Nova, Ciencia Ficción

Barr, Marleen S., ed., 1981. *Future Females: A Critical Anthology*, Bowling Green, Ohio: Bowling Green State University Popular Press

—, 1987. *Alien to Femininity. Speculative Fiction and Feminist Theory*, London: Greenwood

Barr, Marleen S., & Nicholas D. Smith, ed., 1983. *Women and Utopia: Critical Interpretations*, London: University Press of America

Barriuso, Jorge, 1989. 'La mejor literatura erótica en español es cosa de mujeres', *Cambio16*, 31 July, 64-7

Batsleer, Janet, 1981. 'Pulp in the Pink', *Spare Rib*, 109, 52-5

Bayón, Miguel, 1986. 'Mujeres escritoras: la mirada que va desde el rincón', *Cambio 16*, 24 November, 149-52

Beauchamp, Gorman, Kenneth Roemer & Nicholas D. Smith., eds., 1987. *Utopian Studies I*, London: University Press of America

Bell, Donald H., 1987. *Ser varón: La paradoja de la masculinidad* (trans. of *Being a Man: The Paradox of Masculinity*), Barcelona: Tusquets

Bellver, Catherine G. 1982. Rev. of *La función delta* by Rosa Montero, *Hispanic Journal*, 44/1, 150-1

—, 1988. 'Montserrat Roig: A Feminine Perspective and a Journalistic Slant' in Manteiga, Galerstein & McNerney (1988), 152-68

Beltrán, Sonia, 1993. *La mujer española: Bibliografías*, Madrid: Biblioteca Nacional, Guía del Lector N° 5

Benito, Luz Mª Paz, 1993. 'Mujer y cambio en la década de los ochenta', in Guerra & Tezanos (1993), 699-723

Benjamin, Jessica, 1980. 'The Bonds of Love: Rational Violence and Erotic Domination', in *The Future of Difference*, ed. by Hester Eisenstein & Alice Jardine, New York: Barnard College Women's Center, 41-70

—, 1990. *The Bonds of Love: Psychoanalysis, Feminism and the Problem of Domination*, London: Virago

Benstock, Shari, ed., 1988. 'Authorizing the Autobiographical', in*The Private Self: Theory and Practice of Women's Autobiographical Writings*, London: Routledge, 10-33

Bértolo, Constantino, 1993. 'Donde se sueña el sueño', in Dirección Provincial del MEC (Zaragoza), (first publ. in *El País*, 25 February 1990), 4

Bettelheim, Bruno, 1976. *The Uses of Enchantment: The Meaning and Importance of Fairy Tales*, London: Thames and Hudson

Biblioteca de Mujeres, 1989. 'Escritoras de ciencia ficción', *Madrid Feminista*, 9, 4-5

Blau du Plessis, Rachel, 1985. *Writing Beyond the Ending: Narrative Strategies of Twentieth Century Women Writers*, Bloomington: Indiana University Press

Blodgett, Harriet, 1988. *Centuries of Female Days: English Women's Private Diaries*, New Brunswick: Rutgers University Press

Boccia, Maria Luisa, 1987. 'The Gender of Representation', tran. by Sharon Wood, in Bono & Kemp (1987), 352-67

Bonner, Frances, 1992. 'Towards a Better Way of Being: Feminist Science Fiction', in *Imagining Women: Cultural Representations and Gender*, ed. Bonner et al., Cambridge: Polity Press, 94-102

Bono, Paola, & Sandra Kemp, eds., 1991. *Italian Feminist Thought: A Reader*, Oxford: Blackwell

Borderías, Cristina, 1989. 'Etudes et recherches féministes en Espagne/Feminist Studies and Research in Spain', *Cahiers du Grif,* special edn. 'Concept et realité des études féministes', 55-61

Borreguero, Concha et al., 1986. *La mujer española: De la tradición a la modernidad (1960-1980)*, Madrid: Tecnos

Bortolussi, Marisa, 1985. *Análisis teórico del cuento infantil*, Madrid: Alhambra

Bossert, Rex, 1987. 'Godzilla in Cloudcuckooland; or Literary Theory Comes to Utopia', in Beauchamp, Roemer & Smith (1987), 138-46

Braidotti, Rosa, 1994. *Nomadic Subjects: Embodiment and Sexual Difference in Contemporary Feminist Theory*, New York: Columbia University Press

Bravo-Villasante, Carmen, 1988. 'La mujer como autora literaria', *Historia 16*, 145, 49-53

—, 1989. *Ensayos de literatura infantil*, Murcia: Universidad de Murcia

Brée, Germaine, 1988. 'Autogynography' in Olney (1988), 71-9

Briffault, Robert, 1927. *The Mothers: A Study of the Origins of Sentiments and Institutions*, London: Allen & Unwin

Brod, Harry & Michael Kaufman, eds., 1994. *Theorizing Masculinities*, London: Sage

Brodzki, Bella & Celeste Schenk, eds., 1988. *Life/Lines: Theorizing Women's Autobiography*, Ithaca: Cornell University Press

Brooksbank Jones, Anny, 1993. 'Feminisms in Contemporary Spain', paper given at the 1993 ACIS conference, Manchester (copy provided by the author)

—, 1997. *Women in Contemporay Spain*, Manchester: Manchester University Press

Brown, Cheryl L. & Karen Olson, ed., 1978. *Feminist Criticism: Essays on Theory. Poetry and Prose*, London: The Scarecrow Press

Brown, Joan Lipman, ed., 1991a. *Women Writers of Contemporary Spain: Exiles in the Homeland*, London: Associated University Presses

—, 1991b. 'Rosa Montero: From Journalist to Novelist', in Brown (1991a), 240-57

—, 1992. 'Men by Women in the Contemporary Spanish Novel', *HR*, 60/1, 55-70

Brullet Tenas, Cristina & Pilar Carrasquer Oto, eds., 1995. *Sociología de las relaciones de género*, Madrid: Ministerio de Trabajo y Asuntos Sociales & Instituto de la Mujer

Brullet Tenas, Cristina, 1996. 'Roles e identidades de género: Una construcción social' in García de León et al. (1996), 273-308

Buiza, Carlos, 1972. *Antología social de la ciencia ficción*, Algorta: Zero, 21

Bustelo, Carlota, 1979. 'Alternativa feminista', in VV.AA. (1979b), 209-22

—, 1988. 'Yo también estoy por el poder', *Poder y Libertad*, 8, 10-11

—, 1992. 'Intensificar la reflexión y demanda social feminista', in Forum de Política Feminista (1992), 50-3

—, 1994. 'Democracia y participación de las mujeres: Obstáculos y logros. El caso de España', in Instituto de la Mujer (1994b), 17-28

Buxó, A., 1979. 'Problemática de la mujer: Informe bibliográfico', *RICS* (Barcelona), 29, 405-22

Buxo Rey, Mª Jesús, 1976. 'Comportamiento lingüístico de la mujer', *Ethnica* (Barcelona), 11, 7-65

Cabanilles, Antónia, 1990. 'Cartografías del silencio: La teoría literaria feminista', in López & Pastor (1990), 13-23

Calle Fuentes, Mercedes, González Romero, Carmen & Juan Antonio Núñez Triguero, 1988. *Discriminación y acoso sexual a la mujer en el trabajo*, Madrid: Fundación Largo Caballero

Calvera, Leonor, 1982. *El género mujer*, Buenos Aires: Ed. de Belgrano

Calvet, Mª Dolores, 1982. 'El aborto', *Poder y Libertad*, 2, 201-3

Calvo Artes, Montserrat, 1985. 'Magia Sexual', in *III Jornadas Feministas Estatales: 10 años de lucha del movimiento feminista*, collection of papers held at the CIFFE Centro de Documentación

—, 1986. *Mitos sexuales*, unpublished manuscript, held in the Biblioteca Nacional de España

Campos, René A., 1991. 'The Poetics of the Bolero in the Novels of Manuel Puig', *World Literature Today*, 65/4, 637-42

Camps Perarnau, Susana, 1989. *La literatura fantástica y la fantasía*, Madrid: Montena Aula

Camus, Albert, 1942. *Le Mythe de Sisyphe: Essai sur l'Absurde*, 1991 edn, Paris: Gallimard

Candil, Juan Antonio, 1990. 'Entrevista a Rosa Montero: La necesidad de contar', *Madrid Debate* (May), 11

Cantavella, Juan, 1988. 'Rosa Montero: «La literatura es un amante fogoso del que no quiero desprenderme»' (interview), *Diario de Madrid* 24 March, 23

—, 1990. 'Entrevista a Rosa Montero: "Creo en la sabiduría y en el entendimiento humano"', *Ya* 21 February*

Cañellas, A. et al, 1979. 'Los roles sexuales en la literatura infantil: Ideología y pedagogía', *Cuadernos de Pedagogía*, 53, 19-23

Capel, Rosa & Julio Iglesias de Ussel, 1984. *Mujer española y sociedad: Bibliografía (1900-1984)*, Madrid: Instituto de la Mujer

Caplan, Paula, 1981. *Barriers between Women*, Lancaster: MPT Press

Carabí, Àngels & Marta Segarra, eds., 1994. *Mujeres y Literatura*, Barcelona: Universitat de Barcelona

Caravaca, Rubén, 1995. *313 Boleros por ejemplo*, Madrid: Ediciones Guía de Música

Carr, Raymond & Juan Pablo Fusi Aizpurua, 1981. *Spain: Dictatorship to Democracy*, 2nd edn., London: Unwin Hyman

Carrascal, Eduardo. 1981. 'Entrevista con Rosa Montero', *El Rotativo Cultural*, September, 12-13

Carrasco, Bel, 1979. 'Predominio testimonial en la literatura de mujeres', *El País*, 8 June, 35

Casa de las Américas, 1982. *Ensayos de música latinoamericana: Selección del boletín de música de la Casa de las Américas*, Havana: Casa de las Américas, Col. Nuestros Países, Serie Música

Castilla del Pino, Carlos, 1970. 'La "función" de la mujer', *Triunfo*, 31 October, 27-30

—, 1975. 'Acerca del complejo de castración', *El Urogallo* (Madrid), 31-2, 111-15

—, 1979. 'Femenino-masculino', *Argumentos*, 27 (October), 22-4

Castillo de Berchenko, Adriana, 1988. 'En torno a la condición de la mujer escritora en España', *Ventanal: Revista de Creación y Crítica*, 14, 103-27

Castillo Zapata, Rafael, 1990. *Fenomenología del bolero*, Caracas: Monte Avila

Castrortega, Pedro et al, 1989. *Encuentros sobre modernidad y postmodernidad (1987, Madrid)*, Madrid: Fundación de Investigaciones Marxistas

Cate Arries, Francie, 1990. 'Lost in the Language of Popular Culture: Manuel Vázquez Montalbán's Novel Detection', in *Ensayos de la literatura europea e hispanoamericana*, ed. by Felix Menchacatorre, San Sebastian: Universidad del País Vasco, 101-7

Cavero, José, 1996. 'Rosa Montero, periodista y escritora: «Ahora tienen que liberarse los hombres»', *Interviu* 8 January, 50-3

Caws, Mary Ann, 1986. 'Ladies Shot and Painted: Female Embodiment in Surrealist Art', in *The Female Body in Western Culture: Contemporary Perspectives*, ed. by Susan Rubin Suleiman, London: Harvard University Press, 262-87

Centro de Investigaiones Sociológicas, 1991. *Las mujeres españolas: Lo privado y lo público*, Madrid: Ministerio de Asuntoas Sociales & Centro de Investigaciones Sociológicas

Centro de Mujeres de Federico Rubio de Madrid, 1979. 'La comunicación médico/mujer en la consulta ginecológica', in *Alternativas populares a las comunicaciones de masa*, ed. by José Vidal Beneyto, Madrid: Centro de Investigaciones Sociológicas, 495-9

Cerrilo, Pedro & Jaime García Padrino, 1990. *Literatura infantil*, Cuenca: Universidad de Castilla La Mancha

Cervera, Juan, 1991. *Teoría de la literatura infantil*, Bilbao: Mensajero

Cervera, Montserrat et al, 1992. 'Reflexiones sobre el movimiento feminista de los años 80-90', *Mientras Tanto*, 48, 33-49

Chittenden, Jean S., 1986. '*El cuarto de atrás* as Autobiography', *LF*, 12, 78-84

Chodorow, Nancy, 1974. 'Family Structure and Feminine Personality', in *Women, Culture and Society*, ed. by Michelle Zimbalist Rosaldo & Louise Lamphere, Stanford: Stanford University Press, 43-66

—, 1978. *The Reproduction of Mothering: Psychoanalysis and the Sociology of Gender*, Berkeley: University of California Press

Chown, Linda, 1983. 'American Critics and Spanish Women Novelists, 1942-1980', *Signs: Journal of Women in Culture and Society*, 9/1, 91-105

—, 1986. *The Teller in the Tale: The Eye's I in Four Novels by Doris Lessing and Carmen Martín Gaite*, Seattle: University of Washington

Christensen, Inger, 1981. *The Meaning of Metafiction*, Bergen: Universitetsforlaget

Christie, Ruth, Drinkwater, Judith & John Macklin, 1995. *The Scripted Self: Textual Identities in Contemporary Spanish Narrative*, Warminster: Aris & Phillips

Cifrian, Concha, Martínez Ten, Carmen & Isabel Serrano, 1986. *La cuestión del aborto*, Barcelona: Icaria

Ciplijauskaité, Biruté, 1983. 'La novela femenina como autobiografía', *Actas del Congreso Internacional de Hispanistas*, 1, 397-405

—, 1988. *La novela femenina contemporánea (1970-1985): Hacia una tipología de la narración en primera persona*, Barcelona: Anthropos

—, 1989. Rev. of *Amado amo*, *World Literature Today* (Winter), 73-4

—, 1993. 'A media voz', in Dirección Provincial del MEC (first publ. in *El Ciervo*, 39, 1988), 3

Cixous, Hélène, 1975. *Souffles*, Paris: Minuit

—, 1976. 'The Laugh of the Medusa', tran. by Keith & Paula Cohen, *Signs: Journal of Women in Culture and Society*, 1/4, 875-93

—, 1981. 'Castration or Decapitation?', tran. by Annette Kuhn, *Signs: Journal of Women in Culture and Society*, 7/1, 41-55

Clark, Maudemarie, 1990. *Nietzsche on Truth and Philosophy*, Cambridge: Cambridge University Press

CLIJ, 1992. Rev. of *El nido de los sueños* in section 'De 10 a 12 años', *CLIJ*, 37, 60

CLIJ, 1993. 'Lista de honor de CLIJ 1992', *CLIJ*, 49, pull-out section

Clos, Marta, 1997. 'Rosa Montero, periodista i escriptora: "Sempre m'he sentit a prop de l'anarquisme"', *AVUI* (26 May)*

Colaizzi, Guilia, 1994. 'Mujeres y escritura: ¿Una habitación propia? Notas sobre una paradoja', in Carabí & Segarra, 109-22

Colectivo Feminista Barcelona, 1976. 'Les Jornades Catalanes de la Dona', *Vindicación Feminista*, 1, 20-1

Colectivo Feminista de Madrid, 1977. 'El feminismo español en la década de los años 70', *Tiempo de Historia* (Madrid), 27, 29-37

Colectivo Feminista de Madrid, 1979. *El espejismo de la «identidad femenina»: Un nuevo obstáculo en el camino hacia la liberación de las mujeres*, Madrid: booklet produced by the Colectivo

Collin, Françoise, 1994. 'Praxis de la diferencia entre los sexos' in Federación de Organizaciones Feministas del Estado Español, 315-18

Col.lectiu de Dones Joves Desobediencia, 1994. 'Mujeres jóvenes: Iguales ¿en qué?, in Federación de Organizaciones Feministas del Estado Español, 223-38

Comabella, Merché, 1988. 'Feminismo vinculado a la sociedad', *Poder y Libertad*, 8, 18-19

—, 1992.'Reflexiones para una transición en el feminismo', in Forum de Política Feminista (1992), 79-81

Cominges, Jorge de, 1996. 'Rosa Montero, Javier Marías: Mano a mano', *Qué leer* (June), 66-72

'Community Law and Women', 1987. *Women of Europe*, Supplement N° 25, 108-11**

Condé, Lisa P. & Stephen M. Hart, eds., 1991. *Feminist Readings on Spanish and Latin American Literature*, Lampeter: Edwin Mellen Press

Conte, Rafael, 1983. 'Rosa Montero y la lucha por la obra', *El País*, 25 December, 5

Co-ordinadora Una Palabra Otra, 1994. *Espacios en espiral: Dossier cine, literatura y teatro de mujeres*, Barcelona: Co-ordinadora Una Palabra Otra

Costa, Luis F., 1991. '*Para no volver*: Women in Franco's Spain', in Vásquez (1991), 11-28

Cotterell, Arthur, 1986. *A Dictionary of World Mythology*, Oxford: Oxford University Press

Coward, Rosalind, 1984. 'Overwhelming desire', in *Female Desire: Women's Sexuality Today*, London: Paladin, 185-96

Cowie, Elizabeth, 1992. 'Pornography and Fantasy: Psychoanalytic Perspectives', McIntosh & Segal, 132-52

Cranny-Francis, Anne, 1990. *Feminist Fiction: Feminist Uses of Generic Fiction*, Cambridge: Polity Press

Cristóbal, Ramiro, 1993. 'El sexo fuerte', *Cambio16*, 27 December, 20-6

Cruz Malave, Arnaldo, 1988. 'La historia y el bolero en «Sólo cenizas hallarás (bolero)»', *RI*, 142, 63-72

Cummings, Michael S. & Nicholas D. Smith, 1989. *Utopian Studies II*, London: University Press of America

—, 1991. *Utopian Studies III*, London: University Press of America

Cvitanovic, Predrag, ed., 1984. *Universality in Chaos*, Bristol: Adam Hilger

DAIA (Dones per l'autoconeixement i l'anticonceptció), 1979. 'Maternidad, embarazo y parto', in *II Jornadas Estatales de la Mujer, Granada, 7, 8 y 9 diciembre*, collection of papers held at the Biblioteca de la Mujer (Madrid)

Davies, Catherine, 1991a. 'Women Writers in Spain since 1900: From Political Strategy to Personal Inquiry', in *Textual Liberation: European Feminist Writing in the Twentieth Century*, ed. by Helena Forsås-Scott, London: Routledge, 192-226

—, 1991b. 'The Sexual Representation of Politics in Contemporary Hispanic Feminist Narrative', in Condé & Hart, 107-19

—, 1992. 'Foreword', *The Language of a Thousand Tongues: Contemporary European Fiction by Women*, special issue of *Forum for Modern Language Studies*, 28/4, 301-3

—, 1993. 'Entrevista a Rosa Montero' (Madrid, 22 January 1993), *JHR*, 1, 383-8

—, 1994. *Contemporary Feminist Fiction in Spain: The Work of Montserrat Roig and Rosa Montero*, Oxford: Berg, New Directions in European Writing

Delgado, Gema, 1996. 'Mujeres con mando', *Cambio16*, 3 June, 22-29

Delgado Ruiz, Manuel et al, 1991. *La sexualidad en la sociedad contemporánea: Lecturas antropológicas*, Madrid: Universidad Nacional de Educación a Distancia-Fundación Universidad Empresa

Diaz-Ayala, Cristóbal, 1981. *Del areíto a la nueva trova: Historia de la música popular cubana*, Puerto Rico: Cubanacan

Díaz Diocaretz, Myriam & Iris Zavala, eds., 1993. *Breve historia de la literatura española (en lengua castellana) I. Teoría feminista: Discursos y diferencia. Enfoques feministas de la literatura española*, Madrid: Anthropos & Dirección General de la Mujer

Diaz Sánchez, Pilar & Pilar Domínguez Prats, 1988. *Las mujeres en la historia de España, siglos XVIII-XX: Bibliografía comentada*, Madrid: Instituto de la Mujer

Díez Borque, José Mª, 1972. *Literatura y cultura de masas: Estudio de la novela subliteraria*, Madrid: Al Borak

Díez de Ribera, Carmen et al., 1977. 'Informe: La mujer', *Argumentos* (Madrid), 5, 72-83

Dio Bleichmar, Emilce, 1991. *El feminismo espontáneo de la histeria: Estudio de los trastornos narcisistas de la femininidad*, 3rd edn., Madrid: Siglo XXI

Dirección Provincial del MEC (Zaragoza), 1993. *Rosa Montero: Invitación a la Lectura (33)*, Zaragoza: Ministerio de Educación y Cultura

Doane, Mary Ann, 1982. 'Film and the Masquerade: Theorizing the Female Spectator', *Screen*, 23 3/4, 74-88

—, 1991. *Femmes Fatales: Feminism, Film Theory, Psychoanalysis*, London: Routledge

Domínguez, Miguel, 1993. 'Bolero: Golpe bajo al corazón', *Cambio16*, 19 April, 80-82

Douglas, Ann, 1980. 'Punishing the Liberated Woman: Soft-Porn Culture', *The New Republic*, 183, 27-9

Drinkwater, Judith, 1995a. '«Esta carcél de amor»: Erotic Fiction by Women in Spain in the 1980s and 1990s', *LF*, 21, 97-111

—, 1995b. 'Postmodern Identities: Writing by Women and Rosa Montero's Amado Amo', in Christie, Drinkwater & Macklin (1995), 153-66

Durant, Alan, 1984. *Conditions of Music*, London: Macmillan

Dupláa, Cristina, 1988. 'La mujer como objeto literario', *Historia 16*, 145, 54-8

Durán, María Ángeles, 1981. *La mujer en el mundo contemporáneo*, Madrid: Universidad Autónoma de Madrid, Seminario de Esudios de la Mujer

—, 1982. *Nuevas perspectivas sobre la mujer: Actas de las primeras jornadas de investigación interdisciplinaria del Seminario de Estudios de la Mujer de la Universidad Autónoma de Madrid, Vol. I*, Madrid: Seminario de Estudios de la Mujer de la Universidad Autónoma de Madrid

—, 1987, 'Sobre literatura y vida cotidiana' in Durán & Rey (1987), 11-33

Durán Heras, Mª Ángeles, 1982a. *La investigación sobre la mujer en la Universidad Española Contemporánea*, Madrid: Ministerio de Cultura

—, 1982b. *Liberación y utopía*, Madrid: Akal Universitaria

Durán Heras, Mª de los Á., 1976. 'La participación social de la mujer en España', *RICS* (Barcelona), 27-8, 295-313

—, 1978. *El ama de casa: Crítica política de la economía doméstica*, Madrid: Zero-Zyx

Durán, María Ángeles, & María Teresa Gallego, 1986. 'The Women's Movement in Spain and the New Spanish Democracy', in *The New Women's Movement: Feminism and Political Power in Europe and the U.S.A.*, ed. by Drude Dahlerup, London: SAGE, 200-16

Durán, María Ángeles, & José Antonio Rey, eds., 1987. *Literatura y vida cotidiana: Actas de las cuartas jornadas de investigación interdisciplinaria del Seminario de Estudios de la Mujer de la Universidad Autónoma de Madrid*, Zaragoza: Prensas Universitarias de la Universidad Autónoma de Madrid y la Universidad de Zaragoza

Durán Heras, Mª Ángeles & M. D. Temprano, 1987. 'Mujeres, misóginos y feministas en la literatura española', in Durán & Rey (1987), 413-91

Dyer, Richard, 1981. 'Entertainment and Utopia', in *Genre: The Musical: A Reader*, ed. by Rick Altman, London: Routledge & Kegan Paul, 175-89

Echenique, Luisa, Pérez, Carmen & Itziar Zuriarrain, 1989. *Literatura de mujeres: Una bibliografía*, San Sebastian: Txostenak, Seminario de Estudios de la Mujer, Universidad del País Vasco

Egoff, Sheila A., 1981. *Thursday's Child: Trends and Patterns in Contemporary Children's Literature*, Chicago: American Library Association

Ehrlich, Carol, 1979a. 'Anarcha-Feminism: Introduction', in Ehrlich et al. (1979), 233-6

—, 1979b. 'Socialism, Anarchism, Feminism', in Ehrlich et al. (1979), 259-77

Ehrlich, Howard J., Carol Ehrlich, David De Leon & Glenda Morris, eds., 1979. *Reinventing Anarchy: What are Anarchists Thinking These Days?*, London: Routledge & Kegan Paul

Eichler, Magrit, 1981. 'Science Fiction as Desirable Feminist Scenarios', *Women's Studies International Quarterly*, 4/1, 51-64

Elejabeitia, Carmen, 1980. *Quizá hay que ser mujer*, Madrid: Ed. Zero-ZYX

Elam, Diane, 1992. *Romancing the Postmodern*, London: Routledge

Ellis Kate, Barbara O'Dair and Abby Talmer, 1990. 'Feminism and Pornography', *Feminist Review*, 36, 5-18

Elorza, Antonio, 1995. 'Utopía y revolución en el movimiento anarquista español', in Hofman et al. (1995), 79-108

Ende, Michael, 1987. 'Ser niño', *El País* (Extra), 15 July, vi

Érase una vez una niña...libros infantiles y juveniles seleccionados por las librerías de mujeres, Librería de Mujeres, Librería LaSal, Librería Sal de Casa, Coordinadora de Librerías de Mujeres, [n.d.]

Erro-Orthmann, Nora & Juan Cruz Mendizabal, eds., 1990. *La escritora hispánica. Actas de la decimotercera conferencia anual de literatura hispánica en Indiana*, University of Pennyslvania, Miami: Universal

Escario, Pilar, Alberdi, Inés & Ana Inés López-Accotto, 1996. *Lo personal es político: El Movimiento Feminista en la transición*, Madrid: Instituto de la Mujer & Ministerio de Asuntos Sociales

Escudero Álvaro, Consuelo, 1988. 'Mujer y rol', in Instituto de la Mujer (1988), 15-18

Espasa, 1997. *Novedades (mayo-junio)*, Madrid: Espasa Calpe

Estrada, Javier, 1990. 'Rosa Montero, entre el periodismo y la novela', *Plácet* (October-November), 16-19

Evora, Tony, 1993. 'Boleros con sabor', *Cambio16*, 28 June, i-iv

Ezquerro, Milagros, 1991. 'The Culture of Sentiment', *World Literature Today*, 65/4, 647-50

Fagoaga, Concha, 1989. 'Prácticas de la posmodernidad', in Castrortega (1989), 185-8

Fajardo, José Manuel, 1990. 'Rosa Montero: "Los hombres inventan cuentos de hadas para explicarlo todo"', *Cambio16*, 26 February, 100-3

Falcón, Lidia & Elvira Siurana, 1992a. *Catálogo de escritoras españolas en lengua castellana: (1860-1992)*, Madrid: Comunidad de Madrid, Dirección General de la Mujer

—, 1992b. *Mujeres escritoras: Catálogo de escritoras feministas actuales en España*, Madrid: Comunidad de Madrid, Dirección General de la Mujer

Falcón, Lidia, 1981. 'A manera de resúmen del año femenino', *Poder y Libertad*, 2, 5-26

—, 1988. 'Vindicación Feminista o el ideal compartido', *REH*, 22/1, 53-65

—, 1990. 'Escritura de mujer', *Poder y Libertad*, 13, 6-7

—, (París, Carlos, prol.) 1992. *Mujer y poder político: Fundamentos de la crisis de objetivos e ideología del movimiento feminista*, Madrid: Vindicación Feminista

Federación de Organizaciones Feministas del Estado Español, 1994. *Juntas y a por Todas: Jornadas Feministas*, Madrid: Comunidad de Madrid, Dirección General de la Mujer

Feito, Alvaro, 1989. 'Música popular', in *Doce años de cultura española (1976-1987)*, ed. Equipo Reseña, Madrid: Ediciones Encuentro, 275-81

Felski, Rita, 1989. *Beyond Aesthetics: Feminist Literature and Social Change*, [n.p]: Hutchinson Radius

Ferguson, Mary Anne, 1983. 'The Female Novel of Development and the Myth of Psyche', in Abel, Hirsch & Langland (1983), 228-43

Fernández, Victoria, 1992. 'Nombrar de nuevo el mundo: Extravagancias y humor en la primera incursión de Rosa Montero en la literatura infantil', *Babelia* (25 January), 12

Fernández de Avilés, Paloma, 1994. *Literatura infantil: Bibliografías y obras de referencia*, Madrid: Biblioteca Nacional, Guía del Lector N° 3

Fernández Poncela, Anna M., 1992. 'El movimiento feminista en el Estado español', *Fem*, 16/118, 31-4

Fernández Sanz, Matilde, 1994. 'Palabras de la Excma. Ministra de Asuntos Sociales en el acto de apertura', in Instituto de la Mujer (1994b), 7-13

Fernández Villanueva, Concepción, 1982. 'La mujer y la psicología', in Durán Heras (1982b), 81-102

Ferreira, Virginia, 1996. 'Mujer y trabajo: La división sexual del trabajo en el análisis sociológica: De natural a socialmente construida', in García de León et al. (1996), 93-119

Ferrer, Rai, 1985. *Durruti: 1896-1936*, Barcelona: Planeta

Ferreras, Juan Ignacio, 1972. *La novela de ciencia ficción*, Madrid: Siglo XXI

Fetterley, Judith, 1978. *The Resisting Reader: A Feminist Approach to American Fiction*, Bloomington: Indiana University Press

Figueroa, Rafael, 1992. *Salsa and Related Genres: A Bibliographical Guide*, London: Greenwood Press

Fitting, Peter, 1987. 'Positioning and Closure: On the "Reading Effect" of Contemporary Utopian Fiction', in Beauchamp, Roemer & Smith (1987), 23-36

Flax, Jane, 1978. 'The conflict between nurturance and autonomy in mother-daughter relationships and within feminism', *Feminist Studies*, 4/2, 171-89

—, 1987. 'Postmodernism and Gender Relations in Feminist Theory', *Signs: Journal of Women in Culture and Society*, 12.4, 621-43

Folguera, Pilar, ed., 1988a. *El feminismo en España: Dos siglos de historia*, Madrid: Fundación Pablo Iglesias

—, 1988b. 'De la transición política a la democracia: La evolución del feminismo en España durante el periodo 1975-1988', in Folguera (1988a), 111-31

—, 1988c. 'El feminismo en la era del cambio', *Historia 16*, 145, 91-8

Fontcuberta, Mar de, 1987. 'La Ginocrítica: Una perspectiva literaria "otra"', in Durán & Rey (1987), 53-66

Fontradona, Oscar, 1995. 'El machismo esclaviza al hombre: Entrevista a Rosa Montero', *Ajoblanco* (May), 30-5

Forum de Política Feminista, 1992. *Por una política feminista*, Madrid: Forum Política de la Mujer & Instituto de la Mujer

—, 1994. *Feminismo y el estado de bienestar*, Madrid: Forum Política de la Mujer & Instituto de la Mujer

Frade, Cristina, 1993. 'Rosa Montero: «Me pregunto cómo se las arregla la gente sin escribir»', *El Mundo*, 9 July*

Franco, Jean, 1986. 'The Incorporation of Women: A Comparison of North American and Mexican Popular Narrative', in Modleski (1986a), 119-38

Franz, Thomas R., 1993. 'Intertexts and Allusions as Aids to Meaning in Montero's *Temblor*', *ALEC*, 18, 261-79

Freixas, Laura, 1979. 'La nueva moral o el machismo de vanguardia', *Vindicación Feminista*, 28, 95-8

Frye, Joanne S., 1986. *Living Stories, Telling Lives: Women and the Novel in Contemporary Experience*, Ann Arbor: University of Michigan Press

Fuentes Molla, Rafael, 1991. 'Novela española: Entre el testimonio y la experiencia', in Ramos Gascón vol. II, 109-45

Fuertes, Sol, 1982. 'Tras su volumen de entrevistas, Rosa Montero prepara "una novela tragicómica"', *El País*, 9 June, 43

Gabancho, Patrícia, 1982. *La rateta encara escombra l'escaleta: Cop d'ull a l'actual literatura catalana de dona*, Barcelona: edicions 62,

Galán, Natalio, (Cabrera Infante, Guillermo, prol.), 1983. *Cuba y sus sones*, Valencia: Pre-textos/Música

Galeano, Eduardo, 1994. 'Ayudar a mirar' (interview), *El Viejo Topo* (April), 47-55

Galerstein, Carolyn L., 1986. *Women Writers of Spain: An Annotated Bio-Bibliographical Guide* (non-Castilian materials ed. by Kathleen M[c]Nerney), New York: Greenwood Press

Gallego, Maite, García de León, María Antonia, Subirats, Marina & Judith Astelarra, 1996. 'Sobre la especificidad y situación actual de la Sociología del Género', in Brullet Tenas & Carrasquer Oto (1996), 12-33

Gallego, María Teresa, ed., 1982. *Nuevas perspectivas sobre la mujer. Actas de las primeras jornadas de investigación interdisciplinaria sobre la mujer, Vol. II*, Madrid: Seminario de Estudios de la Mujer de la Universidad Autónoma de Madrid

Gallego Méndez, María Teresa, 1983. *Mujer, Falange y franquismo*, Madrid: Taurus

Gambaro, Griselda, 1985. 'Algunas consideraciones sobre la mujer y la literatura', *RI*, 132-3, 471-3

Gamman, Lorraine & Margaret Marshment, eds., 1988. *The Female Gaze: Women as Viewers of Popular Culture*, London: The Women's Press

Gándara, Alejandro, 1988. 'Rosa Montero: «Somos esclavos de lo absurdo»', *El País*, 16 March, 30

Gándara, Consuelo de la, 1981. 'La imagen de la mujer a través de la novela española contemporánea', in Durán (1981), 131-54

García, Evelyne, 1982. 'Lectura: N.Fem.Sing. ¿Lee y escribe la mujer en forma diferente al hombre?', *Quimera*, 23, 54-7.

García, Víctor, 1977. *Utopías y anarquismo*, Mexico City: Editores Mexicanos Unidos

García de León, María Antonia, García de Cortázar, María & Félix Ortega, eds., 1996. *Sociología de las mujeres españolas*, Madrid: Editorial Complutense

García de León, Mª Antonia & Teresa Maldonado, 1989. *Pedro Almodóvar: La otra España cañí (sociología y crítica cinematográfica)*, Ciudad Real: Área de Cultura. Biblioteca de Autores y Temas Manchegos

García Padrino, Jaime, 1992. *Libros y literatura para niños en la España contemporánea*, Madrid: Pirámide

García-Posada, Miguel, 1997. 'Una novela de iniciación: Aventuras,amor y sabiduría vital en la última obra de Rosa Montero, *La hija del caníbal*', *El País*, 17 May, Babelia, 17

Garralón, Ana, 1990. 'Literatura con valores', *CLIJ*, 13, 26-31

Gascón Vera, Elena, 1987. 'Rosa Montero ante la escritura feminina', *ALEC*, 12, 59-78

—, 1992. *Un mito nuevo: La mujer como sujeto/objeto literario*, Madrid: Pliegos

Gil, Rodolfo, 1984. *Los cuentos de hadas: Historia mágica del hombre*, Madrid: Aula Abierta Salvat

Gil Ruiz, Juana María, 1996. *La política de la igualdad en España: Avance y retrocesos*, Granada: Universidad de Granada

Gilman, Charlotte Perkins, 1915. *Herland*, first published as a novel 1979, London: The Women's Press

Gilmore, David D., 1994. *Hacerse hombre: Concepciones culturales de la masculinidad* (trans. of *Manhood in the Making: Cultural Concepts of masculinity*), Barcelona: Paidos

Giménez Bartlett, Alicia, 1993. 'Retazos del mundo de Valle Inclán', *El Mundo*, 1 May, 11

Glenn, Kathleen, 1987. 'Victimised by Misreading: Rosa Montero's *Te trataré como a una reina*', *ALEC*, 12, 191-202

—, 1988. 'Reader Expectations and Rosa Montero's *La función delta*', *Letras Peninsulares*, Spring, 87-96

—, 1990a. 'Conversación con Rosa Montero', *ALEC*, 15, 275-83

—, 1990b. 'Authority and Marginality in Three Contemporary Spanish Narratives', *RLA*, 426-30

—, 1991a. 'Fictions of the Self in *La función delta* and *Primera memoria*', in Torres & King, 197-203

—, 1991b. Rev. of *Temblor*, *ALEC*, 16, 401-2

Gobernado Arribas, Rafael, 1991. 'La incorporación de la mujer a la esfera pública', in Ramos Gascón, vol I, 257-67

Gómez del Manzano, Mercedes, 1987. *El protagonista-niño en la literatura infantil del siglo XX: Incidencias en el desarrollo de la personalidad del niño*, Madrid: Narcea

González Gárate, Anabel, 1978. 'Jornadas de la Condición Femenina', *Ozono* 4/3, 23-4

—, 1979. *El feminismo en España hoy: Bibliografía completa y documentos*, Bilbao: Zero

—, 1980. *Los orígenes del feminismo en España*, Madrid: Zero-ZYX

González Rodríguez, Francisca, 1990. 'La pugna de la mujer por su mismicidad', in Ballarín & Ortiz (1990), 799-809

González Rubio, Victoria, 1990. 'Aventureras en el país de la literatura', *Poder y Libertad*, 13, 22

Grau, Ilda Elena, 1988. 'Utopías y feminismo: Un reto para las mujeres', in *Fem. 10 años de periodismo feminista*, dirección editorial Jaime Aljure Bastos, Mexico: Planeta, colección mujeres en su tiempo, 279-82

Grau Biosca, Elena, 1993. 'De la emancipación a la liberación y la valoración de la diferencia: El movimiento de mujeres en el Estado español', in *Historia de las Mujeres: Siglo XX*, vol. 5, ed. by Françoise Thébaud, Madrid: Taurus, 171-93

Green, Jen & Sarah Lefanu, ed., 1985. *Despatches from the Frontiers of the Female Mind*, London: The Women's Press, intro, 1-7

Greene, Gayle, 1991. *Changing the Story: Feminist Fiction and the Tradition* Bloomington: Indiana University Press

—, 1993. 'Looking at History', in Greene & Kahn (1993), 4-27

Greene, Gayle & Coppélia Kahn, eds., 1993. *Changing Subjects: The Making of Feminist Literary Criticism*, London: Routledge

Grinberg, León & Rebeca, 1980. *Identidad y cambio*, Barcelona: Paidos

Grosz, Elizabeth, 1991. *Jacques Lacan: A Feminist Introduction*, London: Routledge

Grupo Giulia Adinolfi, 1992. 'Construirnos como sujeto, constituirnos en medida del mundo', *Mientras Tanto*, 48, 19-32

Guerra, Alfonso & José Félix Tezanos, eds., 1993. *La década del cambio: Diez años de gobierno socialista 1982-1992*, Madrid: Sistema

Guillaume, Anne, 1988. 'Entrevista a Carme Riera', *Ventanal: Revista de Creación y Crítica*, 14, 71-9

Gullón, Germán, 1987. 'El novelista como fabulador de la realidad: Mayoral, Merino, Guelbenzu...', in Landeira & González del Valle (1987), 59-70

Gunew, Sneja, ed., 1992. *Feminist Knowledge: Critique and Construct*, London: Routledge

Gusdorf, Georges, 1980. 'Conditions and Limits of Autobiography', tran. by James Olney, in Olney (1980a), 28-48

Haraway, Donna, 1991. *Simians, Cyborgs and Women* (London: Free Association Books), includes '"Gender" for a Marxist Dictionary: The Sexual Politics of a Word', 127-44 and 'A Cyborg Manifesto: Science, Technology and Socialist Feminism in the Late Twentieth Century', 149-81

Harnaz, J.L., 1997. 'Novedades editoriales', *Solidaridad Obrera* (June), 7

Hart, Stephen, 1993. *White Ink: Essays on Twentieth Century Feminine Fiction in Spain and Latin America*, London: Tamésis

Hartman, Joan E., 1991. 'Telling Stories: The Construction of Women's Agency', in Hartman & Messer-Davidow (1991), 11-34.

Hartman, Joan E. & Ellen Messer-Davidow, eds., 1991. *(En) Gendering Knowledge: Feminists in Academe*, Knoxville: University of Tennessee

Held, Jacqueline, 1987. *Los niños y la literatura fantástica: Función y poder de lo imaginario*, Barcelona: Paidós Ibérica

Hernández Velasco, Irene, 1996. 'Siglo XXI: La hora de la mujer', *El Mundo*, 8 March, 56

Hey, Valerie, 1983. 'The necessity of romance', *Women's Studies Occasional Papers*, 3, Canterbury: University of Kent

Heymann, Jochen & Montserrat Mullor-Heymann, 1991. *Retratos de escritorio: Entrevistas a autores españoles*, Frankfurt: Vervuert

Hirsch, Marianne, 1989. *The Mother/Daughter Plot: Narrative, Psychoanalysis, Feminism*, Bloomington: Indiana University Press

Hofman, Bert, Joan i Tous, Pere & Manfred Tietz, eds., 1995. *El anarquismo español y sus tradiciones culturales*, Frankfurt: Vervuert

Hofstadter, Douglas R., 1986. 'Mathematical Chaos and Strange Attractors' (November 1981), in *Metamagical Themas: Questing for the Essence of Mind and Pattern*, London: Penguin, 364-95

Hollway, Wendy, 1983. 'Heterosexual Sex: Power and Desire for the Other', in *Sex and Love: New Thoughts on Old Contradictions*, ed. by Sue Cartledge & Joanna Ryan, London: The Women's Press, 124-40

Homans, Margaret, 1983. '"Her Very Own Howl": The Ambiguities of Representation in Recent Women's Fiction', in *Signs: Journal of Women in Culture and Society*, 9/2, 186-205

Huertas Zarco, María, 1994. 'Relaciones entre mujeres' in Federación de Organizaciones Feministas del Estado Español, 91-102

Hurtado, Empar, 1992. 'Las escritoras españolas y la enseñanza de la literatura', in *Del silencio a la palabra: Coeduacación y reforma educativa*, ed. by Montserrat Moreno, Madrid: Instituto de la Mujer, 380-93

Hutcheon, Linda, 1984. *Narcissistic Narrative: The Metafictional Paradox*, London: Methuen

—, 1990. *A Poetics of Postmodernism: History, Theory, Fiction*, London: Routledge

Iglesias de Ussel, Julio, 1976. 'Actitudes discriminatorias contra la mujer de los varones españoles', *RICS* (Barcelona), 27-8, 179-99

—, 1979. *El aborto: Un estudio sociológico sobre el caso español*, Madrid: Centro de Investigaciones Sociológicas

—, 1980. *Elementos para el estudio de la mujer en la sociedad española: Análisis bibliográfico*, Madrid: Dirección de juventud y promoción sociocultural

—, 1983. 'La sociología de la sexualidad en España; notas introductorias', *REIS* (Madrid), 21, 103-33.

Imaz, Virginia, 1996. 'Las mujeres y el humor', in Ortega, Sebastián & De la Torre (1996), 203-6

Imbert Martí, Gerard, 1980. 'Hacia una masculinidad deliberada', *El Viejo Topo*, extra 10, 40-7

—, 1981. 'El cuerpo como producción social', *El Viejo Topo*, extra 13, 12-20

—,1990. *Los discursos del cambio: Imágenes e imaginarios sociales en España de la transición (1976-1982)*, tran. Beatriz Simó, Torrejón de Ardoz, Madrid: Akal

Insituto de la Mujer, 1983. *Seminario Europeo: La Comunidad Europea y las Mujeres Españolas, 10, 11 y 12 de noviembre de 1983, Madrid*, Madrid: Instituto de la Mujer

—, 1985. *Primeras Jornadas- de Mujer y Salud, mayo 1984*, Madrid: Instituto de la Mujer

—, 1987. *Plan para la igualdad de oportunidades de las mujeres 1988-1990*, Madrid: Instituto de la Mujer

—, 1988a. *Primeras Jornadas de Mujer y Salud Mental, mayo 1985*, Madrid: Instituto de la Mujer

—, 1988b. *Los hombres españoles*, Madrid: Instituto de la Mujer & Ministerio de Asuntos Sociales

—, 1990a. *II Plan para la igualdad de oportunidades de las mujeres 1993-1995*, Madrid: Instituto de la Mujer

—, 1990b. *La mujer en España: Situación social, Política*, Madrid: Instituto de la Mujer

—, 1990c. *Síntesis de estudios y encuestas del Instituto de la Mujer, 1984-1990*, Madrid: Instituto de la Mujer

—, 1994a. *Diez años del Instituto de la Mujer*, Madrid: Instituto de la Mujer

—, 1994b. *Foro internacional: Mujer, poder político y desarrollo*, Madrid: Instituto de la Mujer & Ministerio de Asuntos Sociales

—, 1995a. *El largo camino hacia la igualdad: Feminismo en España 1975-1995*, Madrid: Instituto de la Mujer & Ministerio de Asuntos Sociales

—, 1995b. *Spanish Women on the Threshold of the 21st Century*, Madrid: Instituto de la Mujer

Izquierdo, Mª Jesús, 1979. 'Los derechos de la mujer en la Constitución de 1978', *Revista de la Facultad de Derecho de la Universidad Complutense* (Madrid), 2 (monográfico), 205-23

—, 1988. '20 años después del Women's Lib', in VV.AA. (1988), Barcelona: Ayuntamiento, Centro de documentacio de la dona, 11-21

—, 1989. 'La violencia sexista en el lenguaje', in Mateos & Sagasti (1989), 75-84

—, 1994. 'Uso y abuso del concepto del género', in *Pensar las diferencias*, ed. by Mercedes Vilanova, Barcelona: Universitat de Barcelona & Institut Català de la Dona, 31-53

Izquierdo, Mª Jesús & Francesc Borrás, 1984. 'Lo masculino y lo femenino en la ciencia ficción', *Langaiak*, 6, 21-30

—, 1987. 'La «ciencia ficción» de las relaciones entre los sexos', *Mujeres Mulleres Dones Emakumeak*, 15, 35-9

J.C., 1993. '*Bella y oscura*, la madurez de Rosa Montero como novelista' (interview), *Diari de Tarragona*, 6 May, 35

Jackson, Rosemary, 1981. *Fantasy: The Literature of Subversion*, London: Methuen

Jacobs, Naomi, 1989. 'Beyond Stasis and Symettry: Lessing, Le Guin, and the Remodelling of Utopia', in Cummings & Smith (1989), 109-17

Jacobus, Mary, ed., 1979. *Women Writing and Writing about Women*, London: Croom Helm, includes 'The Difference of View', 10-21

Jáuregui, Fernando & Pedro Vega, 1985. *Crónica del antifranquismo*, vol. 1, Barcelona: Argos Vergara

Jay, Paul L., 1982. 'Being in the Text: Autobiography and the Problem of the Subject', *MLN*, 97, 1045-63

Jelinek, Estelle, ed., 1980. *Women's Autobiography: Essays in Criticism*, Bloomington: Indiana University Press

Johnston, Hank, Laraña, Enrique & Joseph Gusfield, 1994. 'Identidades, ideologías y vida cotidiana en los nuevos movimientos sociales', in *Los nuevos movimientos sociales: De la ideología a la identidad*, ed. by Enrique Laraña & Joseph Gusfield, Madrid: Centro de Investigaciones Sociológicas, 3-42

Jones, Ann Rosalind, 1986. 'Mills and Boon meets Feminism', in *The Progress of Romance: The Politics of Popular Fiction*, ed. by Jean Radford, London: Routledge & Kegan Paul, 195-218

Jones, Libby Falk, 1991. 'Breaking Silences in Feminist Dystopias', in Cummings & Smith (1991), 7-11

Jones, Margaret E.W., 1983. 'Del compromiso al egoísmo: La metamorfosis de la protagonista en la novelística femenina de postguerra', in Pérez (1983), 125-34

Juliano, Dolores, 1988. 'Modelos e identidad', in VV.AA. (1988), 22-34

Kaplan, E. Ann, ed., 1988. *Postmodernism and Its Discontents*, London: Verso

Kaplan, Gisela, 1992. *Contemporary Western European Feminism*, London: UCL Press

Kaplan, Temma, 1971. 'Spanish Anarchism and Women's Liberation', *Journal of Contemporary History*, 6, 101-10

—,1977. 'Other Scenarios: Women and Spanish Anarchism', in *Becoming Visible. Women in European History*, ed. by Renate Bridenthal & Claudia Koonz, Boston: Houghton Mifflin, 400-21

Kegan Gardiner, Judith et al., 1982. 'An Interchange on Feminist Criticism: On "Dancing through the Minefield"', *Feminist Studies*, 8/3, 629-75.

Kennard, Jean E., 1981. 'Convention Coverage or How to Read Your Own Life', *New Literary History*, 8, 69-88

Kercher, Dona M., 'Montero and the Bolero: A Musical Feminism?' (undated manuscript supplied by Rosa Montero)

Kessler, Carol Farley, ed., 1984. *Daring to Dream: Utopian Stories by United States Women: 1836-1919*, London: Pandora Press

Kimmel, Michael S., 1994. 'Masculinity as Homphobia: Fear, Shame and Silence in the Construction of Gender Identity', in Brod & Kaufman (1994), 119-141

King, Roger, 1991. 'Utopian Fiction as Moral Philosophy: Imagination and Critique', in Cummings & Smith (1991), 72-8

Knights, Vanessa, 1993. Unpublished interview with Rosa Montero, 22 October

—, 1994. Unpublished interview with Rosa Montero, 3 July

—, 1998. 'Interview with Rosa Montero, Madrid, 23 July 1997', *Tesserae: Journal of Latin American and Iberian Studies*, 4/1, 77-82

Kolbenschlag. Madonna, 1983. *Goodbye Sleeping Beauty: Breaking the Spell of Feminine Myths and Models*, London: Marion Boyars

Kolodny, Annette, 1986. 'Dancing Through the Minefield: Some Observations on the Theory, Practice, and Politics of a Feminist Literary Criticism', in *The New Feminist Criticism. Essays on Women, Literature and Theory*, ed. by Elaine Showalter, London: Virago, 144-67, originally published in *Feminist Studies*, 6 (1980), 1-25

Kornegger, Peggy, 1979. 'Anarchism: The Feminist Connection', in Ehrlich et al. (1979), 237-49

Koskoff, Ellen, 1987. *Women and Music in Cross-cultural Perspective*, New York: Greenwood Press

Kress, Susan, 1981. 'In and Out of Time: The Form of Marge Piercy's Novels', in Barr (1981), 109-22

Labanyi, Jo, 1993. 'Postmodernism, Pastiche and the Problem of Cultural Identity', talk given at the Instituto Cervantes, London in the cycle 'La cultura española en su contexto europeo' on 7 June

Lamberet, Renée, 1975. 'Soledad Gustavo, sa place dans la pensée anarchiste espagnole', *Convivium* (Barcelona), 44-5, 17-35

Landeira, Ricardo & Luis T. González del Valle, eds., 1987. *Nuevos y Novísimos: Algunas perspectivas críticas sobre la narrativa española desde la década de los sesenta*, Boulder: Society of Spanish and Spanish American Studies

Laplanche, Jean, & Jean Bertrand Pontalis, 1986. 'Fantasy and the Origins of Sexuality', in *Formations of Fantasy*, ed. by Victor Burgin, Donald James & Cora Kaplan, London: Methuen, 5-34

Larrauri, Maite, 1993. 'Mujeres en la escena política', *El País*, 2 July, 16

Lauretis, Teresa de, 1986. *Feminist Studies/Critical Studies*, Bloomington: Indiana University Press

—, 1990. 'Upping the Anti (sic) in Feminist Theory', in *Conflicts in Feminism*, ed. by Marianne Hirsch & Evelyn Fox Keller, London: Routledge, 255-70

—, 1991. 'Film and the Visible', in *How do I Look? Queer Film and Video*, ed. Bad Object Choices, Seattle: Bay Press, 223-64

Lefanu, Sarah, 1988. *In the Chinks of the World Machine: Feminism and Science Fiction*, London: The Women's Press

Lejeune, Philippe, 1980. *Je est un autre: L'autobiographie, de la littérature aux médias*, Paris: Éditions du Seuil

Le Guin, Ursula, 1969. *The Left Hand of Darkness*, 1992 edn., London: Orbit

Leighton, Marian, 1979. 'Anarcho-feminism', in Ehrlich et al. (1979), 253-8

León, Argeliers, 1982. 'Notas para un panorama de la música popular', in Casa de las Américas, 235-45

—, 1984. *Del canto y el tiempo*, Havana: Letras Cubanas

LID, 1990. 'Entrevista a Rosa Montero: "Escribir es una aventura sin conocer trayecto y meta"', *Córdoba*, 27 February*

Light, Alison, 1984. 'Returning to Manderley: Romance Fiction, Sexuality and Class', *Feminist Review*, 16, 7-25

Livingston, Dennis, 1978. 'The Utility of Science Fiction', in *Handbook of Futures Research* ed. by Jib Fowles, London: Greenwood Press, 163-78

Longhurst, C. A., 1991. 'Women and Social Change in Contemporary Spain', *ACIS*, 4/1, 17-25

Longo, Aurora, 1983. 'Reflexiones acerca de la maternidad', *Langaiak*, 2, 18-21

Lonzi, Carla, 1970. 'Let's Spit on Hegel', tran. by Veronica Newman, in Bono & Kemp (1991), 40-59

López, Aurora & Mª Ángeles Pastor, eds., 1990. *Crítica y ficción literaria: Mujeres contemporáneas españolas*, Granada: Seminario de Estudios de la Mujer, Feminae

López, Juan Manuel, 1993. 'Rosa Montero recrea la pasión en *Bella y oscura*', *Diario de Mallorca*, 16 April*

López Jiménez, Francisca, 1995. *Mito y discurso en la novela feminina de posguerra en España*, Madrid: Pliegos de Ensayo

López Pintor, Rafael & Ricardo Buceta, 1975. *Los españoles de los años 70*, Madrid: Tecnos

López Tamés, Román, 1990. *Introducción a la literatura infantil*, Murcia: Universidad de Murcia

Lorite Mena, José, 1987. *El orden femenino: Origen de un simulacro cultural*, Barcelona, Anthropos

Lovenduski, Joni, 1986. *Women and European Politics. Contemporary Feminism and Public Policy*, Brighton: Wheatsheaf

Lozano, Irene, 1995. *Lenguaje femenino, lenguaje masculino: ¿Condiciona nuestro sexo la forma de hablar?*, Madrid: Minerva

Lucas Verdú, P., 1981-82. 'El valor constitucional de la igualdad y la condición femenina', *Revista de Política Comparada* (Madrid), 7, 27-49

Lury, Celia, 1991. 'Reading the Self: Autobiography, Gender and the Institution of the Literary', in *Off-Centre: Feminism and Cultural Studies*, Sarah Franklin, Celia Lury & Jackie Stacey, London: Harper Collins, 97-108

Lynn, Ruth Nadelman, 1979. *Fantasy for Children: An Annotated Checklist*, New York: R.R. Bowker

Maillard, Mª Luisa, 1978. 'Desgracia y gracia de los anticonceptivos', *Ozono* 36, 28-30

Man, Paul de, 1979. 'Autobiography as Defacement', *MLN*, 94, 919-30

Manteiga, Roberto, 1988. 'The Dilemma of the Modern Woman: A Study of the Female Characters in Rosa Montero's Novels', in Manteiga, Galerstein & McNerney (1988), 113-23

Manteiga, Roberto, Carolyn Galerstein & Kathleen McNerney, eds., 1988. *Feminine Concerns in Contemporary Spanish Fiction by Women*, Potomac: Scripta Humanistica

Mañà, Teresa, 1992. 'Niñas de papel', *CLIJ*, 41, 42-7

Maquieira, Virginia & Cristina Sánchez, eds., 1990. *Violencia y sociedad patriarcal*, Madrid: Editorial Pablo Iglesias

Marcus, Jane, 1982. 'Storming the Toolshed', in *Feminist Theory: A Critique of Ideology*, ed. by Nannerl O. Keohane, Michelle Z. Rosaldo & Barbara C. Gelpi, Brighton: The Harvester Press, 217-35

Mardones, José Mª, 1991. 'El neo-conservadurismo de los posmodernos', in Vattimo et al. (1991), 21-40

Marímon, Carmen, 1992. 'Leer/escribir como mujer', *Canelobre*, 23-4, 109-15

Marqueño Rozalén, María Ángeles, 1994. 'Autoestima y sexualidad para las mujeres jóvenes', in Federación de Organizaciones Feministas del Estado Español (1994), 227-31

Marqués, Josep-Vicent, 1980. 'El fetismo no es un humanismo', *El Viejo Topo*, 40, 28-30

—, 1987. *¿Qué hace el poder en tu cama?*, Barcelona: Icaria

Marqués, Josep-Vincent & Raquel Osborne, 1991. *Sexualidad y sexismo*, Madrid: Universidad Nacional de Educación a Distancia-Fundación Universidad Empresa

Martí, Sacramento, 1984. 'La mujer entre la biología y la cultura: La mujer nace y se hace', *Langaiak*, 6, 10-14

Martín Gaite, Carmen, 1985 (1st edn. 1983). *El cuento de nunca acabar: Apuntes sobre la narración, el amor y la mentira*, Barcelona: Destinolibro

—, 1994 (1st edn. 1987). *Desde la ventana: Enfoque femenino de la literatura española*, Madrid: Espasa-Calpe, Colección Austral, Pensamiento Contemporáneo

Martín-Maestro, Abraham, 1984. 'La novela española en 1982 y 1983', *ALEC*, 9, 149-74

Martinell Gifre, Emma, 1992. Prologue to Martín Gaite (1994), 9-21

Martínez, José Tono, 1989. 'Prácticas de la posmodernidad', in Castrortega (1989), 189-93

Martínez, Mayra A., 1994. *Cubanos en la música*, Havana: Letras Cubanas

Martínez Menchen, Antonio, 1971. *Narraciones infantiles y cambio social*, Madrid: Taurus

Martínez Ten, Carmen, 1988. 'Maternidad y cambio de roles de género', in *Terceras Jornadas Parlamentarias: Mujer y Socialismo, 6 y 7 de octubre 1988, Grupo Parlamentario Socialista*, Madrid: Mariar, 111-14

—, 1990. 'La participación política de la mujer en España', in Astelarra (1990), 39-82

Mateos, Txoli & Begoña Sagasti, eds., 1989. *Nosotras también escribimos*, Bilbao: Servicio Editorial, Universidad del País Vasco

Mayans Natal, María Jesús, 1991. *Narrativa feminista española de posguerra*, Madrid: Pliegos

McCaffery, Larry, 1982. *The Metafictional Muse*, Pittsburgh: The University of Pittsburgh Press

McClintock, Anne, 1992. 'Gonad the Barbarian and the Venus Flytrap: Portraying the Female and Male Orgasm', in McIntosh & Segal (1992), 111-31

McIntosh, Mary, & Lynne Segal, eds., 1992. *Sex Exposed: Sexuality and the Pornography Debate*, London:Virago

Meese, Elizabeth, 1986. *Crossing the Double-Cross: The Practice of Feminist Criticism*, London: University of North Caroline Press

Mellor, Anne K., 1982. 'On Feminist Utopias', *Women's Studies*, 9, 241-62

Méndez, José, 1993. 'Los azares monstruosos', in Dirección Provincial del MEC (Zaragoza), (first publ. in *El País*, 25 February 1990), 4

Méndez, Lucía, 1996. 'Conferencia sobre mujer y la prensa', in Ortega, Sebastián & De la Torre (1996), 89-93

Mendoza-Prado, Marcelo, 1994. 'El periplo oculto de Durruti', *El País*, 27 November, 18-19

Mestre, Carmen, 1982. 'Feminismo hoy', in *La mujer en el mundo actual: Notas sobre feminismo*, ed. by Pina López Gay, Madrid: Universidad Internacional Menéndez Pelayo, 97-102

Middleton, Richard, 1990. *Studying Popular Music*, Milton Keynes: Open University Press

Miguel, Amando de, 1974a. *Sexo, mujer y natalidad en España*, Madrid: Edicusa

—, 1974b. 'Sobre lo masculino y lo femenino en la relación sexual y social', *Sistema* (Madrid), 4, 75-88

Miguel Martínez, Emilio de, 1983. *La primera narrativa de Rosa Montero*, Salamanca: Salamanca University

Miller, Beth, ed., 1983. *Women in Hispanic Literature: Icons and Fallen Idols*, London: University of California Press

Miranda, María Jesús, 1987. *Crónicas del desconcierto*, Madrid: Instituto de la Mujer

MLN, 1978. Special edn., 'Autobiography and the Problem of the Subject', 93-94, (May)

Modleski, Tania, 1982. *Loving with a Vengeance: Mass Produced Fantasies for Women*, London: Methuen

—, 1986a. *Studies in Entertainment: Critical Approaches to Mass Culture*, Bloomington: Indiana University Press

—, 1986b. 'Feminism and the Power of Interpretation: Some Critical Readings', in Lauretis (1986), 121-38

Moi, Toril, 1990. 'Feminism, Postmodernism and Style: Recent Feminist Criticisms in the United States', in *Criticism in the Twilight Zone: Postmodern Perspectives on Literature and Politics*, ed. by Danuta Zadworne-Fjellestad & Lennart Björk, Stockholm: Almqvist & Wiksell International, 34-51

Molina Petit, Cristina, 1992. 'Lo femenino como metáfora en la racionalidad postmoderna y su (escasa) utilidad para la Teoría Feminista', *Isegoría: Revista de Filosofía Moral y Política*, 6, 129-43

—, 1994a. *Dialéctica de la ilustración*, Barcelona: Anthropos

—, 1994b. '¿Por qué un feminismo ilustrado?', in Federación de Organizaciones Feministas del Estado Español, 319-23

Molinaro, Nina, 1991. *Foucault, Feminism and Power: Reading Esther Tusquets*, London: Associated University Presses

Molloy, Sylvia, 1991. *At Face Value: Autobiographical Writing in Spanish America*, Cambridge: Cambridge University Press

Monegal, Antonio, 1986. 'Entrevista a Rosa Montero', *Plaza*, 11, 5-12

Montano, Alicia G., 1997. 'Rosa Montero: Heridas de Identidad', *Qué leer* (July-August), 22-3

Montero, Justa, 1992. 'La explotación de las diferencias' in Forum de Política Feminista, 81-5

—, 1994a. 'Igualdad y diferencia: Encrucijada del movimiento', *El Viejo Topo*, 73, 39-44.

—, 1994b. 'Aspectos del feminismo socialista y las políticas del bienestar', in Forum de Política Feminista (1994), 15-22

Montero Delgado, Francisco, 1990. 'Típicos tópicos: Sobre los hipotéticos fundamentos biológicos de la personalidad en ambos sexos', in Ballarín & Ortiz (1990), 139-57

Mora, Orlando, 1989. *La música que es como la vida*, Medellín: Ediciones Autores Antioqueños,

Morello-Frosch, Marta, 1981. 'Usos y abusos de la cultura popular: *Pubis angelical* de Manuel Puig', in *Literature and Popular Culture in the Hispanic World: A Symposium*, ed. by Rose Minc, Gaithersburg, MD: Hispamérica & Montclair State College, 31-42

Moreno, Sebastian, 1983. 'Yo no soy ésa: Las mujeres españolas no se identifican con su imagen publicitaria', *Cambio16*, 12 December, 112-17

—, 1988. 'Rosa Montero: «Lo de las dos ministras es una chorrada indignante»' (interview), *Tribuna*, 25 July, 58-9

Moreno Sardà, Amparo, 1986. *El arquetipo viril protagonista de la historia: Ejercicios de la lectura no-androcéntrica*, Barcelona: LaSal, edicions de les dones

—, 1988. *La otra «política» de Aristóteles: Cultura de masas y divulgación del arquetipo viril*, Barcelona: Icaria

Morgan, Ellen, 1978. 'Humanbecoming: Form and Focus in the Neo-Feminist Novel', in Brown & Olson (1978), 272-8

Mujeres Mulleres Dones Emakumeak, 1994. 'Para leer y escribir de otra manera', 13, 10

La mujer feminista, 1985. 'Rosa Montero. Nunca pensé casarme', 21, 7-10

Mulvey, Laura, 1989. *Visual and Other Images*, London: Macmillan Press

El Mundo, 1996. 'La prensa española a la cabeza del despliegue', *El Mundo*, 9 March, 29

Muñoz, Diego, 1990. 'Manuel Puig, el 'bolero literario'', *El País*, 26 April, 36

Myers, Eunice D., 1988. 'The Feminist Message: Propaganda and/or Art? A Study of Two Novels by Rosa Montero', in Manteiga, Galerstein & McNerney (1988), 99-112

Nash, Mary, 1975. 'Dos intelectuales anarquistas frente al problema de la mujer: Federica Montseny y Lucía Sánchez Saornil', *Convivium* (Barcelona), 44-5, 71-101

—, 1991. 'Pronatalism and motherhood in Franco's Spain', in *Maternity and Gender Policies: Women and the Rise of the European Welfare States, 1880s-1950s*, ed. by Gisela Bock & Pat Thane, London: Routledge, 160-77

Navajo, Ymelda, 1978a. 'Entrevista a Cristina Alberdi: "La Constitución es machista"', *Ozono*, 4/30, 25

—, 1978b. '¿Crisis en el feminismo?', *Ozono*, 4/29, 29-32

—, ed., 1982. *Doce relatos de mujeres*, Madrid: Alianza

Navarro, Ana, 1993. 'La mujer y el nuevo paradigma', *El País*, 12 August, 14

Navarro, M., ed., 1988a. *Mujer y realidad social: II congreso mundial vasco*, Vitoria: Servicio Editorial del País Vasco y Gobierno Vasco

—, 1988b. 'El androcentrismo en la historia: La mujer como sujeto invisible', in Navarro (1988a), 15-38

Nichols, Geraldine C., 1992. *Des/cifrar la diferencia: Narrativa femenina de la España contemporánea*, Madrid: Siglo XXI de España

Nogueira, Charo, 1983. 'Rosa Montero: «Quiero hacer novelas lo mejor posible, no escribir panfletos feministas»' (interview), *Diario de Navarra* (Pamplona), 29 November*

Nolte Lensink, Judy, 1987. 'Expanding the Boundaries of Criticism: The Diary as Female Autobiography', *Women's Studies*, 14, 39-53

Núñez, María Teresa, 1988. 'La mujer y el poder', *Poder y Libertad*, 8, 8-9

Núñez, Mª Virtudes & Ramón Guntin, 1992. *Salsa Caribe y otras músicas antillanas*, Madrid: Ediciones Cubicas

Núñez Ladaveze, Luis, 1976. *Utopía y realidad: La ciencia ficción en España*, Madrid: Ed. del Centro

O'Shea, Covadonga, 1976. *La mujer, ¿ha encontrado su identidad?: Apuntes sobre el tema y 11 entrevistas como respuestas*, Barcelona: Fert,

Olba, Mary Sol, 1983. 'Rosa Montero, a ritmo de bolero' (interview), *Pueblo* (Madrid), 24 November

Olmeda Gómez, Carlos, 1989. *La mujer en la bibliografía española: 1984-1988: Bibliografía anotada*, Madrid: Instituto de la Mujer

Olney, James, 1978. 'Autos-Bios-Graphein: The Study of Autobiographical Literature', *South Atlantic Quarterly*, 77, 113-23

—, ed., 1980a. *Autobiography: Essays, Theoretical and Critical*, Princeton: Princeton University Press

—, 1980b. 'Some Versions of Memory/ Some Versions of Bios: The Ontology of Autobiography' in Olney (1980a), 236-67

—, ed., 1988. *Studies in Autobiography*, Oxford: Oxford University Press

Oranich, Magda, 1976. *¿Qué es el feminismo?*, Barcelona: La Gaya Ciencia

Ordóñez, Elizabeth, 1982. 'Reading Contemporary Spanish Narrative by Women', *ALEC*, 7/2, 237-51

—, 1987. '«L'Écriture Féminine»: New Narrative by Women: Inscribing Difference', *ALEC*, 12, 45-58

—, 1988. 'Rewriting Myth and History: Three Recent Novels by Women', in Manteiga, Galerstein & McNerney (1988), 6-28

—, 1991. *Voices of their Own: Contemporary Spanish Fiction by Women*, London: Associated Universities Press

Ordovás, Jesús, 1991. 'Cuarenta años de música popular en España', in Ramos Gascón Vol. II (1991), Madrid: Cátedra, 350-66

Orquín, Felicidad, 1983. 'Nuevas corrientes de la literatura para niños', in *Literatura infantil*, Ramón Gago et al., Madrid: Acción Educativa

—, 1984. 'De las mujeres que escriben, lo femenino y el modelo imposible', *Langaiak*, 6, 31-7

Orovio, Helio, 1981. *Diccionario de la música cubana, bibliográfico y técnico*, Havana: Letras Cubanas

—, 1994. *Música por el Caribe*, Santiago de Cuba: Oriente

—, 1995. *El bolero latino*, Havana: Letras Cubanas

Ortega, Emilio, 1989, *100 Gran Angular*, Madrid: S.M.

Ortega, Félix, 1993. 'Masculino y femenino en la identidad personal de la juventud española', in Ortega et al. (1993), 15-57

—, 1996. Introduction to 'Ideología e imágenes sobre la condición femenina', in García de León et al., 269-71

Ortega, Félix, Fagoaga Concha, García de León, María Antonia & Pablo del Río, 1993. *La flotante identidad sexual: La construcción del género en la vida cotidiana de la juventud*, Madrid: Universidad Complutense & Comunidad de Madrid, Dirección General de la Mujer

Ortega, Margarita, Sebastián, Julia & Isabel de la Torre, eds., 1995. *Las mujeres en la opinión pública: X Jornadas de Investigación Interdisciplinar*, Madrid: Instituto Universitario de estudios de la Mujer, Universidad Autónoma de Madrid

Ortega, Pilar, 1993. 'La escritora y periodista Rosa Montero publica su sexta novela, *Bella y oscura*: «Recordar la felicidad desde la desgracia es insoportable»', *Ya*, 16 April*

Ortiz, Lourdes, 1990. 'Yo a las cabañas bajé', in Maquieira & Sánchez (1990), 137-50

Osborne, Raquel, 1985. 'El discurso de la diferencia: Implicaciones y problemas para el análisis feminista', *Desde el feminismo*, 0, 30-43

—, 1989. *La construcción sexual de la realidad: El debate sobre la pornografía en el seno del feminismo contemporáneo*, Madrid: Editorial de la Universidad Complutense de Madrid

Otero, Carlos, 1993. 'Los aciertos y las limitaciones de Rosa Montero', *El Periódico de Catalunya*, 19 May*

Owens, Craig, 1985. 'The Discourse of Others: Feminists and Postmodernism', in *Postmodern Culture*, ed. by Hal Foster, London: Pluto Press, 57-82

Pacheco, Martín, 1978. 'Jornadas en Valencia: Hasta la autoconciencia', *Ozono*, 4/28, 29-30

Palmer, Paulina, 1989. *Contemporary Women's Fiction: Narrative Practice and Feminist Theory*, Hemel Hempstead: Harvester Wheatsheaf

Palmes, Laura, Soria, Assumpta & Amparo Tuñon, 1977. 'Dossier Feminismo', *El Viejo Topo*, extra 10, 28-38

Pardo, Rosa & Merché Comabella (MDM), 1979, 'Tareas del movimiento feminista', *Argumentos*, 24, 50-3

Pardo, Rosa. 1988a. 'El feminismo en España: Breve resumen, 1953-1985', in Folguera (1988a), 133-40

—, 1988b. 'Feminismo primero, política después', *Poder y Libertad*, 8, 16-17

Parra, Isabel, 1986. 'El control de la natalidad', in Borreguero et al., 61-70

Patai, Daphne, 1983. 'Beyond Defensiveness: Feminist Research Strategies', in Barr & Smith , 148-69

Paz, Abel, 1996. *Durruti en la Revolución Española*, Madrid: Fundación de Estudios Libertarios Anselmo Lorenzo

Pearson, Carol, 1981. 'Coming Home: Four Feminist Utopias and Patriarchal Experience', in Barr (1981), 63-70

—, 1991. *Awakening the Heroes Within: Twelve Archetypes to Help Us Find Ourselves and Transform Our World*, San Francisco: Harper San Francisco

Pearson, Carol & Katherine Pope, 1981. *The Female Hero in American Literature*, London: R.R. Bowker

Pellón, Gustavo, 1983. 'Manuel Puig's Contradictory Strategy: Kitsch Paradigms *versus* Paradigmatic Structure in *El beso de la mujer araña* and *Pubis Angelical*', *Symposium*, 37/3, 186-201

Penelope, Julia, 1990. *Speaking Freely: Unlearning the Lies of the Father's Tongues*, Oxford: Pergamon Press

Peña-Marin, Cristina, 1984. 'La representación de la femininidad', *Langaiak*, 6, 38-41

—, 1986. 'La bella y la publicidad', *Desde el Feminismo*, 1, 68-71

Peña-Marin, Cristina & Carlo Frabetti, 1990. *La mujer en la publicidad*, Madrid: Instituto de la Mujer

Pereda, Rosa María, 1982. '"La imaginación cambia la conciencia del lector", dice Michael Ende', *El País*, 9 June, 39

Peregrín, Julia, 1985. 'Nosotras, nuestros abortos y nuestras palabras', in Instituto de la Mujer (1985), 51-6

Pérez, Janet, ed., 1983 (1st edn. 1978). *Novelistas femeninas de la postguerra española*, Madrid: Porrúa Turanzas

—, 1986. 'The Fantastic in Two Recent Works of Gonzalo Torrente Ballester', in *Aspects of Fantasy: Selected Essays from the Second International Conference on the Fantastic in Literature and Film*, ed. by William Coyle, Westport, Connecticut: Greenwood Press, 31-40

—, 1988. *Contemporary Women Writers of Spain*, Boston: Twayne

Pérez Campo, Ana María, 1992. 'Un apoyo sin cheques en blanco', in Forum de Política Feminista (1992), 85-8

Pérez Oliva, Milagros, 1993. 'La igualdad, una carrera de fondo', *El País*, 14 May, 26-7

Pérez Sanjurjo, Elena, 1986. *Historia de la música cubana*, Miami: La moderna poesía

Pérez Serrano, Mabel, 1979. 'El consenso varón-mujer', in VV.AA. (1979b), 153-73

Pérez Serrano, Mabel, Suzel Punset & Anina Ubeda, 1978. *Mujer y trabajo*, Madrid: Dirección General de Desarrollo Comunitario

Perona, Ángeles J. & Ramón del Castillo Santos, 1996. 'Pensamiento español y representaciones de género', in García de León et al., 325-49

Personal Narratives Group, eds., 1989. *Interpreting Women's Lives: Feminist Theory and Personal Narratives*, Bloomington: Indiana University Press

Pestaña, Angel, 1984. 'La mujer entre la biología y la cultura: Biología y roles sociales', *Langaiak*, 6, 3-9.

Pfaelzer, Jean, 1988. 'The Challenging of the Avant-Garde: The Feminist Utopia', *Science Fiction Studies*, 15/3, 282-94

Piercy, Marge, 1978. *Woman on the Edge of Time*, 1987 edn., London: The Women's Press

Pineda, Empar, 1980. '¿El mito de la femininidad cabalga de nuevo?', *El Viejo Topo*, extra 10, 16-24

—, 1982. 'El discurso de la igualdad. El discurso de la diferencia', in Durán (1982), 257-71

—, 1988. 'El poder patriarcal en el orden social burgués', *Poder y Libertad*, 8, 14-15

Pino, M., 1976. 'Mujeres Libres: Un movimiento feminista en plena Guerra Civil', *Tiempo de Historia*, 2/18, 36-42

Piña, Begoña, 1994. '«El cristal de Agua Fría»: La última ópera del Centro Nacional de Nuevas Tendencias', *Diario 16*, 12 April*

Piñol, Rosa María, 1990. 'Entrevista a Rosa Montero: "«Temblor» es mi primera novela cosmogónica"', *La Vanguardia*, 2 March*

Plaza, José Mª, 1993. 'Rosa Montero: Horror y belleza' (interview), *Leer*, 65, 52-4

Polanco, José Luis, 1993. 'Panorámica histórica de la literatura infantil', in *Un libro para leer muchos más: guía para adentrarse en el mundo de la literatura infantil y juvenil*, Madrid: Alfaguara, 9-16

Polo, María Eugenia, 1997. 'Rosa Montero, escritora y periodista: «Escribir es contrarrestar la negrura de la vida»', *Tribuna de Salamanca*, 22 June, 4-7

Pompeia, Nuria, 1967. *Maternasis*, Barcelona: Kairós

—, 1975. *Mujercitas*, Barcelona: Puch Ediciones

Porter, Phoebe, 1989. Interview with Rosa Montero at the Café Gijón, Madrid, 12 June, (undated manuscript supplied by Rosa Montero)

—, 1990. 'Conversación con Lourdes Ortiz', *LF*, 16, 139-44

Pratt, Annis, 1973. 'Archetypal Approaches to the New Feminist Criticism', *Bucknell Review*, 21, 3-14

Pujal i Llombart, Margot, 1992. *Poder, saber, naturaleza: la triangulación "masculina" de la mujer y su deconstrucción: Análisis de una invención psicosocial*, Bellaterra: Publicacions de la Universitat Autònoma de Barcelona

Puleo, Alicia H., 1992. 'Mujeres en la política: De la cuota a la legitimación', in Forum de Política Feminista (1992), 3-5

—, 1994a. 'Memoria de una ilustración olvidada', *El Viejo Topo*, 73, 27-30

—, 1994b. *Conceptualizaciones de la sexualidad e identidad femenina: Voces de mujeres en la Comunidad Autónoma de Madrid*, Madrid: Comunidad de Madrid, Dirección General de la Mujer, Instituto de Investigaciones Feministas de la Universidad Complutense de Madrid

—, 1994c. 'Género y sexualidad', in Federación de Organizaciones Feministas del Estado Español, 333-7

—, 1994d. 'Las corrientes feministas y su práctica política en el estado de bienestar', in Forum de Política Feminista (1994), 7-14

Radway, Janice, 1983. 'Women Read the Romance', *Feminist Studies*, 9/1 (Spring), 53-78

—, 1984. *Reading the Romance*, Chapel Hill, North Carolina: University of North Carolina Press

Ragué Arias, Mª José 1981a. 'Spain: Feminism in our Time', *Women's Studies International Quarterly*, 4/4, 471-6

—, 1981b. 'Parirás con dolor... (Y Dios creó al ginecólogo)', *El Viejo Topo*, 55, 22-7

Ramírez, Fátima, 1996. 'Hay que cambiar el neomachismo estúpido y pseuderótico' (Interview with Carmen Rico-Godoy), *Cambio16*, 22 July, 58-9

Ramos Gascón, Antonio, ed., 1991. *España Hoy, Vol. I (Sociedad) & Vol. II (Cultura)*, Madrid: Cátedra

Ramos Vázquez, Natalia, 1975. 'El Año Internacional de la Mujer: Limitaciones de una conmemoración', *Documentación Social*, 17, 75-85

Rebollo, Y. & L. Rodríguez, 1980. 'Sugerencias garbosas para un análisis del lenguaje femenino', *El Viejo Topo*, 49, 48-52

Regazzoni, Susanna, 1984. *Cuatro novelistas de hoy: Estudio y entrevistas*, Milan: Cisalpino-Goliardica

Renza, Louis A., 1980. 'The Veto of the Imagination: A Theory of Autobiography', in Olney (1980a), 268-96.

Rey, Carmen, Alonso, Ana & Pilar Walker, 1985. 'Maternidad, situación en España', in Instituto de la Mujer (1985), 23-9

Ribas, José et al, 1993, 'Debate literario: ¿Y ahora de qué vamos?', *Ajoblanco*, 53, 40-7

Rich, Adrienne, 1977. *Of Woman Born: Motherhood as Experience and Institution*, London: Virago

Rico-Godoy, Carmen, 1993. 'El machsimo quiere enterrar al feminismo', *Cambio16*, 27 December, 24

Rico Salazar, Jaime, 1988. *Cien años de boleros*, 2nd edn., Bogota: Centro de Estudios Musicales de Latinoamerica

Riera, Carme, 1981. 'El lenguaje sexual', *Poder y Libertad*, 2, 186-93

—, 1982. 'Literatura femenina: ¿Un lenguage prestado?', *Quimera*, 18, 9-12

—, 1990. 'Femenino singular: Literatura de mujer', in López & Pastor (1990), 25-38

Riley, Denise, 1988. *Am I that Name?: Feminism and the Category of Woman in History*, Basingstoke: Macmillan

Risco, Antonio, 1982. *Literatura y fantasía*, Madrid: Taurus, Colección Persiles

—, 1987. *Literatura fantástica de lengua española*, Madrid: Taurus, Colección Persiles

Rivas, Rosa, 1993. 'El nuevo feminismo salta al ruedo', *El País*, 7 December, 24

Rivera, Milagros, 1994. 'Partir de sí', *El Viejo Topo*, 73, 31-5

Rivera Garretas, María Milagros, 1994. *Nombrar el mundo en femenini: Pensamiento de las mujeres y teoría feminista*, Barcelona: Icaria

Robles Moreno, Dolores, [n.d] 'Escritoras españolas e hispanoamericanas de ciencia ficción' (unpublished manuscript held at the Biblioteca de Mujeres, Madrid)

Rodari, Gianni, 1977. 'Un juguete llamado libro', *Cuadernos de Pedagogía*, 36, 28-31

Rodgerson, Gillian & Elizabeth Wilson, 1991. *Pornography and Feminism: The Case Against Censorship by Feminists Against Censorship*, London: Lawrence & Wishart

Rodiek, Christoph, 1995. 'Enzensberger y Durruti: *El corto verano de la anarquía*', in Hofman et al. (1995), 315-21

Rodríguez, Armonía, 1977. 'Ideología sexista y literatura infantil', *Cuadernos de Pedagogía*, 36, 36-7

Rodríguez, Emma, 1993. '«La fantasía ayuda a salir del agujero negro de la vida», dice Rosa Montero', *El Mundo*, 16 April*

—, 1997. 'El reinado de la novela: Montero, Matute, Pérez Reverte y Muñoz Molina triunfan en la feria', *El Mundo*, 9 June*

Rodríguez Almodóvar, Antonio, 1982. *Los cuentos maravillosos españoles*, Barcelona: Ed. Crítica

Rodríguez Iglesias, Mª Angeles, 1993. *La mujer en la literatura: Una experiencia didáctica*, Pamplona: Gobierno de Navarra, Departamento de Bienestar Social, Deporte y Vivienda, Subdirección de la Mujer

Rodríguez Magda, Rosa Mª, 1992. 'De la modernidad olvidadiza a la usurpación postmoderna', *Canelobre*, 23-4, 53-63

—, 1994. 'Por un feminismo transmoderno', in Federación de Organizaciones Feministas del Estado Español (1994), 303-12

Roig Castellanos, Mercedes, 1986. *A través de la prensa: La mujer en la historia: Francia, Italia, España, Siglos XVIII-XX*, Madrid: Instituto de la Mujer

Roig, Montserrat, 1981a. *¿Tiempo de mujer?*, Barcelona: Plaza y Janés

—, 1981b. 'Nosotras las mujeres', in Roig (1981a), 45-97

—, 1988. 'La mirada de Rosa Montero', *Círculo*, 2, 26-8

Romero, Andrés, 1977. 'Mujer, familia, información y política', *RICS* (Barcelona), 29, 287-95

Romero, Isabel et al., 1987. 'Feminismo y literatura: la narrativa de los años 70', in Durán & Rey (1987), 337-58

Roqueta, Julia, 1997. 'Torero, pistolero y anarquista', *Solidaridad Obrera* (June), 6

Rose, Ellen Cronan, 1983. 'Through the Looking Glass: When Women Tell Fairy Tales', in Abel, Hirsch & Langland (1983), 209-27

Ross, Andrew, 1989. *No Respect: Intellectuals and Popular Culture*, London: Routledge

Rowe, William & Vivian Schelling, 1994 (1st edn., 1991). *Memory and Modernity: Popular Culture in Latin America*, London: Verso

Rubin, Gayle, 1984. 'Thinking Sex: Notes for a Radical Theory of the Politics of Sexuality', in Vance (1984a), 267-319

Rubio Castro, Ana, 1990. 'El feminismo de la diferencia: Los argumentos de una igualdad complejo', *Revista de Estudios Políticos (Nueva Época)*, 70, 185-207

Ruiperes, Mª, 1979. 'Federica Montseny: Cultura y anarquía', *Tiempo de Historia*, 5/52, 16-31

Ruiz, Almudena, 1996. 'Rosa Montero acusa al Gobierno de «crear un ambiente de guerra civil»', *El Diario*, 17 January

Russ, Joanna, 1981. 'Recent Feminist Utopias', in Barr (1981), 71-85

Russell, Diana E. H. & Nicola Van de Ven, eds., 1976. *The Proceedings of the International Tribunal on Crimes Against Women*, East Palo Alto, CA: Frog in the Well

Russell, Elisabeth, 1989. 'Utopías y antiutopías feministas en la literatura anglosajona del siglo XX', in Mateos & Sagasti (1989), 95-105

—, 1994. 'El sueño de un lenguaje común', in Carabí & Segarra (1994), 101-8

Russo, Mary, 1986. 'Female Grotesques: Carnival and Theory', in Lauretis (1986), 213-29

Sadie, Stanley, ed., 1980. *The New Grove Dictionary of Music and Musicians*, vol. 2, London: Macmillan

Sadlier, Darlene J., 1992. 'Portugal', in *Bloomsbury Guide to Women's Literature*, ed. by Claire Buck, London: Bloomsbury Publishing, 89-92

Sadoff, Diane F., 1978. 'Mythopoeia, the Moon and Contemporary Women's Poetry', in Brown & Olson (1978), 142-60

Sáez Buenaventura, Carmen, 1982. 'Para un análisis epistemológico de la maternidad', in Durán (1982), 135-45

Saiz Cidoncha, Carlos, 1988. *La ciencia ficción como fenómeno de comunicación y de cultura de masas*, Madrid: Editorial de la Universidad Complutense de Madrid

Saladrigas, Robert, 1983. 'Con la vana ilusión de un bolero', *La Vanguardia* (Barcelona), 15 December*

Sallé, Mª Angeles & José Ignacio Casas, 1986. *Efectos de la crisis económica sobre el trabajo de la mujer*, Madrid: Instituto de la Mujer

San José, Begoña, 1992. Introduction to 'La relación de las mujeres políticas con otras mujeres, en particular con el movimiento feminista', in Forum de Política Feminista (1992), 77-8

San Ramón, Josefina, 1979. 'Amor y desamor', in *III Jornadas Feministas Estatales: 10 años de lucha del movimiento feminista*, collection of papers held at the CIFFE, Centro de Documentación

Sanahuja, Encarna, 1982. 'Las Amazonas: ¿Pioneras del feminismo?', *Poder y Libertad*, 3, 84-90

Sánchez, Magalie, 1988. 'Los recursos de comunicación en un cuento para niños: *La conejita Marcela* de Esther Tusquets', *Ventanal: Revista de Creación y Crítica*, 14, 193-202

Sánchez Arnosi, Milagros, 1981. Rev. of *La función delta*, *Insula*, 415, 16.

Sánchez López, Rosario, 1990. *Mujer española: Una sombra de destino en lo universal*, Murcia: Universidad de Murcia

Sánchez-Pardo González, Esther, 1991. *Postmodernismo y metaficción*, Madrid: Editorial de la Universidad Complutense de Madrid

Santa Cruz, Isabel, 1992. 'Sobre el concepto de la igualdad: Algunas observaciones', *Isegoría: Revista de Filosofía Moral y Política*, 6, 145-52

Santos, Alonso, 1981. 'Novela en la transición, transición en la novela (1975-1980)', *Nueva Estafeta*, 31-2, 86-91

Santos, Carlos, 1994. 'Las chicas son guerreras', *Cambio16*, 15 August, 12-17

Santos, Domingo, 1982. *Lo mejor de la ciencia ficción española*, Barcelona: Martínez-Roca

Sanz Villanueva, Santos, 1997. 'Apariencias y grandeza del mundo: Rosa Montero, *La hija del caníbal*', *La Esfera*, 17 May, 12

Sargent, Lyman Tower, 1983. 'A New Anarchism: Social and Political Ideas in Some Recent Feminist Eutopias', in Barr & Smith (1983), 3-33

Sargent, Pamela, ed., 1975, 'Women in Science Fiction', *Futures*, 7/5, 433-41

—, 1978. *Women of Wonder: SF Stories by Women about Women*, Harmondsworth: Penguin

—, 1979. *More Women of Wonder: SF Novelettes by Women about Women*, Harmondsworth: Penguin

Satué, Francisco J., 1993. 'Bella y oscura profesión' (interview), *El Siglo de Europa*, 3 May, 52-3

Sau Sánchez, Victoria, 1980. 'Para una teoría del modo de producción patriarcal', *El Viejo Topo*, 47, 19-23

—, 1986a. *Ser mujer: El fin de un imagen tradicional*, Barcelona: Icaria

—, 1986b. 'Maternología', in *Aportaciones para una lógica del feminismo* Barcelona: LaSal edicions de les dones, 62-72

—, 1988. 'La construcción del «yo» femenino: Hacerse a sí misma', in Navarro (1988a), 89-104.

—, 1990. *Diccionario ideológico feminista*, Barcelona: Icaria

Saussure, Ferdinand de, 1991. 'Nature of the Linguistic Sign', in *Modern Criticism and Theory: A Reader*, ed. by David Lodge, London: Longman, 1991, 10-14, originally published in *Course in General Linguistics*, tran. by Roy Harris, [n.p.]: Gerald Duckworth & Co. Ltd/Open Court Publishing Co, 1983

Saval, Lorenzo & Juan García Gallego, eds., 1986. *Litoral: Revista de la Poesía y el Pensamiento*, special edn., 'Literatura escrita por mujeres en la España contemporánea'

Scanlon, Geraldine M., 1986. *La pólemica feminista en la España contemporánea (1868-1974)*, Madrid: Akal

Scholes, Robert, 1979. *Fabulation and Metafiction*, Urbana: University of Illinois Press

Schubert, Adrian, 1990. *A Social History of Modern Spain*, London: Unwin Hyman

Schweickart, Patrocinio, 1983. 'What If...Science and Technology in Feminist Utopias', in *Machina ex Dea: Feminist Perspectives on Technology*, ed. by Joan Rothschild, Oxford: Pergamon Press

Scott, Joan W., 1988. 'Deconstructing Equality-versus-Difference: Or, The Uses of Poststructuralist Theory for Feminism', *Feminist Studies*, 14/1, 33-50.

Segal, Lynne, 1990. *Slow Motion: Changing Masculinities, Changing Men*, London: Virago

—, 1992. 'Sweet Sorrows, Painful Pleasures: Pornography and the Perils of Heterosexual Desire', in McIntosh & Segal (1992), 65-91

Senabre, Ricardo, 1992. Rev. of *El nido de los sueños*, ABC literario, 14 February, 8

—, 1993. Rev. of *Bella y oscura*, ABC literario *

Sendón de León, Victoria, Sánchez, María, Guntín, Montserrat & Elvira Aparici, 1994. *Feminismo holístico: De la realidad a lo real*, Bilbao: Agora

Sendón de León, Victoria, 1981. *Sobre diosas, amazonas y vestales: Utopías para un feminismo radical*, Madrid: Zero-ZYX

—, 1994. 'Feminismo: Un extraño holograma', *El Viejo Topo*, 74, 65-70

SESM, 1986. 'El movimiento feminista en España de 1960 a 1980', in Borreguero et al. (1986), 29-40

Shinn, Thelma J., 1986. *Worlds Within Women: Myth and Mythmaking in Fantastic Literature by Women*, New York: Greenwood Press

Simmons, Judy, 1990. *Diaries and Journals of Literary Women from Fanny Burney to Virginia Woolf*, London: Macmillan

Smith, Paul Julian, 1992. *Laws of Desire: Questions of Homosexuality in Spanish Writing and Film 1960-1990*, Oxford: Clarendon Press

—, 1994. *Desire Unlimited: The Cinema of Pedro Almodóvar*, London: Verso

Smith, Sidonie, 1987. *A Poetics of Women's Autobiography: Marginal Literature and the Fictions of Self-Representation*, Bloomington: Indiana University Press

Solano, Yolanda, Rodríguez, Rocío, Rodríguez, Irene & Paloma Santiago, 1997. *La larga marcha hacia la igualdad: IV conferencia mundial sobre las mujeres, Beijing 95. Evaluación del proceso en España*, Madrid: Instituto de la Mujer y Ministerio de Trabajo y Asuntos Sociales

Solé Puig, Carlota, 1988. *Ensayos de teoría sociólogica: Modernización y postmodernidad*, Madrid: Paraninfo

Solsona, Montserrat & Rocío Treviña, 1990. *Estructuras familiares en España*, Madrid: Instituto de la Mujer

Somay, Bülent, 1984. 'Towards an Open-Ended Utopia', *Science Fiction Studies*, 11/1, 25-38

Sontag, Susan, 1994. 'Notes on "Camp"' (1964) in *Against Interpretation*, London: Vintage

Soriano, Mercedes, 1977. *Las madres solteras*, Barcelona: Dopesa, Colección Los Marginados

Spires, Robert, 1984. *Beyond the Metafictional Mode: Directions in the Modern Spanish Novel*, Lexington: University of Kentucky Press

Stanford Friedman, Susan, 1988. 'Women's Autobiographical Selves: Theory and Practice', in Benstock (1988), 34-62

Stanley, Liz, 1992. *The Auto/Biographical I: The Theory and Practice of Feminist Autobiography*, Manchester: Manchester University Press

Stanton, Domna, 1986. 'Difference on Trial: A Critique of the Maternal Metaphor in Cixous, Irigaray and Kristeva', in *The Poetics of Gender*, ed. by Nancy K. Miller, New York: Columbia University Press, 157-82

—, ed., 1987. *The Female Autograph: Theory and Practice of Autobiography from the Tenth to the Twentieth Century*, Chicago: The University of Chicago Press

Stimpson, Catharine R., 1991. 'Feminisms and Utopia', in Cummings and Smith (1991), 1-6

Strachey, James, ed., 1981. *The Standard Edition of the Complete Psychological Works of Sigmund Freud*, 11th edn., London: Hogarth Press and the Institute of Psychoanalysis, 24 vols.

Studlar, Gaylyn, 1990. 'Masochism, Masquerade and the Erotic Metamorphoses of Marlene Dietrich', in *Fabrications: Costume and the Female Body*, ed. by Jane Gaines & Charlotte Herzog, London: Routledge, 229-49

Subirats, Marina, 1990. 'Problemas y reivindicaciones de las mujeres: Una cinta sin fin', in Astelarra (1990), 117-31

Suñén, Luis, 1981. 'Rosa Montero: Contar la vida', *El País*, 28 March*

—, 1984. 'La realidad y sus sombras: Rosa Montero y Cristina Fernández Cubas', *Insula*, 446, 5

Suvin, Darko, 1979. *Metamorphoses of Science Fiction: On the Poetics and History of a Literary Genre*, London: Yale University Press

—, 1988. *Positions and Presuppositions in Science Fiction*, London: Macmillan

Synapse, Gabinete de Investigación Cualitativa, 1985. 'Estudio de las actitudes de las españolas ante el feminismo', summarised in Instituto de la Mujer (1990b), [no page reference as this is a collection of cards]

Talbot, Lynn, 1988. 'Entrevista con Rosa Montero', *LF*, 14, 90-6

—, 1989. 'Journey into the Fantastic: Cristina Fernández Cubas' *Los altillos de Brumal*', *LF*, 15, 37-47

Threlfall, Monica, 1980. '¿Crisis del feminismo o crisis de las feministas?', *Zona Abierta*, 23, 125-8

—, 1984. 'Women and Political Participation', in *Spain: Conditional Democracy*, ed. by Christopher Abel & Nissa Torrents, London: Croom Helm, 136-59.

—, 1985. 'The Women's Movement in Spain', *New Left Review*, 151, 44-75

Thompson, Keith, ed., 1993. *Ser hombre* (trans. of *To Be a Man*), Barcelona: Kairos

Todorov, Tzvetan, 1975. *The Fantastic: A Structural Approach to a Literary Genre*, trans. by Richard Howard, Ithaca, New York: Cornell University Press

Torre, Cristina de la, 1985. 'Women as Innovators: Spain's Rosa Montero', published in *SAMLA*, (31 October), (Atlanta, Georgia). [I have been unable to obtain the final published version of this essay and am quoting from the manuscript copy provided by Rosa Montero.]

Torres, Sixto E. & S. Carl King, 1991. *Selected Proceedings of the Thirty-Ninth Annual Mountain Interstate Foreign Language Conference, Clemson, South Carolina, September 28-30, 1989*, [n.p., n.pub.]

Traba, Marta, 1981. 'Hipótesis sobre una escritura diferente', *Quimera*, 13, 9-11

Tremosa, Laura y Montserrat Roig, 1977. '¿Qué es la mujer?', *Argumentos*, 5, 72-7

Tribuna de Debate, 1981. '¿Feminismo de la igualdad versus feminismo de la diferencia?', *Dones en Lluita*, first issue, 8-13

Tsuchiya, Akiko, 1990. 'Montserrat Roig's *L'ópera cotidiana* as Historiographic Metafiction', *ALEC*, 15, 145-59

Tubert, Silvia, 1988. 'Trastornos de la identidad femenina', in Instituto de la Mujer (1988), 23-7

Umbral, Francisco, 1973. *Carta abierta a una chica progre*, Madrid: Ed. 99

Urdanibia. Iñaki, 1991. 'Lo narrativo en la posmodernidad', in Vattimo et al. (1991), 41-75

Urraca, Beatriz, 1995. 'Angélica Gorodischer's Voyages of Discovery: Sexuality and Historical Allegory in Science Fiction's Cross-Cultural Encounters', *Latin American Literary Review*, 23/45, 85-102

Urruzola, Mª José, 1988. 'El miedo al feminismo', in VV.AA. (1988), in 'Dossier de la prensa', 17 [First published in *Diario del Alto Aragón* (Huesca), 8 March 1988]

Usandizaga, Aránzazu, 1993. *Amor y literatura: La búsqueda de la identidad femenina*, Barcelona: Promociones y Publicaciones Universitarias

Valcárcel, Amelia, 1991. *Sexo y filosofía: Sobre «mujer y poder»*, Barcelona: Anthropos

—, 1994. 'Feminismo y poder político', in Instituto de la Mujer (1994b), 41-8

Valis, Noël & Carol Maeir, eds., 1988. *In the Feminine Mode: Essays on Hispanic Women Writers*, Lewisburg, Pa.: Bucknell University Press

Valle, Teresa del & Carmela Sanz Rueda, 1991. *Género y sexualidad*, Madrid: Fundación Universidad Empresa

Valls, Fernando, 1991. 'La literatura erótica en España entre 1975 y 1990', *Insula*, 530 (February), 29-30

—, 1995. 'La última narrativa de Rosa Montero: Notas sobre *Temblor, El nido de los sueños* y *Bella y oscura*', *Lectora: Revista de dones y textualitat*, 1, 95-103

Vance, Carole S., ed., 1984a. *Pleasure and Danger: Exploring Female Sexuality*, London: Routledge and Kegan Paul

—, 1984b. 'Pleasure and Danger: Toward a Politics of Sexuality', in Vance (1984a), 1-27

Vanguardia, La, 1988. 'Victoria Camps: el paradigma débil' (interview), in VV.AA. (1988), in 'Dossier de la prensa', 4 [First published in *La Vanguardia* (Barcelona), 17 May 1988]

¿Vanidades?, 1990, 'Entrevista a Rosa Montero', 6, 17-18, 23-4

Vásquez, Mary S., ed., 1991. *The Sea of Becoming: Approaches to the Fiction of Esther Tusquets*, London: Greenwood Press

Vattimo, Gianni et al., eds., 1991. *En torno a la posmodernidad*, Barcelona: Anthropos, Colección Autores, textos y temas, Hermeneusis, 9

Vázquez Montalbán, Manuel, 1970. 'La mujer en las canciones españolas', *Triunfo* (Madrid), 31 October, 39-43

Verdú Maciá, Vicente, 1978. *Las solteronas,* Barcelona: Dopesa

Vidal Santos, M., 1980. 'La novela policiaca española', *Camp de l'Arpa*, 77-8, 53-5

Vila San-Juan, Sergio, 1981a. 'Rosa Montero: «No existe una "mafia violeta"»', *El Correo Catalán*, 2 April*

—, 1981b. 'Rosa Montero' (interview), *Diagonal* (April-May), 22-4

Villán, Javier, 1983a. 'Rosa Montero: Perplejidades y angustias de una triunfadora' (interview), *Odiel* (Huelva), 15 December*

—, 1983b. 'Rosa Montero te tratará como a una reina', *Levante* (Valencia), 4 December*

Villena, Miguel Ángel, 1997.'Rosa Montero sostiene que a los 40 años "se descubre la mediocridad y la mezquindad": En su nueva novela, *La hija del caníbal*, narra una "iniciación en la madurez"', *El País*, 20 May, 36

VV.AA., 1979a. 'La sexualidad femenina (encuesta): El placer es mío, caballero', *Vindicación Feminista*, 28, 14-36

VV.AA., 1979b. *Perspectivas de una España democrática y constitucionalizada: Ciclo de conferencias pronunciadas en el club «Siglo XXI» durante el curso 1978-1979*, Madrid: Unión Editorial, Colección Nuestro Siglo

VV.AA., 1988. *Jornadas "20 años después del Women's Lib"*, Barcelona: Ayuntamiento, Centro de documentació de la dona

VV.AA., 1990a. *Historia de la música pop Salvat, vol. 1, Hasta 1955: Los primeros pasos*, Barcelona: Salvat

VV.AA., 1990b. *Poder y Libertad*, special edn., 'Feminismo y literatura', 13

VV.AA., 1994. *Quimera*, special edn., 'Cátalogo de sombras: Treinta escritoras del Siglo XX en lengua castellana', 123

VV.AA., 1995. 'Aborto: ¿Todavía es un crimen?', *Ajoblanco* (November), 50-7

Watson, Julia, 1988. 'Shadowed Presence: Modern Women Writer's Autobiographies and the Other', in Olney (1988), 181-9

Waugh, Patricia, 1984. *Metafiction: The Theory and Practice of Self-Conscious Fiction*, London: Methuen

—, 1989. *Feminine Fictions: Revisiting the Postmodern*, London: Routledge

—, 1992. *Practising Postmodernism, Reading Modernism*, London: Edward Arnold

Whitford, Margaret, 1992. 'Mother-Daughter Relationship', in Wright (1992), 262-6

Williams, Claire, 1994. *Sexual/Social Intercourse: Communication in Rosa Montero's 'Crónica del desamor'*, thesis submitted in June 1994 for the degree of M.Phil. in European Literature, Faculty of Modern and Medieval Languages, University of Cambridge

Williams, Linda, 1990. *Hard Core: Power, Pleasure and 'The Frenzy of the Visible'*, London: Pandora

Williamson, Judith, 1986. 'Femininity and Colonization', in Modleski (1986a), 99-118

Wolff, Janet, 1990. *Feminine Sentences: Essays on Women and Culture*, Oxford: Polity Press

'Women in Graphics', 1989. *Women of Europe*, Supplement N° 30, 14, 36, 38, 41, 53, 54, 89**

Women of Europe, N° 50, 15 March-15 July 1987, 30-31; N° 67, December 1990-January 1991, 28-29; Brussels: Commission of the European Communities, Directorate General of Information, Communication and Culture, Women's Information Service**

Wright, Elizabeth, ed., 1992. *Feminism and Psychoanalysis: A Critical Dictionary*, Oxford: Blackwell

Zatlin, Phyllis, 1982. 'The Contemporary Spanish Metanovel', *Denver Quarterly*, 17/3, 63-73

—, 1985. 'Rev. of *Crónica del desamor* and *La función delta*', *Hispanófila*, 84, 121-3

—, 1987. 'Women Novelists in Democratic Spain: Freedom to Express the Female Perspective', *ALEC*, 12, 29-44

—, 1992. 'The Novels of Rosa Montero as Experimental Fiction', *Monographic Review/Revista Monográfica*, 8 ('Experimental Fiction by Hispanic Women Writers'), 114-24

—, 1993. 'Gothic Inversion of the Future: Rosa Montero's *Temblor*', *Romance Notes*, 33/2, 119-23

Zavala, Iris M., 1990. 'De héroes y heroinas en lo imaginario social: El discurso amoroso del bolero', *Casa de las Américas*, 30/179, 123-9

—, 1991. *El bolero: Historia de un amor*, Madrid: Alianza

* No page reference as this is a photocopy supplied by Rosa Montero

** Page references refer to the sections on Spain

INDEX

abortion 49, 62-64, 65
active-passive binary 142, 145, 163
agency 6, 7, 86, 94, 104, 143, 145, 160
Allende, Isabel 205
Almodóvar, Pedro 52, 120-121, 123, 257
Amado amo 35, 56, 71, 82, 170-176, 220, 228, 237-239, 252
ambivalence 32, 55, 68, 142, 211-212, 220
anarchism 186-189, 206, 243-244, 267-268
androgyny 185
Anglo-American feminism 27
Anglo-American film theory 145
anti-hero 172
arquetipo viril 29, 80
autobiography 74, 92-96

Barceló, Elia 178
Bella y oscura 36, 52, 204-209, 211-214, 220, 241, 244-246, 263, 265-266
bolero 153, 170, 229-231, 257-258
boom of women's writing 1, 23-27, 247
Burke, Elena 121

camp 121-123, 134

canción española 120
Carroll, Lewis 192
castration 163
castration anxiety 150
castration complex 70, 225, 262
censorship 80
cinema 52, 96, 208, 210, 272
clerical-repressive model of sexuality 159
cognitive estrangement 179-181
communication 133, 253-254
consciousness-raising 24, 231
Constitution (1978) 19, 130, 221
consumer culture 120-121
contraception 49, 59-63, 64
Crónica del desamor 25, 35-36, 44, 51-74, 78, 82-89, 94, 99-100, 101, 103-106, 113, 133, 145, 149, 169, 170, 173, 175, 219-221, 237, 251
Cuba 117-120
culture of evasion 120

deconstruction 79, 106, 197
desencanto 17, 20, 25, 113, 169, 190
desire 115, 116, 157, 174, 209, 230, 257-258
detective fiction 148, 206
diary 92, 94, 104
difference feminism 18, 27-35, 86, 184, 219, 246-247

don Juan 154
double militancy 14-17, 219
dystopia 184, 188

El cristal de Agua Fría 182, 248-249
El nido de los sueños 36, 176-177, 190-196, 206, 220, 249
El viaje fantástico de Bárbara 263-264
Ende, Michael 177, 197
equality politics 16-17, 27-35, 172, 219, 246-247
erotic narrative 142-144
escapism 120-121, 124, 134, 181, 205
Escher, M.C. 229
esperpento 113, 123
exhibitionism 145, 158
existentialism 175, 205

fairy tales 191-193, 249
Falange 49
fantastic 177, 180-181, 195, 204, 228
fantasy 116, 125, 177-196, 207, 258-259
    castration 152
    masturbatory 155, 160
    rape 157-160
    sexual 142, 158, 163, 219
feeling 121-122
female friendship 87
female sexuality 53, 62, 142-145
feminist criticism 6, 233

feminist politics 7
feminist reader 90, 100
fiction of debate 53
first person narrative 90, 209, 220, 264-265, 268
Franco 14, 18, 30, 46, 48-51, 80, 120, 131, 156, 169, 178
French feminist theory 18, 27, 150
French psychoanalytic theory 145

García Márquez, Gabriel 205
gender 66-67
gender stereotypes 145, 149-150, 155, 163, 184, 188, 191, 211-213
Granada jornadas (1979) 16
grotesque 52, 123, 220
Guillot, Olga 118, 121-123, 125-127
gynaecologists 60-62
gynandry 31
gynocriticism 7

hembrismo 22
heroine 171
Highsmith, Patricia 228
Historias de mujeres 273-274
Hollywood 119, 120
homosexuality 56, 62
humour 4, 52, 70, 87, 117, 123, 135, 170, 192
hyperrealism 114, 204
hysteria 150, 156, 171

identity 26, 32, 56, 73, 81
  collective 5-6, 86
  cultural 8, 54
  floating 172
  gender 7, 66
  masculine 56, 144, 151-152, 172, 174
  performative 96-98
  personal 5-6, 86, 92, 94-95, 189, 193, 210
  quest 171
  shifting 6, 95, 214, 221, 269-273
identity politics 9, 56, 57, 73, 169, 178, 196, 218, 221-222
imaginary 195
independent feminists 17, 18
Instituto de la Mujer 18-19, 21, 25, 28-29, 172
intertextuality 114, 182
irony 52, 72, 96, 114, 121, 128, 135, 205, 211
Italian feminism 18, 27

Jornadas «Diez años de lucha del Movimiento Feminista» 33
Jornadas para la Liberación de la Mujer 15
Jornades Catalans de la Dona 15
journalism 2, 9, 13, 35, 52, 82, 224-225

knowledge 91, 99, 197, 209

La función delta 35, 74, 78, 82-84, 89-105, 113, 122, 133, 149, 169-170, 173, 175, 210, 219-220, 229, 271, 274
La hija del caníbal 36, 204-207, 209-211, 214, 220, 265-273
la Lupe 126
Laforet, Carmen 133
language
  creativity 208, 259-261
  sexism 233-235
Las barbaridades de Bárbara 263
Law of the Father 161
Le Guin, Ursula 177
lesbian 185
life narratives 73, 83, 169-171, 208

Machado, Antonio 121
Machín, Antonio 115, 121, 134
magic 177, 192, 205
magical realism 205
male gaze 144, 145, 151, 157-159, 162
Martín Gaite, Carmen 93, 104, 118, 124, 133
masturbation 62, 69, 143, 157-158, 162
maternal trope 45
maternity 26, 214
matriarchy 68, 184
Matute, Ana María 95
memory 92, 94-96, 207
menstruation 188, 213

metafiction 24, 25, 78-85, 89-91, 105-106, 114, 209, 219, 232
Miguel, Luis 120
Moix, Ana María 16
mother-child bond 71, 174, 185, 189
mother-daughter relationship 156, 163, 188
motherhood 44-71
mystique of motherhood 30, 46, 64
myth
    feminine 26, 188, 226-227
    hero 177, 187, 193
    maternal 65, 68
    patriarchal 26, 35, 135, 179, 188
    quest 176, 190, 192, 240-241
    romantic 124
    Sisyphus 175

Nabokov, Vladimir 228
naming 193, 232, 259-260
National Catholicism 49
novela negra 113
novela rosa 112-113, 133
novum 179

object-relations theory 156
Oedipal complex 148, 161, 214, 225
Ortiz, Lourdes 22

paidética 46
palabra de mujer 27, 221

Partido Feminista de España 17
passion 256-257, 274-275
patriarchal family 57, 156, 195
'Paulo Pumilio' 169
phallologocentrism 26, 83
Plan para la igualdad de oportunidades de las mujeres (1988-1990) 25, 28
Plan para la igualdad de oportunidades de las mujeres, (1993-1995) 28
pleasure 116, 145, 159
popular culture 56, 113-116, 124, 135-136, 145, 163, 170, 189, 219
pornography 59, 153, 157, 161, 235-236
postfeminism 21, 222
postmodernism 8, 81, 86, 91, 114, 182-183, 221
poststructuralism 6, 79
poststructuralist theory 5
power
    hegemonic 29
    hierarchy 174, 183, 186
    maternal 45, 66, 68-71, 185, 213, 261-262
    patriarchal 32, 61, 161, 172
    political 30
professional feminism 21
pronatalist policy 51
psychoanalysis 70
Puig, Manuel 113, 117

radical feminism 16, 19, 30, 46, 244

reader identification 54, 84, 89, 135
realism 53-54, 73, 83, 205-206
   subjective 92
Roig, Montserrat 4, 16, 26, 56, 60, 82, 143, 160
role models 47-48, 68, 131, 135, 179, 220
romantic fiction 124, 134, 153
romantic love 130-133

Sánchez, Luis Rafael 117
Saussurean linguistics 78
science fiction 177-190
scopophilia 157, 161
Sección Femenina 30, 44, 48-51
shifter 128
silence 87-88, 100, 120, 173, 221
single militancy 14, 219
single mother 57-58
solitude 103, 124, 131-133, 254-255
Spanish feminist movement 13, 14-23, 187, 219, 221, 235
Spanish feminist theory 19
speculative fiction 101, 179
spinster 155, 163
subject-object binary 142, 145, 155, 160, 163
subjectivity 7, 33, 57, 82-83, 144, 221

taboos 52, 53, 89, 143
Te trataré como a una reina 35, 52, 82, 104, 112, 136, 142-163, 170, 171, 177, 204, 219, 229, 231, 251
Temblor 36, 44, 114, 169, 171, 176-190, 193, 194, 196-197, 204, 206, 208, 212, 220, 240, 244
testimonial literature 24, 53, 145, 169, 179, 219, 237
theatre 96, 208, 210
transition 14-17, 59-64
transmodern feminism 86
truth 5, 91, 175, 182, 197, 205
Tusquets, Esther 143

utopia 32, 184-185, 187-190, 222

Valle Inclán, Ramón 52, 113
Vargas Llosa, Mario 117
Vindicación Feminista 16
violence 125, 134, 144
voyeurism 144, 145, 148, 157, 161-162

Women's Studies 19

SPANISH STUDIES

1. Gerardo Piña Rosales, **La obra narrativa de Segundo Serrano Poncela: Crónica del Desarraigo**
2. **A Bilingual Edition of Fray Luis de León's** *La perfecta casada*: **The Role of Married Women in Sixteenth-Century Spain**, edited and translated with introduction and notes by John A. Jones and Javier San José Lera
3. John Gilmour, **Manuel Fraga Iribarne and the Rebirth of Spanish Conservatism 1939-1990**
4. Vanessa Knights, **The Search for Identity in the Narrative of Rosa Montero**
5. **Personal Memories of the Days of the Spanish Civil War, in Catalan and English: Lluís Puig Casas,** introduced, edited and annotated by Idoya Puig